Dining Out in Freeport/Lucaya

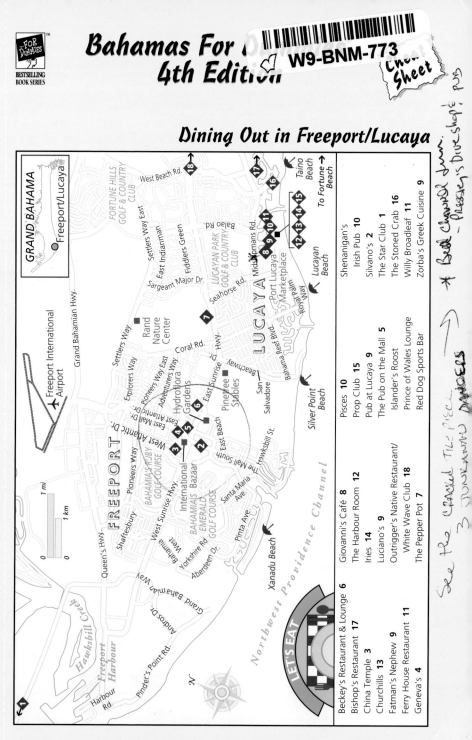

GRAND BAHAMA — Freeport/Lucaya

Shenanigan's
Irish Pub **10**
Silvano's **2**
The Star Club **1**
The Stoned Crab **16**
Willy Broadleaf **11**
Zorba's Greek Cuisine **9**

Pisces **10**
Prop Club **15**
Pub at Lucaya **9**
The Pub on the Mall **5**
Islander's Roost
Prince of Wales Lounge
Red Dog Sports Bar

Giovanni's Café **8**
The Harbour Room **12**
Iries **14**
Luciano's **9**
Outrigger's Native Restaurant/
White Wave Club **18**
The Pepper Pot **7**

Beckey's Restaurant & Lounge **6**
Bishop's Restaurant **17**
China Temple **3**
Churchills **13**
Fatman's Nephew **9**
Ferry House Restaurant **11**
Geneva's **4**

Bill Channel Inn — Pressley's Diveshop & Pub

See the Grand the Piece
3 Junkanoo Dancers

LET'S EAT

Dining Out in Nassau

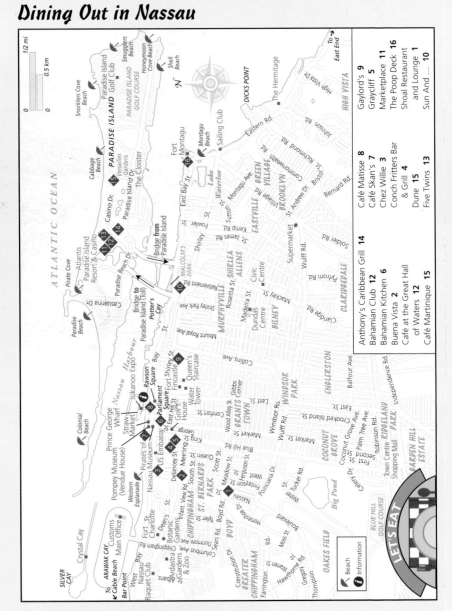

Gaylord's **9**
Graycliff **5**
Marketplace **11**
The Poop Deck **16**
Shoal Restaurant and Lounge **1**
Sun And … **10**

Café Matisse **8**
Café Skan's **7**
Chez Willie **3**
Conch Fritters Bar & Grill **4**
Dune **15**
Five Twins **13**

Anthony's Caribbean Grill **14**
Bahamian Club **12**
Bahamian Kitchen **6**
Buena Vista **2**
Café at the Great Hall of Waters **12**
Café Martinique **15**

FOR DUMMIES

The fun and easy way™ to travel!

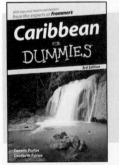

Bahamas
FOR
DUMMIES®
4TH EDITION

by Darwin Porter and Danforth Prince

Wiley Publishing, Inc.

Bahamas For Dummies, 4th Edition

Published by
Wiley Publishing, Inc.
111 River St.
Hoboken, NJ 07030-5774
www.wiley.com

About the Authors

Darwin Porter, while still a teenager, began writing about The Bahamas for the *Miami Herald* and has been a frequent visitor ever since. His writing partner is **Danforth Prince,** formerly of the Paris bureau of the *New York Times,* who has co-authored numerous Frommer's best-sellers with Darwin, including those to the Caribbean, Bermuda, and the Virgin Islands.

Publisher's Acknowledgments

We're proud of this book; please send us your comments through our Dummies online registration form located at www.dummies.com/register/.

Some of the people who helped bring this book to market include the following:

Editorial

Editors: Suzanna R. Thompson, Production Editor; Christine Ryan, Development Editor

Copy Editor: Elizabeth Kim

Cartographer: Andrew Murphy

Senior Photo Editor: Richard Fox

Cover Photos
Front: © David Stoecklein/Corbis
Back: © Davis Sacks/Getty Images

Cartoons: Rich Tennant
(www.the5thwave.com)

Composition Services

Project Coordinator: Ryan Steffen

Layout and Graphics: Carl Byers, Stephanie D. Jumper, Barbara Moore, Heather Ryan, Julie Trippetti

***Special Art:* Anniversary Logo Design:** Richard Pacifico

Proofreaders: David Faust, Christine Pingleton, Techbooks

Indexer: Techbooks

Publishing and Editorial for Consumer Dummies

Diane Graves Steele, Vice President and Publisher, Consumer Dummies

Joyce Pepple, Acquisitions Director, Consumer Dummies

Kristin A. Cocks, Product Development Director, Consumer Dummies

Michael Spring, Vice President and Publisher, Travel

Kelly Regan, Editorial Director, Travel

Publishing for Technology Dummies

Andy Cummings, Vice President and Publisher, Dummies Technology/General User

Composition Services

Gerry Fahey, Vice President of Production Services

Debbie Stailey, Director of Composition Services

Contents at a Glance

Maps at a Glance

Table of Contents

Introduction

L ying just off the tip of Florida and stretching southeast across
258,998 sq. km (100,000 sq. miles) of the Atlantic Ocean, The
Bahamas are often called the South Sea Islands of the Atlantic. Many of
The Bahamas' thousands of miles of perfect coral sand beaches remain
free of footprints.

Charting its own course from Britain since 1973, the archipelago is made
up of a landmass of 700 islands. The prospect of deciding which island is
right for you isn't as daunting as that figure suggests. Most of the islands —
or islets, in some cases — aren't inhabited. Of those islands that are
inhabited, only a few are graced with places to stay.

Don't come here looking for mountainous interiors like the ones found in
Jamaica or Puerto Rico. Instead of hills, The Bahamas offer seascapes that
seem to stretch forever. For the most part, beaches of white, golden, or,
in some rare cases, pink sands ring the islands. If you're flying over them
like a bird, you can see translucent waters shimmering in the sunlight —
pale aquamarine, blue sapphire, or what an aerial photographer once
called "dancing green."

Entire books containing only photographs of these swirling water patterns have been published. As more and more of the world's seas
become polluted, the Bahamian waters alone make this island nation
worth a trip.

In *Bahamas For Dummies,* 4th Edition, we help you discover the islands,
focusing on the high points but also warning you about some of the low
points. Of course, we hit all the hot spots, like the well-touristed **Nassau,
Paradise Island,** and **Freeport/Lucaya** on **Grand Bahama Island.** But we
also take you to the less-visited and harder-to-reach islands, such as the
Exumas in the southern Bahamas, perfect for those visitors seeking an
escape for some serious R & R.

About This Book

You can use this book in three ways:

  ✔ **As a trip planner:** Whether you think you know where you want to
    go in The Bahamas or you don't have a clue, this book helps you
    zero in on the right island (or islands) for you. Expect plenty of
    insider advice — the kind you'd get from a trusted friend — about
    where to go and what to avoid. We guide you through all the neces-
    sary steps of making your travel arrangements, from finding the

cheapest airfare, to figuring out a budget, to packing like a pro. All the chapters are self-contained, so you don't have to read them in order. Just flip to them as you need them.

✔ **As an island guide:** Pack this book alongside your sunscreen and it'll come in just as handy while you're away. Turn to the appropriate island chapters whenever you need to find the best beaches, a tasty place to eat, a great snorkel or sail, a challenging golf course, a hot nightspot, or tips on any other diversions.

✔ **For an overview:** If you want a feel for The Bahamas, peruse this guide from start to finish to figure out which of the archipelago's pleasurable pursuits are right for you.

Be advised that travel information is subject to change at any time — and this is especially true of prices. We suggest that you write or call ahead for confirmation when making your travel plans. The authors, editors, and publisher cannot be held responsible for the experiences of readers while traveling. Your safety is important to us, however, so we encourage you to stay alert and be aware of your surroundings. Keep a close eye on cameras, purses, and wallets — all favorite targets of thieves and pickpockets.

Conventions Used in This Book

Bahamas For Dummies is a reference guide that allows you to read chapters in any order you want. Instead of providing guidebook "hieroglyphics," the book is user-friendly, keeping abbreviations and symbols to a minimum.

The following credit card abbreviations noted are used for the establishments that accept them:

✔ AE: American Express

✔ DC: Diners Club

✔ DISC: Discover

✔ MC: MasterCard

✔ V: Visa

Dummies Post-it® Flags

As you're reading this book, you'll find information that you'll want to reference as you plan or enjoy your trip — whether it be a new hotel, a must-see attraction, or a must-try walking tour. Mark these pages with the handy Post-it® Flags included in this book to help make your trip planning easier!

We use $ signs to indicate the costs of hotels and restaurants so that you can quickly determine whether you want to unpack your luggage at a hotel or dine on the local cuisine (see the price table later in this section). The $ system lists a range of costs so you can make fast comparisons.

The rates we use in our hotel recommendations are for two guests spending one night in a standard double room during the high season, which lasts from mid-December to mid-April. In the off season, tariffs are sometimes lowered anywhere from 20 to 60 percent.

Most rates listed include only the room. In some cases, however, the stated price includes breakfast. And in the rare cases of all-inclusive hotels, the rates we present may initially seem very high, but we note that one price includes everything: your room, meals, drinks, and all those extra expenses, such as tips, taxes, most activities, airport pick-ups, and returns for your departing flight. For restaurants, we give the price range for a main course per person.

The following table shows the system of $ signs that we use to indicate a range of costs for one night in a hotel or the price of a dinner main course at a restaurant.

Cost	Hotel	Restaurant (Main Courses)
$	$100 or less per night	Less than $15
$$	$101–$200	$15–$25
$$$	$201–$300	$26–$35
$$$$	$301 and up	$36 and up

Foolish Assumptions

We made the following assumptions in preparing this guide:

- ✔ You may be a first-time visitor to The Bahamas in need of the "building blocks" to help you create a trip at a price that you can afford.

- ✔ You may have been to The Bahamas before, but you haven't explored them in a long time and you want sound advice about what's new and good and what's changed since your last trip.

- ✔ You're a busy person and don't want to read a lot of background and less-than-urgent information. After all, a vacation shouldn't be homework. You want a book that focuses quickly on the places that'll give you the best experience in the islands.

- ✔ Finally, we assume that you're seeking value — that you want to get the biggest bang for your buck in The Bahamas. So we help you steer clear of pricey tourist traps.

If you fall into any of these categories, *Bahamas For Dummies* is for you.

How This Book Is Organized

This book is divided into seven parts. The chapters within each part cover specific subjects in detail. You don't have to read this book in any particular order. In fact, think of these pages as an island buffet: You can consume whatever you want, and no one cares whether you eat the guava duff for dessert before you consume the conch chowder.

Part I: Introducing The Bahamas

In this part, we offer our opinions on the best attractions and experiences The Bahamas have to offer, and we give you an overview of Bahamian customs, music, festivals, cuisine, and "thirst-busters." We also compare and contrast the most popular islands of The Bahamas so that you can decide which place (or places) best suits your tastes. Sure, they all have gorgeous beaches, but that's where the similarities end.

We also tell you the best and worst times of the year to travel to The Bahamas. We explain *high season* (when prices go up) and *low season* (when prices go down again), and we highlight the advantages and dis-advantages of traveling during these times of year. We also provide a calendar of events in case you want to plan your trip to coincide with a festival, tournament, or local holiday.

Part II: Planning Your Trip to The Bahamas

Part II lays out everything you need to know about how to plan a worry-free trip. Because money is a primary consideration, we tell you how to access your funds, and we provide tips on how you can stay within your budget. We also help you decide how to travel to The Bahamas. If you're flying, you discover how to get hold of the best fares, or if you're travel-ing by cruise ship, we show you how to link up with some of the best deals for your "floating hotel" to The Bahamas.

To help you plan a stay that's tailored to your preferences, we explain in detail the various accommodations awaiting you, from simple Bahamian inns and guesthouses to mega-resorts. We offer trip-planning tips for newlyweds, soon-to-be-newlyweds, families, singles, gays and lesbians, seniors, and travelers with disabilities. You also find out everything you need to know about the boring but vital stuff, such as getting a passport and purchasing travel insurance.

Parts III through VI: The Islands

These parts are where we dish out the main course. The chapters in Parts III through VI are the juiciest morsels of the book because they're packed with all the fun stuff that makes a vacation a vacation. For each island or island group — New Providence, Grand Bahama (Freeport/

Lucaya), the Abacos, the Eleuthera chain (including Harbour Island), the Exumas, Bimini, San Salvador, and some of the less-visited islands for escapists — you get the lowdown on hotels, what to expect when you arrive (from landing at the airport to dealing with local taxi drivers), what restaurants to try and, of course, where to go and what to do, including beaching it.

For each island, we include a section called "Fast Facts." These quick tips give you handy information that you may need, including phone numbers to use in an emergency, where to find area hospitals and pharmacies, where to find ATMs, and more. For the bigger islands, you find "Fast Facts" at the end of the "Settling In" chapters. For the smaller islands, you can locate them at the ends of the chapters.

Part VII: The Part of Tens

As in every *For Dummies* book, this lighthearted part is just for fun. We share our ten favorite island experiences with you, along with ten common myths about The Bahamas.

Icons Used in This Book

Throughout this book, icons highlight useful information. Here's what each symbol means:

Keep an eye out for the Bargain Alert icon as you seek out money-saving tips and great deals.

Best of the Best highlights the best the destination has to offer in all categories — hotels, restaurants, attractions, activities, shopping, and nightlife.

Watch for the Heads Up icon to identify annoying or potentially dangerous situations, such as tourist traps, unsafe neighborhoods, monetary rip-offs, and other things to beware.

Look to the Kid Friendly icon for attractions, hotels, restaurants, or activities that are particularly hospitable to children or people traveling with kids.

When you see the Tip icon, you find useful advice on things to do and ways to schedule your time.

The Worth the Search icon points out secret discoveries or useful resources that are worth the extra bit of effort to find.

Where to Go from Here

Nothing's like a vacation in the islands — when you plan it with the right advice and inside tips, that is. Whether you're a veteran traveler or a rookie, this book helps you put together just the kind of trip you have in mind. So, start turning these pages, and before you know it, you'll feel that warm island breeze on your face.

Part I

Introducing
The Bahamas

The 5th Wave   By Rich Tennant

"My thinking has changed a little this year."

In this part . . .

We arm you with everything you need to know about The Bahamas before you begin making your travel plans. We tell you about the best the islands have to offer, and we introduce you to the islands' customs, music, and cuisine.

After giving you an overview of this sunny archipelago, we describe the highlights and drawbacks of each island and help you decide exactly where you want to go. We also give you an enjoyable quiz that helps you pinpoint the island or islands that match your preferences. Finally, we help you choose the best time of year to travel to your island getaway.

Chapter 1

Discovering the Best of The Bahamas

*I*n The Bahamas, you can island-hop by boat or scuba dive along what some devotees believe are the remains of the lost continent of Atlantis. Or perhaps your idea of a perfect island vacation is to plunk yourself down on a pink-sand beach with a frosted drink in hand. Whether you're looking for adventure or relaxation — or a bit of both — this chapter points you to the best The Bahamas has to offer. Throughout the book, look for the "Best of the Best" icons that highlight our picks.

The Best Beaches

✔ **Cable Beach** (New Providence): This crescent-shaped, sandy, 6.5km (4-mile) strip of shoreline is even better than Paradise Island's Cabbage Beach, which is more crowded. The prime beach-front strip of Cable Beach came into prominence during the post–World War II boom on the island, and today the beach is a beehive of activities ranging from water-skiing to banana-boat rides. Cable Beach isn't always kid-safe, however — during the winter months waters are sometimes rough. See Chapter 13.

✔ **Cabbage Beach** (Paradise Island): The sandy strands of Paradise Island, across the waters from New Providence, are called Cabbage Beach (no one's quite sure how the beach got its name). Cabbage Beach is the showpiece of Paradise Island; a spectacular strip of sand running in front of the swanky Ocean Club Resort that's ideal for swimming, sunning, and watersports, such as Jet-Skiing and parasailing. The big drawback to this beach is that it's overcrowded in winter. There's no admission charge, but non-guests may be charged to use the facilities of hotels along the beach. Cabbage Beach stretches for 3km (2 miles), rimming the north coast from the Atlantic lagoon all the way to the intimate Snorkeler's Cove. See Chapter 13.

✓ **Xanadu Beach** (Grand Bahama): In Samuel T. Coleridge's *Kubla Khan*, Xanadu is an idyllic, exotic, and luxurious place, and so is this aptly named stretch of white sands. Xanadu Beach is located on the most populated sector of this sprawling island and is convenient to the resorts of Freeport and Lucaya. The surf is most often tranquil, and the white sands stretch for 1.6km (1 mile). During the winter, Xanadu Beach is crowded, but it's a year-round magnet, with kid-friendly waters from spring to fall. The best watersports on the island are here. See Chapter 17.

✓ **Tahiti Beach** (Elbow Cay): Think South Pacific in The Bahamas. Lying at the far southern end of remote Elbow Cay Island in the yachting haven of the Abacos, this relatively undiscovered beach is Paradise Found. After three days on this strip of white sands, you lose all sense of time and space, and may be tempted to devote the rest of your life to beachcombing. The sands of Tahiti Beach are set against a backdrop of thick walls of palm trees. See Chapter 19.

✓ **Treasure Cay Beach** (Treasure Cay): Tucked away on a remote island in the Abacos, Treasure Cay Beach is one of the best beaches in The Bahamas, or even the Caribbean. Treasure Cay Beach is so large — 5.5km (2½ miles) — that you never feel crowded, even during the high season. Nowhere else in the Abacos (or most anywhere else) can you find sand this soft and white. Unpolluted water in striking shades of blue and green washes up on this peaceful shore. See Chapter 21.

✓ **Pink Sand Beach** (Harbour Island): In our view, no beach in the Out Islands — or even in Nassau, Grand Bahama, or Paradise Island — tops this lovely strip of pink sands that stretches for a whopping 5km (3 miles). Swimming is idyllic year-round because the natural harbor is protected by reefs that break up the turbulent sea's waves. Going sunning in the morning is best because afternoon can be a bit shadowy. See Chapter 22.

✓ **Ten Bay Beach** (Eleuthera): These golden sands, lying just north of Savannah Sound, are waiting for your beach towel. Don't expect watersports kiosks, fast-food stands, and vendors pushing handicrafts. Instead, expect relatively undiscovered sands opening onto generally tranquil waters. In the 1960s, this beach was one of the most fashionable in The Bahamas, but the exclusive clubs that once flourished here are long gone, leaving . . . well, the beach. See Chapter 23.

The Best Places to Get Away from It All

✔ **One&Only Ocean Club** (Paradise Island; ☎ 800-321-3000 or 242-363-2501): This hideaway is the most exclusive on New Providence and the adjoining Paradise Island. A true pocket of posh, the Ocean Club was once a private club owned by A&P zillionaire Huntington Hartford, but today it's a glitzy sanctuary of elegance and charm. Surrounded by splendid terraced gardens, it offers a country-club ambience, prime beachfront, and gourmet dining. See Chapter 11.

✔ **Viva Wyndham Fortuna Beach** (Grand Bahama Island; ☎ 242-373-4000): Away from the hordes of Freeport or Lucaya, this resort hotel sits on 11 hectares (26 secluded acres) and opens onto one of the best white sandy beaches on the island. A stay at this hideaway on the water is like being in a world far removed from bustling Lucaya. Like an Italian version of Club Med. See Chapter 15.

✔ **Hope Town Hideaways** (Elbow Cay; ☎ 242-366-0224): This series of gingerbread villas lies across the harbor from where the ferryboats from Marsh Harbour arrive. The "hideaways" in this resort's name is apt. It is reached only by boat and lies on its own 11-acre site. The grounds are beautifully landscaped and some of the villas are large enough to sleep six guests comfortably. See Chapter 19.

✔ **Green Turtle Club & Marina** (Green Turtle Cay; ☎ 800-963-5450 or 242-365-4271): Boasting the most complete yachting facility in its archipelago, this resort is one of the most charming of the "in" spots. Green Turtle Club has some of the best fishing and diving facilities. The villas include kitchens, and standard rooms are decorated in the colonial style. Two small, white sandy beaches are within walking distance. See Chapter 20.

✔ **Treasure Cay Hotel Resort & Marina** (Treasure Cay; ☎ 800-327-1584 or 242-365-8801): Boaters, golfers, fishermen, divers, yachties, and just plain escapists retreat to this luxurious resort on remote Treasure Cay. This resort boasts 5.5km (3½ miles) of spectacular sandy beach, and guests stay in privately owned condos when the owners aren't using them. The standout attractions here are the superb 18-hole golf course and the 150-slip marina. See Chapter 21.

✔ **Pink Sands** (Harbour Island; ☎ 800-OUTPOST or 242-333-2030): Posh and sophisticated, this plush hideaway opens onto a 5km (3-mile) stretch of pink sandy beach sheltered by a barrier reef. This luxury resort features a main house and one- and two-bedroom villas spread across 10 hectares (25 acres) of property. This resort serves the best meals in Harbour Island. See Chapter 22.

✔ **Four Seasons Resort Great Exuma at Emerald Bay** (Exuma; ☎ 800-819-5053 or 242-366-6800): The grandest resort to open in the Out Islands, this 183-room resort is waking up this sleepy archipelago, whose tranquil waters are loved by yachties. At the Four Seasons' centerpiece is an 18-hole golf course designed by Greg Norman, and the resort's full-service spa and health club is also the finest in the Out Islands. See Chapter 24.

✔ **Club Med–Columbus Isle** (San Salvador; ☎ 800-CLUB-MED or 242-331-2000): One of the most remote — and luxurious — Club Meds in the Western Hemisphere opens onto one of the most pristine beaches in the southern Bahamas. This getaway attracts tennis buffs along with scuba divers, honeymooners, and escapists. Other enticements include the lavishly decorated public lounges and the supremely comfortable bedrooms. See Chapter 25.

The Best Honeymoon Resorts

✔ **Sandals Royal Bahamian Hotel** (New Providence; ☎ 800-SANDALS or 242-327-6400): If you're "any couple in love," you can receive the most lavish and catered honeymoon in New Providence or Paradise Island. The way to go, of course, is to book one of the 27 secluded honeymoon suites with semiprivate plunge pools. The staff handles on-site wedding celebrations, and you're supplied with everything from the minister to the flowers, not to mention champagne and a wedding cake. See Chapter 11.

✔ **Wyndham Nassau Resort & Crystal Palace Casino** (New Providence; ☎ 800-222-7466 or 242-327-6200): If you and your loved one want glitter and bright lights instead of romantic isolation, this mega-resort is for you. Honeymooners flock here for its wide array of drinking, dining, and gambling options. Of course, when it's time to put up the DO NOT DISTURB sign and retreat to a king-size bed, that's all right, too. Ask about honeymoon package deals. See Chapter 11.

✔ **Dunmore Beach Club** (Harbour Island; ☎ 800-891-3100 or 242-333-2200): The quintessential elegant hideaway. Dunmore Beach club stands on its own 3.2 hectares (8 acres) of landscaped rooms and opens onto the most beautiful beach in The Bahamas — and pink at that. You sleep in romantic cottages with private patios and can use the hot tubs in the units to get better acquainted with your mate. See Chapter 22.

✔ **One&Only Ocean Club** (Paradise Island; ☎ 800-321-3000 or 242-363-2501): On lush acres between the golf course and a white sandy beach, this resort is a chic — though costly — address. Ocean Club is a haven of tranquillity, with fine dining, formal gardens, luxury rooms and suites, and even reflecting pools that stretch toward a cloister assembled stone by stone from Europe. No staff on the island pampers honeymooners more, but if you want to be left alone with your mate, the staff gently retreats. See Chapter 11.

✔ **Abaco Inn** (Elbow Cay; ☎ **800-468-8799** or 242-366-0133): For barefoot elegance in the sands and romance, this sophisticated little hideaway is one of the gems of the yachting haven known as the Abacos. Luxury villa suites with sunrise and sunset views are the way to go. If you and your loved one find a hammock in the gardens, the day is yours. See Chapter 19.

✔ **Bluff House Beach Hotel** (Green Turtle Cay; ☎ **800-745-4911** or 242-365-4247): This hotel, located in a romantic spot on a secluded beach, is an escapist's dream. The hotel has a nautical charm with British colonial overtones. The best honeymoon accommodations are the spacious suites, with cathedral ceilings and balconies overlooking the Sea of Abaco, and a beach nearby. The 4 hectares (10 acres) on which the hotel sits are some of the most desirable real estate in The Bahamas. See Chapter 20.

✔ **Pink Sands** (Harbour Island; ☎ **800-OUTPOST** or 242-333-2030): This resort is the one place in all The Bahamas where we'd personally go for a honeymoon. Chris Blackwell, who brought reggae star Bob Marley to world attention, created the most sophisticated hideaway in the Out Islands. It opens onto the pink sands of one of the country's greatest beaches, which stretches for 5km (3 miles). The inn's luxurious accommodations are set on an 11-hectare (28-acre), beautifully landscaped estate. See Chapter 22.

The Best Family Resorts

✔ **Radisson Cable Beach Resort** (Cable Beach; ☎ **800-333-3333** or 242-327-6000): A well-organized kids' camp lures families to this sprawling 691-room resort, which opens onto some of the best sands along Cable Beach right outside Nassau. The resort's children's activities are the best organized on New Providence (though they're nowhere near the equal of Atlantis on Paradise Island). An added plus is that many of the bedrooms contain two double beds, making them suitable for families of four. Dining is no problem here because of the vast array of possibilities. See Chapter 11.

✔ **Atlantis Paradise Island Resort & Casino** (Paradise Island; ☎ **800-ATLANTIS** or 242-363-3000): Imagine yourself and your kids washed up on the shores of the lost continent of Atlantis. The Bahamas don't offer any other choices that are more fun for a family vacation than this sprawling mega-resort, a true fantasy world that's nautical with a vengeance. The children's programs (for ages 4–12) are the most spectacular in the country. Better yet, kids can spend hours cavorting through a "sea world" of underground grottoes that sprawls across 5.7 hectares (14 acres) and includes aquariums, underwater viewing tunnels, and cascading waterfalls. See Chapter 11.

✔ **Ritz Beach Resort** (Lucaya; ☎ 242-373-9354): Think Disney on Grand Bahama Island. Surrounded by semi-tropical gardens, the Ritz is in the midst of all the fun, next door to a water park and the Pirates of The Bahamas Theme Park (all that's missing is Johnny Depp). Efficiencies, one-bedroom suites, or multi-level studio penthouses with private pools are available to suit the needs of your family. See Chapter 15.

✔ **Lofty Fig Villas** (Marsh Harbour; ☎ 242-367-2681): This family-owned bungalow colony is for self-sufficient types who want more of a Robinson Crusoe holiday. Vacationing families meet like-minded people around the outdoor barbecue or the freshwater pool. Each bungalow comes with a fully equipped kitchen and a private screened-in porch. See Chapter 18.

✔ **Banyan Beach Club Resort** (Treasure Cay; ☎ 888-625-3060 or 242-365-8111): Right on a beach that's widely hailed as one of the world's top ten, this resort offers spacious condos that are well suited for families. All the condos come with complete kitchens, and you can get burgers and hot dogs served at the beach bar and grill. For larger families, two-bedroom accommodations with an additional sleeping area are available. See Chapter 21.

✔ **Four Seasons Resort Great Exuma at Emerald Bay** (Great Exuma; ☎ 800-819-5053 or 242-366-6800): This resort is the only major resort in the Exumas, or in all the southern Bahamas, that caters to families, and it does so exceedingly well with its well-organized children's programs. If your budget allows, book one of the idyllic beachfront properties that has one or two bedrooms. The array of activities, the great beaches, the wide variety of dining options, and the overall comfort make this resort a winning choice. See Chapter 24.

The Best Restaurants

✔ **Chez Willie** (Nassau; ☎ 242-322-5364): One of the most elegant and romantic restaurants in New Providence, Chez Willie recaptures some of the magic of Nassau in the 1940s during the heyday of the Duke and Duchess of Windsor. The host, Willie Armstrong, is the epitome of graciousness, and the French and Bahamian cuisine is elegantly presented and beautifully prepared. See Chapter 12.

✔ **Sun and . . .** (Nassau; ☎ 242-393-1205): This restaurant, which serves Continental (mainly French) cuisine and seafood, is a Nassau classic with an overlay of British charm. The chef uses exceptional products along with a finely honed technique in the kitchen and is known for his to-die-for soufflés. See Chapter 12.

✔ **Sole Mare** (Cable Beach; ☎ 242-327-6200): The most elegant choice for dining on the beachfront strip outside Nassau also serves the finest Northern Italian cuisine on island. Candlelit tables and a guitarist playing soft tunes add to its romantic allure. See Chapter 12.

✔ **Dune** (Paradise Island; ☎ **242-363-2501,** ext. 64739): This elegant dining choice is located on the lobby level of the chic Ocean Club. French-born master chef and restaurant guru Jean-Georges Vongerichten created this fine dining experience. With its trendy décor and sweeping view of the ocean, Dune is a study in culinary classicism, where flavors, aromas, and textures are perfectly combined. See Chapter 12.

✔ **Bahamian Club** (Paradise Island; ☎ **242-363-3000**): A notch down from the superb Dune, this strictly upscale establishment is one of the leading restaurants in The Bahamas and is our favorite at the sprawling mega-resort of Atlantis. It presents a superb French and international cuisine nightly against a backdrop that evokes the British colonial era. The restaurant serves the island's finest cuts of meats. See Chapter 12.

✔ **Rock House Restaurant** (Harbour Island; ☎ **242-333-2053**): On the increasingly chic Harbour Island, the restaurant in the Rock House Hotel serves superb international cuisine. Its hip *bodega* aura evokes Miami, but it's thoroughly grounded on the island. At lunch you can get a rock lobster sandwich, but at night the chefs display their culinary prowess with an array of satisfying dishes. See Chapter 22.

The Best Diving

✔ **New Providence:** Right off the coast of Nassau lies a spectacular underwater world with many stunning dive sites that offer a panorama of rainbow-hued fish, large sponges, and a wide variety of coral reef life along with ocean holes, wrecks, old shipwrecks, caves, and cliffs. One of the greatest dive sites is Shark Wall, which is 16km (10 miles) off the coast of New Providence. Other good dive sites are Southwest Reef, Razorback, Booby Rock Reef, and Rose Island Reef.

The coastline of New Providence, called "the best-kept diving secret in The Bahamas," is home to some fascinating wrecks that you can explore in shallow water, including the *Mahoney* and the *Alcora*. The *Never Say Never Again* wreck was a backdrop for the James Bond film: A 34m (100-ft.) freighter, seized as a drug runner, was sunk by the film crew. Nearby, you can explore the remains of an airplane prop created for another Bond thriller, *Thunderball*. The best outfitter is **Bahama Divers** (☎ **242-393-5644**). See Chapter 13.

✔ **Grand Bahama:** On Grand Bahama, you can hook up with **Underwater Explorer's Society** (UNEXSO; ☎ **800-992-DIVE** or 242-373-1244), which is one of the premier dive outfitters in The Bahamas. Its escorted dives include a series of dramatic reef trips, shark dives, shipwreck dives, and even night dives. See Chapter 17.

✔ **Theo's Wreck** (Grand Bahama): This is one of the most famous wrecks in The Bahamas, and it lies off Freeport. The site is ideal for photo ops. In 1982, the 70m (230-ft.) freighter was deliberately sunk just to attract marine life. It succeeded: The wreck teems with sea turtles, moray eels, eagle rays, and horse-eyed jacks, among other creatures of the deep. For spur and groove coral beds, you can also explore other dive sites, including Gold Rock, Pygmy Caves, and Silver Point Reef. If you're an experienced diver, you can explore these sites independently; otherwise, hook up with the previously recommended UNEXSO. See Chapter 17.

✔ **Marsh Harbour:** You can explore the *Abacos Train Wreck* in 4.5 to 6m (15–20 ft.) of water. This wreck consists of two almost-intact locomotives lying on their sides. Another wreck in the area, *Adirondack,* also lies in shallow water some 3 to 7.5m (10–25 ft.) deep. Marsh Harbour is also the jumping-off point for the government-protected **Sea Preserve** and **Fowl Cay Land,** both teeming with sea life in shallow reefs. Divers have actually kissed barracudas here (not recommended!). Look for "The Towers," two coral towers rising 23m (75 ft.). The best outfitter is **Dive Abaco** (☎ **800-247-5338** or 242-367-2787). See Chapter 18.

✔ **Exuma Cays Land and Sea Park:** A major attraction of The Bahamas, this park, inaugurated in 1958, is the first of its kind in the world. The 35km-long (22-mile), 13km-wide (8-mile) natural preserve attracts scuba divers to its 453 sq. km (175 sq. miles) of sea gardens with spectacular reefs, flora, and fauna. You can access it only by boat. See Chapter 24.

✔ **San Salvador:** Some of the best diving in the southern Bahamas centers around this remote island, which is the site of Riding Rock, a dive resort, and a Club Med. Some 40 well-preserved dive sites are no more than 45 minutes away by boat from either resort. You can experience *wall diving* here — diving amid stunning sea walls at sites where the coral reef drops steeply. The underwater photography is great here, and you can even arrange to night dive. The best outfitter is **Guanahani Dive Ltd.** (☎ **242-331-2631**). See Chapter 25.

The Best Snorkeling

✔ **New Providence/Paradise Island:** Most of the big hotels and resorts at Cable Beach and on Paradise Island lend or rent snorkeling equipment. A number of intriguing sights await you, especially at Love Beach on New Providence. Also attracting snorkelers are such areas as Rose Island Reefs, Booby Rock Channel, the Goulding Reef Cays, and Gambier Deep Reef, plus some underwater wrecks lying in shallow water. **Bahamas Divers** (☎ **242-393-5644**) can give you the most helpful advice on snorkeling possibilities. The company's branch on Paradise Island is located at the Sheraton Grand

Resort (☎ 242-393-8724). Also consider **Hartley's Undersea Walk** (☎ 242-393-8234), which allows you to walk through an underwater world. See Chapter 13.

✔ **Grand Bahama:** Resort hotels on island can hook you up with snorkeling excursions, such as the ones offered by **Ocean Motion Water Sports Ltd.** (☎ 242-374-2425), which is the best outfitter for snorkeling. In addition, the outlet can connect you with any number of other watersports, from banana-boating to water-skiing. The clear water around Grand Bahama is wonderful for snorkeling because it has a rich marine life. Snorkelers are fond of exploring Ben's Cave, a stunning cavern that's part of Lucayan Caves, as well as the coral beds at places like Silver Point Reef and Gold Rock. See Chapter 17.

✔ **Elbow Cay:** With its 209km (130-mile) string of beautiful cays and some of the best beaches in The Bahamas, the Abacos are ideal for snorkeling, especially in the waters off Elbow Cay. Visibility is often great because the cay lies close to the cleansing waters of the Gulf Stream. Mermaid Beach, a particularly colorful reef, is a favorite. **Sea Horse Boat Rentals** (☎ 242-367-2513) provides equipment and the best snorkeling advice. See Chapter 19.

✔ **Green Turtle Cay:** Because the Abacos have one of the world's largest barrier reefs, the island chain — and especially Green Turtle Cay — is a snorkeler's delight. Some of the colorful reefs start at depths of just 1.5m (5 ft.). Immerse yourself in a world of schools of fish along with coral caverns, huge tube and barrel sponges, and fields of elk and staghorn coral. Snorkelers can contact **Green Turtle Divers** (☎ 242-365-4271) or **Brendal's Dive Center** (☎ 242-365-4411). See Chapter 20.

✔ **Stocking Island:** George Town is the capital of Exuma, which is celebrated for its crystal-clear waters so beloved by yachties. From George Town, Stocking Island lies across Elizabeth Harbour, which is only 1.5km (1 mile) away. Stocking Island is a long, thin, barrier island that attracts snorkelers who explore its blue holes (ocean pools of fresh water floating on heavier salt water). The island is also ringed with undersea caves and coral gardens in stunning colors. Stocking Island also has some of the most gorgeous white-sand beaches in the southern Bahamas. See Chapter 24.

✔ **San Salvador:** Following in the footsteps of Columbus, snorkelers find a rich paradise on this relatively undiscovered island, with its unpolluted and unpopulated kilometers and kilometers of beaches that are ideal for swimming, shelling, and close-in snorkeling. A week's stay is enough time to become acquainted only with the possibilities, including Bamboo Point, Fernandez Bay, and Long Bay, which are all within a few kilometers of Cockburn (the main settlement) on the western side of the island. At the southern tip of San Salvador is one of our favorite places for snorkeling, Sandy Point, and its satellite, Grotto Bay. See Chapter 25.

The Best Fishing

✔ **New Providence/Paradise Island:** The waters around New Providence are thick with game fish. In-the-know fishermen long ago learned the best months to pursue their catches: November through February for wahoo found in the reefs, June and July for blue marlin, and May through August for the oceanic bonito and blackfin tuna. Nassau is ideal for sportfishing. Most boat charters allow their passengers to start fishing within 15 minutes after leaving the dock. The best outfitter is **Born Free Charters (☎ 242-393-4144)**, where anchoring and bottom-fishing are also options. See Chapter 13.

✔ **Grand Bahama:** Off the coast, the clear waters are good hunting grounds for snapper, grouper, yellowtail, wahoo, barracuda, and kingfish. The tropical waters along Grand Bahama lure anglers in search of "the big one" because the island is home to some of the biggest game fish on earth. Many fishermen catch dolphins (not the Flipper kind, though). And Deep Water Cay is a fishing hot spot. The best outfitter is **Reef Tours, Ltd. (☎ 242-373-5880)**. See Chapter 17.

✔ **Green Turtle Cay:** The deep-sea fishing possibilities off the coast of this cay draw anglers from all over the world. An abundance of giant game fish as well as tropical fish live in these beautiful waters. Both dedicated fishermen and more casual sportfishermen come to the little island, seeking yellowfin tuna, a few dolphinfish, and the big game wahoo, among other catches. Green Turtle Cay boasts some of the best fishing guides in The Bahamas: weather-beaten men who've spent a lifetime fishing the surrounding waters. The best place to hook up with one of these guides is **Green Turtle Club (☎ 242-365-4271)**. See Chapter 20.

✔ **Treasure Cay:** In the Abacos, some of the best fishing grounds are in the sea bordering this remote island. At the **Treasure Cay Marina (☎ 242-365-8250)**, fishermen from all over the world hire experienced skippers to take them out in their searches for barracuda, grouper, yellowtail, snapper, tuna, marlin, dolphinfish, and wahoo. Deep-sea, sea-bottom, and drift fishing are yours for the asking. The cay's own bonefish flats are just a short boat cruise from the marina. See Chapter 21.

✔ **Exuma:** Anglers from all over America descend on this beautiful archipelago for deep-sea or bottom-fishing. Fishermen hunt down kingfish, wahoo, dolphinfish, tuna, and bonito in the deepest waters off the coastline of the Exumas. Many visitors also fly here just to go bonefishing. Among other outfitters who can hook you up with fishing outings is **Club Peace & Plenty (☎ 242-345-5555)**, which rents the necessary equipment and can arrange experienced guides to accompany you. See Chapter 24.

The Best Sailing

✔ **New Providence:** Although sailing in the waters off New Providence isn't the equal of yachting-favorites the Exumas and the Abacos, boaters can still find much to delight in. More organized-boating excursions are offered in New Providence than anywhere else in The Bahamas, especially by outfitters, such as **Barefoot Sailing Cruises** (☎ 242-393-0820) and **Majestic Tours Ltd.** (☎ 242-322-2606). You can also choose from an array of sunset cruises, like the ones **Flying Cloud** (☎ 242-393-4430) offers, which feature its fleet of catamarans. The most popular — and the most scenic — trip is sailing to tranquil Rose Island, which is 13km (8 miles) east of the center of Nassau and is reached after sailing past several small uninhabited cays. In addition, Blue Lagoon Island, 4.8km (3 miles) northeast of Paradise Island, is a magnet for boaters because it offers seven white-sand beaches along with seaside hammocks. The drawback to this island, however, is that cruise-ship passengers flock here and many beach buffs come over on day trips. See Chapter 13.

✔ **Grand Bahama:** On the beautiful waters off this large island, you can go sailing aboard *Ocean Wonder* (☎ 242-373-5880), which is supposedly the world's largest twin-diesel engine glass-bottom boat. This boat offers the best and most panoramic view of underlife off the coast of Grand Bahama Island — a view most often reserved for scuba divers. You can also go sailing aboard *Bahama Mama,* a two-deck 22m (72-ft.) catamaran, on a Robinson Crusoe Beach Party. The catamaran also sails at sunset on a booze cruise. **Superior Watersports** (☎ 242-373-7863) operates this catamaran. See Chapter 17.

✔ **Marsh Harbour:** One of the finest anchorages in the Out Islands is found in Marsh Harbour, which is called "The Boating Capital of The Bahamas." **The Moorings** (☎ 888-952-8420 or 242-367-4000) is one of the leading charter sailboat outfitters in the world, renting boats to sail the waters of the Abacos. Passengers discover white sand beaches and snug anchorages on uninhabited cays. Sailing here is one of the great experiences of visiting The Bahamas. See Chapter 18.

✔ **Exuma:** Yachties flock to these beautiful sailing waters to see some of the most dramatic coastal scenery in The Bahamas. The National Family Island Regatta, the most popular boating spectacle in The Bahamas, is held here annually. Most recreational boating is in the government-protected Exumas Cays Land and Sea Park, an area of splendid sea gardens and rainbow-hued coral reefs that stretches south from Wax Cay to Conch Cay. You can rent motorboats at **Minns Water Sports** (☎ 242-336-3483) in George Town. See Chapter 24.

The Best Shopping

✔ **Nassau:** Nassau is home to more shops than anyplace else in The Bahamas. If you're seeking anything from a Swiss watch to British-made china, you can find it at one of the shops along Bay Street in the heart of Nassau. Some of the merchandise — but hardly all of it — sells at discounts that range from 30 to 50 percent. You can purchase a lot of the merchandise for the same price or lower in your hometown, so the wise shopper who knows his prices can make off with the bargain merchandise. Surprisingly, goods actually made in The Bahamas are hard to come by. If you're in the market for Bahamian handicrafts, you can stroll by the famous Straw Market in Nassau, but watch which items you pick up — that handicraft may have MADE IN TAIWAN stamped on it. See Chapter 13.

✔ **Grand Bahama:** The only island in The Bahamas to rival the shopping in Nassau is the **Freeport/Lucaya** area. Much of the same merchandise that's sold in New Providence — including international imports of china, perfume, crystal, gemstones, or watches — is also for sale here at virtually the same prices. We're drawn more to the **Port Lucaya Marketplace** these days than to the more famous **International Bazaar** at Freeport. The situation at both markets is very tricky. We've found merchandise 20 to 40 percent lower than Stateside prices displayed along with so-called "discounted" and "duty-free" products that were actually cheaper in our hometown. See Chapter 17.

The Best Nightlife

✔ **Cable Beach:** The partying crowd packs the bars and restaurants at the resorts along this beachfront strip at night. Most of the action is around the **Crystal Palace Casino** (☎ 242-327-6200) in the center of Cable Beach. This resort and casino obviously evoke Las Vegas and stand up well when compared to other glittering casinos in the Caribbean. See Chapter 13.

✔ **Paradise Island:** The most glamorous casino in The Bahamas is **Atlantis Paradise Island Resort** (☎ 242-363-3000), which is the largest casino in the Caribbean. When you tire of blackjack, you can also join the party at the resort's **Dragons Night Club** (see Chapter 13).

✔ **Grand Bahama:** Most of the after-dark diversions on this island spin around its casino: the **Isle of Capri Casino** at the Westin & Sheraton at Our Lucaya Resorts (☎ 242-373-1333). In winter, guests can catch periodic stage shows, which pack the house with Las Vegas–style revues. Another popular gathering place is **Count Basie Square** at the Port Lucaya Marketplace, where musicians perform live three nights a week. And did we mention that it's free? See Chapter 17 for more information about nightlife on Grand Bahama.

Chapter 2

Digging Deeper into The Bahamas

*F*ollowing in the footsteps of Columbus, Ponce de León arrived in The Bahamas searching for the legendary Fountain of Youth, which led to the discovery of Florida and the Gulf Stream. Chances are your own discoveries won't be quite as legendary. But part of the fun of visiting The Bahamas is getting a taste of island life — and that means listening to Junkanoo music, eating conch prepared in countless ways, meeting the friendly locals (who'd rather not be called "natives"), discovering guava duff (our favorite dessert), finding the bar that makes the best Bahama Mamas and, in general, putting yourself on "island time," which is one slow-moving clock.

In this chapter, we've assembled some easy-to-digest cultural information — historical background, culinary tidbits, local lingo, and films or books you may want to check out before your trip — that we hope will help you better appreciate your own island discoveries.

History 101: The Main Events

This island nation has an exciting history — a tale of conquistadors, pirates, rumrunners, and post-colonial prosperity. Here's the story.

The early years

Columbus first landed in the New World somewhere in The Bahamas on October 12, 1492. He landed on an island called "Guanahani" by the local inhabitants, who were Arawak Indians known as Lucayans. Columbus renamed the island San Salvador. Over the years, exactly which island

Columbus landed on has been much disputed. Recent research places the first landing on Samana Cay, 105km (65 miles) southeast of the island that today is known as San Salvador. (Just to make things more confusing, San Salvador is also sometimes called Watling Island.)

The Lucayans Columbus encountered are believed to have come to the islands from the Greater Antilles in the eighth century A.D. They were seeking refuge from the Carib Indians then living in the Lesser Antilles. The Lucayans were peaceful people who welcomed the Spaniards and taught them a skill soon shared with the entire seafaring world: how to make hammocks from heavy cotton cloth.

The Spanish conquistadors, who claimed the islands for their king and queen, didn't repay the Lucayans kindly. Finding neither gold nor silver mines nor fertile soil, the conquistadors cleared out the population of the islands, taking some 40,000 doomed Lucayans to other islands in the Spanish empire to work in mines or dive for pearls.

Ponce de León voyaged here in 1513 looking for the legendary Fountain of Youth. His journey led to the European discovery of Florida and the Gulf Stream — but not the magic fountain. Ponce de León's historian described the waters of the Little Bahama Bank — just north of Grand Bahama — as *bajamar* (pronounced "bahamar," which is Spanish for "shallow water"). This word seems to be a reasonable source of the name "Bahamas." Other than this mention, however, practically no references were made to the islands first discovered by Columbus for 135 years.

The coming of the English

England formally claimed The Bahamas — by then unpopulated — in 1629. No settling took place, however, until the 1640s, following a religious dispute that arose in Bermuda. Dissident English and Bermudian settlers (known as the Eleutheran Adventurers) sailed to an island called Cigatoo, changed the name to Eleuthera (from the Greek word for freedom), and launched a tough battle for survival. Many settlers became discouraged and went back to Bermuda, but a few hardy souls remained, living on fish and salvage from shipwrecks.

Other people from Bermuda and England eventually followed, and they helped settle New Providence Island in 1656. They planted crops of cotton, tobacco, and sugar cane and established Charles Towne (named in honor of Charles II) at the harbor.

Pirates and privateers

The promising agricultural economy of The Bahamas was short-lived. Several of the governors of The Bahamas during the late 17th century were corrupt, and soon the island became a refuge for English, Dutch, and French buccaneers who plundered Spanish ships. The Spaniards repeatedly attacked New Providence for revenge, and many of the settlers left. Those settlers who remained found supplying the rich pirates to be a good source of income. Privateers, a slightly more respectable type of freebooter (they had their sovereign's permission to prey on enemy ships), also found the many islets, tricky shoals, and secret harbors of the islands to be good hiding places from which they could stage their attacks on ships sailing between the New and Old Worlds.

Late in the 17th century, the settlers changed the name of Charles Towne to Nassau to honor King William III, who also held the title Prince of Nassau. At the time, some 1,000 pirates still called New Providence their home base.

Finally, the appeals of merchants and law-abiding islanders in favor of Crown control were taken seriously, and in 1717 the lord proprietors turned over the government of The Bahamas, both civil and military, to King George I, who commissioned Captain Woodes Rogers as the first royal governor.

Rogers captured hundreds of the lawless pirates. He sent some pirates to England to be tried; eight were hanged, and the king pardoned others after they promised to lead law-abiding lives. Later, Rogers was given the authority to set up a representative assembly, the precursor of today's Parliament. Despite such interruptions as the fledgling U.S. Navy capturing Nassau in 1776 (for only a few days) and the Crown Colony surrendering to Spain in 1782 (which lasted almost a year), the government of The Bahamas since Rogers's time has been conducted in an orderly fashion. In early 1783 under the Treaty of Paris, Spain permanently ceded The Bahamas to Britain, ending some 300 years of disputed ownership.

Loyalists, blockade runners, and bootleggers

After the American Revolution, several thousand Loyalists from the former colonies immigrated to The Bahamas. Some of the immigrants, especially Southerners, brought slaves with them and tried their luck at planting sea-island cotton in the Out Islands. Growing cotton was unsuccessful (the plants fell prey to the chenille bug), but the former deep South planters learned to fish, grow vegetables, and provide for themselves in other ways.

The first white settlers of The Bahamas also brought slaves with them, but when slavery was abolished throughout the British Empire in 1834, they were freed. The settlers achieved a fairly peaceful transition, although many years passed before any real equality between blacks and whites existed.

During the American Civil War, blockade running brought prosperity to The Bahamas. Nassau became a vital base for the Confederacy, with vessels taking manufactured goods to South Carolina and North Carolina and bringing back cotton. The Union victory ended blockade running and plunged Nassau into an economic depression.

Important dates in Bahamian history

700 Lucayans emigrate to The Bahamas from the Greater Antilles, seeking refuge from the cannibalistic Caribs.

1492 Columbus makes his first landfall in the New World, traditionally said to be at San Salvador, although many historians dispute this theory.

1513 Ponce de León searches for the Fountain of Youth and discovers the Gulf Stream.

1629 England claims The Bahamas, which were then destitute of population.

1640s The first Western settlements are established.

1656 New Providence Island (site of Nassau) is settled.

1717 King George I orders Captain Woodes Rogers, the first royal governor, to chase the pirates out of Nassau.

1776 The fledgling United States Navy captures Nassau but soon departs.

1782 The British Crown Colony surrenders The Bahamas to Spain.

1783 Spain signs the Treaty of Paris, ceding The Bahamas to Britain.

1833 The United Kingdom Emancipation Act frees slaves throughout the British Empire.

1861–65 Blockade-running during the U.S. Civil War brings prosperity to The Bahamas.

1920–33 Rumrunning during Prohibition in the U.S. revives a slumping Bahamian economy. The 1920s are a busy and prosperous time for bootleggers.

1933 The repeal of Prohibition causes an economic collapse on the islands.

1940 The Duke of Windsor, after renouncing the British throne, becomes governor of The Bahamas as war rages in Europe.

1964 Sir Roland Symonette becomes the country's first premier. The Bahamas are granted internal self-government.

1967 Lynden Pindling, named premier in a close election, begins a long, notorious reign.

1968 African-Bahamian rule becomes firmly entrenched.

1972 Bahamians vote for total independence from Britain.

1973 On July 9, the Union Jack in New Providence is lowered for the last time, ending more than three centuries of British rule.

1992 After 25 years, controversial Prime Minister Pindling goes down in defeat. Hubert Ingraham, campaigning against corruption and recession, replaces him.

1994 Hotel mogul and entertainer Merv Griffin sells Paradise Island properties.

1995 Developers of the famed Sun City complex in Swaziland become hotel czars of Paradise Island.

2002 Perry Gladstone Christie becomes the third prime minister in the nation's history.

The islands' next real economic boom resulted from Prohibition in the U.S. Just like the blockade runners who preceded them — only with faster boats and more of them — rumrunners plied the waters between The Bahamas and the southeastern U.S. From the enforcement of the 18th Amendment in 1920 to the repeal of that law in 1933, bootleggers used Nassau, Bimini, and Grand Bahama as bases for running contraband alcoholic beverages across the Gulf Stream. The U.S. Coast Guard and the bootleggers waged a ceaseless battle on each other. The repeal of Prohibition dealt another shattering blow to the vulnerable Bahamian economy.

The war, the duke, and the woman he loved

On August 17, 1940, the Duke and Duchess of Windsor arrived in Nassau following his appointment as governor of the colony. The duke abdicated his throne as King Edward VIII so he could marry the woman he loved, the divorcée American Wallis Simpson. The people of The Bahamas were shocked that such a once-powerful figure was assigned to govern their impoverished colony, which was viewed then as a backwater of the British Empire. The duke tried to bring self-sufficiency to The Bahamas and provide more employment for its out-of-work population.

World War II healed the wounds left over from the bootlegging days. The Bahamas served as an air and sea station in the Atlantic; as a result, the country inherited two airports built by the U.S. Air Force. The islands also were strategically important when Nazi submarines intruded Atlantic coastal and Caribbean waters. Today, some of the outlying islands still house U.S. missile-tracking stations.

A declaration of independence

In the years after World War II, party politics developed in The Bahamas as independence from Britain seemed more possible, and change came at the ballot box. In 1967, Lynden Pindling won a close election to become prime minister. During the general election of 1972, the Bahamian people voted for total independence. The people of The Bahamas agreed to be a part of the British Commonwealth, presided over by Queen Elizabeth II. Her representative in The Bahamas would be a governor-general, a position with mostly symbolic power. In 1992, after years of corruption under Pindling and countless exposés in the *Miami Herald,* Hubert A. Ingraham became prime minister. In office, he pledged to promote quality tourism for his nation.

In May 2002, Perry Gladstone Christie led the Progressive Liberal Party to victory, becoming the third prime minister to govern the island nation. Public opinion seems divided on Christie's reign. Many voters praise him as a progressive, modern leader; others have attacked him, including scorching editorials in *The Nassau Guardian.* Christie has been accused of receiving a vast amount of campaign money from known drug dealers, an accusation that the prime minister denies.

Building Blocks: Local Architecture

The unique geography and history of The Bahamas contributed to a distinctive architectural feature — the Bahamian clapboard house — that is today one of the most broadly copied styles in the tropics. But this design wasn't perfected and standardized until the early 19th century.

The earliest clapboard-sided houses were usually angled to receive the trade winds. Large window openings and high ceilings increased airflow, and awning-style push-out shutters shaded the windows and helped direct breezes indoors, even during rainstorms. Unlike larger, more impressive houses where foundations were massive edifices of coral, brick, or stone, the first floors of Bahamian cottages were elevated on low stilts or light masonry pilings to allow more air circulation. Raising the building also kept the floor joists, beams, and planks above floodwaters during a hurricane surge.

Ruggedly built of timbers whose ends were often pegged (not nailed) together and pinned to stone pilings several feet above the ground, Bahamian-style clapboard houses survived when many rigid and unyielding stone-built structures collapsed during hurricanes. Modern engineers claim that the flexibility of these structures increases their stability in high winds.

Within The Bahamas, you can check out some of the best-preserved and most charming examples of the Bahamian cottage style in Harbour Island (off the coast of Eleuthera) and, to a lesser extent, in Spanish Wells and Green Turtle Cay.

Living on Island Time

Island clocks aren't wound as tightly as clocks in other parts of the world. Life in The Bahamas moves much more slowly than many visitors are used to. Waiters, salespeople, and hotel desk clerks operate at what some outsiders consider too leisurely a pace. Especially in Nassau and Freeport, you may find some poorly trained, less-than-accommodating staff members here and there. But getting annoyed is a waste of energy. Most travelers soon learn to go with the flow and get in step with island time. If you're going to enjoy your vacation, you have to crank your expectations about time — and sometimes service — down a notch.

Words to the Wise: The Local Language

Bahamian dialect has its own cadence and musical rhythm. Sometimes an educated Bahamian dining with you will speak a lilting Queen's English and then suddenly lapse into Bahamian dialect when he hits on an emotional subject.

Accents in The Bahamas resemble those of the Caribbean region, just south of these Atlantic isles. However, a trained ear can easily pick up the difference. Some Bahamians sound as if they were imported from Brooklyn. For example, *woik* is what you do *fuh* a living, and a waiter will *soive* you.

Sometimes the letters *v* and *w* are interchanged. "So you wisitin', ay?" translates into "So you're visiting, are you?" If a Bahamian tells you he's going "spilligatin'," he means that he's planning to "carry on bad" — he intends to party and have an all-out good time. If he says he wants "to conversate" (a common Bahamian variation of the verb "to converse") with you for a while, he wants to chat.

Some of the Loyalist villages, such as the ones found in Eleuthera, including Spanish Wells, retain certain pronunciations that were in use in the England of Shakespeare's day. For instance, the glass that someone serves your rum punch in may be called a *goblet.*

Taste of The Bahamas: Local Cuisine

When it's time to chow down in The Bahamas, settings range from casual family-run restaurants featuring local treats to elegant candlelit dining rooms offering gourmet international fare. The main source of food is the ocean. The steak you order may be juicy, but it didn't come from an island cattle farm. Instead, it was flown in to the airport and taken to the restaurant, along with lamb and other meats, as well as most of the fruits and vegetables on your plate.

You find plenty of good food here and some mediocre eats as well — imported or not. Menus throughout the islands are varied. You may dine on an Indian or Greek appetizer one night, an Italian or Tex-Mex main course another night, and a French dessert the next night.

Are you traveling with fussy kids? Don't worry. Burgers and fries, pizza, fried chicken, pasta, sandwiches, and other child-friendly fixings are easy to find, especially in Nassau and Freeport/Lucaya, where you find some fast-food chains.

For the tastiest, most authentic (and least expensive) island cuisine, head to the smaller, locally run restaurants, where the home-style cooking revolves around the sea. Even the so-called island dishes at the larger hotels and restaurants have American and Continental influences.

Eating like a local

Restaurants specializing in island cuisine commonly serve conch, fish (especially grouper), and lobster. Among other local favorites are crab and rice, okra soup, chicken and dough (dumplings), mutton, wild boar, and souse, but these dishes are harder to find outside of people's homes. If you stop by a local restaurant in the morning and see men eating souse or conch salad, chances are they're trying to kill hangovers; locals believe that the hot peppers do the trick.

In the dining sections of the chapters, we sprinkle in a number of local eateries serving authentic and affordable Bahamian cuisine. In Nassau, sample island cuisine at **Shoal Restaurant and Lounge** or the **Bahamian Kitchen** (see Chapter 12). On Grand Bahama Island, bite down at **Beckey's Restaurant & Lounge** or **Fatman's Nephew** (see Chapter 16). After you reach many of the Out Islands, Bahamian food is all you can order in some of the smaller places, except for a first-class resort here and there, including the ones found on Harbour Island. Other top locations to check out island treats include

- Stands on Potter's Cay, the dock beneath the Paradise Island exit bridge on New Providence.

- Many restaurants in The Bahamas' Out Islands (see Chapters 22 through 25).

- Kiosks during Bahamian festivals such as Junkanoo (at Christmas and New Year's) and the National Family Island Regatta (in George Town, Exuma, in Apr).

It's all about conch

The star of the culinary show is *conch* (pronounced "konk"). On every island at the edge of the water near boat docks, you see huge mounds of discarded conch shells — the kind with the shiny pink spiral interior that you put to your ear to hear the waves. Residents claim that conch gives men "strong back" — in other words, this tasty mollusk can raise the roof in the boudoir. No wonder the meat is transformed into so many local favorites, including

- **Conch chowder:** A rich, spicy soup with vegetables and bits of conch.

- **Conch fritters:** Golf ball–sized fried appetizers made with chopped conch, herbs, flour, baking powder, and water.

- **Conch salad:** Minced raw conch marinated in lime juice and mixed with chopped onions and peppers.

- **Cracked conch:** Pounded until tender, battered, and deep fried like a breaded veal cutlet.

- **Scorched conch:** Raw meat washed with seawater and lime juice, cut into large pieces and scored with a knife, and then rubbed with hot pepper and topped with sliced fresh tomatoes and onions. (You may catch fishermen on docks preparing this delicacy.)

- **Steamed conch:** Tenderized by beating or boiling, and then cooked with sautéed onions, bell peppers, hot peppers, thyme, tomatoes, and sometimes okra or carrots.

- **Stewed conch:** Made with a seasoned, flour-thickened gravy.

Dining on other Bahamian favorites

Fish, another staple, turns up for dinner, lunch, and even breakfast. Grouper and snapper are the usual suspects. *Boil fish* (cooked with salt pork, onions, and green peppers) is a popular morning eye-opener that comes with grits. Many places also often serve delicately sweet *johnnycake* (a mildly sweet bread) on the side. Also eaten as the day's first meal is stewed fish that comes in a rich brown gravy. Steamed fish (which may sound bland, but is far from it), however, isn't eaten before noon and is cooked with a tomato base.

Local lobster is a bit tougher than the Maine variety, but it's prepared in lots of tasty ways: steamed, breaded, sautéed in butter, or topped with grated cheese. To make minced lobster — a Bahamian winner served in the shell — chefs shred the meat and cook it with tomatoes, green peppers, and onions.

A limited number of chickens are raised locally in The Bahamas, mostly on Eleuthera. *Chicken souse* is a popular dish made with chicken, onion, sweet peppers, bay leaves, allspice, and other ingredients, as the cook's imagination dictates. This dish simmers in a pot for about an hour; the cook then adds lime juice, and it simmers a little longer. Pig's feet souse is also a favorite dish.

Goats and sheep are also raised on the Out Islands. On a menu, "mutton" can refer to either type of meat and is often curried. Bahamians catch wild boar on some of the islands and hunt game birds, such as ducks and pigeons. They also eat raccoon stew.

Most meats, including pork, veal, and beef, are imported. Even with these meats, however, Bahamian cooks show their ingenuity with interesting variations. For example, at an Out Island inn, we recently enjoyed pork that was marinated with vinegar, garlic, onion, celery tops, cloves, mustard, and Worcestershire sauce and then baked and served with gravy. Even a simple baked ham is given a Bahamian touch — cooked with fresh pineapple, coconut milk, coconut flakes, mustard, honey, and brown sugar.

Many vegetables are grown in The Bahamas; others are imported. If you have a cucumber, you can be almost certain that it's from one of Edison Key's farms in North Abaco. They supply cucumbers to not only their own country, but also to about 5 percent of the stateside market. Bahamians also grow their own sweet potatoes, corn, cassava, okra, and peppers (both sweet and hot), among other produce. Lunch and dinner come with heaping portions of peas and rice, potato salad, coleslaw, or macaroni and cheese — and sometimes all of them.

Guava duff is the dessert specialty of The Bahamas. This dessert, which resembles a jellyroll, is made with guava pulp that has been run through a food mill or sieve. Nobody seems to agree on the best method of cooking it. One way you can make this dessert is to cream sugar and butter, and then add eggs and spices, such as cinnamon and cloves or nutmeg. Make a stiff dough by adding flour and mix the dough with the guava pulp, which you then place in the top of a double boiler and cook over boiling water for hours. You can also boil or steam the dough, and some cooks insist that you bake it. Guava duff is served with hard sauce (a blend of butter, confectioners' sugar, vanilla, and rum).

Other tasty Bahamian desserts and breads include coconut tarts, benne seedcakes, and potato bread.

Drinking island cocktails

Vacationers and residents alike satisfy their thirst with beer, much of it imported from the U.S., Germany, and The Netherlands.

These imports have a higher alcohol content than the same brands of foreign beer sold in the U.S. The Bahamas' high-quality brew is called *Kalik,* named for the sound cowbells make in Bahamian Junkanoo music.

If you're not a beer drinker, colorful rum and fruit juice concoctions are the rage. Depending on who makes them, the ingredients and proportions vary; most bartenders won't reveal the secrets of their success. Besides rum punch, the top three tropical island cocktails are

- ✔ **Bahama Mama:** Vat 19 (a white rum), citrus juice (often pineapple), bitters, a dash of nutmeg, crème de cassis, and a hint of grenadine

- ✔ **Goombay Smash:** Coconut rum, pineapple juice, lemon juice, Triple Sec, Vat 19, and a dash of syrup

- ✔ **Yellowbird:** Crème de banana liqueur, Vat 19, orange juice, pineapple, apricot brandy, and Galliano

Of course, you can find colas and other sodas, bottled (and sometimes freshly squeezed) juices, and bottled water on all islands. Although tap water is safe for brushing your teeth, most people drink bottled or filtered water.

Jumping to Junkanoo

The Bahamians maintain great pride in their original musical idioms, often comparing their vitality to the more famous musical traditions of Jamaica, Puerto Rico, and Trinidad. Other than spirituals, which share roots with slave music from colonial North America, by far the most famous musical products are Goombay and its closely linked sibling, Junkanoo.

Goombay music is an art form with melodies and body movements that are always accompanied by the beat of goatskin drums and, when available, the liberal consumption of rum. The most outlandish expressions of Goombay occur the day after Christmas (Boxing Day), especially in

Nassau on Bay Street. Dancers outfit themselves in masquerade costumes with bizarre accessories and glittering colors that evoke the plumage of jungle birds. Goombay musicians and dancers are almost always male, a custom dating from the days of slavery, and before that, originating in West Africa. However, in the "Jump-In Dance," performers dance in a circle at the center of which a solo dancer performs. To the rhythm of drums, the star dancer selects another person to take his place. Today this person is likely to be a female, who will then dance in the circle and select a male to replace her.

Junkanoo music is to The Bahamas what reggae is to Jamaica. In other words, you can't miss hearing it. All hotels and resorts, and even some restaurants, offer this music as part of the evening's entertainment. Some musical groups even call themselves "Junkanoo." Hearing it performed by locals in resorts or hotels is a lot safer than wandering the back streets of Nassau at night looking for a local club. The music will probably be just as authentic at the resort.

You can get a taste of Junkanoo at **Café Johnny Canoe** on Cable Beach, where the weekly Friday-night parade turns this New Providence restaurant into a party (Chapter 12). If you want a close-up look at the elaborate costumes, stop by the **Junkanoo Expo at Prince George Dock** in Nassau (see Chapter 13).

Background Check: Recommended Books

The checkered past of the archipelago — from pirates to shipwreckers and rumrunners — comes alive again in Paul Albury's *The Story of The Bahamas* (Macmillan Caribbean). This 294-page book is the best of its kind for a quick overview. Author Robert H. Fuson dug into the archives and came up with *The Log of Christopher Columbus* (International Marine Publishing), dating from 1492, of course. On seeing The Bahamas for the first time, the explorer wrote: "I made sail and saw so many islands that I could not decide where to go first."

For a lighter read, try Ernest Hemingway's *Islands in the Stream* (Charles Scribner & Sons), the classic novel in which "Papa" created the fascinating fictional character of Thomas Hudson, tracing his life from his years as a painter in Bimini in the 1930s through his anti-submarine activities off the Cuban coast during World War II. The character of Hudson is much like Hemingway himself.

Isles of Eden: Life in the Southern Family Islands of The Bahamas by Harvey Lloyd, with a foreword by former Prime Minister Lynden Pindling (Benjamin), chronicles the island people who live in this rarely visited archipelago, which stretches 144km (90 miles) southeast of Nassau all the way to Haiti. Lloyd blends unusual island photographs with social commentary, history, and personal recollections.

Beach reads

Before heading for the sands, pick up a copy of Desmond Bagley's *Bahama Crisis* (Fontana/Collin). This mystery spins around the character of Tom Mangan, who lures rich guests to his hotel in The Bahamas, where disaster strikes in a series of strange accidents.

Barry Estabrook's *Bahama Heat* (St. Martin's Press) is whimsical and a good read, dealing with the usual drug-running schemes in The Bahamas, but with more plot than most. The cast of characters ranges from a rum-guzzling, charismatic pastor to a crazed lesbian pilot.

Great descriptions of The Bahamas, especially underwater, appear in the fast-paced *Bahamas Blue,* by D. C. Poyer (St. Martin's Press). Poyer is a well-known writer of sea adventures, and in this action-packed thriller he demonstrates both his love of the sea and his contempt for the drug runners who abuse it.

One of the most evocative novels on The Bahamas is *Paradise Overdose: A Novel* by Brian Antoni (Grove Press). Drug trafficking once again figures into this tale of a young bachelor, Chris Angostura, whose life centers around women and cocaine. The tropical paradise comes alive in the descriptions of beaches and turquoise seas, but the profanity isn't for the faint of heart.

If you go to The Bahamas for a close encounter with nature, *The Ephemeral Islands: A Natural History of The Bahamas* by David G. Campbell (Media Publishing Ltd.) is the best fauna-and-flora book you can find. A well-written survey of the natural history of the island also comes with beautifully illustrated color plates.

The Yachtsman's Guide to The Bahamas (Tropic Isle Publishers, revised annually) is an essential guide for all visitors considering boat tours of The Bahamas. This guide is the standard one used by most yachties, but Stephen Pavlidis is cutting in on the market with *The Abaco Guide: A Cruising Guide to the Northern Bahamas including Grand Bahama, the Bight of Abaco, and the Abacos* (Seaworthy Publications). Pavlidas is a veteran of these seas, and his charts are the most accurate ones published. Because he's an active ham-radio operator, yachties in the Abacos often talk to him.

Chapter 3

Choosing Where to Go

● ●

In This Chapter

▶ Getting to know The Bahamas
▶ Picking the right island(s) for you
▶ Rating the islands

● ●

*W*hen measured against any region of the Caribbean, the Bahamian archipelago — which lies entirely in the Atlantic Ocean — is the number-one destination for visitors.

In this chapter, we help you decide which island is best for you by giving you a rundown of the highlights and drawbacks of each of the most popular (and most accessible) islands. If you want casinos and mega-resorts, for example, you may want to head for Paradise Beach, the most expensive area in The Bahamas. But if you seek a remote, tranquil location with pink sandy beaches and quiet inns, then Harbour Island may be for you, although it's also expensive. A fun quiz at the end of this chapter helps you narrow down your island options.

For details on where to stay, where to dine, and where to play on each of the islands covered in this book, check out Parts III through VI.

Introducing The Bahamas

Many people think that The Bahamas are in the Caribbean Sea when, in fact, they're surrounded by the Atlantic Ocean. But culturally, The Bahamas are part of the Caribbean.

The Bahamas are an archipelago of some 700 islands (many mere islets) and 2,500 coral reefs. These reefs extend for about 1,290km (800 miles) on a northwest/southeast slant. The archipelago lies between the Atlantic Ocean and the Straits of Florida, with channels separating The Bahamas from Cuba and the island of Hispaniola (jointly owned by the Dominican Republic and Haiti). Only about 20 of the islands are inhabited.

George Washington called The Bahamas the "isles of perpetual June." They have a warmer climate than their northern latitude would suggest because equatorial sea currents bathe them. And the refreshing trade winds blowing in from the Atlantic rescue them from torrid summer seasons — the effect is kind of like natural air-conditioning.

The northern locale of these islands means that during winter months, the weather is sometimes cooler than it is in the always-warm Caribbean. (For more details about the best times to travel, turn to Chapter 4.) Without question, most of these islands have beautiful beaches, superb snorkeling, great scuba diving, and big-time boating and fishing. Each island also boasts its own special character and atmosphere. This variety means that you can easily tailor a trip to almost any desire or budget.

Finding the Right Island for You

The most frequently visited island in The Bahamas is **New Providence,** which includes the resort areas of **Nassau** and **Cable Beach** on its northern shore, and the offshore **Paradise Island.** New Providence is a world of gambling casinos, cruise-ship arrivals, mega-resorts, Las Vegas–like entertainment, and fancy restaurants.

The area's cousin, which offers the same diversions but without so much glitter, is the second-most visited island: **Grand Bahama,** with its vacation "villages" of **Freeport** and **Lucaya.**

Don't be misled by all the hype in Nassau and Freeport about shopping bargains. You do save on tax, but prices on many international goods are list, so you often pay what you would back home.

New Providence and Grand Bahama are where most of the dry-land sightseeing is concentrated, from forts and museums to aquariums, gardens, and nature reserves. A couple of straw markets plus scores of stores and boutiques are additional attractions. New Providence and Grand Bahama are also the most accessible islands from the United States because of frequent flights and ship or ferry connections.

If the thought of taking an elevator to the beach leaves you cold, you may want to pass on the high-rises and impersonal crowds of Nassau, Paradise Island, and Freeport/Lucaya and head to the **Out Islands** instead.

The Out Islands are the most beautiful part of The Bahamas. Miles of empty, golden sand beaches trim the clear waters. Except for scattered small towns — villages, really — and only a few large-scale beach resorts, nature has been left almost intact. Chickens, donkeys, sheep, and goats wander freely through front yards and on roads. Boats, bicycles, golf carts, and feet are more prevalent than cars on some islands.

The most visited of the Out Islands include, in order, the **Abacos** (with Marsh Harbour, on Great Abaco, as its capital), **Eleuthera** (with its major vacation spot of Harbour Island), and the **Exumas** (popular with the boating crowd). Less visited and more alluring to those visitors who seek offbeat locations is **San Salvador,** which is home to a Club Med, the only major resort in the southern Bahamas.

The Out Islands aren't as easy to get to as Nassau, Paradise Island, or Freeport/Lucaya. In some cases, you have to take a plane (or two), a taxi to a dock, a ferry, and then another taxi to your hotel. But the inconvenience of transportation is a small price to pay for the peacefulness of a more secluded part of The Bahamas.

Knowing New Providence

A trio of destinations — **Nassau, Cable Beach,** and **Paradise Island** — are The Bahamas' main vacation areas, outranking its nearest rival, Freeport/Lucaya, in charm, class, and grandeur. Nassau, Cable Beach, and Paradise Island are adjoined, so you can stay in one and play in all three.

An architectural delight of old-world charm, Nassau is also The Bahamas' largest cruise-ship port. When ships are in port, the center of the city is congested, with shops, restaurants, and other businesses overflowing.

New Providence is a mix of the ultra-modern and colonial quaint. The majority of The Bahamas' roughly 260,000 residents live on New Providence. **Nassau,** the archipelago's colonial capital, consists of a historic center that stretches for about a dozen blocks and is four blocks wide. Many government buildings have a rather grand neocolonial style of architecture, and even smaller buildings boast wide balconies, louvered windows, and wood construction. Aging forts, small museums, gardens, and a zoo can amuse you when you're not bouncing along the waves on Jet Skis or off snorkeling or scuba diving.

The part of the city that attracts most visitors lies along the waterfront and Bay Street, the main street of Nassau, which is a block away from the water. As you proceed inland from Nassau, the buildings become less grand, and the incomes of the families dwindle. Families on the lower end of the economic ladder live on the fringes of Nassau.

Emerging in recent years is New Providence's answer to Miami Beach: **Cable Beach.** Reached by heading west from Nassau along West Bay Street, Cable Beach opens onto a broad strand of golden sands lined with mega-resorts. Plenty of casino action and a wide array of watersports facilities are available for fun on the beach.

Cable Beach's major competition is the even glitzier **Paradise Beach,** which lies on **Paradise Island,** reached by a bridge. Although technically part of New Providence, Paradise Beach is a world unto itself. This beach has come a long way since it was called Hog Island.

Paradise Beach boasts the priciest real estate in The Bahamas. Its old-world charm is long gone, and today it's home to a colony of high-rises, condos, second homes of the wintering wealthy, and gambling casinos. Its centerpiece is the mammoth Atlantis Paradise Island Resort & Casino (see Chapter 11).

Whether you're looking for an old-fashioned guesthouse or a splashy multi-story beach resort, you can find it in New Providence. Restaurants and fast-food eateries cater to a range of tastes, from the burger-on-the-run crowd to romantic couples enjoying Continental cuisine by candlelight overlooking a lagoon.

Sports lovers can find plenty of golf, tennis, and horseback riding to keep them busy. Only a few nightclubs in Nassau itself are special. But after dark, Cable Beach and Paradise Island light up with elegant bars, dance floors, casinos, and Las Vegas–style stage shows.

Drawing everyone from American college students on spring break to middle-aged gamblers, many hotels offer economical air/land package deals. Nassau has a very limited number of hotels and not much in the way of a beach. Most resorts are clustered along Cable Beach and on Paradise Island. If you're looking for a moderately priced place to stay, find it on Cable Beach — not on Paradise Island.

Bottom line: New Providence isn't the place for a cozy retreat. But if you want plenty of diversions and you don't mind crowds, it sizzles more than anywhere else in The Bahamas. (For more information on New Providence, see Part III.)

New Providence delivers a punch because it offers

- ✔ **Plenty of sights:** Nassau lures travelers with old forts, impressive colonial buildings, small museums, manicured gardens, and a small zoo.

- ✔ **A variety of vacation playgrounds:** Choose among action-packed Cable Beach, historic downtown Nassau, and glitzy Paradise Island.

- ✔ **Shops galore:** Here you find The Bahamas' largest selection of duty-free stores and designer boutiques, plus the largest straw market.

But New Providence is far from being paradise. Here's a look at the downsides:

- ✔ **No warm and cuddly hotel service:** With thousands of visitors arriving in Nassau every day, staffs at restaurants and hotels have grown jaded by tourism. You won't get the kind of service you may get at an Out Island inn, where all the staff knows you by name.

- ✔ **Crowds and congestion:** If you live in a metropolis and want to escape crowds on your vacation, Nassau isn't for you. When cruise ships pull in at the same time, passengers overrun shops at the

New Providence and Paradise Islands

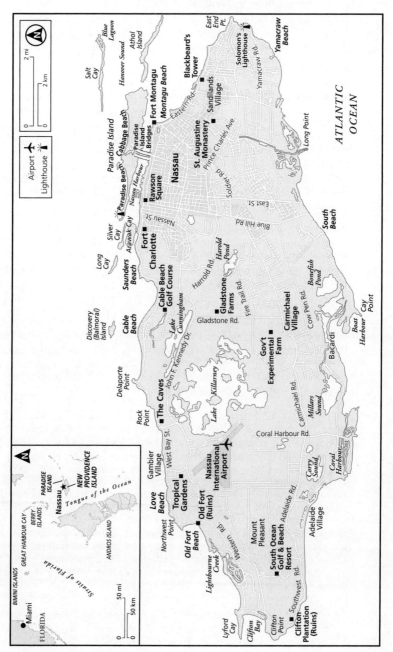

Straw Market and in the center of town. Visitors also crowd the golf courses, beaches, and popular restaurants.

✔ **A walk on the wild side:** You can find safer places to be at night than downtown Nassau. It has the highest crime rate in all The Bahamas. Our advice is to take a taxi to where you're going after dark in the center of Nassau.

Getting to know Grand Bahama

After New Providence, the second-most popular attraction in The Bahamas is the large island of **Grand Bahama,** which contains **Freeport,** the second-largest city in The Bahamas. When compared to Nassau, Freeport is rather unsophisticated. But its beaches at **Lucaya** are top-notch, as are its duty-free shopping, glittering casinos, and two national parks. When you want to capture some of the spirit of The Bahamas of yesterday, you can escape from all this modernity by heading to the funky little village of **West End.**

Grand Bahama has a much younger and trimmer look than Nassau. Stately palms and pines border broad, landscaped boulevards. Modern high-rise hotels, apartment buildings, and condominiums overlook beaches and marinas. Smooth lawns sprouting flowering shrubs surround stucco homes topped with terra-cotta tiles. The flip side of this beauty is that Grand Bahama doesn't offer much history. Too much of its architecture is either kitschy or bland, with little local flavor.

The hotels in Grand Bahama endured a slump at the end of the 20th century, but many of them are bouncing back after being vastly restored or completely rebuilt. Even better news is that hotel rates on the island tend to be moderate — none of the lodgings carry the high price tags that shock you on New Providence.

Likewise, Grand Bahama has many good restaurants but not world-class ones like those in New Providence. You can still eat well, especially if you follow our recommendations. As for nightlife, Grand Bahama has some, but no one ever mistakes it for Las Vegas.

Duty-free shopping remains one of the major attractions of Grand Bahama, especially at the emerging **Port Lucaya Marketplace** and also at the famous but rather tacky **International Bazaar at Freeport.**

Grand Bahama is perfect for the active vacationer. Topping most lists is excellent scuba diving, snorkeling trips by kayak to offshore islets, the chance to pet Flipper's cousins in the **Dolphin Experience** (see Chapter 17), the island's landscaped gardens and nature reserves, deep-sea fishing and, of course, the golden sand beaches.

Bottom line: Grand Bahama is short on island spice but compensates with its diversity of activities, ranging from gambling to watersports. (For more information on Grand Bahama, see Part IV.)

Grand Bahama Island

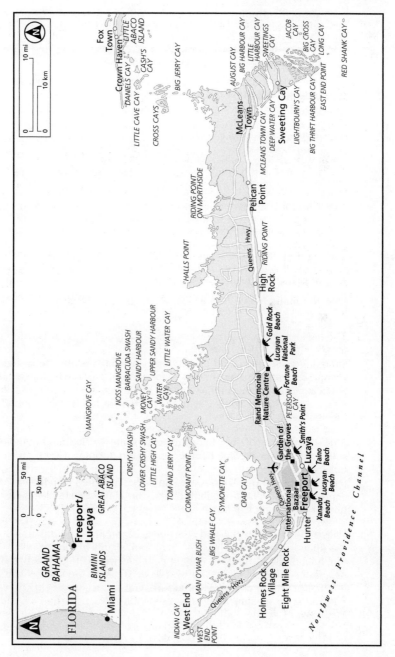

Grand Bahama is a hit with travelers because

- ✔ **Young destination:** Developed during the 1960s, the ox-jaw shaped island has been called a "mecca for fast-lane vacationers."

- ✔ **International appeal:** Many Americans, Canadians, and Europeans live and work here alongside Bahamians.

- ✔ **Fewer hotels:** The main beach resort area, Lucaya, isn't nearly as crowded with hotels as New Providence's Cable Beach or Paradise Island.

But Grand Bahama has its downsides:

- ✔ **Little history:** Unlike Nassau with its buccaneering past, the history of Grand Bahama is rather colorless, except when the Confederate States used it as a supply depot.

- ✔ **Less local appeal:** The cultural scene here is much blander than in Nassau or the Out Islands, where you can find lots of local flavor and island spice.

- ✔ **A jumping-off point for day-trippers:** Unlike New Providence and the Out Islands, Grand Bahama attracts a lot of day-trippers who are on cheap cruises from Florida.

- ✔ **Not many beach hotels:** Not all the best hotels are on the golden sands.

Arriving in the Abacos

Spanning 1,683 sq. km (650 sq. miles), the **Abaco Islands** form the second-largest landmass in this island nation. The boomerang-shaped chain is at the northernmost tier of The Bahamas, stretching 321km (200 miles) from Walker's Cay in the northwest to Cherokee Sound in the southeast.

A true water world, the Abacos make a prime destination for sailing, scuba diving, snorkeling, fishing, and island hopping. Green Turtle Cay boasts one of the fanciest hotels in the Out Islands but, for the most part, lodgings in the Abacos are laid-back. Travelers arriving in September and October will find many hotels and restaurants closed because of the lack of business.

Unlike the relatively flat and charmless island of Grand Bahama, the Abacos are among the most beautiful islands in the nation. The man-made attractions are appealing as well. One of The Bahamas' best golf courses is in the Out Islands at Treasure Cay. And, if you're into history and colonial architecture, you can enjoy the tidy New England-style seaside villages on Elbow Cay, Green Turtle Cay, and Man-O-War Cay.

The Abaco Islands

Here's a rundown of the Abaco Islands:

- ✔ **Marsh Harbour:** Marsh Harbour is the capital of the Abacos. But don't expect congestion, even though it contains the only traffic light in the Out Islands. A legendary port among boaters, Marsh Harbour lies on **Great Abaco Island** and is a shipbuilding center. The town lacks the New England charm of either New Plymouth or Hope Town (see Elbow Cay and Green Turtle Cay in this list) and instead has the feel of a small Florida town.

  Everything is relatively new in Marsh Harbour, most of it dating from the middle of the 1980s. The town's growth originally was fueled by drug money; it only recently discovered tourism. To meet the demands of modern tourism, some excellent restaurants have opened, as well as hotels, shops, bars, cafes, and boat outfitters. For more information on Marsh Harbour, see Chapter 18.

- ✔ **Elbow Cay:** All motor vehicles are banned from the center of Hope Town, the island's Cape Cod–like village. Along the narrow, paved streets, you find harborside restaurants and saltbox cottages painted in tropical tones, with pink and yellow bougainvillea dripping over stone or picket fences. Many Americans, Canadians, and Europeans, who first arrived as vacationers decades ago, own some of the biggest and most attractive homes.

  People get around this small island by golf cart, bicycle, and foot, but the boat is the primary means of locomotion. Amid a bobbing mass of boats, Hope Town's red-and-white striped lighthouse probably has had more photographs taken of it than any other sight on the island. You can hike or bike to isolated **Tahiti Beach,** where shelling at low tide is great fun. For more information on Elbow Cay, see Chapter 19.

- ✔ **Green Turtle Cay:** The 18th-century New England–style village of New Plymouth is idyllic for strolling. You can find out about the Abacos' seafaring past at the **Albert Lowe Museum,** housed in an old cottage. Across the street, the **Memorial Sculpture Garden** honors noteworthy Bahamians.

  Boats take people around Green Turtle Cay more than wheels and feet do. Coral colonies starting in relatively shallow water make for some of the best snorkeling in The Bahamas, and diving is exceptional. You can spend a day on a deserted beach on an uninhabited island. You can swim with stingrays, and the captain of your boat can spear lobster and fish and then grill them for you right on the beach.

- ✔ Its rooms decked with Oriental rugs and Queen Anne chairs, **Green Turtle Club and Marina** is among the most upscale places to stay in the Out Islands. Tiny Green Turtle Cay doesn't have fairways, but if you're a golfer, you can take the ferry and a taxi (or charter a boat) to the championship golf course at Treasure Cay. For more information on Green Turtle Cay, see Chapter 20.

✔ **Treasure Cay:** A little sterile for our tastes, Treasure Cay feels too much like a playground designed exclusively for visitors. Not much of a local settlement was here before this resort developed during the 1960s, so you won't find any historic sites or old island communities. If not for the golden crescent beach and the rich blues of the water, you may forget that you're in The Bahamas.

This lack of local color doesn't seem to bother the vacationers who come to fish and play golf on one of the country's best courses. They stay in the attractive hotels, condos, and villas on the marina and beach. Treasure Cay is close to the dock where you can catch the ferry to Green Turtle Cay, and you can easily rent a boat to sail to Elbow Cay, Man-O-War Cay, and other nearby islands. Rooms are hard to come by in May during the **Treasure Cay Billfish Championship.** For more information on Treasure Cay, turn to Chapter 21.

Bottom line: Nirvana for divers, snorkelers, and anglers, the Abacos offer many opportunities to sail off to different islands, each with its own special allure. Many islands are uninhabited while others have man-made attractions that run a distant second to natural beauty.

The Abacos are a good choice if you're hoping for

✔ **An underwater wonderland, fish tales, and great greens:** The Abacos have some of the most alluring scuba diving, snorkeling, and fishing around and, in Treasure Cay, there's a championship golf course.

✔ **Scenic villages:** Historic seaside settlements on Elbow Cay, Green Turtle Cay, and Man-O-War Cay are filled with pretty clapboard cottages surrounded by white-picket fences.

✔ **Spectacular sailing:** With so many appealing islands clustered together, the Abacos are called "the Sailing Capital of the World."

Locals who love their islands claim that the Abacos are Paradise Found and that they have no downsides. Even so, you may not like

✔ **The travel time:** Getting to these islands can take a while. You may need a plane, a ferry, and a taxi to reach your destination.

✔ **Potential seasickness:** Almost everybody in the Abacos uses boats to travel more than they rely on wheels, so if you're prone to seasickness you may want to choose a different destination.

✔ **Hardly any hotels:** You don't have many choices for lodging, and most options are small and low-key.

Hanging out on Harbour Island

Harbour Island is small — barely 5 sq. km (2 sq. miles) — but it's one of the most beautiful islands in The Bahamas. Its major attraction is a long, broad, pink beach, tinted by pulverized coral and shells. The snorkeling and scuba diving are first-rate. You can even reach shipwrecks on a scuba outing. Perched on a bluff overlooking the water are several of the country's prime — and most expensive — inns and small hotels. (Many accommodations and restaurants close here during the fall.) Wander into **Dunmore Town,** and you stroll past historic churches, 18th-century cottages with lacy gingerbread trim, and tropical flowers nuzzling picket fences.

Harbour Island is affectionately known to residents as *Briland.* Briland lures mainly American and Canadian vacationers, and more than a few of them have snapped up prime real estate here. However, the island maintains a distinct Bahamian look and feel. At the harbor's edge, old men shoot the breeze while slapping dominos onto card tables. Chickens and horses wander through front yards. Women trade gossip while selling straw goods and shell jewelry from outdoor stalls. If those wares aren't upscale enough for you, go boutique browsing for Haitian paintings, Balinese silver, and French wine vinegar.

In Harbour Island, you can don your drop-dead duds for candlelit cocktails one night and cool out over *Kaliks* (the local brew) in a smoky pool hall the next. However, hipbones don't usually start slipping until the weekend, when anything from waterside hotel decks to cavelike local bars morph into dance clubs. Mom-and-pop kitchens whip up Bahamian favorites, such as cracked conch (pounded, battered, and fried) and peas and rice. Hotels lure diners with gourmet creations. And don't be surprised if your waiter knows you went sailing before you tell him — folks are friendly, and word travels fast. But don't worry: With quiet roads, romantic lookout points, and empty sandy strands, you can find plenty of places to keep your privacy intact. For more information on Harbour Island, see Chapter 22.

Bottom line: With some of The Bahamas' finest small beach hotels, a time-warp waterfront village, and a pink sand beach, you can't go wrong with Harbour Island — if you can afford it.

Harbour Island's highlights include

- ✔ **Pink sand:** The hue of this stunning 5km (3-mile) beach is rosy, and it runs the whole length of the eastern side of the island.

- ✔ **Eye candy:** Picture this scene: New England meets the tropics, with white picket fences around colonial clapboard houses that are shaded by palm trees.

- ✔ **Small-town hospitality:** Briland is so petite and friendly that residents may start greeting you by name before you can say "cracked conch."

Harbour Island

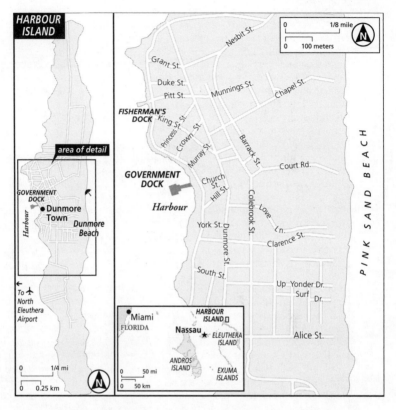

Before you decide on Harbour Island, however, consider the following:

- ✔ **Cost:** Harbour Island is one of the most expensive islands in The Bahamas.

- ✔ **Travel fatigue:** A trip here from the U.S. requires a plane or two, a taxi, a ferry, and another taxi.

- ✔ **Quiet nights:** What little nightlife there is wakes up mainly on the weekends.

Eloping to Eleuthera

Eleuthera is a wisp of an island chain that stretches for a distance of 161km (100 miles) from north to south. It lies only 81km (50 miles) east of Nassau, but in terms of atmosphere, it's a thousand miles removed from that busy scene.

Eleuthera

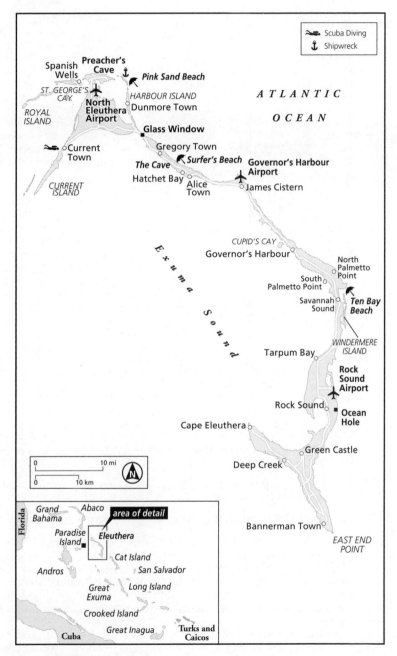

Spanish Wells
Preacher's Cave
Pink Sand Beach
ST. GEORGE'S CAY
HARBOUR ISLAND
ROYAL ISLAND
North Eleuthera Airport
Dunmore Town
Glass Window
Current Town
Gregory Town
The Cave
Surfer's Beach
Governor's Harbour Airport
Hatchet Bay
Alice Town
James Cistern
CURRENT ISLAND

ATLANTIC OCEAN

Exuma Sound

CUPID'S CAY
Governor's Harbour
North Palmetto Point
South Palmetto Point
Savannah Sound
Ten Bay Beach
WINDERMERE ISLAND
Tarpum Bay
Rock Sound Airport
Rock Sound
Ocean Hole
Cape Eleuthera
Green Castle
Deep Creek
Bannerman Town
EAST END POINT

Scuba Diving
Shipwreck

0   10 mi
0   10 km
N

Florida
Grand Bahama
Abaco
area of detail
Paradise Island
Eleuthera
Cat Island
Andros
San Salvador
Great Exuma
Long Island
Crooked Island
Great Inagua
Turks and Caicos
Cuba

Even though the atmosphere is relatively quiet, Eleuthera remains one of the most developed of the Out Islands when stacked against the Exumas or the southern Bahamas.

However, Eleuthera's heyday is long gone. The chic social scene is now but a memory with the closing of such ritzy resorts as the Cotton Club and the Winderemere Club in South Eleuthera. Today, the rich and famous head for Harbour Island because the entire mainland of Eleuthera doesn't really have a state-of-the-art hotel.

At no point is Eleuthera more than 6km (4 miles) wide. Despite the island's size, some 10,000 people eke out a living on Eleuthera, which hasn't always been a friendly place to do so. What Eleuthera offers in great abundance is a galaxy of beaches, an "endless summer," and multi-hued seas ranging from deep blue to aquamarine.

On Eleuthera, you don't have to bother with historical sites or museums because none exist. What we like to do is drive the Queens Highway for the whole length of the island. We know of no more dramatic drive in all The Bahamas. For the most part, you hug the coastline and get stunning views of the seascape or landscape. The seaside villages you come across have known better days, but it's their decaying gingerbread charm that attracts us in the first place. In Eleuthera, you get the impression that everyone was once here but now is gone. You can wander about the most remote places, which you have all to yourself.

For more information on Eleuthera, see Chapter 23.

Bottom line: Come here if you're the ultimate escapist, seeking unspoiled beaches, few people, diversions mainly of your own creation, and life in The Bahamas the way it used to be.

Consider a visit to Eleuthera if you're hoping for

- ✔ **Remote seaports and villages from long ago:** With its fashionable heyday long gone, the settlements of Eleuthera exist in a time warp. Far removed from casino wheels and mega-resorts, the little inns of Eleuthera take us back to the 1950s.

- ✔ **Scenery and sights:** Why come here? For the miles and miles of unspoiled beaches, for gingerbread-trimmed houses hung with bougainvillea, for bargains galore, for rolling hills, for lush green forests, for sheltered coves, and for offshore coral reefs.

- ✔ **Friendly people:** Instead of being locked away in a high-rise hotel, you get to meet the locals. The island doesn't have any big towns — only small settlements that welcome visitors.

For a look at the downside of Eleuthera, consider

- ✔ **The absence of any top-rated hotels:** If you want luxury, Eleuthera sends you to Harbour Island. To live on "mainland" Eleuthera, you most often settle for "rental units," which are clean but rather basic — definitely not luxurious.

✔ **No catering:** Visitors find that everything is pretty much of a do-it-yourself affair on Eleuthera. "Things," as they're called here, aren't very well organized. A lot of personal initiative is needed to make your vacation wheels spin.

✔ **Difficult transportation:** Except for the main highway, roads are often a disaster. Because no major car-rental companies exist, you often have to negotiate with a local for a rental.

Exploring Exuma

Looking out the window of your plane, you can see that the water is different colors before you even get to **Exuma.** Strung out like stepping-stones, these islands are surrounded by some of The Bahamas' most beautiful waters.

With a cay for every day of the year — and most of them uninhabited — Exuma is prime sailing territory. A bridge joins **Great Exuma** and **Little Exuma,** the two largest islands in the chain. Hotels and island action are concentrated in and around **George Town,** Exuma's pretty capital on Great Exuma. If you happen to vacation here in April, you can catch the festivities of the **National Family Island Regatta.** Far up north — and accessible only by chartered boat — the gorgeous **Exuma Cays Land and Sea Park** covers 160 sq. km (177 sq. miles) of islands and marine life. See Chapter 24 for more on Exuma's attractions.

You can make arrangements for sailing, snorkeling, diving, and fishing through your hotel. Be forewarned, though, that George Town's few hotels aren't located on the best beaches. For the best sandy stretches, you have to take a ferry to undeveloped **Stocking Island,** which has a sole hotel just across the harbor.

Bottom line: Exuma is a fine choice if sailing, R & R, and absorbing natural beauty are more important to you than man-made sights and late-night entertainment.

Exuma has many idyllic qualities, including

✔ **Water colors:** Bring your camera, or no one at home will believe you when you describe the range of aquatic hues.

✔ **Small size:** Petite hotels — a couple of hotels are on their own islands — and friendly residents quickly make you feel at home.

✔ **Parties:** Well, sometimes, at least. On most Saturday nights, everyone heads to Club Peace and Plenty's dance party, and in April, the festivities of the National Family Island Regatta bring many a far-flung Bahamian home to Exuma.

Exuma

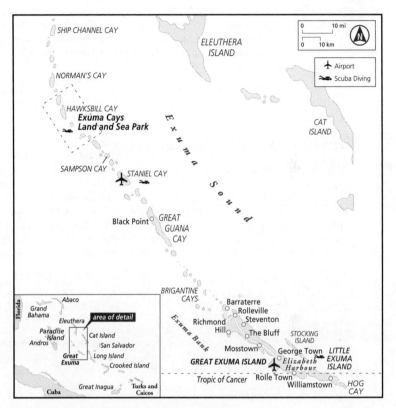

But Exuma isn't always convenient because

- ✔ **The marine park isn't nearby:** You may hear talk of the Exuma Cays Land and Sea Park, but unless you charter a boat (or both a boat and a small plane), you can't get there from George Town, where most vacationers stay.

- ✔ **You may have to take a boat to the beach:** George Town, where most hotels reside, isn't known for its beaches, and not all hotels are on the sand. Better beaches surround Stocking Island, which is a short ferry ride across the harbor.

- ✔ **It can get crowded:** During the National Family Island Regatta each spring, George Town can get as packed as Cable Beach in February.

Savoring San Salvador

Lying 322km (200 miles) southeast of Nassau is the Bahamian island of **San Salvador,** which is often confused with the Central American country of the same name. Some folks say that this scuba-diving mecca is the first place that Christopher Columbus stepped ashore in the "New" World. (The world that wasn't new at all, of course, to the Native Americans living there for at least five centuries.) Historians bitterly debate whether the famed explorer ever came here, however, with some experts believing his first landfall was actually at Samana Cay, another Bahamian island 105km (65 miles) to the south. But don't tell that to residents of San Salvador. They point you with pride to all the island's monuments that commemorate the world-changing event.

Columbus's visit, if it happened at all, didn't change San Salvador very much. Most of this island is nearly as undeveloped as it was back in the days when Lucayan Indians called it home. The interior is still interlaced with a network of quiet lakes, and the main village, **Cockburn Town,** couldn't be much drowsier. Climb to the top of **Dixon Hill Lighthouse,** and you get a sweeping view of the island and its pristine coastline. Bicycling is another good way to see San Salvador.

Today, many visitors are avid divers who wax poetic about the variety and bright colors of the coral and other marine life. Visitors don't frequent the best dive sites as much as the ones around New Providence because San Salvador has only a couple of hotels. True, one hotel is the sprawling **Club Med,** but not all the guests here are interested in scuba. Although the other hotel, the locally run **Riding Rock Inn Resort and Marina,** has long been a favorite among serious divers, it's not large enough to cause scuba gridlock at any diving sites.

The island's two main beach hotels give vacationers a choice: Do you want a small, unassuming scuba-lover's hangout that's dead-quiet during the day (Riding Rock), or do you want a huge low-rise resort decorated with an impressive collection of international folk art that's like a playground for adults (Club Med)? The bar at Riding Rock is the island's social center, and it hosts parties once or twice a week where vacationers hang out with locals. Although something's happening every night at Club Med, you can forget that you're in The Bahamas after dark because most people here aren't locals. For more information on San Salvador, check out Chapter 25.

Bottom line: Since Club Med hit the scene, San Salvador isn't just for divers anymore, but the underwater sights are still the main draw beyond cooling out amid pristine surroundings.

San Salvador may be a good choice if you find the following activities enticing:

San Salvador

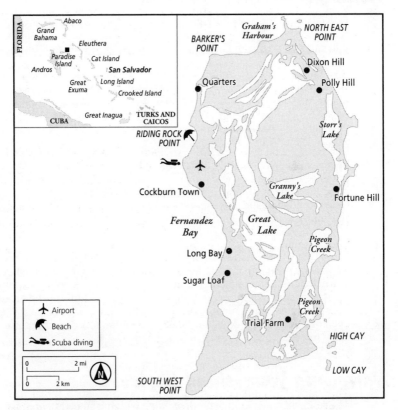

- ✔ **Serene scuba:** More than three dozen unspoiled dive sites are less than 45 minutes from shore.

- ✔ **Fabulous digs:** A great all-inclusive resort — one of the top of Club Med's line — sits along an excellent sandy stretch.

- ✔ **Striking beaches:** Finding shores that are more naturally stunning is hard to do.

But, consider these downsides:

- ✔ **Few hotels:** Your choice of accommodations is basically between an upscale Club Med and a modest diving-oriented resort.

- ✔ **No real towns:** Cockburn Town is more like a sleepy residential neighborhood.

- ✔ **Little island action:** Don't come here looking for any activities other than what Club Med offers.

Visiting More than One Island

One island is certainly enough for most visitors, especially if you stay in Nassau on New Providence or Freeport/Lucaya on Grand Bahama, where you can find sights and activities to keep you busy beyond the waves.

If you need variety to spice up your life, consider an island that makes a good home base for exploring other landfalls by boat, such as an island in the Abacos or the Exumas. From many islands, checking out a second island (or third or fourth) is as easy as hopping in a water taxi or a ferry, or taking a snorkeling cruise.

For example, on a visit to New Providence, based at either Cable Beach or Nassau, all you have to do is cross a bridge to enter another world — Paradise Island. From New Providence, you can also take boats to offshore cays. If you have the time, you can plan three nights in cosmopolitan New Providence and then spend the rest of your vacation week in, say, Harbour Island near Eleuthera.

Keep in mind that getting from some islands to others can be tricky, especially when you need to fly. Visiting more than one Out Island by air usually means that you have to return to Nassau between islands because most remote islands don't have air links, except by expensive charter planes. Therefore, you may spend a lot of time sitting around Nassau International Airport because some flights are once a day (or even once every few days) and delays are common. See Chapter 6 for more information.

Narrowing Your Island Choices

The following quiz helps you determine which islands are best suited to your vacation style and interests.

Step 1: Get to know your "Rate the Islands" scorecard.

The scorecard at the end of the quiz has a column for each island and a row for each of the categories in our island-rating system. Use this score-card to compile a rating for each island, based on the special-interest categories that follow.

On a scale of 1 to 4 points, the top vacation destinations are rated in various categories, such as dining, nightlife, price, sights, diving, and more. The lowest rating is 1, and the highest is 4. When an island isn't listed, it flunked completely. For example, golfers don't go to Harbour Island because it has no greens.

Step 2: Score islands based on what interests you.

Rate islands only in categories of interest to you. For example, if you don't play golf, skip that one. Write the scores for each island in the appropriate row under each column in your scorecard. For example, if you're looking for luxury, go across row 1 of your scorecard and put 4 under New Providence, 3 under Harbour Island, 2 under San Salvador, and 1 under Grand Bahama.

Keep racking up points until you review all the categories and give each island a score for every category of interest to you.

1) If you want to be in the lap of luxury . . .

Rating	Island	Why?
4	New Providence	Cable Beach and Paradise Island are graced with the most elegant pockets of posh in The Bahamas, with the Atlantis Paradise Island Resort & Casino being the country's most spectacular hotel.
3	Harbour Island	Some of The Bahamas' most distinctive small hotels overlook the pink sand beach.
2	San Salvador	Home of one of Club Med's snazziest resorts and the only first-class hotel in the southern Bahamas.
1	Grand Bahama	Our Lucaya resort is more affordable than comparable beach resorts on New Providence.

2) If you're watching your wallet but still want to stay on the sand . . .

Rating	Island	Why?
4	Grand Bahama	Beach resorts may not be as plentiful here as they are on New Providence, but they're easier on your pocketbook.
3	New Providence	With a good choice of affordable shoreline hotels, Cable Beach is a better bet than pricier Paradise Island.

(continued)

(continued)

Rating	Island	Why?
2	Elbow Cay	Several small hotels on this tiny cay hug near-empty beaches of golden sand — if you don't mind getting here by plane, taxi, and ferry.
1	Eleuthera	This narrow island, or series of islands, has virtually no expensive hotel — at least since the luxury resorts went belly up and a hurricane blew away Club Med. You're housed at a lot of mom-and-pop inns on local beaches.

3) If you want an island (almost) all to yourself . . .

Rating	Island	Why?
4	Exuma	Hotel Higgins Landing on Stocking Island and Latitude Exuma Resort on Rolle Cay are true getaways.
3	Elbow Cay	On this petite island that has more boats than cars, you can stay in small, isolated beach hotels that are really intimate inns.
2	Green Turtle Cay	Coco Bay Cottages are tucked away in a quiet corner of this sleepy island on a near-empty beach.
1	Harbour Island	You may not have your own island, but staying at the intimate Landing, a historic seven-room harborfront inn, may make you think the panoramic sunset is for your eyes only.

4) If you want to party the night away . . .

Rating	Island	Why?
4	New Providence	Here you find plenty of dance clubs, bars, island musical revues, and Las Vegas–style casinos. Atlantis Paradise Island Resort & Casino alone can keep you entertained for weeks!
3	Grand Bahama	This island doesn't offer as much after-dark action as New Providence does, but you can still choose from some good selections, including gambling.

Rating	Island	Why?
2	**Green Turtle Cay**	Here you're down to mainly midweek and weekend partying, with dance bands at the hotels.
1	**Exuma**	Club Peace & Plenty is the place to be on Saturday night if you like to shake it up to a poolside calypso band. Also, you can check out the weekly rake and scrape at Eddie's Edgewater, a local dive.

5) If you like dining really well . . .

Rating	Island	Why?
4	**New Providence**	This island offers plenty of first-rate restaurants, plus a good selection of local eateries.
3	**Harbour Island**	The Bahamas' best collection of small beach hotels — plus the historic Landing, a harborside dining spot — offer some of the country's most creative cooking.
2	**Green Turtle Cay**	Bluff House, New Plymouth Club & Inn, and Green Turtle Club & Marina create a culinary buzz.
1	**Grand Bahama**	From steak in an elegant dining room to oceanfront seafood, it's all here.

6) If you're looking for the most unspoiled beaches . . .

Rating	Island	Why?
4	**Harbour Island**	The broad beach is 5km (3 miles) long, almost deserted, and the sand is actually pink. For once, you can believe all that tourist stuff.
3	**Elbow Cay or Green Turtle Cay**	Many empty sandy stretches encircle uninhabited islands offshore or border populated-but-low-key locales on the cays themselves.
2	**Exuma**	For a drop-dead gorgeous white-sand beach, ferry over to Stocking Island from George Town.
1	**San Salvador**	Club Med–Columbus Isle hugs one of The Bahamas' most striking golden strands.

7) If you want to experience island spice . . .

Rating	Island	Why?
4	New Providence	Funky Nassau is The Bahamas' political (and cultural) capital and is the place to be during the Christmas/New Year's Junkanoo festival.
3	Exuma	You can visit here during the National Family Island Regatta every April for a real island vibe. Any time of year is fine because cute little George Town is never overrun with visitors.
2	Harbour Island	Chickens and horses wander in front yards, and residents soon call you by name.
1	Green Turtle Cay	This place is home to friendly folks who enjoy showing off their little gem of an island.

8) If you want to tee off . . .

Rating	Island	Why?
4	Grand Bahama	The island boasts more golf courses than any other in The Bahamas. The first golf course ever to open in The Bahamas, The Reef Course, made its debut here back in 1969.
3	Treasure Cay	The desert-type, windy Dick Wilson course at the Treasure Cay Golf Club is a winner.
2	New Providence	This island offers a trio of good courses, plus plenty of hotels and activities, both wet and dry.
1	Green Turtle Cay	You can take the ferry and a taxi (or a chartered boat) to the championship Treasure Cay golf course.

9) If you like sightseeing . . .

Rating	Island	Why?
4	New Providence	It's the home of Nassau, The Bahamas' stately colonial capital, with historic forts, gardens, museums, and horse-drawn carriages galore.
3	Green Turtle Cay	New Plymouth looks like an 18th-century New England seaside village. It lives in a time capsule, and its museum evokes the days of the Loyalists who escaped here instead of becoming part of the new American Republic.

Rating	Island	Why?
2	Elbow Cay	Elbow Cay is another Loyalist Cay, settled by blond, blue-eyed people whose descendants are still here. It's like Lilliput, and its red-and-white striped lighthouse is the most photographed sight in the Abacos.
1	Harbour Island	Harborside Dunmore Town boasts 18th-century gingerbread cottages and The Bahamas' oldest Anglican church.

10) If you want the best scuba diving or snorkeling . . .

Rating	Island	Why?
4	San Salvador	Scuba divers in the Columbus spirit go exploring here, finding more than a dozen shipwrecks, including the most famous, the *Frascate,* along with canyons and reefs to the southwest that are spectacular.
3	Green Turtle Cay	Excellent reefs teeming with a varied marine life line its Atlantic shores. Loggerhead turtles still crawl ashore to nest. Snorkelers have great visibility in these waters.
2	Harbour Island	Certified divers ride in underwater scooters, and rushing waters make Current Cut an exhilarating scuba site.
1	Exuma	Many excellent reefs are just 20 or 25 minutes away from the George Town area, so long boat rides don't cut into your underwater time.

11) If you want the best sport fishing . . .

Rating	Island	Why?
4	Treasure Cay	Anglers snag wahoo, billfish, and other big game all over the Abacos, where the Treasure Cay Billfish Championship is one of The Bahamas' most popular fishing tournaments.
3	Green Turtle Cay	The Green Turtle Club & Marina hosts a major fishing tournament each spring.
2	Exuma	Just outside George Town, try bonefishing right from the shore. Deep-sea fishing is excellent as well.
1	Grand Bahama	Waters off Grand Bahama turn up impressive catches in barracuda, snapper, grouper, yellowtail, wahoo, and kingfish. Some of the best deep-sea fishing charters in The Bahamas are found here.

12) If you want to island hop . . .

Rating	Island	Why?
4	Elbow Cay	Frequent ferries connect Marsh Harbour with Elbow Cay and Man-O-War Cay, and you can charter a boat to Treasure Cay for golf or to Green Turtle Cay for more quaint beauty.
3	New Providence	A bridge links you to Paradise Island, boats cruise to various beach-rimmed uninhabited islets, and planes fly to Grand Bahama and all Out Islands.
2	Eleuthera	Eleuthera itself is like a string of little islands, but in the north, you can take the ferry to remote, isolated Spanish Wells or chic Harbour Island.
1	Exuma	Wherever you go in the Exumas, you seem to land on another island in about 15 minutes of boating. These islands are the sailing capital of The Bahamas.

13) If you're craving peace and quiet . . .

Rating	Island	Why?
4	Exuma	Check out the gorgeous surrounding waters stocked with serene, uninhabited islets.
3	Green Turtle Cay	Historic seaside New Plymouth village enhances Mother Nature's handiwork on this tranquil island.
2	Elbow Cay	The quaintest of all Bahamian villages, this place seems more like a Hollywood set than reality. The population is scarce, and you have much of the place to yourself, except for some feral cats, curly-tailed lizards, and cooing doves.
1	Eleuthera	The celebrities of yesteryear have long since departed, leaving this island asleep in the sun. You not only get sun but also sands and only a few other people.

14) If you're traveling with children . . .

Rating	Island	Why?
4	New Providence	You can visit an aquarium, zoo, and dolphin encounter program, as well as enjoy children's camps at Atlantis, the Radisson, and elsewhere.

Rating	Island	Why?
3	Grand Bahama	Our Lucaya's children's program and the Dolphin Experience make a kid's stay enjoyable.
2	Elbow Cay	Here you can find family-friendly villas, but you won't find much to do beyond the beach.
1	Exuma	The cottages of Latitude Exuma Resort, the only place to stay on peaceful, undeveloped Rolle Cay off George Town, are kid-friendly.

15) If you want to get there quickly and easily . . .

Rating	Island	Why?
4	New Providence	Airlines offer plenty of daily flights (a little more than three hours from New York or 50 minutes from Miami).
3	Grand Bahama	Not as many daily flights are available here, but the trip is shorter (a 40-minute flight from Miami).
2	Exuma	You can catch just one or two flights a day to this island, but travel time from Miami is a comfortable hour and 40 minutes.
1	San Salvador	Weekly charters take three hours and 15 minutes from New York or an hour and 45 minutes from Miami. Small airlines also connect San Salvador with Florida twice a week and with Nassau daily.

Step 3: Tally the scores to determine your final favorite(s).

After you review all the categories and plug scores into your scorecard for all islands in the categories that matter to you, add up each of the results.

And the winner is . . . the island with the highest total score. Chances are this island is the one that most caters to your vacation needs. If a second island scores high, consider dividing your time between the two islands — that is, if they're close or accessible enough. If a third island scores high as well, you have an excuse to plan your next vacation there.

"Rate the Islands" Scorecard

POINTS FOR:	Elbow Cay	Eleuthera	Exuma	Grand Bahama	Green Turtle Cay	Harbour Island	New Providence	San Salvador	Treasure Cay
1) Luxury									
2) Beach Bargains									
3) Solitude									
4) Nightlife									
5) Great Food									
6) Best Beaches									
7) Island Spice									
8) Golf									
9) Sightseeing									
10) Diving/Snorkeling									
11) Fishing									
12) Island Hopping									
13) Peace and Quiet									
14) Families									
15) Easy Access									
TOTAL SCORE:									

Chapter 4

Deciding When to Go

● ●

In This Chapter

▶ Evaluating the seasons
▶ Charting the weather
▶ Planning your trip around special events

● ●

*T*he Bahamas have their high season in winter and their low season in summer, but any time of the year can be a good time for a visit — that is, if the weather holds. The off season can bring hurricanes, but you receive plenty of warnings before these storms arrive.

This chapter highlights not only the weather but also the best year-round happenings, from Junkanoo parades to sailing regattas.

Revealing the Secrets of the Seasons

Bahamian weather falls into two main seasons: winter (high season) and summer (low season). The Bahamas are in the Atlantic Ocean, just north of the warmer Caribbean region. For this reason, high season can mean surprisingly cool weather, especially in the northern Bahamas. But cool spells, if they descend at all, blow away rather quickly, and you're back on the beach after a day or two. The southern Bahamian islands, on the other hand, truly live up to their reputation of being "June all year round."

Visiting during high season

High season is roughly November through April, which is the cooler, drier, and more expensive time of year to visit. Although average temperatures in The Bahamas may vary only about 12°F throughout the year, winter temperatures can sink into the 60s (about 18°C). Especially during winter months, early morning and evening temperatures are often cool enough to require sweaters or jackets, even when you wear beach gear during the day. See Tables 4-1 and 4-2 for more info on the weather.

If you're not willing to risk a few days that are better suited to golf and tennis than to sand and surf, you may not want to book your vacation during January or February.

Spring break occurs during the high season (from late Feb to mid-Apr). This time of year is when many hotels, restaurants, and beaches are packed with vacationing American college students who have clearly checked their inhibitions at the airport. If you're not looking to party, you may want to avoid the area. But if you're here during these festive weeks, you can treat yourself to an extra dose of entertainment, including sporting events, beach parties, and musical performances.

Table 4-1				Average Monthly Temperatures							
Jan	Feb	Mar	Apr	May	June	July	Aug	Sep	Oct	Nov	Dec
70°F	70°F	72°F	75°F	77°F	80°F	81°F	82°F	81°F	78°F	74°F	71°F
21°C	21°C	22°C	24°C	25°C	27°C	27°C	28°C	27°C	26°C	23°C	22°C

Table 4-2				Average Monthly Rainfall							
Jan	Feb	Mar	Apr	May	June	July	Aug	Sep	Oct	Nov	Dec
4.1cm	3.6cm	5cm	12.2cm	23.4cm	5cm	15.5cm	16cm	19.1 cm	21.1cm	5.8cm	3.8cm
(1.9")	(1.6")	(1.4")	(1.9")	(4.8")	(9.2")	(6.1")	(6.3")	(7.5")	(8.3")	(2.3")	(1.5")

In-season advantages

If you live in the northern climates that are swept with wintry blizzards, nothing is more appealing than a white sandy beach under a summer-like sun on a palm tree-studded Bahamian island in February. The best reasons to visit during the high season are

✔ The winter weather in The Bahamas has been called "a perpetual June." The daytime temperature usually doesn't dip below 70°F (21°C).

✔ All restaurants, services, sports activities, entertainment, shops, and facilities operate at full blast from mid-December to mid-April.

✔ The in-season is ideal for singles and honeymooners because families with children are gone and a more romantic atmosphere prevails.

✔ Both the rainy season and the hurricane season are over. Except for a rare cloudy day, you mostly have sand, sea, and sunshine. Some visitors add an extra "s" to that allure — sex.

✔ The cuisine at resorts is better than ever. The resorts bring in top chefs from both Europe and America during the winter months to tease your taste buds.

In-season disadvantages

Of course, the greatest allure is enjoying sun and sand when much of the United States and Canada is in a deep freeze. But here are the downsides:

✔ You find lots of people crowding around you in airport lounges, on the most popular beaches, at the resorts' buffet tables, at the best restaurants (the lucky stiffs reserved the best tables before you called), and in the casinos.

✔ Reservations become extremely important at resorts, car-rental agencies, nightclubs, the best restaurants, and even for sports activities, such as scuba-diving courses.

✔ You pay top dollar for everything from your hotel room to your car rental. Hotel rates skyrocket, especially around the Christmas holidays. Nothing, including the merchandise in shops, is discounted in winter.

✔ Expect a more frantic pace at the resorts when the guest count reaches maximum capacity. Personalized service goes the way of the trade winds.

Checking out the islands during low season

Low season — May to October — is warmer and wetter and, therefore, is a less expensive time to travel to The Bahamas. Most rain falls between June and October. Showers are usually brief, often coming in the late afternoon, and sometimes the sun doesn't even bother to stop shining during downpours.

As pleasant as you may find the balmy subtropical summer, the low season is also hurricane season. Officially, hurricane season lasts from June to November, but these storms are most likely to arrive during late August, September, or October. Although summer or fall travel can save you a few bucks, it can also cancel your trip. You can, of course, insure yourself in case you're forced to cancel your Bahamian vacation because of a hurricane (see Chapter 9).

The good news is that hurricanes aren't all that common in The Bahamas. Even if one is predicted to hit during your vacation, you usually have enough warning (with the help of satellite forecasts) to rearrange your plans. If you choose to travel during this time of year, you can keep an eye on weather patterns by visiting the National Weather Service Web site at www.nws.noaa.gov.

Off-season advantages

Although The Bahamas may seem more inviting during the winter, here are the many reasons that your trip may be much more enjoyable if you go during the off season:

- A less-hurried way of life prevails. You have a better chance to savor the food, culture, and customs.
- Swimming pools and beaches are less crowded.
- Resorts offer year-round activities, like snorkeling, boating, and scuba diving, often at reduced rates.
- Resort boutiques often feature summer sales.
- You frequently can get a table at a top restaurant without a reservation.
- You don't have to wait for a rental car, tee time, or an open tennis court.
- Some package-tour prices are as much as 20 percent lower, and individual excursion fares are also reduced between 5 and 10 percent.
- You may have an easier time booking accommodations and flights.
- The very best of attractions — sea, sand, and surf, and plenty of sunshine — remain undiminished in the off season.

Off-season disadvantages

Although the advantages of off-season travel outweigh the disadvantages, here are some drawbacks to summer travel:

- You may end up staying at a construction site: Caribbean hoteliers save their serious repairs and major renovations until the off season.
- Hotels often reduce their services and staff.
- Not all resort restaurants and bars are fully operational.

Perusing a Calendar of Events

The following are special events that you may want to keep in mind when you plan your vacation.

Bahamians celebrate familiar holidays, such as New Year's Day, Good Friday, Easter, and Christmas, but you should also prepare for closed businesses, shorter hours, or wild partying on Easter Monday, Whitmonday (seven weeks after Easter), Labour Day (the first Fri in June), Independence Day (July 10), Emancipation Day (the first Mon in Aug), Discovery Day (Oct 12), and Boxing Day (Dec 26).

January

New Year's Day Junkanoo Parades: These parades are held throughout The Bahamas, but the most spectacular one is on Bay Street in downtown Nassau, New Providence. The annual Junkanoo Parade begins in the wee hours (around 1 a.m.). People dance down the street to the sounds of cowbells, goatskin drums, and whistles while wearing elaborate masks and costumes that they've taken months to create. With roots in Africa, this festival (also held on Boxing Day, Dec 26) is the Bahamian version of Rio de Janeiro's Carnival and New Orleans's Mardi Gras. A traditional breakfast of *boil fish* and *johnnycake* (see Chapter 2) caps off the parade. For more details about the Nassau parade, contact the **Local Tourist Office** at ☎ 242-324-1714. For information about the **Grand Bahama parade,** call ☎ 242-352-8044.

Want to jump up with the Nassau crowd? Visitors are welcome to participate. Call **X-plorers Junkanoo** to make arrangements at ☎ 242-361-0907 or 242-325-3567.

Annual New Year's Day Sailing Regatta: Some 40 locally built sailing sloops duke it out for the championship during the Annual New Year's Day Sailing Regatta (Nassau and Paradise Island), organized by The Bahamas Boat Owners Association. For details call ☎ 242-394-0445.

Polar Bear Swim: On New Year's Day, with beach party spectators cheering them on, daring (crazy) swimmers plunge into Cable Beach waters, cooled by huge blocks of ice, during the Polar Bear Swim in Nassau. For details, call Tom Muir of the **Canadian Men's Club** at ☎ 242-322-6504.

February

Farmer's Cay Festival: This festival is a rendezvous for yachtsmen cruising the Exumas and a homecoming for the people of Farmer's Cay. Boat excursions depart Nassau for the festival at 8 p.m. from Potter's Cay on the first Friday in February and return to Nassau the next day. For information, contact Terry Bain in **Little Farmer's Cay** at ☎ 242-355-4006 or 242-355-2093; or the **Exuma Tourist Office** at ☎ 242-336-2430.

March

Annual George Town Cruising Regatta: More than 500 visiting yachts flock to Exuma for a splashy week of fun and competition during the Annual George Town Cruising Regatta. The regatta occurs during late February to March. For details, call the **Exuma Tourist Office** at ☎ 242-336-2430.

Annual Garden of the Groves Art Festival: The daylong festival takes place at the flourishing Garden of the Groves in Grand Bahama. Bring the kids for the local arts and crafts, music, food, and pony rides, as well as a sky-diving exhibition. This event occurs in early March. For more information, call ☎ 242-373-5668.

Annual Art Exhibition: Hope Town, Elbow Cay, shows off its creativity with a display of watercolors, oils, wood-carvings, and sculpture during this mid-March art exhibition. Call **Abaco Inn** at ☎ 242-366-0133.

Bacardi Rum Billfish Tournament: The prestigious week-long tournament attracts the who's who of deep-sea fishing. The Port Lucaya Marina in Grand Bahama is the event's headquarters. The tournament takes place in mid- to late March. For more information, call ☎ 305-234-7386.

Easter Junkanoo Parade: If you can't get to The Bahamas on Boxing Day (Dec 26) or New Year's Day, you can still catch Junkanoo festivities at Marsh Harbour during the Easter Junkanoo Parade (late Mar or Apr). Contact the **Abaco Tourist Office** at ☎ 242-367-3067.

April

Annual Abaco Anglers Fishing Tournament: Men, women, and children can compete in the popular Annual Abaco Anglers Fishing Tournament, which takes place in late April. Contact the Abaco Tourist Office at ☎ 242-367-3067.

The **Bahamas Family Island Regatta:** Every single Bahamian living abroad seems to come home for this event. If you're planning to visit George Town, Exuma, during this week-long event, book your room months in advance. As the handcrafted sloops, owned and sailed by Bahamians, compete in Elizabeth Harbour, you can eat, drink, and socialize nonstop. Food stands, set up along the waterfront, tempt you with fresh pineapple, grilled chicken, peas and rice, and conch in all its incarnations. Events include a parade, Junkanoo and police bands, and nightly parties. If you're in Nassau but want to hop over for the festivities, special excursions can get you here by motorboat or plane. The regatta takes place in late April. Contact the **Exuma Tourist Office** at ☎ 242-336-2430 or 242-336-2457.

May

Treasure Cay Billfish Championship: Taking place in the waters off beautiful Treasure Cay in the Abacos, the popular, challenging Treasure Cay Billfish Championship draws serious anglers, but amateurs can also participate. Entertainment and other festivities surround the tournament. Contact the **Bahamas Billfish Championship** at ☎ 954-920-5577. Dates vary, so call for information.

Long Island Regatta: This regatta in the Out Islands sees some 40 to 50 sailing sloops from throughout The Bahamas compete in three classes for trophies and cash prizes. Onshore, you find sporting events, dancing to indigenous "rake 'n' scrape" music, and local food specialties, all of which make for a carnival-like atmosphere. This event takes place in late May. For more information, call ☎ 242-394-1535.

June

Eleuthera Pineapple Festival: This festival is held in Gregory Town, Eleuthera, and is a celebration devoted to the island's succulent pineapple. It features a Junkanoo parade, craft displays, dancing, a pineapple-recipe contest, tours of pineapple farms, and a "pineathalon" — a half-kilometer (¼-mile) swim, a 5.5km (3½-mile) run, and a 6.5km (4-mile) bike ride. This festival occurs in early June. For more information, call ☎ 242-332-2142.

July

Independence Week: Festivities, parades, and fireworks mark Independence Week throughout the islands. The celebrations culminate on Independence Day, which is July 10.

Annual Racing Time in Abaco: This event is an eight-day series of five boat races at Marsh Harbour. The event lures plenty of sailors during The Bahamas' Independence Week. Beach parties, dances, and live music accompany the races. Contact the **Abaco Tourist Office** at ☎ 242-367-3067.

August

Emancipation Day: The first Monday in August commemorates the emancipation of slaves in 1834. A highlight of this holiday is an early morning "Junkanoo Rushout" starting at 4 a.m. in Fox Hill Village in Nassau, followed by an afternoon of cookouts and fun events, such as climbing a greased pole and the plaiting of the maypole.

Fox Hill Day: This day is a big blast, celebrating the abolition of slavery. A daylong series of entertaining events is planned along with a giant food fest, serving Bahamian specialties. The celebration takes place on the second Tuesday in August in the Fox Hill area about 8km (5 miles) from the center of Nassau.

September

The Grand Bahama Jazz and Rhythm Blues Festival: Jazz, R&B, reggae, and calypso musicians from around the globe descend on Grand Bahama for this four-day festival during the third week in September. There is music in the morning, music in the afternoon, and most definitely music at night — much of it extraordinary. For more information, call ☎ 242-352-8044.

October

Annual McLean's Town Conch Cracking Championship and Festival:
Visit the small fishing village of McClean's Town in Grand Bahama to watch fast-fingered contestants race each other to extract the greatest number of conchs from shells in the shortest amount of time. The festival takes place on Discovery Day (in commemoration of Columbus's first landing in the New World), celebrated on the second Monday in October. For details, call the **Grand Bahama Island Tourism Board** at ☎ 242-352-8044.

November

Guy Fawkes Day: The best celebrations of Guy Fawkes Day occur in Nassau. On many islands, Bahamians hold nighttime parades throughout the streets, culminating in the hanging and burning of Guy Fawkes, an effigy of the British malefactor who was involved in the Gunpowder Plot of 1605 in London. This celebration occurs in early November. For more details, call ☎ 242-356-5216.

Bahamas Wahoo Championship: Test your skill at snagging one of the ocean's fastest fish, wahoo, which can cut through the waves at speeds up to 113km (70 miles) per hour. The annual Bahamas Wahoo Championship is held in three different legs in November, January, and February. The first leg usually kicks off in early to mid-November. For complete details, call ☎ 954-236-9292 or 305-234-7386; or check out the Web site at www.bahamaswahoo.com.

Bimini Big Game Fishing Club All Wahoo Tournament: During this tournament, anglers try to bait one of the fastest fish in the ocean. The Port Lucaya Resort and Yacht Club is the headquarters for this event, which usually occurs over four days during the third week of November. For information, call ☎ 800-737-1007 or 242-373-6618, or visit www.bahamaswahoo.com.

Annual One Bahamas Music and Heritage Festival: This three-day festival is staged at both Nassau and Paradise Island to celebrate national unity. Highlights include concerts featuring top Bahamian performing artists, as well as island walks and other activities. The festival takes place during the last week of November. For more information, contact the Nassau/Paradise Island Tourist Office at ☎ 242-356-5216, ext. 4100.

December

Boxing Day: The famed Junkanoo Parade kicks off on Boxing Day, December 26 (see the Jan events for more info on the parade). Bahamians inherited this holiday from England's Queen Victoria's Day, when the upper class would give gifts of cash or presents — in boxes, of course — to the lower class, usually servants.

Part II
Planning Your Trip to The Bahamas

The 5th Wave
By Rich Tennant

WHILE TRYING TO FIND THE RENTAL RETURN AREA AT MIAMI INTERNATIONAL AIRPORT, FRANK AND MONA DISCOVER THE BAHAMAS.

In this part . . .

*I*n this part, we help you book your ideal vacation in The Bahamas. We tell you the fastest and most economical ways to reach your chosen island, and then explain how to estimate your trip's price tag and how to stay within your budget.

We also offer tips for getting married or honeymooning in The Bahamas, as well as special advice for families, seniors, and travelers who are single, gay or lesbian, or disabled. Finally, we help you tie up loose ends to ensure a hassle-free vacation with details about getting a passport, considering travel insurance, and staying safe.

Chapter 5

Managing Your Money

- -

In This Chapter

▶ Figuring out your budget
▶ Saving money without skimping on fun
▶ Choosing between paper and plastic
▶ Knowing what to do when you lose your wallet

- -

A fabulous vacation in The Bahamas doesn't have to put you in the poor house. Taking a few moments to figure out your expenses in advance, deciding how to carry your money, and finding out what to do if your wallet is lost or stolen can ensure a trouble-free vacation without a financial hangover.

Planning Your Budget

To get an idea of your expenses, try taking a mental stroll through your entire trip. Start with the cost of transportation from your home to the airport, your airline tickets, and transfers to your accommodations. Add your daily hotel rate, meals, activities and entertainment, and your return to the airport. Then add in your transportation home from the airport. And finally, just to be on the safe side, add another 15 to 20 percent for other costs that may crop up. Table 5-1, "What Things Cost in The Bahamas," contains a few representative examples of prices on transportation, dining, and entertainment options.

The lowest airfares and the cheapest resort rates are in effect from April 15 to December 15. If you must go during the Christmas and New Year's holidays, expect the steepest airfares and hotel rates. Resort prices tend to fall right after New Year's and then pick up again in February.

In general, you pay more for your hotel room than your other expenses. Unless you're at an all-inclusive hotel, you can escape your resort's usually expensive dining tabs by sneaking away to a little Bahamian kitchen where you can dine reasonably well on authentic island fare.

Special deals come and go in The Bahamas, even in the peak winter season. Always check for last-minute deals; otherwise, you may end up staying in a $275 double room on Paradise Island next door to a couple who got a room with an even better view for less than $190.

Table 5-1	What Things Cost in The Bahamas		
Travel Expense	*U.S. or Bahamian $*	*U.K. £*	*Canadian $*
Taxi from airport to Nassau's center	$20	£11	$23
Local phone call	25¢	14p	33¢
Double room at Atlantis Resort (expensive)	$360	£198	$414
Double room at Nassau Palm Resort (moderate)	$159	£87.45	$182.85
Dinner for one at Chez Willie (expensive)	$60	£33	$69
Dinner for one at Bahamian Kitchen (inexpensive)	$22	£12	$25.30
Bottle of beer in a bar/hotel	$3.50–$3.95	£1.90–£2.20	$4–$5.45
Rolls of ASA 100 Color Film (36 exposures)	$7	£3.85	$8.05
Movie ticket	$6.50	£3.60	$7.50

Lodging

The biggest chunk of your budget goes to your accommodations. As you flip through the island chapters, dollar signs ($ to $$$$$) indicate the price category of each hotel. For an explanation of these price categories, turn to the Introduction at the beginning of this book. Notice that hotel rates are all over the map and may include more than just your room. Some rates cover breakfast or breakfast and dinner. Also, some rates include taxes and gratuities but others don't. The highest-priced properties we list are *all-inclusive* resorts, which means that you can't compare their rates to the ones of other hotels without taking into account that one price includes all meals, beverages, and most activities.

The prices of rooms within a single resort can vary as much as the prices of hotels. Should you shell out top dollar to stay in an oceanfront suite? Your answer depends on your budget and desire to fall asleep to the sound of the surf or wake up to the sun shimmering on the water. But if you find a garden room steps away from the shore just as attractive and comfortable, you can save the extra cash for something else.

The least you can expect to pay for a double room is about $85 (in the low season) or $150 (in high season) per night at a small hotel — that is, on a *rack rate,* or the top price a hotel charges for a room. See Chapter 7 for a discussion of rack rates and how to avoid paying them.

Transportation

Because The Bahamas lie right off the coast of Florida, getting here for a beach holiday is most often cheaper than flying farther south to the Caribbean. For specifics on saving money on flights, see Chapter 6.

After you pay for airfare, your transportation costs should be low. Taxis, hotel shuttles, and public buses are readily available on some islands. Many vacationers don't rent cars for good reason: Gas is extremely expensive in The Bahamas.

Most package deals include transfers between the airport and your hotel. Ferries to Harbour Island, Green Turtle Cay, Elbow Cay, and Man-O-War Cay run $8 to $16 round-trip.

On New Providence (Nassau, Cable Beach, and Paradise Island), you can get to most sights and attractions on foot or by public bus. Cab fares to and from sights can add up fast, but you can always take a taxi tour of several attractions. Half-day taxi tours begin at about $40 for adults. Most taxi expenses are for transportation to and from restaurants.

Take advantage of the free shuttle buses offered by some resorts. You can find such shuttles on Paradise Island and Cable Beach on New Providence as well as in George Town, Exuma.

Dining

In each island chapter in Parts III through VI, we recommend our favorite restaurants. Dollar signs ($ to $$$$) indicate whether the restaurant is cheap, expensive, or somewhere in between (see the Introduction for an explanation of these price categories).

The prices we quote are for main courses at dinner, unless we state otherwise. When a restaurant has $$, for example, these signs mean that most of the dinner courses are in that price range, but some may be more or less expensive. To get a picture of your total expenses, remember to estimate your beverage, appetizer, dessert, and tip as well.

À la carte hotel breakfast buffets can be expensive, but they're often elaborate. With everything from made-to-order omelets and waffles to carved meats, an array of fresh fruit, and a variety of bread and cereals, you often don't need to eat again until dinner.

On the larger islands (New Providence or Grand Bahama), you can sample some top-rate cuisine. But dinner for two at a top-drawer restaurant can easily run more than $100 — before the tip. Costs for these meals are high because much of the food is imported. Quite a few chefs are from Europe, however, so you're treated to the imaginative creations of some of the Continent's best. Some of the best food comes from the marriage of European and island cuisine.

Check out local restaurants outside the hotels and away from resort areas. Not only do you come across savory home-style food, but you also save money. Many of these local establishments aren't much on décor, and you may sit in metal chairs and dine on plastic tablecloths, but the atmosphere is friendly and the price is usually right.

Staying in a rental unit with a kitchen or kitchenette can help you cut costs. Even if you don't feel like cooking every meal, you can save plenty of money by not eating out for every breakfast or lunch. Likewise, if your room has only a refrigerator, fill it with drinks, snacks, and fruit from the local grocery store.

Sightseeing and outdoor fun

Of course, the two main activities in The Bahamas — swimming in that beautiful, impossibly blue sea and basking on those sandy beaches — are absolutely free. However, if you're interested in activities like sightseeing attractions, scuba diving, snorkeling, windsurfing, and water-skiing, they usually cost extra.

In recent years, more and more of the all-inclusives are offering terrific freebies like scuba and windsurfing lessons, free water-skiing, and free snorkeling gear for the week. Some all-inclusive resorts even toss in a free round of golf.

The costs for activities and attractions can differ greatly from resort to resort and from island to island. The following are some popular activities and what you can expect to pay for them:

- **Golfing on the go:** Greens fees run $85 to $145 at most courses for 18 holes, including a shared cart, plus about $25 to $35 for club rentals. If that price range isn't expensive enough for you, try the course at the **Ocean Club** on Paradise Island, where greens fees run around $245. Some courses offer reduced fees for 9 holes in the afternoon, and rates for both 9 and 18 holes drop during the off season (roughly May–Oct). Arrange tee times as far in advance as you can.

- **Indulging in watersports:** Even at all-inclusive resorts, you have to pay extra for scuba diving, which starts at $88 for a two-tank dive. To sail off to a reef for snorkeling, expect to spend at least $30. If you want to rent snorkel gear at the beach, you pay about $15. For deep-sea fishing, expect to spend at least $75 per person. For details on boat rentals, windsurfing, water-skiing, and golf (on New Providence, Grand Bahama, and the Abacos), turn to the island-specific chapters.

- **Taking a tour:** Save a day to take an island tour, especially if you aren't renting a car. Even though taking an island tour may seem very touristy, it's cheaper and more convenient to take an organized tour than to take taxis, especially on Grand Bahama, where the major attractions are spread out across the island. Island tours begin at $40. See the individual island chapters in Parts III through VI for information on destination-specific tours.

Shopping

In 1992, the government abolished all import duties on a variety of items, making for duty-free shopping. You save tax on perfumes, crystal, leather goods, watches and clocks, jewelry, fine linens and tablecloths, china, camera equipment, and binoculars and telescopes. If you're in the market for any of these goods, you can pay anywhere from 25 to 50 percent less in The Bahamas than in the U.S. You can also take home up to two liters of liquor duty-free, as long as you're of legal drinking age in your country of citizenship.

Save your most serious purchases for Nassau and Freeport/Lucaya, which have the most variety of merchandise and the best discounts. Stores on Cable Beach and Paradise Island charge more for their merchandise because of higher rents, and shops in the Out Islands can't afford to be as generous in their discounting.

Nightlife

The center of Nassau is rather dead and dull at night, although Cable Beach and Paradise Island are jumping, as is the Freeport/Lucaya area. In the Out Islands, a drink in a pub or bar suffices for entertainment.

Because The Bahamas don't have much spectacular nightlife, you're not likely to spend a great deal on it — and, in fact, you can bring your budget under control by not doing so. That is, unless you gamble. Then the sky's the limit.

In general, cover charges for clubs range from $10 to $25. You can find a lot of cheap entertainment because the lounges of the big resorts often have live Bahamian bands entertaining you after dark. The price of admission is the price of a drink.

Taxes

On your hotel bill, you pay resort taxes, gratuities, and sometimes an energy surcharge. Some hotels include these extras in the quoted rates, while others add them on to your bill. Make sure that you're aware of any extra charges that you pay, because they can easily inflate your hotel bill by $20, $30, or even $60 or more per night, depending on the cost of your room.

Total charges vary from hotel to hotel, but you can roughly expect to pay a 12 percent resort tax and about $8 per day per guest (over age 12) for housekeeping gratuity and energy surcharges for use of electricity.

 Don't gamble away your last few dollars in cash because you need extra cash to leave the country. The airports collect a **departure tax** from all passengers over age 12. You pay $15 if you're leaving from New Providence (Nassau) or Out Islands and $18 from Grand Bahama.

Cutting Costs — But Not the Fun

You can save money without shortchanging yourself of a good time. Here are a few ways:

- ✔ **Go during the off season.** If you can travel at non-peak times (from mid-Apr to mid-Dec, for example), you find hotel prices are almost half the price they are during peak months.

- ✔ **Look for a package deal.** For many destinations, you can book airfare, hotel accommodations, ground transportation, and even some sightseeing just by making one call to a travel agent or packager, for a price much less than if you put the trip together yourself. (Chapter 6 is your source for more on package deals.)

- ✔ **Reserve a room with a refrigerator and coffeemaker.** You don't have to slave over a hot stove to cut a few costs; several hotels have minifridges and coffeemakers. Buying supplies for breakfast saves you money — and probably calories, too.

- ✔ **Always ask for discount rates.** Membership in AAA, frequent-flier plans, trade unions, professional organizations, AARP, or other groups may qualify you for savings on car rentals, plane tickets, hotel rooms, and even meals. Ask about everything; you may be pleasantly surprised.

- ✔ **Get a room off the beach.** Accommodations within walking distance of the shore can be much cheaper than accommodations right on the beach. Beaches are public, so you don't need to stay in a hotel that's on the sand to spend most of your vacation at the beach.

- ✔ **Ask if your kids can stay in the room with you.** A room with two double beds usually doesn't cost any more than a room with a queen-size bed. And many hotels don't charge you the additional-person rate if the additional person is pint-size and related to you. Even if you have to pay $10 or $15 extra for a rollaway bed, you can save hundreds by not taking two rooms.

- ✔ **Use a pay phone to call home.** Avoid using the phone in your hotel room to call outside the hotel. Charges can be astronomical, even for local calls, which are sometimes at least $1 a pop (instead of 25¢ at a pay phone). When you call long distance, you may think that you're saving money by using the toll-free number of your calling card instead of dialing direct. However, most hotels charge you at least $1 to connect you to an outside line for the toll-free call. On top of whatever your calling card bills you, the hotel also charges you just for picking up the phone — whether or not you reach the person you wanted.

✔ **Try expensive restaurants at lunch instead of dinner.** Lunch tabs are usually a fraction of what dinner costs at a top restaurant, and the menu often boasts many of the same specialties.

✔ **Walk a lot.** A good pair of walking shoes can save you lots of money on taxis and other local transportation. As a bonus, you get to know your destination more intimately, as you explore at a slower pace.

✔ **Steer clear of the casinos.** If you can't resist gambling, head to an island without casinos. Only New Providence and Grand Bahama offer casinos.

Handling Money

In The Bahamas, you can use U.S. dollars interchangeably with the local Bahamian dollar — they have the same value. So you don't have to worry about exchanging your U.S. cash. If you're carrying a currency other than greenbacks, check out the "Converting currency" section later in this chapter.

As you near the end of your trip, ask for your change in only American dollars if you're headed back to the States. Otherwise, you can end up with unwanted Bahamian currency that you need either to spend or exchange at the airport, and, if you exchange it there, you lose some of it to service charges.

Carrying cash, traveler's checks, or credit cards?

You're the best judge of how much cash you feel comfortable carrying or what alternative form of currency is your favorite. Credit and debit cards, traveler's checks, and cash are all welcome in The Bahamas, but some forms of payment are more convenient (or cheaper) than others.

Using ATMs

The easiest and best way to get cash away from home is from an ATM (automated teller machine), sometimes referred to as a "cash machine," or "cashpoint." Nassau and Freeport have handy 24-hour ATMs linked to an international network that almost always includes your bank at home. For the most part, the Out Islands lack this convenience. **Cirrus** (☎ 800-424-7787; www.mastercard.com) and **PLUS** (☎ 800-843-7587; www.visa.com) are the two most popular networks. Check the back of your ATM card to see which network your bank belongs to. The networks' toll-free numbers and Web sites give specific locations of ATMs where you can withdraw money while on vacation. You can use them to withdraw just the amount that you need every couple of days, which eliminates having to carry around a large green stash.

Of course, many ATMs are little money managers (or dictators, depending on how you look at it) that may allow you to withdraw only a certain amount of money — a maximum of $200, say — per day. Check with your bank about withdrawal limits before you set off on your vacation.

Another important reminder before you go ATM crazy: Many banks now charge a fee ranging from 50¢ to $3 whenever a nonaccount holder uses his ATMs. Your own bank may also assess a fee for using an ATM that isn't one of its branch locations. In some cases, you get charged twice just for using your bank card when you're on vacation. Reverting to traveler's checks may be cheaper (although certainly less convenient to get hold of and use).

The most common bank branches in The Bahamas are offices of First Caribbean International Bank. All these branches assess small fees for their transactions.

Toting traveler's checks

Traveler's checks are a holdover from the days when people wrote personal checks instead of going to an ATM. On New Providence (Nassau, Cable Beach, and Paradise Island) or Grand Bahama (Freeport/Lucaya), finding a 24-hour ATM is easy, so you don't need to carry traveler's checks or a wad of cash. On smaller islands, such as Eleuthera or the Abacos, ATMs are few and far between, if not nonexistent, so carrying traveler's checks may be a good idea. Be aware, however, that in The Bahamas, some restaurants tack on an additional service charge when you pay with a traveler's check.

You can get traveler's checks at almost any bank. **American Express** offers denominations of $20, $50, $100, $500, and (for cardholders only) $1,000. You pay a service charge ranging from 1 percent to 4 percent. You can also get American Express traveler's checks over the phone by calling ☎ **800-221-7282;** Amex gold and platinum cardholders who use this number are exempt from the 1 percent fee.

Visa offers traveler's checks at Citibank locations nationwide, as well as at several other banks. The service charge ranges between 1.5 percent and 2 percent; checks come in denominations of $20, $50, $100, $500, and $1,000. Call ☎ **800-732-1322** for information. AAA members can get hold of Visa checks for a $9.95 fee at most AAA offices or by calling ☎ **866-339-3378. MasterCard** also offers traveler's checks. Call ☎ **800-223-9920** for a location near you.

If you choose to carry traveler's checks, be sure to keep a record of their serial numbers separate from your checks in the event that they are stolen or lost. You get a refund faster if you know the numbers.

Charging ahead with credit cards

Credit cards are a safe way to carry money: They also provide a convenient record of all your expenses, and they generally offer relatively good exchange rates. You can also withdraw cash advances from your credit cards at banks or ATMs, provided you know your PIN. If you've forgotten yours, or didn't even know you had one, call the number on the back of your credit card and ask the bank to send it to you. It usually takes 5 to 7 business days, though some banks will provide the number over the phone if you tell them your mother's maiden name or some other personal information.

 Even though the Bahamian dollar is equivalent to the U.S. dollar, the two currencies are still different. If you use a credit or debit card, when you receive your monthly statement, note that the bank or credit card company added a currency conversion fee (usually about 2 percent) to your charges.

Some credit card companies recommend that you notify them of any impending trip abroad so that they don't become suspicious when the card is used numerous times in an unusual location. If the company becomes suspicious, it may block your charges. Even if you don't call your credit card company in advance, you can always call the card's emergency number if a charge is refused.

Converting currency

Conversion ratios between the U.S. or Bahamian dollar and other currencies fluctuate, and their differences could affect the relative costs of your holiday. The figures in Table 5-2 were valid at the time of this writing, but they may not be valid by the time you depart. This table would still be useful for conversions of small amounts of money, but if you plan to make any major transactions, check for more updated rates prior to any serious commitments.

Table 5-2		Foreign Currencies versus the U.S./Bahamian Dollar					
$U.S./ $B	*U.K. £*	*Canadian $*	*E.U. €*	*$U.S./ $B*	*U.K. £*	*Canadian $*	*E.U. €*
1.00	0.55	1.15	0.83	10.00	5.50	11.50	8.30
2.00	1.10	2.30	1.66	15.00	8.25	17.25	12.45
3.00	1.65	3.45	2.49	25.00	13.75	28.75	20.75
5.00	2.75	5.75	4.15	100.00	55.00	115.00	83.00

Dealing with a Lost or Stolen Wallet

Be sure to contact all your credit card companies the minute you discover that your wallet's been lost or stolen. Then file a report at the nearest police precinct. Your credit card company or insurer may require a police report number or a record of the loss. Most credit card companies have an emergency number to call if you lose your card or it gets stolen; they may be able to wire you a cash advance immediately or deliver an emergency credit card in a day or two. Call the following emergency numbers:

  ✓ **American Express:** ☎ 800-221-7282

  ✓ **MasterCard:** ☎ 800-307-7309

  ✓ **Visa:** ☎ 800-847-2911

If you need emergency cash over the weekend when all banks and American Express offices are closed, you can have **Western Union** wire money to you (☎ **800-325-6000;** www.westernunion.com).

Identity theft and fraud are potential complications of losing your wallet, especially if you lose your driver's license along with your cash and credit cards. Notify the major credit-reporting bureaus immediately; placing a fraud alert on your records may protect you against liability for criminal activity. The three major U.S. credit-reporting agencies are

  ✓ **Equifax:** ☎ **888-766-0008;** www.equifax.com

  ✓ **Experian:** ☎ **888-397-3742;** www.experian.com

  ✓ **TransUnion:** ☎ **800-680-7289;** www.transunion.com

Finally, if you lose all forms of photo ID, call your airline and explain the situation. The airline may allow you to board the plane if you have a copy of your passport or birth certificate and a copy of the police report that you filed.

Chapter 6

Getting to The Bahamas

*U*nless you're a long-distance swimmer, you have to get to The Bahamas by air (commercial, chartered, or private plane) or by sea (cruise ship or ferry). Of course, the quickest, easiest, and most convenient way to reach The Bahamas is by plane. Many people enjoy cruising to The Bahamas, although these trips mean spending a lot more time on the surf than on the turf.

Flying to The Bahamas

New York and Miami are the most popular U.S. gateway cities from which to fly to Nassau (New Providence and Paradise Islands) and to Freeport/Lucaya (Grand Bahama Island). Several other U.S. cities, including Philadelphia and Atlanta, also offer direct service.

Nassau is the busiest and most popular entry point. From here, you can make travel arrangements to many of the remote Out Islands. Freeport, on Grand Bahama, also has its own airport, which serves flights from the U.S. mainland, too.

Flight time to Nassau from Miami is about 35 minutes; from New York, two hours and 30 minutes; from Atlanta, two hours and 5 minutes; from Philadelphia, two hours and 45 minutes; from Charlotte, two hours and 10 minutes; from central Florida, one hour and 10 minutes; and from Toronto, three hours.

Connecting airlines and islands

To help you get started making your travel arrangements, we break this section down island by island so that you can tell how easy — or how difficult — it is to reach the vacation spot you have in mind.

We list information about only nonstop flights and direct flights (where you may touch down once, but you don't have to change planes). Therefore, if you're not starting from one of the cities mentioned in the preceding section, you probably have to change planes or even airlines to get to the island of your choice. Keep in mind that no matter where you start, to get to some of the smaller cays, you have to fly to one island and then take a ferry or switch to a small airline. (See the individual island chapters for complete details.) Planes flying from Florida to The Bahamas and from Nassau (New Providence) to other Bahamian islands often carry fewer than 30 or 40 passengers.

Also, remember that flight schedules always change, so use the information in this section to get a rough idea of what's available. Some routes are seasonal, with fewer flights or no flights at all, at various times of the year. For up-to-the-minute details, call the airlines directly or check their Web sites.

Flying to Nassau, New Providence (for Nassau, Cable Beach, and Paradise Island): American Eagle (☎ 800-433-7300; www.aa.com) offers about 12 flights each day from Miami to Nassau, as well as less frequent service from Ft. Lauderdale, Orlando, and Tampa. **Bahamasair** (☎ 800-222-4262; www.bahamasair.com) flies from West Palm Beach, Miami, Ft. Lauderdale, and Orlando to Nassau. **Continental Airlines** (☎ 800-525-0280; www.continental.com) offers daily flights to Nassau from Newark, Miami, Ft. Lauderdale, and West Palm Beach. **Delta** (☎ 800-241-4141; www.delta.com) has several flights to Nassau, providing service from Atlanta, Orlando, and New York's LaGuardia Airport. **JetBlue** (☎ 800-JET-BLUE; www.jetblue.com), has one direct flight daily to Nassau, from JFK in New York. **U.S. Airways** (☎ 800-428-4322; www.usairways.com) offers daily flights to Nassau from Philadelphia and Charlotte, North Carolina. **Air Canada** (☎ 888-247-2262 in the U.S.; www.aircanada.com) is the only carrier that offers service to Nassau from Toronto and Montreal.

British Airways (☎ 800-247-9297 in the U.S. or 0870-850-9850 in the United Kingdom; www.britishairways.com) flies directly only to Nassau, offering four weekly flights from London. The airline also has at least one flight daily to Miami, where a staggering number of connections are available to Nassau and many other points within the archipelago on several carriers. Prospective visitors from Australia or New Zealand usually fly to London, where they take a connecting flight across the Atlantic to Nassau on British Airways.

Flying to Paradise Island: Most visitors to Paradise Island arrive in Nassau and commute to Paradise Island by ground transport. However, **Chalk's International Airlines** (☎ 800-424-2557 or 242-363-3115; www.chalksoceanairways.com) flies daily from Ft. Lauderdale International Airport directly to Paradise Island. This airline offers about five flights on weekdays and around eight flights on Saturdays and Sundays. The airplanes are Grumman G-73Ts; each aircraft carries up to 17 passengers.

Flying to Freeport, Grand Bahama (for Freeport and Lucaya): A number of airlines fly to Grand Bahama International Airport from the continental U.S., including **American Eagle** (☎ 800-433-7300; www.aa.com) and **Bahamasair** (☎ 800-222-4262; www.bahamasair.com). Both airlines have daily flights from Miami. **GulfStream Continental Connection** (☎ 800-231-0856; www.gulfstreamair.com) flies to Freeport from both Ft. Lauderdale and Miami. **U.S. Airways** (☎ 800-428-4322; www.usairways.com) flies daily from New York's LaGuardia Airport; Charlotte, North Carolina; and Philadelphia. And **U.S. Airways Express** (☎ 800-428-4322; www.usairways.com) wings in from West Palm Beach to Freeport.

Many visitors arrive in Nassau and then hop a **Bahamasair** flight to Freeport. These 35-minute hops run $140 round-trip.

Flying to Marsh Harbour, the Abacos (for Elbow Cay): Air Sunshine (☎ 800-327-8900; www.airsunshine.com), a small commuter airline, offers daily flights from Ft. Lauderdale to Marsh Harbour, where you can catch the ferry to Elbow Cay. **Bahamasair** (☎ 800-222-4262; www.bahamasair.com) flies to Marsh Harbour from West Palm Beach or Nassau. You can find other connections aboard **American Eagle** (☎ 800-433-7300 or 242-367-2231; www.aa.com) with flights from Miami to Marsh Harbour. **Continental Connections** (☎ 800-525-0280; www.continental.com) flies into Marsh Harbour from several locales in Florida. **U.S. Airways Express** (☎ 800-428-4322; www.usairways.com) flies from West Palm Beach to Marsh Harbour.

Flying to Treasure Cay, the Abacos (for Green Turtle Cay and Treasure Cay): Air Sunshine (☎ 800-327-8900 or 242-365-8900; www.airsunshine.com) offers daily flights from Ft. Lauderdale to Treasure Cay (you can take a ferry from Treasure Cay to Green Turtle Cay). **Bahamasair** (☎ 800-222-4262; www.bahamasair.com) flies in daily from Nassau and West Palm Beach. You can find other connections aboard **Twin Air** (☎ 954-359-8266; www.flytwinair.com), which wings in from Ft. Lauderdale. **Continental Connection** (☎ 800-525-0280; www.continental.com) flies to Treasure Cay from several Florida locales.

Getting to Eleuthera and Harbor Island: Bahamasair (☎ 800-222-4262; www.bahamasair.com) flies daily from Nassau to North Eleuthera, where you catch the ferry to Harbour Island. **U.S. Airways Express** (☎ 800-428-4322; www.usairways.com) flies daily from Miami and West Palm Beach to North Eleuthera.

Flying to George Town, Exuma: The most popular way to visit the Exumas is to fly aboard **Bahamasair** (☎ 800-222-4262; www.bahamasair.com), which offers twice-daily service from Nassau to George Town. Flights usually begin leaving Nassau sometime around 6:30 a.m., depending on the day. Be sure to call ahead, because flight schedules can change. **American Eagle** (☎ 800-433-7300; www.aa.com) serves Exuma from Miami daily. Other minor carriers that serve the archipelago include

Lynx Air International (☎ 888-596-9247; www.lynxair.com), which has flights on Fridays, Saturdays, and Sundays, with links from Ft. Lauderdale. **Air Sunshine** (☎ 800-327-8900 or 954-434-8900; www.airsunshine.com) flies from Ft. Lauderdale, but only on Mondays and Thursdays. You can return to Ft. Lauderdale aboard this airline on Mondays and Fridays.

Flying to San Salvador: Bahamasair (☎ 800-222-4262; www.bahamasair.com) offers flights six days a week from Nassau. Flight times constantly change. The island's most popular hotel, **Club Med** (☎ 800-CLUBMED [888-WEB-CLUB] or 242-331-2000) flies guests in on weekly charter flights from Miami. In winter, charter flights from New York are available once a week.

Getting the best deal on your airfare

Competition among the major U.S. airlines is unlike that of any other industry. Every airline offers virtually the same product (basically, a coach seat is a coach seat is a . . .), yet prices can vary by hundreds of dollars.

Business travelers who need the flexibility of buying their tickets at the last minute and changing their itineraries at a moment's notice — and who want to get home before the weekend — pay (or at least their companies pay) the premium rate, known as the *full fare*. But if you can book your ticket far in advance, stay over Saturday night, and travel midweek (Tues–Thurs), you can qualify for the least expensive price — usually a fraction of the full fare. On most flights — even the shortest hops within the U.S. — the full fare is close to $1,000 or more, but a 7- or 14-day advance-purchase ticket may cost you less than half of that amount. Obviously, planning ahead pays.

Periodically, the airlines hold sales in which they lower the prices on their most popular routes. These fares have advance-purchase requirements and date-of-travel restrictions, but you can't beat the prices. As you plan your vacation, keep your eyes open for these sales, which tend to take place in seasons that have low travel volume — from May to October for The Bahamas.

Consolidators, also known as "bucket shops," are great sources for international tickets, although they usually can't beat the Internet on fares within North America. Start by looking in travel sections in the Sunday newspaper; U.S. travelers should focus on the *New York Times, Los Angeles Times,* and *The Miami Herald.*

Bucket-shop tickets are usually nonrefundable or are rigged with stiff cancellation penalties, often as high as 50 to 75 percent of the ticket price. And some bucket shops put you on charter airlines with questionable safety records. Ask plenty of questions before you fork over your money.

Travel (☎ 800-781-4040; www.statravel.com), the world's leader in student travel, offers good fares for travelers of all ages. **ELTExpress**

(**Flights.com;** ☎ **800-TRAV-800;** www.eltexpress.com) has excellent fares worldwide, particularly to Europe. **FlyCheap** (☎ **800-FLY-CHEAP;** www.1800flycheap.com) is owned by package-holiday megalith MyTravel and so has especially good access to fares for sunny destinations. **Air Tickets Direct** (☎ **800-778-3447;** www.airticketsdirect. com) is based in Montreal and leverages the currently weak Canadian dollar for low fares; it also books trips to places that U.S. travel agents won't touch, such as Cuba.

Frequent-flier membership doesn't cost a cent, but it does entitle you to better seats, faster response to phone inquiries, and prompter service if your luggage is stolen or your flight is canceled or delayed, or if you want to change your seat. And you don't have to fly to earn points; **frequent-flier credit cards** can earn you thousands of miles for doing your everyday shopping. With more than 70 mileage awards programs on the market, consumers have never had more options. Investigate the program details of your favorite airlines before you sink points into any one. Consider which airlines have hubs in the airport nearest you, and, of those carriers, which have the most advantageous alliances, given your most common routes. To play the frequent-flier game to your best advantage, consult Randy Petersen's **Inside Flyer** (www.insideflyer. com). Petersen and friends review all the programs in detail and post regular updates on changes in policies and trends.

Booking your flight online

The "big three" online travel agencies, **Expedia** (www.expedia.com), **Travelocity** (www.travelocity.com), and **Orbitz** (www.orbitz.com), sell most of the air tickets bought on the Internet. (Canadian travelers should try www.expedia.ca and www.travelocity.ca; U.K. residents can go for expedia.co.uk and opodo.co.uk.) Each has different business deals with the airlines and may offer different fares on the same flights, so shopping around is wise. Expedia and Travelocity will also send you an **e-mail notification** when a cheap fare to your favorite destination becomes available. Of the smaller travel agency Web sites, **SideStep** (www.sidestep.com) receives good reviews from users. It purports to "search 140 sites at once," but in reality only beats competitors' fares as often as other sites do.

If you're willing to give up some control over your flight details, use a service like **Priceline** (www.priceline.com; www.priceline.co.uk for Europeans) or **Hotwire** (www.hotwire.com). Both companies offer rock-bottom prices in exchange for traveling on a "mystery airline" at a mysterious time of day, often with a mysterious change of planes en route. The mystery airlines are all major, well-known carriers, and the airlines' routing computers are a lot better than they used to be. But your chances of getting a 6 a.m. or 11 p.m. flight are pretty high. Hotwire tells you the flight prices before you buy; Priceline usually has better deals than Hotwire, and you now also have the option to pick your flights, times, and airlines from a list of low prices that Priceline offers.

Just a ferry ride away

A great way to get from the Florida coast to Freeport is aboard a modern ferryboat, the sleek *Cloud X,* which transports you there in three hours. Launched in 2004, the ferry sets sail from the port of Palm Beach Thursday to Monday at 9 a.m., with a return voyage from Freeport at 6:15 p.m. The round-trip fare is $119 for adults, $80 for children ages 6 to 12, and free for kids 5 and under. A $38 port charge is levied on passengers of all ages. A trio of comfortable lounges, two bars, and a casino are on board to entertain. This 367-passenger vessel sails under a U.S. flag. For more information, call ☎ 866-GO-FERRY (866-463-3779) or visit www.cloudx.com.

Great last-minute deals are also available directly from the airlines themselves through a free e-mail service called *E-savers.* Each week, the airline sends you a list of discounted flights, usually leaving the upcoming Friday or Saturday and returning the following Monday or Tuesday. You can sign up for all the major airlines at one time by logging on to **Smarter Travel** (www.smartertravel.com), or you can go to each individual airline's Web site. Airline sites also offer schedules, flight booking, and information on late-breaking bargains.

Other helpful Web sites for booking airline tickets online include:

✓ www.biddingfortravel.com

✓ www.cheapflights.com

✓ www.hotwire.com

✓ www.kayak.com

✓ www.lastminutetravel.com

✓ www.opodo.co.uk

✓ www.site59.com

Cruising to The Bahamas

Cruises to The Bahamas are usually either three- or four-day weekend getaways or week-long itineraries. If you go on a week-long cruise, the ship may stop at Nassau, Freeport, and/or one of several privately owned Bahamian islands for a day at the beach en route to Caribbean ports farther south.

If you've never been to The Bahamas, consider taking a cruise to Nassau, where you can also enjoy Paradise Island and Cable Beach on the same visit. Nassau has better shopping possibilities, better restaurants, and more entertainment than any other site in The Bahamas.

We provide a summary of cruise lines that sail to The Bahamas in the upcoming section, but for detailed information, consider picking up a copy of *Cruise Vacations For Dummies* or *Frommer's Caribbean Cruises & Ports of Call.*

Regardless of the ship you choose, your cruise will most likely depart from the cruise capital of the world, **Miami.** A handful of vessels also depart for Bahamian waters from Port Everglades (adjacent to Ft. Lauderdale), Port Canaveral, and, in very rare instances, New York. Many cruise-ship passengers combine a three- or four-day cruise with visits to Orlando's theme parks, Miami's South Beach, the Florida Everglades, or the Florida Keys and Key West.

Nearly all cabins aboard ships today have two twin beds that you can push together, plus storage space (of varying size), a shower and a toilet (ditto), and sometimes a TV showing a rotating stock of programs. If you want to keep costs to a minimum when booking, ask for one of the smaller, inside cabins (one without windows). If you're the type who likes being active all day and staying out late to enjoy the ship's bars and nightclubs, you won't miss the sunshine anyway. On the other hand, passengers of means can get suites that have an amazing array of pampering options (including hot tubs on their own private verandas!).

Because cruise lines buy in bulk, they typically offer some of the best deals on airfare to your port of embarkation. They also typically offer extension packages that allow pre- or post-cruise stays at a hotel or resort.

Getting around Freeport/Lucaya or Nassau is relatively easy, and the official shore excursions that most ships offer are dull and sometimes restrictive, so decide what you want to do (shopping, swimming, snorkeling, or gambling) and head off on your own during your stop at each port of call. You certainly have time to relax at the beach or to enjoy watersports (the chapters that follow give you details on what companies or outfitters to contact for equipment, so don't feel dependent on the cruise line for everything).

In Nassau, cruise ships anchor at piers along **Prince George Wharf.** Taxi drivers meet all arrivals and can transport you into the heart of Nassau — the center of most shopping and sightseeing activities. Duty-free shops also lie just outside the dock area, but for shopping, you're better off going inside the city's commercial and historic core.

As you disembark, a tourist information office is visible in a tall pink tower, where you can pick up maps of New Providence Island or of Nassau itself. The tourist information office conducts one-hour walking tours from here if you'd like an overview of the city, with a guide pointing out historic monuments. Outside this office, an ATM can supply you with U.S. dollars if your cash is running low. (For more information on money issues, see Chapter 5.)

On Grand Bahama Island, your cruise ship will dock at a dull industrial-looking wasteland on the western part of the island, far removed from the center of all the action at Freeport or Lucaya. For shopping, sightseeing, the best beaches, or gambling, you must take a $10 taxi ride to the resort areas. Taxis await all arriving cruise ships.

Reviewing the major cruise lines

Here's a rundown of the major cruise lines that serve The Bahamas. Most of them focus on either Nassau or Freeport (or both).

- ✔ **Carnival Cruise Line** (☎ 888-CARNIVAL; www.carnival.com): The cruise line that everyone's heard of offers a big, loud, flashy cruise party with lots of gambling, glitz, and crowds, so if you're looking for some quiet, reflective time, this cruise may not be your cup of rum. Carnival's best bet for The Bahamas is aboard the *Fantasy,* which sails on three-night loops to Nassau and four-night excursions to both Freeport and Nassau. Similar in appeal is the *Fascination,* which visits Nassau and attracts passengers seeking a "long weekend" at sea and in port.

- ✔ **Disney Cruise Line** (☎ 800-951-3532; www.disneycruise.com): Launched with lots of publicity in 1999, the *Disney Wonder* is saturated with the total Disney vibe and is specifically marketed to families. It succeeds in mingling state-of-the-art technology and audiovisuals with lots of Disney razzle-dazzle. Disney also offers the best-designed family cabins of any cruise ship, the biggest children's facilities, and even a number of adults-only areas, including one swimming pool, a piano bar, a comedy club, and various social venues. The three- and four-night Bahamian cruises depart from Port Canaveral, Florida.

- ✔ **Norwegian Cruise Line** (☎ 800-327-7030; www.ncl.com): Norwegian Cruise Line offers seven-night Florida-Bahamas transits aboard the *Norwegian Dawn,* visiting Nassau and Great Stirrup Cay (the cruise line's private island). Generally inexpensive and emphasizing sports, these ships attract a lot of active travelers in the 24-to-45 age bracket. Activities and cuisine are routine but adequate. Passengers who book on this cruise line want to travel to a hot-weather destination in winter but don't want to spend lavish sums for the experience. A wide variety of cabins are available at a range of prices to cater to a more diverse clientele than those usually found aboard Holland America or Celebrity ships.

- ✔ **Royal Caribbean International** (☎ 866-3562-7626; www.royalcaribbean.com): This is another cruise line that offers The Bahamas (Nassau and Freeport) as a specific destination instead of including the archipelago as a one-night stopover. Things run smoothly on this middle-of-the-road cruise line, which has a less frenetic atmosphere than Carnival's mega-ships but a livelier one than Celebrity or Holland America. The company is well run, and it offers enough on-board activities to suit virtually any taste and age level. Although accommodations and facilities are more than adequate, they're not upscale, and cabins aboard some of the line's older vessels tend to be a bit more cramped than the industry norm.

Getting the best deal on your cruise

Cruise lines operate like airlines, setting rates for their cruises and then selling them in a rapid-fire series of discounts, offering almost whatever it takes to fill their ships. For this reason, great deals come and go in the blink of an eye, and most deals are available only through travel agents.

If you have a travel agent who you trust, leave the details to her. If not, try contacting a travel agent who specializes in booking cruises. Some of the most likely contenders include the following:

- ✔ **Cruises, Inc.,** 1415 NW 62 St., Ft. Lauderdale, FL 33009 (☎ **866-325-6893;** www.cruisesinc.com)

- ✔ **Cruises Only,** 1011 E. Colonial Dr., Orlando, FL 32803 (☎ **800-278-4737;** www.cruisesonly.com)

- ✔ **The Cruise Company,** 10760 Q St., Omaha, NE 68127 (☎ **800-289-5505;** www.thecruisecompany.com)

- ✔ **Kelly Cruises,** 1315 W. 22nd St., Suite 105, Oak Brook, IL 60523 (☎ **800-837-7447;** www.kellycruises.com)

- ✔ **Hartford Holidays Travel,** 129 Hillside Ave., Williston Park, NY 11596 (☎ **800-828-4813;** www.hartfordholidays.com)

- ✔ **Mann Travel and Cruises,** 4400 Park Rd., Charlotte, NC 28209 (☎ **866-591-8129;** www.manntravelandcruises.com)

Choosing a Package Deal

For The Bahamas, package deals can be a smart way to go. In many cases, a package that includes airfare, hotel, and transportation to and from the airport costs less than the hotel alone that you book yourself. The reason is because tour operators buy packages in bulk and then resell them to the public.

Package tours can vary widely. Some package tours offer better classes of hotel than others; others provide the same hotels for lower prices. Some packages book flights on scheduled airlines; others sell charters. In some packages, your choice of accommodations and travel days may be limited. Some packages let you choose between escorted vacations and independent vacations; others allow you to add just a few excursions or escorted day trips (also at discounted prices) without booking an entirely escorted tour.

If you're dreaming of getting away from it all on one of The Bahamas' undeveloped Out Islands, finding good package deals may be hard. Most packagers concentrate on the larger hotels on the more popular islands, such as New Providence or Grand Bahama.

To find package tours, check out the travel section of your local Sunday newspaper or the ads in the back of national travel magazines, such as *Travel + Leisure, National Geographic Traveler,* and *Condé Nast Traveler.* **Liberty Travel** (call ☎ 888-271-1584 to find the store nearest you; www.libertytravel.com) is one of the biggest packagers in the Northeast and usually boasts a full-page ad in Sunday papers.

Some packagers specialize in types of trips, such as scuba-diving adventures, golf getaways, or casino excursions. Likewise, a few of the larger hotels, such as the all-inclusive Club Med on San Salvador, offer money-saving hotel packages that include charter flights. If you already know where you want to stay, call that resort and ask whether it offers land/air packages.

Another good source of package deals is the airlines themselves. Most major airlines offer air/land packages. Several big online travel agencies — Expedia (www.expedia.com), Travelocity (www.travelocity.com), Orbitz (www.orbitz.com), Site59 (www.site59.com), and Lastminute.com (www.lastminute.com) — also do a brisk business in packages. If you're unsure about the pedigree of a smaller packager, check with the Better Business Bureau in the city where the company is based or go online to www.bbb.org. If a packager won't tell you where it's based, don't book with it.

Here are some of the packagers that we prefer:

- ✔ **American Airlines Vacations** (☎ 800-321-2121; www.aavacations.com) can arrange packages to Nassau, Cable Beach, and Paradise Island (New Providence); Freeport/Lucaya (Grand Bahama); and Exuma. These economical deals include discounted airfare, hotel, and, if you like, a rental car, as well as meals (at certain accommodations).

- ✔ **American Express Vacations** (☎ 800-335-3342; www.americanexpress.com) books trips to a couple of the smaller Bahamian islands that many packagers ignore: Green Turtle Cay in the Abacos and Harbour Island off the coast of Eleuthera. Of course, the company also sets up air/land packages to the most popular resort areas: Nassau, Cable Beach, and Paradise Island (New Providence); and Freeport/Lucaya (Grand Bahama). Nonstop charter flights from Newark, New York, and Miami can take you to Nassau or Freeport.

- ✔ **British Airways** (☎ 0870-850-9850 in the U.K. or 800-247-9297 in the U.S.; www.britishairways.com) offers travelers direct flights from Gatwick Airport outside London to Nassau. Call the airline or visit the Web site for information on package deals.

✔ **Caribbean Dive Tours** (☎ 800-433-DIVE; www.worlddive.com) makes one-stop shopping especially attractive, because this company arranges scuba-diving trips for individuals or groups that include airfare, hotel, meals (in some cases), and all dives and gear.

✔ **Club Med** (☎ 888-WEB-CLUB; www.clubmed.com) features all-inclusive options on Paradise Island and San Salvador.

✔ **Continental Airlines Vacations** (☎ 800-301-3800; www.covacations.com) customizes hotel and air packages to Nassau, Cable Beach, and Paradise Island that include transfers to and from the airport. Depending on what hotel you choose, you can throw in breakfast or both breakfast and dinner.

✔ **Delta Vacations** (☎ 800-221-6666; www.deltavacations.com) coordinates packages from New York or Atlanta to Nassau, Cable Beach, and Paradise Island that include air, hotel, and transfers between your accommodations and the airport.

✔ **Frontiers International** (☎ 800-245-1950 or 724-935-1577; www.frontierstrvl.com) features fly- and spin-fishing tours of The Bahamas and specializes in saltwater-fishing destinations.

✔ **Grand Bahama Vacations** (☎ 800-545-1300; www.grandbahamavacations.com) books charter flights with Laker Airways to Freeport/Lucaya (Grand Bahama) twice a week from Ft. Lauderdale, Baltimore, Cleveland, Cincinnati, Hartford, Memphis, Nashville, Raleigh, Richmond, and Pittsburgh, as well as every other Saturday from West Palm Beach. When you reserve your flight, you can also book a bed at one of more than a dozen Grand Bahama hotels.

✔ **Just-A-Vacation, Inc.** (☎ 800-683-6313; www.justavacation.com) specializes in all-inclusive resorts on the islands of The Bahamas, mainly Nassau/Paradise Island and Grand Bahama Island.

✔ **Kuoni Travel** (☎ 01306-742-222; www.kuoni.co.uk) is another British specialist that offers both land and air packages to The Bahamas, including such destinations as Nassau and Freeport, and to some places in the Out Islands. They also offer packages for self-catering villas on Paradise Island.

✔ **Maduro Dive Fanta-Seas** (☎ 800-327-6709; www.maduro.com) can set up a complete dive trip with one phone call. Packages for individuals or groups include airfare, hotel, meals (if you want them), and all dives and gear.

✔ **U.S. Airways Vacations** (☎ 800-455-0123; www.usairwaysvacations.com) arranges air/hotel packages, with nonstop service to Nassau from Philadelphia or Charlotte, North Carolina.

Chapter 7

Booking Your Accommodations

*W*hen visiting an archipelago as vast and, in some cases, as difficult to reach as parts of The Bahamas are, choosing where to hang your hat becomes all-important. Visiting The Bahamas isn't like visiting a city where you can check out of a hotel you don't like the next morning and take a taxi to another one.

Throughout this guide, we give you honest and candid descriptions about what to expect from a hotel. We hope to match you up with the right location for your island fantasy because if you land in the wrong place, especially if you've already prepaid, your vacation may be disappointing. This chapter tells you what you need to know about the types of accommodations awaiting you on each island. In Grand Bahama and New Providence, you have plenty of choices. In the Out Islands, the lack of accommodations greatly restricts you.

Getting to Know Your Options

The Bahamas offer a wide selection of accommodations, ranging from small private guesthouses to large luxury resorts. Hotels vary in size and facilities, from deluxe (offering room service, sports, swimming pools, entertainment, and so on) to fairly simple Out Island inns.

Hotel properties in the islands aren't rated according to any rigid classification system or "star system." The word "deluxe" is often used (or misused) when "first class" may be the more appropriate term. "First class" itself often isn't first class. For those reasons and others, we present fairly detailed descriptions of the properties in destination-specific chapters throughout the book to give you an idea of what to expect.

However, even in the deluxe and first-class resorts and hotels, don't expect top-rate service and efficiency. "Things," as they're called in the islands, don't seem to work as well here as they do in certain fancy resorts of California, Florida, and Europe.

Travelers to The Bahamas have the following options:

- Hotels, resorts, and inns
- All-inclusive resorts
- Villas, condos, and timeshares
- Guesthouses

No matter which option you choose, our accommodations' price ranges apply throughout the book. Check out Table 7-1 for an explanation of the dollar sign symbols and the amenities you can expect at each price level.

Table 7-1	Key to Hotel Dollar Signs	
Dollar Sign(s)	**Price Range**	**What to Expect**
$	$100 or less than $100	These accommodations are relatively simple and inexpensive. Rooms are likely to be small, and you may not have a TV in your room. In some cases, you may not have a phone in your room.
$$	$101–$200	These midrange accommodations are a bit classier and offer more room, more extras (such as irons, hair dryers, or microwaves), and a more convenient location — perhaps on the beach — than the preceding category.
$$$	$201–$300	Higher-class still, these accommodations begin looking plush. Think chocolates on your pillow, a classy restaurant, and maybe even expansive views of a white sandy beachfront.
$$$$	$301 and up	These top-rate, most often beachfront, accommodations come with luxurious amenities, such as valet parking, on-premise spas, and in-room hot tubs and CD players — but you pay through the nose for 'em.

Hotels, resorts, and inns: Enjoying your stay

If you want to live in luxury, your best and sometimes only bets are found on New Providence, with its array of hotels and resorts spread from Cable Beach to Nassau to Paradise Island. The second-largest concentration of hotels and resorts is on Grand Bahama Island, mainly around Freeport or Lucaya.

Except for certain pockets of luxury, such as Harbour Island off the coast of Eleuthera, resort pickings grow slim as you explore the Out Islands. Hotels are small except Club Med on San Salvador and the Four Seasons Resort in the Exumas. Most of the Out Islands have inns rather than large hotels. Some inns are very basic, often in dull concrete blocks, but our recommendations have style and a bit of class.

We recommend mainstream hotels, resorts, and inns for

- ✔ Families that want plenty of amusements for their kids and sitters close at hand

- ✔ Sports lovers who seek golf or watersports facilities

- ✔ Honeymooners or couples who want to focus on each other

- ✔ First-time visitors to The Bahamas

- ✔ Travelers with disabilities

Hotels and resorts also have a downside:

- ✔ Authentic island flavor doesn't exist in most of these places.

- ✔ Guests tend to be resort-bound and don't get to sample an island's offerings or charms.

- ✔ All the extra expenses add up quickly. You may get a shock when it's time to pay up.

All-inclusives: Simplifying your vacation

The all-inclusive resort concept finally has a foothold in The Bahamas. At such resorts, one price includes everything — your room, all meals, entertainment, many watersports (although some cost extra), and sometimes even drinks. Some people find that the cost of all-inclusive holidays is cheaper than paying individually for each item, and others appreciate knowing in advance what their final bill will be.

The first all-inclusive resort hotel in The Bahamas was **Club Med** (☎ 888-WEB-CLUB), with its property on Paradise Island. This resort isn't a swinging-singles kind of place; it's popular with everybody from honeymooners to families. There's another Club Med on San Salvador, in the southern Bahamas, with more of a luxurious hideaway atmosphere.

The biggest all-inclusive resort of them all, **Sandals** (☎ 888-SANDALS; www.sandals.com), came to Cable Beach in 1995. This Jamaican company is now walking its sandals across the Caribbean. The most famous of the all-inclusives (but not necessarily the best), it caters only to "Any two people in love."

Good candidates for all-inclusive resorts are

- Honeymooners
- Families
- Inexperienced travelers
- The budget-conscious
- The super-stressed

What are the downsides?

- Because you pay for everything in advance, you may feel obligated to spend all your time at the resort and not venture out to see what's happening beyond the compound.

- At an all-inclusive resort, you live in a cocoon and miss what makes your island special.

- Exuberant activity coordinators feel their job is to keep you occupied day and night. This "organized fun" may not be for you.

Villas: Vacationing with the comforts of home

You may want to rent a villa, a good-sized apartment in someone's condo or timeshare, or even a small beach cottage (more accurately called a *cabaña*).

Private apartments come with or without maid service, so ask upfront exactly what to expect. This option is more no-frills than a villa or condo. The apartments may not be in buildings with swimming pools, and they may not have a front desk to help you.

Many cottages or cabañas open onto a beach, although others cluster around a communal swimming pool. Most cottages are fairly simple, containing no more than a plain bedroom plus a small kitchen and bathroom. In the peak winter season, make reservations at least five or six months in advance.

VHR Worldwide (☎ **800-633-3284** or 201-767-9393; www.vhrww.com) offers the most comprehensive portfolio of luxury villas, condominiums, resort suites, and apartments for rent not only in The Bahamas, but also in the Caribbean. **Hideaways Aficionado** (☎ **800-843-4433** in the U.S. or 603-430-4433; www.hideaways.com), a travel club, publishes *Hideaways Insider,* a 148-page pictorial directory of home rentals throughout the world with full descriptions so you know what you're renting. Rentals range from cottages to staffed villas to whole islands. Annual membership in Hideaways International costs $185 and includes perks such as discounts on condos and resorts, and services such as airline ticketing and car rentals.

Sometimes local tourist offices will also advise you on vacation-home rentals if you write or call them directly.

We recommend villas for

- Families
- Groups of friends
- Honeymooners or couples craving privacy
- Independent travelers who want to connect with the island

But staying at a home-away-from-home also has its downsides:

- You don't get the extensive dining facilities and other amenities of a resort.
- A villa may not offer daily maid service and other niceties (like a pool or Jacuzzi) that you consider vital to your relaxation.
- Few villas are located right on the beach; resorts usually snag the prime real estate.
- You definitely won't get (or be subjected to, depending on your point of view) the nightly entertainment that almost every Bahamian hotel trumpets.
- You're more isolated, so you'd better really like your traveling companion (if you have one).
- Of all the travel options, villas are the least likely to live up to their brochure promises.

We recommend condos and cabañas for

- Families. You can feed your kids what you want and not suffer disapproving looks from the honeymooners at the next table when junior flips his soggy cereal onto the floor.
- Groups of friends.
- Older couples looking for quiet.
- Long-term vacationers. Cooking your own meals is a great money-saving tactic for an extended stay on an island.
- Independent travelers who want to connect with the island and its people.

What are some drawbacks to staying at a condo or cabaña?

- You have all the comforts of home, but also all the work.
- Amenities are limited.
- You entrust your tropical dream to someone else's decorating taste.
- When dinnertime comes, you're the staff as well as the diner.

Guesthouses: Living like a Bahamian

The B&B-style guesthouse is where many Bahamians stay when they're traveling in their own islands. In The Bahamas, however, the term "guesthouse" can mean anything. Sometimes so-called guesthouses are really simple motels built around swimming pools. Others are small individual cottages, with their own kitchenettes, constructed around a main building in which you often find a bar and restaurant serving local food.

In the Out Islands, the guesthouses are no-frills. The ones we recommend are clean and decent for families or single women. Many of these guesthouses are very basic. Salt spray takes a serious toll on metal or fabric, and chipped paint is commonplace. Bathrooms can fall into the vintage category, and sometimes the water isn't heated — but when the weather is 85°F to 92°F outside, you don't need hot water anyway.

On the other hand, some of these places are quite comfortable. A few guesthouses are almost luxurious; and, in addition to giving you the opportunity to live with a local family, they boast swimming pools, private bathrooms in all rooms, and air-conditioning.

We recommend guesthouses for

- ✔ Older couples who like the bed-and-breakfast concept
- ✔ Long-term vacationers on tight budgets
- ✔ The independent traveler who needs a home base

Here are some of the drawbacks to staying at a guesthouse:

- ✔ You may be far from the beach, without a pool.
- ✔ The digs may not be glamorous.
- ✔ You may not get along with your host.
- ✔ Housekeeping standards vary widely.
- ✔ If a problem occurs, you're stuck dealing one-on-one with the homeowner.

Locating Lodging that Suits You

Where you want to sleep often determines your choice of island. The type of accommodations you have in mind means that you should consider some islands and write off others. For example, perhaps you're dreaming of napping in your personal hammock at the edge of a secluded beach right in front of your individually decorated bungalow. Your choices are very limited on New Providence and Grand Bahama. However, The Bahamas' Out Islands offer lots of small, peaceful, beachfront lodgings.

If your ideal vacation includes a hotel with a wide variety of restaurants, Las Vegas–style extravaganzas, and nightly dancing, steer clear of The Bahamas' Out Islands and head to Cable Beach on New Providence, Paradise Island, or Grand Bahama.

Certain hotels allow children under a set age to stay free or at reduced rates in a room with an adult. Many dining rooms offer children's menus with lower prices and smaller portions than the regular fare. Policies vary, so be sure to ask when making reservations.

Rooming on the main islands

Rooms in the larger hotels on New Providence, Paradise Island, and Grand Bahama are air-conditioned (some also have ceiling fans) and come with satellite TV and direct-dial telephones. Most rooms have two double beds or one king-size bed, plus a balcony or patio. Many rooms are also equipped with irons and ironing boards, coffeemakers, minibars or refrigerators, hair dryers, and in-room safes. Some rooms have Internet access and sometimes even CD players. Hotels have U.S. newspapers — usually from Miami or New York — available. Expect to find plenty of activities, along with restaurants, shops, salons, and (on the premises or nearby) watersports operators. Many hotels also have wheelchair-accessible rooms. Likewise, some hotels offer supervised children's programs.

In some cases, you're on your own, without on-premises restaurants or activities desks to provide information, help you set up excursions, call taxis, or assist with other arrangements.

Bahamian landlords offer plenty of villas and condos for rent on the main islands, but first-time visitors may want to skip them because you should be familiar with the island and getting around by car.

The more elegant and expensive villa rentals offer maid service, and in some cases, even your own cook — for an extra fee, of course. At cheaper rentals, you may have to do your own cleaning and cooking.

Choosing the less developed islands

You won't find high-rise hotels in the Out Islands. A few islands offer posh digs with rooms and facilities as snazzy as the ones on busier islands — for example, Pink Sands on Harbour Island (see Chapter 22) or Green Turtle Club & Marina on Green Turtle Cay in the Abacos (see Chapter 20). Still, these low-rise lodgings are far less formal than upscale hotels on New Providence, Paradise Island, or Grand Bahama.

Accommodations on the less developed islands may or may not have air-conditioning, but ceiling fans or good cross-ventilation does the trick if they don't. Some rooms have two double beds, and others have only one. In rare cases, some rooms offer only twin beds. In the Out Islands, many hotel rooms don't have telephones, TVs, or radios. In hotels that do have TVs in the rooms, the channels are centrally controlled (usually at the bar), so don't be surprised if the mystery you're watching suddenly turns into a soccer game just before the murderer's identity is revealed. If any of these amenities are important to you, ask about them before you make your reservation.

In many cases in the Out Islands, you don't have to worry about losing your room key because you don't get one in the first place. (No one locks doors.) Forgot your beach reading? You're likely to find a selection of dog-eared paperbacks that previous vacationers left in your room. You can even take one of those books home with you — as long as you leave one of yours in its place.

You may be surprised to know that quite a few hotels have *honor bars,* where no bartender is on duty. Guests simply take or mix their own drinks, write them down, and pay for them when they check out. With this trusting attitude, it's no wonder that staff members at these small, easygoing hotels quickly get to know guests. Staff members aren't shy about sharing tips about their favorite parts of the islands, either.

Independent families or groups of friends traveling together find villas, condos, and hotel rooms with kitchens convenient places to stay on the quieter, less developed islands. On less-developed islands, hotels are small enough that managers themselves are usually willing to help you make arrangements for watersports, dining, transportation, and other activities that may or may not be on the premises.

 If you or someone in your group is in a wheelchair, ask about the specifics of the landscape and the facilities at hotels on the less developed islands. Some hotels, such as a few on Harbour Island and Green Turtle Cay in the Abacos, have hilly grounds or lots of steps.

Understanding the Meal Plans

As you're shopping around for your accommodations (whether while consulting this guide or other sources like hotel Web sites), note that prices are listed according to meal-plan options.

Many Bahamian resorts offer a **European Plan** (EP) rate, which means that you pay only for the price of a room. Most of our hotel recommendations have the EP rate listed. If you choose this option, you're free to dine at other resorts or restaurants. Another plan is the **Continental Plan** (CP), which means that your room and a continental breakfast of juice, coffee, bread, jam, and so on is included in a set price. A variation of this plan is the **Breakfast Plan** (BP), which is a full traditional American-style breakfast — eggs, bacon, pancakes, French toast, and hash browns. Guests who don't want to "dine around" at breakfast time prefer the Continental and Breakfast plans.

Another major option is the **Modified American Plan** (MAP), which includes breakfast and one main meal of the day, either lunch or dinner. The final choice is the **American Plan** (AP), which includes breakfast, lunch, and dinner. At certain resorts, you can save money by booking either MAP or AP because the per-meal cost may be cheaper. If you dine à la carte for lunch and dinner at various restaurants, your final dining bill is likely to be much higher than if you stayed on the MAP or AP.

Aside from the savings in cost, meal plans have drawbacks if you like to eat in a variety of places as a part of your holiday. You face the same dining room every night, unless the resort you're staying in has many different restaurants on the dining plan. Many resorts have specialty restaurants that serve a variety of cuisines, but these more expensive restaurants aren't included in MAP or AP and charge à la carte prices.

Dining at your hotel cuts down on transportation costs because taxis are especially expensive. Nonetheless, if dining out and having many different culinary experiences is your idea of a vacation and you're willing to pay the higher price, avoid AP plans or at least make sure that the hotel where you're staying has more than one dining room.

Before booking a room, investigate what you're likely to save by booking a dining plan. The meal-plan options may have a significant impact on your choice of accommodations.

Finding the Best Room at the Best Rate

The *rack rate* is the maximum rate a hotel charges for a room. This rate is the one you get when you walk in off the street and ask for a room for the night. Hotel managers are happy to charge you the rack rate, but you can almost always do better. Perhaps the best way to avoid paying the rack rate is surprisingly simple: Just ask whether they can quote you a better price. You may be pleasantly surprised.

In all but the smallest accommodations, a room's price depends on how you make your reservation. A travel agent may be able to negotiate a better price with certain hotels than you can get by yourself. (The hotel gives the agent a discount in exchange for steering her business toward that hotel.) Making a reservation online through a hotel or airline Web site often allows you to take advantage of special discounts. Reserving a room through a hotel chain's central toll-free number may not yield the best rate because the representative may not be aware of local discounts. Your best bet is to call both the local number and the toll-free number to see which one gives you a better deal.

Package deals abound, and they're always cheaper than rack rates. Going to a reliable travel agent to find out what, if anything, is available in the way of a land-and-air package before booking particular accommodations is sometimes a good idea. For more on package deals, see Chapter 6.

To save money on accommodations, timing is also vital. The winter season in The Bahamas runs roughly from the middle of December to the middle of April, and hotels charge their highest prices during this peak period. During the winter months, make reservations two months in advance if you can. You can't book early enough if you want to travel over Christmas or in February.

The off season in The Bahamas — roughly from mid-April to mid-December (although the off season varies from hotel to hotel) — amounts to a sale. In most cases, hotels slash their rates by a startling 20 to 60 percent. This deal is a bonanza for cost-conscious travelers, especially for families who can travel in the summer. For more tips on helping you decide when to take your vacation in The Bahamas, see Chapter 4.

Ask whether you can get an upgrade or a free night's stay if you stay an extra few days. If you travel during the marginal periods between low and high season, you can sometimes delay your travel plans by a week or ten days and get a substantial rate reduction. For example, if you book a $300 room on April 12, the price may lower to $180 by April 17 because mid-April marks the beginning of the low season in The Bahamas.

Surfing the Web for hotel deals

Shopping online for hotels is generally done one of two ways: by booking through the hotel's own Web site; or through an independent booking agency (or a fare-service agency like Priceline). These Internet hotel agencies have multiplied in mind-boggling numbers of late, competing for the business of millions of consumers surfing for accommodations around the world. This competitiveness can be a boon to consumers who have the patience and time to shop and compare the online sites for good deals — but shop they must, for prices can vary considerably from site to site. And keep in mind that hotels at the top of a site's listing may be there for no other reason than that they paid money to get the placement.

In addition to **Travelocity, Expedia, Orbitz, Priceline,** and **Hotwire,** the following Web sites will help you with booking hotel rooms online:

- www.hotels.com
- www.quickbook.com
- www.travelaxe.net
- www.travelweb.com
- www.tripadvisor.com

It's a good idea to **get a confirmation number** and **make a printout** of any online booking transaction.

In the opaque Web site category, **Priceline** and **Hotwire** are even better for hotels than for airfares; with both, you're allowed to pick the neighborhood and quality level of your hotel before offering up your money. Priceline's hotel product even covers Europe and Asia, though it's much better at getting five-star lodging for three-star prices than at finding anything at the bottom of the scale. On the down side, many hotels stick Priceline guests in their least desirable rooms. Be sure to go to the BiddingForTravel Web site (www.biddingfortravle.com) before bidding on a hotel room on Priceline; it features a fairly up-to-date list of hotels that Priceline uses in major cities. For both Priceline and Hotwire, you pay upfront, and the fee is nonrefundable. *Note:* Some hotels do not provide loyalty program credits or points or other frequent-stay amenities when you book a room through opaque online services.

Reserving the best room

Somebody has to get the best room at a hotel or a resort, so it may as well be you. Here's how to go about getting the best room:

- ✔ Inquire about ceiling fans, air-conditioning, and whether the windows open.

- ✔ Find out whether the room faces the water or the garage in back. If you're not going to spend a lot of time in your room, getting the back view makes sense because it's cheaper. Upper-floor rooms with views cost more, too.

- ✔ Ask for a room, floor, or annex that was recently renovated.

- ✔ Ask about nonsmoking rooms.

- ✔ Avoid rooms overlooking outdoor nighttime entertainment or the bar or lounge, if you're a light sleeper.

 Most Bahamian hoteliers wait until the slow season (summer) to do major renovations. If you're traveling other than in the winter months, check to see whether your hotel is in the midst of renovating. If it is, request a room away from the worksite. Those construction workers are early risers.

Chapter 8

Catering to Special Travel Needs and Interests

. . . .

In This Chapter

▶ Bringing the kids along

▶ Honeymooning or getting hitched on the islands

▶ Traveling if you're single, gay or lesbian, a senior, or have other special needs

. . . .

*O*ne-size-fits-all doesn't pertain to vacations in The Bahamas. Individual travelers or even people traveling with companions or children often have special needs.

Some questions immediately come to mind. Where can couples honeymoon or even tie the knot? What discounts or privileges can people who've reached the golden age get? How wheelchair accessible are the islands? Or are the islands gay friendly? In this chapter, we discuss the challenges and opportunities that some travelers may encounter in The Bahamas.

Traveling with the Brood: Advice for Families

If you have enough trouble getting your kids out of the house in the morning, dragging them hundreds of miles away may seem like an insurmountable challenge. But family travel is immensely rewarding, giving you new ways of seeing the world through smaller pairs of eyes.

A traveling brood plays a big part in your choices of accommodations, dining, and activities. To help make matters easier, remember to look for the Kid Friendly icon we use throughout this book. This icon calls attention to hotels and resorts, restaurants, or attractions that are especially family friendly.

Kids vacationing at some beach resorts need not settle for just a sandy shore. They're treated to organized programs so comprehensive that they rival summer camp. Some larger accommodations offer children's programs year-round.

Some programs are no more than a bored baby sitter in a room full of toys or video games. Other programs have enthusiastic, well-trained staff members who engage children in age-appropriate diversions, from face painting and storytelling to beach Olympics and computer-assisted science projects. Some resorts charge an additional fee for their programs, but others are free to guests. Most resorts usually offer morning and afternoon sessions, and meals and night sessions may also be available. Most programs take children from around age 5 up to about age 12.

The best kids' programs are at **Atlantis Paradise Island Resort & Casino** (Chapter 11) on Paradise Island, New Providence; **Radisson Cable Beach** (see Chapter 11) on New Providence; and **Westin Grand Bahama Island at Our Lucaya Resort & Sheraton Grand Bahama Island at Our Lucaya Resort** (see Chapter 15) on Grand Bahama.

Here are some questions to ask when you're evaluating a children's program:

- ✔ What is the ratio of caretakers/counselors to children?
- ✔ Are kids divided into age groups?
- ✔ Exactly what activities do they engage in?
- ✔ How much time do the kids spend at the pool or beach, and what kind of expert supervision do they have nearby or in the water?
- ✔ Are meals included?
- ✔ Do the children leave the drop-off area, and if so, where else do they go?

Flying with children

If you're traveling with an infant, bring along a car seat to use on the plane. Because many airlines allow children under age 2 to fly free when sitting on an adult's lap, you may be tempted not to purchase a seat for your child. Doing so really isn't safe, however, because turbulence can easily injure a child. You may wonder why you should bother buying a ticket for your child when empty seats are often available. The problem is that if the plane is full, you're out of luck.

Don't forget gum or lollipops for kids to chew or suck during takeoff and landing to combat ear-pressure pain. And pack a deck of cards or some favorite toys to keep them entertained. You may be used to hearing their mantra of "Are we there yet?" but the whines of bored children can drive other passengers crazy. Flight attendants are quite accommodating if you need to refrigerate baby bottles or if you have other child-related requests.

Remember to specify any food allergies, to slather your younger editions with sunscreen and, of course, to make sure that the caretakers know where to find you in case of an emergency.

If you need a baby sitter for your smallest tots, you can hire one through your hotel. Expect to pay around $12 to $15 an hour, plus $3 for each additional child.

You can find good family-oriented vacation advice on the Internet from sites like the **Family Travel Network** (www.familytravelnetwork.com), which features excellent articles; **Traveling Internationally with Your Kids** (www.travelwithyourkids.com), a comprehensive site that offers sound advice for long-distance and international travel with children; and **Family Travel Files** (www.thefamilytravelfiles.com), which offers an online magazine and a directory of off-the-beaten-path tours and tour operators for families.

Making Age Work for You: Tips for Seniors

Senior travelers to The Bahamas tend to gravitate toward New Providence and Grand Bahama. For example, the **Nassau Beach Hotel** on Cable Beach receives many repeat guests who've visited for decades, and the **British Colonial Hilton** in downtown Nassau gets plenty of older vacationers as well.

Although all the major U.S. airlines flying to The Bahamas canceled their senior-discount and coupon-book programs, many hotels still offer discounts for seniors. For the most part, The Bahamas charge the same admission for all adults attending museums, theaters, and other attractions. Of course, asking about senior discounts doesn't hurt. You may be pleasantly surprised.

Members of **AARP** (formerly known as the American Association of Retired Persons), 601 E St. NW, Washington, DC 20049 (☎ **888-687-2277** or 202-434-2277; www.aarp.org), get discounts on hotels, airfares, and car rentals. AARP offers its members a wide range of benefits, including *AARP: The Magazine* and a monthly newsletter. Anyone over 50 can join.

Many reliable agencies and organizations target the 50-plus market. **Elderhostel** (☎ **877-426-8056**; www.elderhostel.org) arranges study programs for those aged 55 and over (and a spouse or companion of any age) in the United States and in more than 80 countries around the world. **ElderTreks** (☎ **800-741-7956**; www.eldertreks.com) offers small-group tours to off-the-beaten-path or adventure-travel locations, restricted to travelers 50 and older. **INTRAV** (☎ **800-456-8100**; www.intrav.com) is a high-end tour operator that caters to the mature, discerning traveler, not specifically seniors, with trips around the world that include guided safaris, polar expeditions, private-jet adventures, and small-boat cruises down jungle rivers.

Recommended publications offering travel resources and discounts for seniors include: the quarterly magazine *Travel 50 & Beyond* (www.travel50andbeyond.com); *Travel Unlimited: Uncommon Adventures for the Mature Traveler* (Avalon); *101 Tips for Mature Travelers,* available from Grand Circle Travel (☎ 800-221-2610 or 617-350-7500; www.gct.com); and *Unbelievably Good Deals and Great Adventures That You Absolutely Can't Get Unless You're Over 50* (McGraw-Hill), by Joann Rattner Heilman.

Accessing The Bahamas: Advice for Travelers with Disabilities

Travelers with disabilities have an easier time getting around on some islands in The Bahamas than others. Many of the larger hotels on New Providence, Paradise Island, and Grand Bahama offer ground-floor guest rooms, wide bathrooms, and elevators that make wheelchair accessibility relatively easy. These islands also have plenty of sidewalks, marina boardwalks, and paved pathways.

On the other hand, most hotels on the smaller islands have hilly grounds, narrow, unpaved pathways, and steps leading to guest rooms or dining areas. Several accommodations on Harbour Island, for example, sit at the top of a bluff with long staircases that lead down to the beach. Therefore, if you find a hotel that sounds good, call to ask about the specifics of accessibility. If you're in a wheelchair or you have trouble walking but you want to get as close to the sand as possible, look for hotels with accessible beachfront pool patios.

The Out Islands are more difficult to reach. The planes that service these islands are usually small, and passengers board and disembark on narrow, somewhat rickety staircases. In some instances, you need to change planes once or twice and catch a ferry, as well as take a taxi or two.

If you're a wheelchair-bound traveler heading to New Providence, you can contact **The Bahamas Association for the Physically Disabled** (☎ 242-322-2393) to rent a specially equipped van for airport pickup or to arrange for transportation around the island. Make reservations as far in advance of your trip as possible. You can get temporary ramps and other portable aids through this association, too.

Many travel agencies offer customized tours and itineraries for travelers with disabilities. Among them are **Flying Wheels Travel** (☎ 507-451-5005; www.flyingwheelstravel.com), **Access-Able Travel Source** (☎ 303-232-2979; www.access-able.com), and **Accessible Journeys** (☎ 800-846-4537 or 610-521-0339).

Organizations that offer assistance to disabled travelers include **MossRehab** (www.mossresourcenet.org), **American Foundation for the Blind** (**AFB**; ☎ 800-232-5463; www.afb.org), and **SATH** (**Society for Accessible Travel and Hospitality**; ☎ 212-447-7284; www.sath.org). **AirAmbulanceCard.com** is now partnered with SATH and allows you to preselect top-notch hospitals in case of an emergency.

For more information specifically targeted to travelers with disabilities, the community Web site **iCan** (www.icanonline.net/channels/travel/index.cfm) has destination guides and several regular columns on accessible travel. Also check out the quarterly magazine *Emerging Horizons* (www.emerginghorizons.com) and *Open World Magazine,* published by SATH.

Following the Rainbow: Resources for Gay and Lesbian Travelers

If you're gay or lesbian, how comfortable will you feel in The Bahamas? The official word is that everyone is welcome, but the reality is somewhat different, depending on where you go and what you do when you get there.

Homosexuality isn't necessarily illegal, but gay sex acts performed in public can carry a jail sentence of up to 20 years. This law is rarely enforced any more, but as long as it remains on the books, you have to exercise extreme caution.

In The Bahamas, many residents are uncomfortable with public displays of affection between same-sex couples. In fact, "Don't ask, don't tell" reigns. Therefore, if you can't imagine a vacation that doesn't include strolling down the beach hand-in-hand with your main squeeze, The Bahamas may not be for you. Head for Key West or South Miami Beach, which will welcome you with open arms.

Nevertheless, The Bahamas can be a great vacation choice if you're discreet in public about your sexuality. On the most popular islands (New Providence, Paradise Island, and Grand Bahama), not only can you get lost in the crowds, but you're more likely to run into other gay vacationers and residents. Quietly ask around, and folks can direct you to other small hangouts, some of which are open only every other weekend.

The International Gay & Lesbian Travel Association (**IGLTA**; ☎ 800-448-8550 or 954-776-2626; www.iglta.com) is the trade association for the gay and lesbian travel industry and offers an online directory of gay- and lesbian-friendly travel businesses; go to its Web site and click on "Members."

Many agencies offer tours and travel itineraries specifically for gay and lesbian travelers. Among them are **Above and Beyond Tours** (☎ 800-397-2681; www.abovebeyondtours.com), **Now, Voyager** (☎ 800-255-6951; www.nowvoyager.com), and **Olivia Cruises & Resorts** (☎ 800-631-6277 or 510-655-0364; www.olivia.com).

Gay.com Travel (☎ 800-929-2268 or 415-644-8044; www.gay.com/travel or www.outandabout.com) is an excellent online successor to the popular *Out & About* print magazine. It provides regularly updated information about gay-owned, gay-oriented, and gay-friendly lodging, dining, sightseeing, nightlife, and shopping establishments in every important destination worldwide.

The following travel guides are available at many bookstores, or you can order them from any online bookseller: *Spartacus International Gay Guide* (Bruno Gmünder Verlag; www.spartacusworld.com/gayguide) and *Odysseus,* both good, annual English-language guidebooks focused on gay men; and the *Damron* guides (www.damron.com), with separate, annual books for gay men and lesbians.

Planning the Perfect Getaway: Tips for Honeymooners

The Bahamas offer so many different types of hotels and resorts that you're certain to find just the right honeymoon retreat to jump-start your new lives together. Of course, you don't have to be hitched to indulge in these hideaways.

All-inclusive resorts — where one price covers your room, meals, beverages, entertainment, most activities, tips, taxes, and airfare — are popular among newlyweds. To stay busy day and night, you need never leave these self-contained vacation playgrounds until you have to go home. Check out Chapter 11 for the descriptions of elegant, couples-only **Sandals Royal Bahamian** and the more moderately priced **Breezes;** both resorts are located on New Providence. On Grand Bahama, think about **Viva Wyndham Fortuna Beach** (see Chapter 15). On San Salvador, consider **Club Med–Columbus Isle** (see Chapter 25).

If you don't necessarily want an all-inclusive resort but you want a blizzard of action, check into **Atlantis Paradise Island Resort & Casino** (see Chapter 11) off New Providence. You can also find plenty to see and do in and around the **Westin** and **Sheraton at Our Lucaya** on Grand Bahama (see Chapter 15).

Some couples prefer quieter, more remote resorts, where the sun, the sand, and each other's company are the main draws. If you prefer this scenario, the elegant **One&Only Ocean Club** is an excellent honeymoon haunt on New Providence (see Chapter 11). Small is beautiful at cozy resorts like **Green Turtle Club** and **Bluff House** on Green Turtle Cay in the Abacos (see Chapter 20), as well as **Pink Sands** and **Runaway Hill Club** on Harbour Island (see Chapter 22).

 Quite a few accommodations, particularly the larger ones, feature honeymoon packages. These packages aren't usually money-savers, but they do include special extras, such as a corner room, king-size bed, champagne, maybe a first-rate meal or two, and transportation in limousines between your hotel and the airport. Each hotel boasts a somewhat different set of perks, so when you make your reservation, you have to ask exactly what your package includes.

Saying "I Do" Bahamian Style

The Bahamas are popular honeymoon destinations for just-married spouses, but plenty of couples save the wedding for the island as well. Romantic settings, ranging from the beach at sunset to a harborside gazebo to a poolside patio or an elegant yacht, make tying the knot here tempting. With colorful coral and tropical fish as a backdrop, couples have even signaled "I do" underwater while decked out in scuba gear. Many of the larger hotels (and some of the smaller ones, too) provide a wedding coordinator to help you secure all your paperwork, find an official to perform the ceremony, and hire photographers — both still and video — and the florist. Coordinators also organize the reception and make any other arrangements that you need.

Reviewing the marriage requirements in The Bahamas

You and your intended must both be in The Bahamas for at least 24 hours before you can apply for a marriage license. You can fill out applications Monday through Friday.

For details, contact the office of the **Registrar General** (☎ 242-322-3316 in Nassau or ☎ 242-352-4934 on Grand Bahama). If you plan to marry in one of the Out Islands, call the **Bahamas Out Islands Promotions Board** (☎ 800-688-4752).

 If you and your partner are U.S. citizens, you need to get an affidavit to confirm this — and the fact that you're both single — from the American Embassy in Nassau. *Note:* The U.S. Embassy is closed on both American and Bahamian holidays. You must present proof of identity, such as a passport and, if necessary, proof of divorce. You don't need to take any blood tests, however. The **Weddings and Honeymoon Unit of The Bahamas Ministry of Tourism** (call ☎ 888-687-8425 or 242-302-2000 for a brochure) can also provide you with information.

For assistance with planning your nuptials in The Bahamas, call your hotel or one of the following tourist offices:

- Nassau, New Providence (☎ 242-302-2000)
- Freeport/Lucaya, Grand Bahama (☎ 242-352-8044)
- The Abacos (☎ 242-367-3067)
- Andros (☎ 242-368-2286)
- Bimini (☎ 242-347-3529)
- Eleuthera (☎ 242-332-2142)
- Harbour Island (☎ 242-333-2621)
- Exuma (☎ 242-336-2430)
- San Salvador (☎ 242-356-0435)

Working out the wedding costs

An island wedding in a stunning setting can cost thousands of dollars less than a traditional wedding at home. Table 8-1 gives you a general idea of how much money you can expect to spend on the ceremony:

Table 8-1	The Cost of a Bahamian Wedding
Marriage license	$100
Affidavit (per person)	$55 and up (U.S. Embassy or Notary Public)
Marriage officer	Weekdays: $160 Weekends: $200
Florist	Bouquet: $30 and up Boutonniere: $10
Limousine	$90 an hour
Tuxedo rental	$85 and up
Video	$350 and up
Photographer	$300 and up
Music	Steel drum band: $550 an hour Organ music in church: $150 an hour Violinist or vocalist: $100 an hour Violin and flute: $200 an hour

Traveling Solo

You don't need kids or a partner to have a great vacation on these islands, especially in Nassau or Freeport/Lucaya. Plenty of couples stay at the smaller, quieter hotels on these islands, so you don't have nearly as many opportunities to meet other single visitors as you may at larger accommodations. However, you can find groups of unattached friends vacationing together. Because hotels in the Out Islands are so much smaller and more intimate than on the busier islands, meeting people in these locations is easier.

If you're shy, join a snorkeling sail, a scuba trip, or an excursion to an uninhabited island for a beach picnic. Before you can say "Goombay Smash," you'll be chatting with new friends.

On the downside, you pay more for a hotel room or an air/hotel package if you go it alone than if you travel with a friend because single rates are higher than double rates divided by two. But the good news is that you can find many affordable hotels on New Providence (particularly in downtown Nassau and some on Cable Beach), so you shouldn't have trouble finding a place that suits your wallet.

Club Med–Columbus Isle (see Chapter 25) on San Salvador attracts plenty of singles. This all-inclusive beach resort offers many diversions designed to get people together. In addition, this place is perfect for two single friends who travel together but like their privacy. (The hotel offers single rooms joined by a shared bathroom.)

If you're a socially minded single, Nassau is a good choice — you can be as busy or as lazy as you want. **Breezes,** a moderately priced all-inclusive resort on Cable Beach (see Chapter 11), is a popular choice because it offers a medley of group activities.

 During March and April, droves of U.S. college students on spring break descend on New Providence. So if you've outgrown toga parties and drinking contests, you may want to skip this scene.

Chapter 9

Taking Care of the Remaining Details

*B*efore you can start wiggling your toes in the sand, you need to handle a few details. In this chapter, we deal with all the nitty-gritty details of your travel plans, such as insurance and car rentals.

Preparing for Arrival and Departure

If you're a U.S., Canadian, or British citizen, you don't *need* a passport to enter The Bahamas, as long as you have two other acceptable forms of identification. However, a passport is required to get back into the United States and Canada. If you don't have a passport, you must take the following papers with you:

✔ A certified or original copy of your birth certificate (it must have a raised seal)

✔ An official photo ID, such as a valid driver's license

✔ A return or ongoing airplane ticket

Getting a Passport

A valid passport is the only legal form of identification accepted around the world. Getting a passport is easy, but the process takes some time. For an up-to-date country-by-country listing of passport requirements, go to the "Foreign Entry Requirement" Web page of the U.S. State Department at www.travel.state.gov.

New passport requirements

During the lifetime of this book, a change in Homeland Security regulations will require Americans returning from The Bahamas to show passports when reentering the United States. At press time, the new rules were set to go into effect on January 8, 2007. Visit http://travel.state.gov for more information.

When you enter the country, you receive an Immigration Arrival/Departure Card to fill out and sign. Do this paperwork before it's your turn with the Customs official. Be sure to keep your carbon copy in a safe place because an official will collect it when you leave The Bahamas.

Save enough cash for the departure tax that you have to pay when you exit the country. The tax is $15 from New Providence or any Out Island and $18 from Grand Bahama.

Applying for a U.S. passport

If you're applying for a first-time passport, follow these steps:

1. **Complete a passport application in person at a U.S. passport office (a federal, state, or probate court or a major post office).** To find your regional passport office, either check the **U.S. State Department Web site,** www.travel.state.gov, or call the **National Passport Information Center (☎ 877-487-2778)** for automated information.

2. **Present a certified birth certificate as proof of citizenship.** Bringing along your driver's license, state or military ID, or social security card is also a good idea.

3. **Submit two identical passport-sized photos, measuring 2 inches by 2 inches in size.** You often find businesses that take these photos near a passport office. *Note:* You can't use a strip from a photo-vending machine because the pictures aren't identical.

4. **Pay a fee.** For people 16 and over, a passport is valid for ten years and costs $97. For those 15 and under, a passport is valid for five years and costs $82.

 When applying for a passport, allow plenty of time before your trip; processing normally takes three weeks but can take longer during busy periods (especially spring).

If your passport is in your current name and was issued within the past 15 years (and you were over age 16 when it was issued), you can renew your passport by mail for $67. Whether you're applying in person or by mail, you can download passport applications from the U.S. State Department Web site at www.travel.state.gov. For general information, call the **National Passport Agency (☎ 202-647-0518)**.

Applying for other passports

If you're a citizen of Australia, Canada, New Zealand, or the United Kingdom, the following lists information on applying for a passport:

✔ **Australians** can visit a local post office or passport office, call the **Australia Passport Information Service** (☎ **131-232** toll-free from Australia), or log on to www.passports.gov.au for details on how and where to apply.

✔ **Canadians** can pick up applications at passport offices throughout Canada, at post offices, or from the central **Passport Office, Department of Foreign Affairs and International Trade,** Ottawa, Ontario K1A 0G3 (☎ **800-567-6868;** www.ppt.gc.ca). You must send two identical passport-sized photos and proof of Canadian citizenship along with your application. Processing takes five to ten days if you apply in person or about three weeks by mail.

✔ **New Zealanders** can pick up a passport application at any **New Zealand Passports Office** or download it from the office's Web site (www.passports.govt.nz). Contact the Passports Office at ☎ **0800-225-050** in New Zealand or 04-474-8100.

✔ **United Kingdom** residents can pick up applications for a standard ten-year passport (five-year passport for children under 16) at passport offices, major post offices, or a travel agency. For information, contact the **United Kingdom Passport Service** (☎ **0870-521-0410;** www.ukpa.gov.uk).

Traveling with minors

It's always wise to have plenty of documentation when traveling in today's world with children. For changing details on entry requirements for children traveling abroad, keep up-to-date by going to the U.S. State Department Web site: www.travel.state.gov/foreignentryreqs.html.

To prevent international child abduction, governments have initiated procedures at entry and exit points. These often (but not always) include requiring documentary evidence of relationship and permission for the child's travel from the parent or legal guardian not present. All children must have their own passport. To get a passport, the child *must* be present — that is, in person — at the center issuing the passport. If both parents are not present, a notarized statement from the parents is required.

All questions parents or guardians may have can be answered by calling the **National Passport Information Center** at ☎ 877-487-6868 Monday to Friday 8am to 8pm eastern standard time.

Renting a Car — or Not

Whether or not you need a car depends on which island you're visiting. Many visitors to New Providence, Paradise Island, Freeport/Lucaya, or one of the Out Islands don't bother renting a car. Here are four reasons why you may not want to rent a car, either:

- ✔ **You don't truly need it.** In New Providence/Paradise Island, a car is more of a burden than a help. Driving around congested Nassau is difficult, parking is limited, and you can walk to most attractions and shops. If you're on Cable Beach, taking a few limited taxi rides is probably cheaper in the long run than renting a car. Grand Bahama Island is spread out, and most locals need a car to get around. But most places of interest are centered around Freeport/Lucaya, which you can easily traverse with public transportation or taxi. You can also easily explore the vast part of Grand Bahama Island on an organized day tour (far cheaper than renting a car). On Harbour Island you don't need a car, but on "mainland" Eleuthera you may want to rent a car for a day just to tour the entire length of the island.

- ✔ **Driving is on the left.** If you're unfamiliar with this form of driving, you're more likely to have an accident.

- ✔ **Reservations may not be honored.** Unless you deal with a major car-rental company, you may arrive on an island and find that the car you reserved was rented to someone else. Many car-rental entrepreneurs figure that a "bird in hand is better than one in the bush," as one staff member recently told us at Marsh Harbour. Angry potential motorists at car-rental desks is a common sight in The Bahamas, especially during the overbooked winter months.

- ✔ **Insurance hassles and accidents.** On Grand Bahama Island and on New Providence Island, you can deal with the big U.S.-based chains, such as Hertz and Avis. If you have an accident, you may have the same problems with insurance companies that you encounter in the U.S.

  But driving around in the Out Islands and dealing with relatively unknown car-rental companies or parties could lead to anything. Settling claims may be extremely difficult, especially if you're at fault for causing property damage or bodily injury. You may not want to take these risks because you can rent a taxi for a day tour on every island. Or, for example, if you're in George Town in the Exumas, you can often walk to where you want to go.

Getting the best deal

If you decide to rent a car, be aware that car-rental rates vary even more than airline fares. The price for a rental car depends on the size of the car, the length of time that you keep it, where and when you pick it up and drop it off, where you take it, and a host of other factors. Asking a few key questions may save you hundreds of dollars:

- ✔ Weekend rates may be lower than weekday rates. If you're keeping the car five or more days, a weekly rate may be cheaper than the daily rate. Ask whether the rate is the same for pickup Friday morning as it is Thursday night.

- ✔ Check whether the rate is cheaper if you pick up the car at a location in town rather than at the airport.

- ✔ Ask whether age is an issue. Many car-rental companies add on a fee for drivers under 25, and some companies don't rent to them at all.

- ✔ If you see an advertised price, be sure to ask for that specific rate; otherwise the company may charge you the standard (higher) rate. Don't forget to mention membership in AAA, AARP, professional organizations, and trade unions. These memberships usually entitle you to discounts ranging from 5 percent to 30 percent.

- ✔ Check your frequent-flier accounts. Not only are your favorite (or, at least, most-used) airlines likely to have sent you discount coupons, but also most car rentals add at least 500 miles to your account.

- ✔ As with other aspects of planning your trip, using the Internet can make comparison shopping for a car rental much easier. You can check rates at most of the major agencies' Web sites. Plus, all the major travel sites — **Travelocity** (www.travelocity.com), **Expedia** (www.expedia.com), **Orbitz** (www.orbitz.com), and **Smarter Travel** (www.smartertravel.com), for example — have search engines that can dig up discounted car-rental rates. Just enter the car size you want, the pickup and return dates, and location, and the server returns a price. You can even make the car reservation through any of these sites.

Adding up the charges

In addition to the standard rental prices, other optional charges apply to most car rentals (and some not-so-optional charges, such as taxes). Many credit card companies cover the *Collision Damage Waiver* (CDW), which requires you to pay for damage to the car in a collision. Check with your credit card company before you leave so you can avoid paying this hefty fee (as much as $20–$25 a day).

The car-rental companies also offer additional *liability insurance* (if you harm others in an accident), *personal accident insurance* (if you harm yourself or your passengers), and *personal effects insurance* (if someone steals your luggage from your car). Your insurance policy on your car at home probably covers most of these unlikely occurrences. However, if your own insurance doesn't cover you for rentals or if you don't have auto insurance, definitely consider the additional coverage (ask your car-rental agent for more information). Driving around without liability or personal accident coverage is never a good idea. Even if you're a good driver, other people may not be, and liability claims can be complicated.

Playing It Safe with Travel and Medical Insurance

Three kinds of travel insurance are available: trip-cancellation insurance, medical insurance, and lost luggage insurance. The cost of travel insurance varies widely, depending on the cost and length of your trip, your age and health, and the type of trip you're taking. You can get estimates from various providers through **InsureMyTrip.com**. Enter your trip cost and dates, your age, and other information, for prices from more than a dozen companies. Here is our advice on all three types of travel insurance.

✔ **Trip-cancellation insurance:** This type of insurance helps you get your money back if you have to back out of a trip, if you must go home early, or if your travel supplier goes bankrupt. The allowed reasons for cancellation range from sickness to natural disasters to the State Department declaring your destination unsafe for travel.

A good resource is **"Travel Guard Alerts,"** which is a list of travel-related companies that Travel Guard International (www.travel insured.com) considers high-risk. You can protect yourself further by paying for the insurance with a credit card; by law, consumers can get your money back on goods and services you don't receive if you report the loss within 60 days after the charge is listed on your credit card statement.

✔ **Travel medical insurance:** For travel overseas, most health plans (including Medicare and Medicaid) do not provide coverage, and the ones that do often require you to pay for services upfront and reimburse you only after you return home. As a safety net, you may want to buy travel medical insurance, particularly if you're traveling to a remote or high-risk area where emergency evacuation is a possible scenario. If you require additional medical insurance, try **MEDEX Assistance** (☎ **410-453-6300;** www.medexassist.com) or **Travel Assistance International** (☎ **800-821-2828;** www.travel assistance.com); for general information on services, call the company's Worldwide Assistance Services, Inc., at ☎ **800-777-8710.**

✔ **Lost luggage insurance:** Most travelers don't need this insurance. Your homeowner's or renter's insurance should cover stolen luggage if you have off-premises theft coverage. Check your existing policies before you buy any additional coverage.

If you lose your luggage, immediately file a lost-luggage claim at the airport, detailing the luggage contents. On international flights (including U.S. portions of international trips), airline baggage coverage is limited to approximately $9.07 per pound, up to approximately $635 per checked bag. For most airlines, you must report delayed, damaged, or lost baggage within four hours of arrival. The airlines are required to deliver luggage, once found, directly to your house or destination free of charge.

You can get additional baggage insurance as part of your comprehensive travel-insurance package. Don't buy insurance at the airport; it's usually overpriced. Be sure to take any valuables or irreplaceable items with you in your carry-on luggage, because many valuables (including books, money, and electronics) aren't covered by airline policies.

For more information, contact one of the following recommended insurers: **Access America** (☎ 866-807-3982; www.accessamerica.com); **Travel Guard International** (☎ 800-826-4919; www.travelguard.com); **Travel Insured International** (☎ 800-243-3174; www.travelinsured.com); and **Travelex Insurance Services** (☎ 888-457-4602; www.travelex-insurance.com).

Staying Healthy When You Travel

You can get over-the-counter medications — aspirin, cold remedies, antacids, and so on — at pharmacies and hotels on New Providence and Grand Bahama and in many hotels on other islands. If you need to refill a prescription, bring the generic name of your medication because local pharmacists may know only the generic name. Most hotel shops and pharmacies aren't open at night, so travel with any basics that you may need, such as medicine for diarrhea or upset stomach, sunburn remedies, anti-itch cream to soothe insect bites, and children's aspirin if you're traveling with little ones. Don't forget any prescription drugs that you're taking, and if you think that you may run out, plan ahead to refill your prescription. If you wear contact lenses, pack an extra pair in the event that you lose one.

Before you go

If you have a serious or chronic illness, talk to your doctor before you leave. If you have a condition such as epilepsy, diabetes, or heart problems, wear a **MedicAlert identification tag** (☎ 888-633-4298; www.medicalert.org), which immediately alerts doctors to your condition and gives them access to your records through MedicAlert's 24-hour hot line. Contact the **International Association for Medical Assistance to Travelers** (IAMAT; ☎ 716-754-4883 or, in Canada, 416-652-0137; www.iamat.org) for tips on travel and health concerns and lists of local English-speaking doctors. The U.S. **Centers for Disease Control and Prevention** (☎ 877-394-8747; www.cdc.gov) provides up-to-date information on health hazards by region or country and offers tips on food safety. The Web site **www.tripprep.com**, sponsored by a consortium of travel medicine practitioners, may also offer helpful advice on traveling abroad. You can find listings of reliable clinics overseas at the **International Society of Travel Medicine** (www.istm.org).

Emergencies and medical care

If you get sick, ask a staff member at your hotel to recommend a local doctor — even his own doctor, if necessary. If you can't find a doctor to help you right away, try the emergency room at the local hospital or clinic. Many hospital emergency rooms have walk-in clinics for cases that aren't life-threatening. You may not get immediate attention, but you won't pay the high price of an emergency-room visit.

 If you have health insurance, carry your insurance card in your wallet, but you may have to pay all medical costs upfront and be reimbursed for them later. For information on purchasing additional medical insurance for your trip, see the previous section.

 ## *Addressing other potential hazards*

Here are some ways you can prevent common vacation disasters:

✔ **Drinking the water:** Drinking water from the tap is safe, but you may not like the unfamiliar taste. Many hotels supply bottled or filtered water for guests. Before you take a swig from a bottle, though, check whether the hotel gives you the water free. Some resorts charge $5 or more per bottle. Stocking up on bottled water at a nearby drugstore or grocery store is always cheaper than buying it at your hotel or taking it from your minibar.

✔ **Sunbathing:** As all visitors to the islands know, you can get a wicked sunburn even on hazy days if you don't wear sunscreen. Reapply sunscreen every time you come out of the water, even if your sunscreen is waterproof. Reapply the cream periodically throughout the day, whether you go into the water or not. If you get your hair cornrowed and you're not used to wearing it that way, put some sunscreen on the delicate skin of your newly exposed scalp. Wide-brimmed hats also come in handy, of course.

✔ **Repelling bugs:** Use insect repellent, particularly at dusk, when the mosquitoes and gnats are at their most treacherous.

✔ **Taking a scuba dive:** If scuba diving is part of your vacation, plan your trip so that you don't fly within 24 hours of diving. Your body needs time to recover from being at a high altitude before it hits the lower depths and vice versa.

When you're in the water, the stunning shapes and colors of fish, coral, and sea plants may make you want to reach out and touch. *Don't.* Not only can you destroy delicate marine life by doing so, but you can also put yourself in danger. Even innocuous-looking coral can be razor sharp, and a variety aptly known as *fire coral* can burn your skin. Also be warned that shiny jewelry in the water can attract barracudas and sharks.

✔ **Keeping safe:** Even though you're relaxing on a vacation, keep up your guard. For example, especially in Nassau, don't venture into unknown neighborhoods alone at night. Don't wear flashy jewelry or leave your valuables lying around, even in your locked hotel room. Many larger hotels have in-room safes or front-desk safety deposit boxes.

Staying Connected by Cellphone or E-mail

Travelers have a number of ways to stay in touch while on the road. Of course, using your own laptop, personal digital assistant (PDA), or cellphone gives you the most flexibility. But even if you don't own these devices or prefer not to travel with them, you can stay connected.

Accessing the Internet away from home

Although most cities have cybercafes, you'll only find a few in The Bahamas. Check www.cybercafe.com for locations. Otherwise, you may be at the mercy of your hotel's facilities — but beware of exorbitant rates.

To retrieve your e-mail, find out whether your Internet Service Provider (ISP) has a Web-based interface tied to your existing e-mail account. If it does, follow its instructions for accessing your e-mail. If your ISP doesn't have such an interface, you can use the free **mail2web** service (www.mail2web.com) to view and reply to your home e-mail.

If you need to access files on your office computer, look into a service called **GoToMyPC** (www.gotomypc.com). The service provides a Web-based interface so you can access and manipulate a distant PC from anywhere — even a cybercafe — provided your "target" PC is on and has an always-on connection to the Internet (such as RoadRunner cable access).

If you're bringing your own computer, check your ISP's Web site or call its toll-free number and ask how you can use your current account away from home via a local access number; also ask how much it will cost.

If you're traveling outside your ISP's reach, the **iPass** network has dial-up numbers in most of the world's countries. You have to sign up with an iPass provider, who then tells you how to set up your computer for The Bahamas. For a list of iPass providers, go to www.ipass.com and click on "Individuals." One solid provider is **i2roam** (☎ **866-811-6209** or 920-235-0475; www.i2roam.com). Wherever you go, bring a **connection kit** with the right power and phone adapters, a spare phone cord, and a spare Ethernet network cable.

Most business-class hotels offer dataports for laptop modems, and some hotels in The Bahamas offer high-speed Internet access using an Ethernet network cable. You have to bring your own cables either way, so call your hotel in advance to find out what your options are.

Using a cellphone

The three letters that define much of the world's **wireless capabilities** are GSM (Global System for Mobiles), a big, seamless network that makes for easy cross-border cellphone use throughout Europe and dozens of other countries worldwide. In the U.S., T-Mobile, AT&T Wireless, and Cingular use this quasi-universal system; in Canada, Microcell and some Rogers customers are GSM, and all Europeans and most Australians use GSM.

If your cellphone is on a GSM system, and you have a world-capable multiband phone such as many Sony Ericsson, Motorola, or Samsung models, you can make and receive calls across civilized areas on much of the globe, from Andorra to Uganda. Just call your wireless operator and ask for "international roaming" to be activated on your account. Unfortunately, per-minute charges can be high — usually $1 to $1.50 in Western Europe and up to $5 in places like Russia and Indonesia.

For many, **renting** a phone is a good idea. (Even worldphone owners will have to rent new phones if they're traveling to non-GSM regions, such as Japan or Korea.) While you can rent a phone from any number of overseas sites, including kiosks at airports and at car-rental agencies, we suggest you rent the phone before you leave home. North Americans can rent one before leaving home from **InTouch USA** (☎ **800-872-7626;** www.intouchglobal.com) or **RoadPost** (☎ **888-290-1606** or 905-272-5665; www.roadpost.com). InTouch will also, for free, advise you on whether your existing phone will work overseas; simply call ☎ **703-222-7161** between 9 a.m. and 4 p.m. EST, or go to www.intouchglobal.com/travel.htm.

Buying a phone can be economically attractive, as many nations have cheap prepaid phone systems. Once you arrive at your destination, stop by a local cellphone shop and get the cheapest package; you'll probably pay less than $100 for a phone and a starter calling card. Local calls may be as low as 10¢ per minute, and in many countries incoming calls are free.

Keeping Up With Airline Security Measures

With the federalization of airport security, security procedures at U.S. airports are more stable and consistent than ever. Generally, you'll be fine if you arrive at the airport **two hours before a flight** to The Bahamas.

Bring a **current** passport. Keep your ID at the ready to show at check-in, the security checkpoint, and sometimes even the gate.

E-tickets have made paper tickets nearly obsolete. Passengers with E-tickets can beat the ticket-counter lines by using airport **electronic kiosks** or even **online check-in** from your home computer. Online check-in involves logging on to your airline's Web site, accessing your reservation, and printing out your boarding pass — and the airline may even offer you bonus miles to do so!

If you're using a kiosk at the airport to check in, bring the credit card you used to book the ticket or your frequent-flier card. Print out your boarding pass from the kiosk and simply proceed to the security checkpoint with your pass and a photo ID. If you're checking bags or looking to snag an exit-row seat, you're able to do so using most airline kiosks. Even the smaller airlines employ the kiosk system, but always call your airline to make sure these alternatives are available. **Curbside check-in** is also a good way to avoid lines, although a few airlines still ban curbside check-in; call before you go.

Security lines are getting shorter, but long ones still remain. If you have trouble standing for long periods of time, tell an airline employee; the airline can provide a wheelchair. You can speed up security by **not wearing metal objects,** such as big belt buckles or clanky earrings. If you have metallic body parts, a note from your doctor can prevent a long chat with the security screeners. Keep in mind that only **ticketed passengers** are allowed past security, except for folks escorting passengers with disabilities or children.

Federalization has stabilized **what you can carry on** and **what you can't.** Travelers in the U.S. are allowed one carry-on bag, plus a "personal item" such as a purse, briefcase, or laptop bag. Carry-on hoarders can stuff all sorts of things into a laptop bag; as long as it has a laptop in it, it's still considered a personal item. The Transportation Security Administration (TSA) has issued a list of restricted items; check its Web site (www.tsa. gov) for details.

Airport screeners may decide that your checked luggage needs to be searched by hand. You can now purchase luggage locks that allow screeners to open and re-lock a checked bag if hand-searching is necessary. Look for Travel Sentry certified locks at luggage or travel shops and Brookstone stores (you can buy them online at www.brookstone. com). For more information on the locks, visit www.travelsentry.org.

Part III

New Providence: Nassau, Cable Beach, and Paradise Island

In this part . . .

In this part, we guide you through the details of getting to (and around) New Providence, home of The Bahamas' historic capital. We also help you sift through the wide array of accommodations in Cable Beach, Nassau, and Paradise Island, and point you to the best sights to see after you settle in.

We offer you tips on finding the most authentic local cuisine and give you our top picks of everything from fast food to fine dining. Sure, you can hit the casinos and duty-free shops, but we also steer you to plenty of other diversions, both in the ocean and on dry land.

Chapter 10

Settling into New Providence

*M*ost of The Bahamas is about escapism. Not New Providence Island — it's where the action is. This is the bustling hub of The Bahamas and the country's major tourist attraction. Expect elegant bars, gargantuan gambling parlors, dance clubs, the best restaurants, sprawling resorts, and blocks and blocks of shops with discounted merchandise. The island's a bit of a circus, but that's what many vacationers are seeking.

Paradise Island is sleeker and more upscale than Cable Beach, even though it's overbuilt and overly commercialized. Most visitors opt for the beachfront properties and visit Nassau only for its shops and attractions.

Arriving at the Airport

When Bahamians come to the end of a journey, they say, "Ya reach." You receive a special New Providence welcome as "ya reach" **Nassau International Airport** (☎ 242-377-1759). Spirited live calypso or Bahamian Junkanoo music greets you in the arrivals' hall. The beat of the music will have your shoulders bouncing and your feet tapping.

The airport is hassle-free. From collecting your bags and passing through Customs to finding the taxi or van that will take you to your hotel, everything runs quickly and smoothly. You can find the ATMs at the airport in the arrivals hall, and you also find a Tourist Information Booth (☎ 242-377-6806), open daily from 8:30 a.m. to 10 p.m. The booth's staff dispenses vacation brochures and free maps.

Navigating your way through passport control and Customs

Start filling out your Immigration Arrival/Departure Card as soon as you join one of the lines marked "Visitors." This way, you're ready to roll when it's your turn to present the card along with your passport or birth certificate, photo ID, and your return- or onward-bound airline ticket. Remember where you stick your copy of the immigration card because you need to show it before you leave the country.

Getting through Customs usually takes about 15 minutes, depending on how many different pieces of luggage you have. Even if you declare that you're not bringing in anything illegal, Customs may single you out for a more thorough search.

Getting from the airport to your hotel

Cable Beach, the main resort area on New Providence, is about a 15-minute drive from the airport. **Paradise Island,** joined to New Providence by bridge, is 30 minutes away. If your hotel package includes transportation, you receive a coupon or voucher to use upon arrival. When you find the right bus going to your hotel, show the driver the voucher. Buses are labeled and easy to find. Otherwise, you have to take a taxi, which costs about $22 for two passengers to Cable Beach or about $27 to Paradise Island.

To save money, you can share a cab with another couple heading to the same hotel and pay $3 for each additional person — but pretend that you've known each other since kindergarten. If you reveal that you just met at the airport, the driver may try to charge each couple the full rate. Drivers expect, and sometimes request, a 15 percent tip.

In most cases, you can get around New Providence without a car. If you decide that you need wheels, you can pick up your car at the airport if you rented through a major agency. Try to make your car-rental reservation before leaving home. For more information, see the section "Getting Around New Providence" later in this chapter.

Cruising into New Providence

Sometimes nearly a dozen cruise ships are in port at one time at **Prince George Dock,** also known as **Prince George Wharf.** If you're among the passengers, your ship is as much of an attraction as its destination, meaning that you don't have a whole lot of time for exploring dry land. However, because you disembark near Rawson Square in the heart of Nassau, you're just a stroll away from the **Straw Market** and all the shops and restaurants of **Bay Street,** the main avenue. Read more about these attractions in Chapter 13.

A *jitney,* or public bus, takes you to the sandy shores of Cable Beach or to the foot of the Paradise Island bridge. You can walk across the bridge (and pay the 25¢ toll) to **Paradise Beach,** the most popular beach on Paradise Island. Of course, taxis can take you from downtown Nassau across the bridge (for a $2 toll), but the most convenient way for cruise-ship passengers to get to Paradise Island is to take one of the ferries from Prince George Dock for $1 each way.

Choosing Your Location

The capital city of **Nassau** dominates **New Providence Island.** Most of the beach resorts are at **Cable Beach,** a ten-minute drive west of Nassau. **Paradise Island,** which is connected by bridge to Nassau, is also packed with beachfront hotels.

Nassau, where Bahamians live and work, and the resort areas of Cable Beach and Paradise Island have distinct personalities. A hotel in downtown Nassau can put you on or across from a beach; it can also place you within walking distance of a slew of restaurants, the Straw Market, duty-free shops, horse-and-buggy rides, and historic sites. However, Nassau isn't a safe place to be at night. For many visitors, life on scenic Cable Beach revolves around the casinos, while the draw for others is the long stretch of golden sand. Paradise Island is short on historic attractions but long on water fun, designer shops, nightlife, and first-rate (but expensive) cuisine.

 If you want to stay on the beach but not cause serious damage to your wallet, look for choices on Cable Beach and Nassau. On Paradise Island, the best hotels — whether on or off the beach — are more expensive.

The casino in Cable Beach sits between the Wyndham Nassau Resort and the Radisson. On Paradise Island, the casino is located at the Atlantis Resort. Shuttle buses take you to these gambling meccas if you choose to stay at one of the other hotels.

You can easily reach other attractions, such as museums, old forts, and the **Ardastra Gardens & Zoo** (see Chapter 13) from Cable Beach, downtown Nassau, or Paradise Island. To get to these points of interest, you can take a taxi, guided tour, public bus, or go on foot. You can also make arrangements through your hotel to sail to one of the beach-rimmed offshore islets that offers aquatic activities, including dolphin and stingray encounters. Some of these side trips are popular among cruise-ship passengers, so depending on when you go, these uninhabited islands may host large crowds.

Getting Around New Providence

Two parallel bridges — with traffic flowing in opposite directions — link Nassau and Paradise Island. The older bridge — the *only* bridge for decades before the most spectacular section of the multimillion-dollar Atlantis resort sprouted on Paradise Island in the late 1990s — goes from Paradise Island to Nassau.

The bridge to Paradise Island is about a mile from the center of downtown Nassau. You can walk the whole distance, take a jitney to the foot of the bridge and walk across, or take a taxi from Nassau all the way across. Every time you cross the bridge from Nassau to Paradise Island, you must pay a toll: $2 by taxi or $1 by car. There is no charge for pedestrians.

Here are more tips about the various modes of transportation in New Providence.

Exploring on foot

Historic downtown Nassau is suitable for walking but is congested between 9 a.m. and 5 p.m. on weekdays. (For details on what sights you can expect to see, check out Chapter 13.)

The city's streets are desolate after dark, so lone strolls at night aren't safe. If you like wandering under the stars, Cable Beach and Paradise Island are your best bets.

Taking a bus

Some hotels along Cable Beach and on Paradise Island offer guests free bus service within the resort areas. To go elsewhere, you can take taxis or rent a car and brave Nassau traffic. Or, you can get almost anywhere you want to go on New Providence on a jitney. These small buses or large vans travel up and down West Bay Street (the road in front of Cable Beach hotels) to beaches, through downtown Nassau, and to other parts of the island. They run from approximately 6 a.m. to 7 p.m. At $1 a ride, they're a convenient, inexpensive way to get around. You need exact change or a $1 bill. When you see a jitney coming, flag it down. The buses wait to fill up at depots and are often tightly packed, but with reggae or calypso pumping on the radio, the mood is always festive.

To go east from downtown Nassau toward the Paradise Island bridges, catch a bus at Frederick and Bay streets, near the Straw Market. These buses don't go over the bridge, so you have to walk or take a cab across. To go west toward Cable Beach, catch a bus near the British Colonial

Hilton at Bay Street. If you're traveling from Cable Beach to Paradise Island or vice versa, you must change buses in town.

Taking a taxi

Taxis wait outside Cable Beach and Paradise Island hotels, and they're also plentiful in downtown Nassau. Drivers take the same routes so often that many don't bother to use their meters. Therefore, before you hop into a cab, ask your hotel staff the approximate fare to wherever you're going. From Cable Beach to downtown Nassau, you pay about $10 for two passengers. The trip from Cable Beach to Paradise Island costs about $16.

Driving around

If you want to rent a car, you must drive on the left side of the road, a holdover of British tradition. If you come from small-town America, drivers in Nassau may appear reckless to you. You can make car-rental arrangements at the airport or through your hotel (see Chapter 9 for more information).

Ferrying from island to island

Ferries run between Prince George Dock, in downtown Nassau, and Paradise Island about every ten minutes daily from 9 a.m. to 6 p.m. The round-trip cost is $6. A ferry is the most scenic way to get from Paradise Island to Nassau and vice versa. Go to the dock and climb aboard the next ferry that's leaving for a brief sail across the harbor.

Other fun ways to get around

Here are other options for getting around New Providence and Paradise Island.

- ✔ **Touring town in a horse-drawn carriage:** Riding around in a horse-drawn surrey with fringe on top is the most romantic way to see Nassau. Your horse may even have a droopy flower stuck in his straw hat. Carriages wait for passengers at **Rawson Square,** in the heart of Nassau, not far from where the cruise ships dock. For a 20-minute ride, expect to pay about $15 per person for up to three adults plus one or two children.

- ✔ **Riding bicycles:** Because traffic is often crazy in and around Nassau, two-wheelers aren't the best way to get from place to place. If you want to bike, you can do so in front of any large hotel complex. (Ask the hotel staff for information on bike rentals.) A guided tour is your best bet along scenic and shoreline trails.

A half-day bicycle tour with **Bahamas Outdoors Ltd.** (☎ 242-362-1574) costs $65.

✔ **Buzzing by on a motor scooter:** Some vacationers love zipping around on mini-motorcycles or scooters, but the often speedy Nassau traffic makes them far from safe. If you're feeling brave, wear a helmet and set out on your adventure, staying on the left side of the road. Ask your hotel staff for the closest scooter-rental outfit. Rates run about $45 per day.

Fast Facts: New Providence

American Express

If you need help with traveler's checks or other American Express services, visit the office at Destinations on Shirley Street, between Parliament and Charlotte streets (☎ 242-322-2931). It's open Monday to Friday 9 a.m. to 5 p.m.

ATMs

Major banks throughout Nassau include the Royal Bank of Canada (☎ 242-322-8700), Bank of Nova Scotia (☎ 242-356-1517), and Barclays (☎ 242-356-8000); each has ATMs. However, some accept cards only in the Cirrus network (☎ 800-424-7787), while others take only Plus (☎ 800-843-7587). ATMs at both the Paradise Island and Cable Beach casinos also dispense quick cash. You can also find ATMs at the airports.

Baby Sitting

Hotel staff can help you make arrangements to hire an experienced sitter. Expect to pay around $10 to $15 an hour, plus $3 an hour for each additional child.

Emergencies

For any major emergency, call ☎ 919.

Hospitals

The government-run Princess Margaret Hospital (☎ 242-322-2861) is located on Shirley Street in downtown Nassau. Before your trip to The Bahamas, check out whether your health insurance covers you while you're abroad. If not, you may want to purchase a traveler's insurance plan with emergency medical expense coverage (see Chapter 9 for details).

Information

Contact the Ministry of Tourism at Rawson Square (☎ 242-328-7810) or ask your hotel staff for good local maps and other visitor information.

Internet Access

Check out Cybercafe at The Mall at Marathon (☎ 242-394-6254). Here you can get online from your own laptop or log on to one of the computers. The cost is 15¢ per minute. Some of the larger hotels also offer guests Internet access for a small fee.

Newspapers and Magazines

The Tribune Daily and *The Nassau Guardian,* both published in the morning, are the country's two competing daily newspapers. At your hotel and visitor information stations, you can find various helpful magazines, brochures, and booklets.

Pharmacies

The Prescription Parlourx Pharmacy (☎ 242-356-3973) on East Street South is open daily from 7 a.m. to 11 p.m. You can have whatever you need delivered to your hotel for about the cost of a round-trip taxi ride to the pharmacy.

The delivery charge is $6 from about 7 a.m. to 9 p.m. and $25 until 11 p.m. Another reliable pharmacy that also delivers is Cole Thompson, open 8:30 a.m. to 7 p.m. at Bay and Charlotte streets (☎ 242-322-2062).

Police

In an emergency, call ☎ **919.**

Post Office

The main post office is at the juncture of East Hill Street and East Street in Nassau (☎ 242-322-3344).

Restrooms

Downtown Nassau has free public toilets, which are adjacent to both the cruise ship docks and other docks near the Straw Market on Bay Street. But when nature calls, most locals opt to duck into one of the better-maintained restrooms of the many bars or casinos scattered throughout the city. The toilets in McDonald's on Bay Street are a good bet.

Safety

Just as you should anywhere in the world, exercise caution and common sense. For example, don't wear flashy jewelry to the beach or turn your back on your camera or handbag. Stay away from desolate or run-down areas — whether residential or commercial — at night. Cable Beach and Paradise Island are always packed with visitors and are safer places for walking and exploring after dark.

Taxis

Taxis wait outside Cable Beach and Paradise Island hotels, and they're also plentiful in Nassau. Before you hop into a cab, ask your hotel staff the approximate fare to wherever you're going. From Cable Beach to downtown Nassau, you pay about $10 for two passengers. The trip from Cable Beach to Paradise Island costs about $16.

Chapter 11

Staying in Style in New Providence

*N*ew Providence reigns supreme when it comes to the number of resorts and activities. You can also find a bed-and-breakfast or a small beach hotel away from the crowds.

Surveying the Scene

Most accommodations in New Providence are high-rises with hundreds of rooms. But New Providence also offers villas, town houses, and condos. These options have fewer services, such as restaurants or staff to help make arrangements for tours and activities. Many villas, town houses, and condos are a distance from sights and attractions, and you have to provide your own transportation. Keep in mind that while you have all the comforts of home, you also have all the work that goes along with it. However, these types of accommodations are good for families or groups of friends who prefer doing their own cooking and are looking for a private vacation. For long-term vacationers, these types of accommodations are a great money-saving tactic for an extended island stay.

The rates listed in the reviews below are for two people spending one night in a double room in winter or early spring. These charges are published rates available to anybody who walks in off the street and requests a room. You can get discounted hotel rates in many ways (see Chapter 7 for more details). Rates at Breezes and Sandals Royal Bahamian include meals, beverages, tips, taxes, transportation to and from the airport, entertainment, and most activities.

If a view is important to you, make sure that you clarify this point when you reserve a room. The most expensive rooms invariably have ocean views; the less expensive accommodations open onto a pool or a garden. Sometimes another building obscures views from a room. Ask so that you aren't unpleasantly surprised with a vista of a wall.

Most New Providence hotels don't quote prices for a meal plan, such as MAP (modified American plan or breakfast and dinner). When they do, the extra cost per person is indicated.

The Best Accommodations

Here are our top hotel picks in Nassau, Cable Beach, and Paradise Island, along with some handy maps.

Atlantis Paradise Island Resort & Casino
$$$$$ Paradise Island Beach

The Atlantis is a 2,349-room resort that sprawls from one shore of Paradise Island to the other, opening onto a long stretch of white sandy beach. Stay here if you'd like to lodge in a mega-resort and mini-city. Check into the nearby One&Only Ocean Club (see the listing for this property later in the chapter) if you're seeking more tranquillity and exclusivity.

Dozens of restaurants, bars, lounges, designer boutiques, and a mammoth casino that's open day and night keep many visitors glued to the premises. The resort's comfortable, sleekly decorated rooms vary in size, view, and location. Although all rooms have small balconies, many of the balconies in the plush Royal Towers (the priciest section) are wide enough for only two pairs of feet. The Beach Tower is the least expensive wing, with Coral Towers in the middle. Bathrooms are spacious and well maintained. Room service is available round-the-clock, and you can stay busy on the tennis, volleyball, and basketball courts; the putting green; in exercise classes; or at the spa. However, the centerpiece of the hotel is its dazzling water wonderworld of aquariums, freshwater pools, snorkeling lagoons, water slides, and a white-sand beach.

Take one of the water slides down the life-size replica of a Mayan temple. An 18m (60-ft.), nearly vertical drop zips you along a clear tunnel that slices through a shark tank. To view the sharks at a more leisurely pace, take the 15m (48-ft.) corkscrew slide instead. Other aquatic playgrounds range from a shallow children's pool and beachlike zero-entry pool (instead of having steps, the shallow end gradually slopes from dry land, just like a beach) to a river pool that carries you along in an inner tube, as well as a series of pools linked by water slides. In other words, you're at Disney. The Atlantis's activity-packed children's program is not only the best in The Bahamas but also in the Caribbean.

Twenty restaurants are on-site, so the range of prices and types of cuisine are greater than in many small towns. You can take the kids to chow down

Nassau and Paradise Island Accommodations

Atlantis Paradise Island Resort & Casino **4**

British Colonial Hilton **3**

Comfort Suites Paradise Island **5**

Dillet's Guest House **1**

Nassau Palm Resort **2**

One&Only Ocean Club **7**

Sunrise Beach Club and Villas **6**

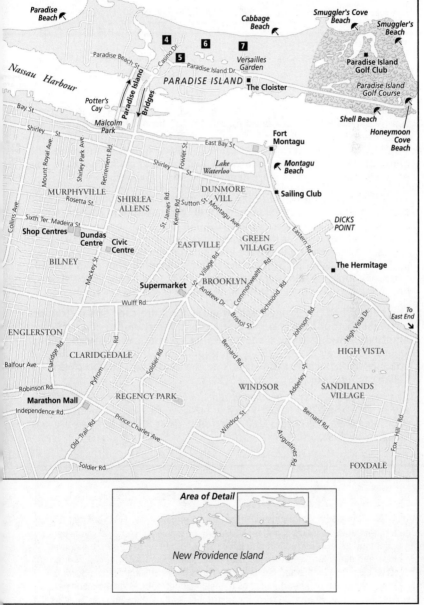

ATLANTIC   OCEAN

Pirate Cove

Paradise
Beach

Cabbage
Beach

Smuggler's Cove
Beach

Smuggler's
Beach

4

6

7

Paradise Beach St.

Casino Dr.

5

Paradise Island Dr.

Versailles
Garden

Paradise Island
Golf Club

Nassau   Harbour

PARADISE ISLAND ■
The Cloister

Paradise Island
Golf Course

Paradise Island

Bridges

Shell Beach

Honeymoon
Cove
Beach

Bay St.

Potter's
Cay

Malcolm
Park

Shirley   St.

Shirley Park Ave.

Retirement Rd.

Mount Royal Ave.

East Bay St.

Fowler St.

Shirley
St.

Fort
Montagu

Lake
Waterloo

Montagu
Beach

Sailing Club

MURPHYVILLE

Rosetta St.

SHIRLEA
ALLENS

St. James Rd.

Kemp Rd.

Sutton St.

DUNMORE
VILL

Montagu Ave.

Collins Ave.

Sixth Ter. Madeira St.

Eastern Rd.

DICKS
POINT

Shop Centres

Dundas
Centre

Civic
Centre

EASTVILLE

GREEN
VILLAGE

The Hermitage

BILNEY

Mackey St.

Village Rd.

Commonwealth Rd.

Richmond Rd.

Supermarket

St. Andrew Dr.

BROOKLYN

Wulff Rd.

Bristol St.

Johnson Rd.

High Vista Dr.

To
East End

ENGLERSTON

Claridge Rd.

Rd.

Soldier Rd.

CLARIDGEDALE

Pyfrom

Bernard Rd.

HIGH VISTA

Balfour Ave.

Robinson Rd.

Marathon Mall

Independence Rd.

REGENCY PARK

WINDSOR

Adderley St.

SANDILANDS
VILLAGE

Bernard Rd.

Old Trail Rd.

Prince Charles Ave.

Windsor St.

St. Augustines Rd.

Fox Hill Rd.

Soldier Rd.

FOXDALE

Area of Detail

New Providence Island

on burgers, or you can dine more elegantly on some of the most superior cuisine in The Bahamas, prepared by top Bahamian, American, or European chefs.

See map p. 134. Casino Drive. ☎ *800-ATLANTIS or 242-363-3000. Fax: 242-363-6300.* www.atlantis.com. *Parking: $10 valet, $7 self-parking. Rack rates: $360–$720 double, $810 suite. AE, DC, DISC, MC, V.*

Breezes Bahamas
$$$$$ Cable Beach

At the eastern end of the strip of Cable Beach hotels, all-inclusive Breezes, run by SuperClubs, is designed mainly for adult couples and singles, but children age 14 or older are welcome, too. The other major all-inclusive, Sandals (reviewed later in this chapter), is more stylish and upscale with better amenities, but that Jamaican chain only accepts male/female couples, whereas Breezes is more democratically open to all.

The hotel opens onto one of the best beaches along the entire coastal strip. You entertain yourself with everything from toga and pajama parties to talent shows and comedy cabarets. There's even an ice-skating rink. Island traditions, such as dancers and musicians dressed in whimsical costumes, make lively appearances in Junkanoo Jamborees and steel-band performances. A large, heated freshwater swimming pool is on-site. You can also snorkel or take scuba lessons. A short walk along the road or the beach takes you to the Crystal Palace Casino (see Chapter 13).

The refurbished hotel rooms with wooden furniture and Formica tops are comfortable, but frankly never rise beyond the standard of a first-class American hotel. Although the price tag sounds expensive at first, it includes all meals, beverages, and most activities. Diners can sample good but unremarkable international cuisine at a food court. The best bet is the Italian dining room.

See map p. 137. W. Bay Street (just east of the Nassau Beach Hotel). ☎ *800-GO-SUPER (800-467-8737) or 242-327-5356. Fax: 242-327-1209.* www.superclubs.com. *Rack rates: $700–$750 double, $800–$1,200 suite. Rates include all meals and most activities. AE, DISC, MC, V.*

Coming attractions

During the life of this edition, Atlantis will begin a new phase of development that will include a significant enlargement and revamping of the present layout. Individual elements will include the construction of a 600-room all-suite luxury hotel, a 400-unit condo hotel, and additional water-themed attractions, including a dolphin encounter. The resort will also add local branches of Bobby Flay's Mesa Grill and Nobu, an avant-garde Japanese restaurant spearheaded by namesake chef Nobu Matsuhisa and partially funded by partner Robert De Niro. If construction and deal-making continue as planned, both will be in place and functioning sometime in 2007.

Cable Beach Accommodations

ATLANTIC OCEAN

BROWN'S POINT

NEW PROVIDENCE ISLAND

area of detail

Goodman's Bay

Sanford Dr.

CABLE BEACH GOLF COURSE

PROSPECT RIDGE

West Bay St.

Rugby Ave.

Devonshire St.

Poinciana Dr.

Skyline Dr.

Oak Hill Rd.

Lake Cunningham

Cable Beach Lagoon

West Bay St.
Hampshire St.
Yorkshire St.
Oxford Ave.

1/4 mi
0.5 km

Sandals Royal Bahamian Hotel **1**
Wyndham Nassau Resort &
Crystal Palace Casino **3**

Breezes Bahamas **5**
Nassau Beach Hotel **4**
Radisson Cable Beach Resort **2**

British Colonial Hilton
$$$ Nassau

The grand dame of all Nassau hotels, this landmark seven-floor, 291-room hotel has been fine-tuned by the Hilton chain. If you're going to The Bahamas for a beach vacation, check into one of the hotels at Paradise Island or Cable Beach. If the shopping and sights of Nassau are more important to you, consider this landmark hotel. A beach that's adequate for sunning and swimming is here, but it's a bit small. The hotel doesn't even try to attract the casino crowd, who prefer either the Atlantis or the Nassau Marriott. Business travelers come here, and so do visitors who are more interested in buying than gambling.

Scenes from such 007 flicks as *Thunderball* and *Never Say Never Again* were shot at this plush and glamorous hotel. There's even a "Double 0" suite filled with Bond memorabilia. The rooms open onto the small beach that's situated on the channel separating New Providence from Paradise Beach. A dignified atmosphere prevails in the bedrooms, which are a bit on the small side, but quite comfortable. They're capped with rich crown moldings and accessorized with tile or stone-sheathed bathrooms, and many offer scenic views of the Nassau harbor. The cuisine at the British Colonial is good standard fare, although it can't compete with top Nassau restaurants (see Chapter 12). The hotel features a medium-sized, unheated freshwater pool.

See map p. 134. 1 Bay St. ☎ 800-HILTONS (800-445-8667) in the U.S. and Canada, or 242-322-3301. Fax: 242-302-9009. www.hilton.com. *Parking: $6. Rack rates: $205–$325 double, $435–$2,000 suite. AE, DC, DISC, MC, V.*

Comfort Suites
$$$–$$$$ Paradise Island

Here you're offered modern "suites," but don't expect yours to have separate rooms or even a balcony. Instead, you get one comfortable motel-like room with sitting and sleeping areas. For families or groups of friends, the rooms offer pull-out sofas. This hotel isn't on the beach and you can't see the ocean from your bedroom, but across from your hotel is the Atlantis Paradise Island Resort & Casino (see this resort's entry earlier in this chapter), which does open onto a beautiful white sandy beach with a sheltered marina. So you're only a five-minute walk from the sands. The freshwater pool is small and unheated. An open-air restaurant serves only breakfast and lunch.

The real draw of Comfort Suites is that, as a guest, you have full access to the amenities at the Atlantis. Comfort Suites is a quieter three-story hotel and is a good choice if you want access to Atlantis facilities without staying at the overwhelming mega-resort. For the most privacy at Comfort Suites, ask for a room that's not along a walkway. Children under age 16 stay free with one or two adults.

See map p. 134. Paradise Island Drive. ☎ 877-424-6423 or 242-363-3680. Fax: 242-363-2588. www.comfortsuites.com. *Rack rates: $250–$300 double. Rates include continental breakfast. AE, DISC, MC, V.*

Dillet's Guest House
$$ Nassau

This bed-and-breakfast sits in a residential neighborhood within strolling distance of Saunders Beach, downtown Nassau, and bus stops. Iris Knowles, who runs Dillet's with her daughter, Danielle, was reared in this handsome home, which was built in 1928 by her father. The inn has only seven rooms, which are decorated with white wicker and pastels. All the guest quarters offer sitting areas, air-conditioning, and ceiling fans. The bathrooms are also attractive but small, each with a shower. Taking up an entire block, the grounds — which include a small, unheated freshwater pool — are planted with tropical greenery. You're treated to a Bahamian breakfast featuring sweet johnnycake and banana bread or potato bread flavored with coconut.

See map p. 134. Dunmore Avenue and Strachan Street. ☎ *242-325-1133. Fax: 242-325-7183.* www.islandeaze.com/dillets. *Rack rates: $125 double. Rate includes breakfast. No credit cards.*

Nassau Beach Hotel
$$–$$$ Cable Beach

Next door to its sibling, the flashier Wyndham Nassau Resort & Crystal Palace Casino (reviewed later in this chapter), and across the road from the Cable Beach Golf Course, the Nassau Beach Hotel has been going strong since the 1940s. Claiming a prime slice of the white sand beach-front, this hotel is one of the more dignified in the area, and has weathered competition from the newer, glitzier resorts nearby. But don't let the Georgian-style architecture, gleaming marble-and-tile lobby, and hushed hues fool you. The Nassau Beach Hotel knows how to party. Check out the nightly Bahamian revue at the popular King & Knights club, the loud Friday-evening Junkanoo parade at Café Johnny Canoe out front, or one of the hotel's various bars. When hunger hits, you can choose from seven on-site restaurants serving standard international cuisine — except for the Beef Cellar, which grills the juiciest, most tender, and succulent steaks on Cable Beach.

The midsize accommodations contain summery rattan pieces, comfortable beds, and a marble bathroom. All rooms come with a balcony or patio, but make sure you ask about the view when you make your reservation. Although you can see the ocean from most rooms, some overlook buildings instead. Watersports are extensive, and the hotel also has six tennis courts (four are floodlit for night play) and a fitness center. Two unheated freshwater pools are also on-site.

See map p. 137. W. Bay Street (near the Crystal Palace Casino). ☎ *888-NASSAU-B (888-627-7282) or 242-327-7711. Fax: 242-327-8829.* www.nassaubeachhotel.com. *Rack rates: $90–$150 double, $250–$400 suite. AE, DISC, MC, V.*

The times, they are a changin' for Cable Beach

Currently, Cable Beach boasts a wide variety of restaurants and sports facilities, lots of glitz and glitter, and the biggest casino, in terms of square footage, in The Bahamas. All of that will be changing between 2007 and 2009, when a multi-tiered redevelopment program will forever change the status of Cable Beach as the "also-ran" next to Paradise Island — though to be fair, even in its present incarnation, Cable Beach has many loyal fans, some of whom think Paradise Island is too snobbish, too contrived, too expensive, and too similar to a Disney-inspired theme park.

Major infrastructure changes will include a revised layout of one of New Providence Island's busiest traffic arteries, West Bay Street. Other plans include the dredging of new lakes, marinas, water traps for a redesigned golf course, the destruction of some of the older buildings within the new Cable Beach compound, and an enlargement of the existing casino. It will also call for the construction of an entire new string of resort hotels, all of them members of the Starwood group, each of which will cater to a different market. A "W" hotel on-site, for example, will be a postmodern testimony to avant-garde design, and, it's hoped, a youthful, trend-setting clientele. An all new Saint Regis hotel will offer more conservative and somewhat more plush comforts geared to the *haute bourgeoisie*. Into the melee will be factored an intelligent re-use of some of the existing structures, including the Marriott. Big changes should be visible by 2008 and 2009, with the more radical transformations in place by 2010.

Nassau Palm Resort
$$–$$$ Nassau

If you like spending your cash on purchases other than your hotel room, this place may be for you. Just west of downtown Nassau, this hotel is within easy reach of shops, restaurants, and historic sites of Bay Street, the main drag. The hotel's right across the street from the small but adequate Junkanoo Beach. If you're ready to hit a casino, head 3km (2 miles) northeast to Paradise Island's casino or 5km (3 miles) west to Cable Beach's casino.

The medium-sized bedrooms have a view of either the beach or Nassau Harbour, and they come with extras that you don't always find in a moderately priced choice, including alarm clocks, phones with two lines, and a desk. Bathrooms are a bit small. With diversions such as Nintendo on hand, the kid suites on the ground floor around the swimming pool are good for families; these rooms have a king-size bed, plus a second (small, windowless) room with bunk beds. The hotel boasts two unheated freshwater pools, one small and one large. The on-site Bay Street Grille is not

reason alone to stay here, although the setting is pleasant — you dine outside in a tropical courtyard overlooking the pool.

*See map p. 134. W. Bay Street (across the street from the beach, on the edge of
downtown Nassau).* ☎ **242-356-0000.** *Fax: 242-323-1408. Rack rates: $154 double,
$182 suite. AE, DISC, MC, V.*

One&Only Ocean Club
$$$$$ Paradise Island

Tucked away on the quiet eastern side of Paradise Island, this elegant colo-
nial-style resort is as understated as the Atlantis is extravagant. For class
and style, nothing matches it on the island. In a past life, Ocean Club was
the private estate of A&P grocery-chain heir Huntington Hartford. The
resort stretches from a white sandy beach to the harbor side of the island.
At the core of the resort are formal terraced gardens, inspired by
Versailles, where stone steps, hand-laid rock ridges, and European bronze
and marble statues set off bougainvillea and hibiscus plants. Striking stone
arches of a 12th-century Augustinian cloister, which Hartford had shipped
from France and reassembled, overlook the gardens and the harbor.

Guest rooms are spacious, with views of the gardens or the beach and
ocean. All rooms come with patios or balconies, and some have king-size
mahogany four-poster beds, cane chairs, tall potted palms, hardwood
floors, and sisal rugs, plus luxurious private bathrooms. Every afternoon,
champagne and strawberries mysteriously appear in your room. The on-
site restaurants offer the finest hotel dining on Paradise Island — better
than the hotel dining rooms in Nassau or Cable Beach. Tennis courts, a
large, heated freshwater pool, and a spa are also on the premises. Take the
shuttle bus or a short walk to the 18-hole championship golf course.
Because Atlantis and Ocean Club share the same owners (Sun
International), Ocean Club guests have full access to all the facilities at
theme-park Atlantis (see its review earlier in this chapter). A courtesy bus
links Ocean Club to Atlantis.

See map p. 134. Ocean Club Drive. ☎ **800-321-3000** *or 242-363-2501. Fax: 242-
363-2424.* www.oneandonlyresorts.com. *Rack rates: $750–$860 double, from
$1,085 suite, from $6,000 villa. AE, MC, V.*

Orange Hill Beach Inn
$ Love Beach

This hotel, set on 3½ landscaped hillside acres, lies about 13km (8 miles)
west of Nassau and 1.5km (1 mile) east of Love Beach, which has great
snorkeling. It's perfect for those who want to escape the crowds and stay
in a quieter part of New Providence Island; it's easy to catch a cab or jitney
to Cable Beach or downtown Nassau. The welcoming owners, Judy and
Danny Lowe, an Irish-Bahamian partnership, jokingly refer to their opera-
tion as "Fawlty Towers Nassau."

This place was built as a private home in the 1920s and became a hotel in 1979 after the Lowes added more rooms and a swimming pool. The 33 rooms and apartments come in a variety of sizes, although most are small. The bathrooms, likewise, are small but well maintained. Each unit has a balcony or patio, and a few apartments are equipped with kitchenettes. Many of the guests are European, especially in summer. It has been renovated with updated furniture in the rooms, and bathrooms have been upgraded as well. On-site is a bar serving sandwiches and salads throughout the day, and a restaurant that offers simple but good dinners. Management here maintains regular jitney service, without charge, to and from the local grocery stores. Some units have kitchenettes.

W. Bay Street, just west of Blake Road (P.O. Box N-8583). ☎ *888-399-3698 or 242-327-7157. Fax: 242-327-5186.* www.orangehill.com. *Rack rates: $139 double, $146 apt.*

Radisson Cable Beach Resort
$$$–$$$$ Cable Beach

With a broad, white sandy beach and an extensive children's program, the Radisson resort is a good choice for families. Offering beach olympics, arts and crafts, treasure hunts, storytelling, and other well-supervised activities, the complimentary half- or full-day programs at Camp Junkanoo are open to children between the ages of 4 and 11. Children under age 12 stay free, with one or two adults. The Radisson's tropical waterscape features five freshwater swimming pools and also includes rock formations, waterfalls, and whirlpools.

Some 700 guest rooms in two nine-story wings form a U that cups the pools and beautiful sandy shore. Views from lower floors showcase the gardens while higher rooms overlook the ocean. Bedrooms are modern and comfortable, with large windows, balconies, and a midsize bathroom. The hotel features a fitness center on the premises and a golf course is across the road. When you're not working out or teeing off, go snorkeling, scuba diving, sailing, or play some tennis. You can dine at several good restaurants and, at night, listen to live music at the hotel. If you prefer, however, you can head to the adjoining casino complex for other eats, shops, and entertainment.

See map p. 137. W. Bay Street (adjacent to the Crystal Palace Casino). ☎ *800-333-3333 or 242-327-6000. Fax: 242-327-6987.* www.radisson-cablebeach.com. *Rack rates: $175–$250 double, from $550–$950 suite. Rates are all-inclusive. AE, MC, V.*

Sandals Royal Bahamian Hotel
$$$$$ Cable Beach

Opening onto a white sand beach, this Jamaican chain member is a more upscale all-inclusive hotel than Breezes Bahamas. With its Romanesque statues, European spa, first-class restaurants, and two large, unheated freshwater pools surrounded by columns, Sandals Royal Bahamian is an elegant but more expensive alternative. A shuttle ride or a leisurely stroll west of the Crystal Palace Casino, the hotel is removed from the busiest section of Cable Beach. Sandals appeals to newlyweds, and many couples get married on the hotel's grounds. With romantic touches such as four-poster beds and luxurious bathrooms, the individual rooms, suites, and villas at Sandals are exclusively for couples.

As soon as you enter the lobby that's decked out in marble with chandeliers hanging from fresco-painted ceilings, you feel regal. You can spend a week here and splash in a different pool every single day. You can sail off to the hotel's private island, complete with its own pool and restaurant, or go snorkeling, scuba diving, or water-skiing. The cuisine at more than half a dozen restaurants ranges from home-style Bahamian and Japanese Teppanyaki to classic French and Northern Italian. Although the food is plentiful, entirely presentable, and prepared with first-rate ingredients, the Sandals kitchen never rises to the sublime. After dark, head to the theater for live performances by local bands, dancers, and other entertainers, or spend a quiet evening at the piano bar.

See map p. 137. W. Bay Street (a short drive or comfortable walk from the Crystal Palace Casino). ☎ *800-SANDALS or 242-327-6400. Fax: 242-327-6961.* www.sandals.com. *Rack rates: $4,760–$8,820 per couple for seven days in double room, including all meals, beverages, and activities. Minimum two-night stay. AE, DISC, MC, V.*

Sunrise Beach Club and Villas
$$$$–$$$$$ Paradise Island

This sprawling low-rise resort, drawing mostly European vacationers, is the kind of place you picture when you think of a tropical getaway. Narrow paths snake through the colorful grounds that are thick with palm trees, hibiscus, crotons, and bougainvillea. This property offers only 35 units for rent, so the atmosphere is far quieter than it is at Paradise Island resorts, such as Atlantis.

The one-, two-, and three-bedroom villas and town houses are set in different areas and have varying architectural styles and décor. Some units are tucked into the flourishing gardens, while the preferred ones overlook the two pools (one with a cave, waterfall, and children's wading section) or the sand beach. Cabbage Beach, one of the best beaches in The Bahamas, is only a short stroll to the east. Accommodations vary in size, but all have the same comfort level. A winding staircase may lead to the bedroom in your unit, or your master bathroom may sport a whirlpool tub. Glass and rattan, chrome, and stained glass highlight some accommodations, while others feature more hardwood. All come with kitchens — some larger, some smaller.

Living up to its name, the resort's Jungle Bar makes a scenic spot for a drink, a conch burger (a fried conch sandwich), or other light fare.

See map p. 134. Casino Drive. ☎ *800-451-6078 or 242-363-2234. Fax: 242-363-2308.* www.sunrisebeachclub.com. *Rack rates: $315–$365 one-bedroom apt, $551 two-bedroom apt. AE, MC, V.*

Wyndham Nassau Resort & Crystal Palace Casino
$$$$ Cable Beach

Adjacent to the casino that also adjoins the Radisson (which has a better beach), this large, sprawling hotel is an epic extravaganza. Without going outside, you can walk directly from the hotel towers to an array of restaurants, shops, and a fitness center. Most people hang out around the large, heated freshwater pool with its swirling aqua-slide. If you're traveling with kids, consider the modest children's program and playground.

The Wyndham doesn't have all the glitz of mega-resort Atlantis, but it is the island's second-largest hotel. With its rainbow-hued towers and wings, it's far flashier than the Radisson and is good for party-loving types. The hotel sells entertainment aggressively but houses you well in its accommodations towers, most of which are far enough away from the noisy public areas for light sleepers. We prefer the Casino Tower and Tower F because they have the grandest seafront vistas. You'll find some of the country's most lavish suites here, and you can live out your fantasies — for example, you can become Valentino in the Sheik-in-the-desert suite decorated for a sultan.

See map p. 137. W. Bay Street (neighboring the Radisson). ☎ **800-222-7466** *or 242-327-6200. Fax: 954-915-2929.* www.wyndhamnassauresort.com. *Parking: $5 valet, free self-parking. Rack rates: $179–$250 double, $250–$500 suite. AE, DC, MC, V.*

Chapter 12

Dining Out in New Providence

- -

In This Chapter

▶ Finding the best food beyond your hotel dining room
▶ Locating restaurants with island ambience

- -

*F*rom familiar fast-food chains to first-class international dining rooms, New Providence offers vacationers dozens of dining choices. The less-expensive places are in and around downtown Nassau, while the widest selection of expensive restaurants is on Paradise Island. What you won't find are restaurants devoted to a healthy cuisine, although almost every dining room offers dishes that would win the approval of your doctor.

Getting a Taste for New Providence

You have a choice of three areas for dining: Nassau, Paradise Island, and Cable Beach. Most visitors patronize the Nassau restaurants during the day while on shopping and sightseeing jaunts, preferring to dine at Cable Beach and Paradise Island in the evening.

Nassau can be dangerous after dark because of muggings. However, a few restaurants in Nassau, such as **Chez Willie,** are so special that you may want to dine there. In that case, take a taxi to the restaurant. When you finish dinner, have the staff summon a cab to return you safely to your hotel.

First-class restaurants always require reservations, especially during the winter months.

Most restaurants host happy hour (actually two or three hours starting around 5 p.m.), which is a good time to sample whatever tropical rum-based concoction the establishment features. Dining rooms often close between meals, but fast-food joints can satisfy your hunger. A few restaurants in the casino complexes don't allow young children.

See Chapter 2 for details about local specialties and the Introduction for an explanation of the price categories we use.

Dining at Nassau's Best Restaurants

Bahamian Kitchen
$ Nassau BAHAMIAN

For real local flavor and a down-home taste, head to this little eatery next to Trinity Church. This restaurant is one of our favorite local dives, enjoying a popularity that exceeds Café Skan's (see the review later in this chapter). The Bahamian Kitchen is one of the best places to try that Bahamian delicacy, freshly made conch salad. Some of the other delights include *stew fish* (fish marinated in spices and vegetables), a creamy curried chicken, okra soup, or pea soup and dumplings. Most dishes come with peas and rice. If you want to eat like your Bahama mama may have cooked for you, try such fare as corned beef and grits, all served with johnnycake. Baked pork chops and grouper also appear on the menu. Nearly all dishes (except the lobster) are at the low end of the price scale below. If the weather is nice, you can order takeout and have a Bahamian picnic on the beach.

See map p. 148. Trinity Place, off Market Street. ☎ *242-325-0702. Lunch and dinner main courses: $10–$42. AE, MC, V. Open: Mon–Sat 11:30 a.m.–10 p.m.*

Buena Vista
$$$$$ Nassau CONTINENTAL

Only Graycliff and Sun and . . . (see reviews later in this chapter) do Continental cuisine better. For more than half a century, this two-story, 19th-century mansion has been a citadel of fine food, which diners enjoy by candlelight in mellow surroundings decorated with antique paintings. A pianist entertains softly in winter, recapturing the flavor of the early '40s when the Duke and Duchess of Windsor ran The Bahamas. In fair weather, request a table on the garden terrace and order the bartender's special: a rum punch with coconut milk. Meals are served on the kind of delicate china that your grandmother keeps locked behind glass in a cabinet. The cookery is natural, straightforward, and classic, making the best use of quality ingredients. Highlights include tender rack of lamb, roast duckling in a zesty orange sauce, stone crab with mustard sauce (our favorite), and an especially delectable filet mignon in a peppercorn sauce. Chefs prepare these dishes to perfection (if you like heavy sauces), although they hardly tax the imagination of the kitchen staff, who has been making them for years. Since 1946, the house's special dessert has been Mrs. Hauck's orange pancakes with a Grand Marnier sauce.

See map p. 148. Delancy and Meeting streets, behind the Roman Catholic cathedral, a block west of Government House. ☎ *242-322-2811. Reservations recommended.*

Jackets requested for men. Main courses: $28–$40; fixed-price dinner: $39–$49. AE, MC, V. Open: Mon–Sat 7–9:30 p.m.

Café Matisse
$$$ Nassau   INTERNATIONAL/NORTHERN ITALIAN

This century-old former private home is a local favorite, attracting both Bahamian government employees (it's right behind Parliament House) and visitors. The joint efforts of a Bahamian chef and his Italian-born wife result in a harmonious cuisine that reaches from the islands to the Mediterranean. The restaurant gets its name from the Matisse reproductions that hang on the walls. Café Matisse serves pizzas, including the best *frutti di mare* pie in town, topped with fresh local seafood. But the cuisine of Greg and Gabrielle Curry is far more advanced and challenging than that. You can open your meal with their savory curried shrimp with a fragrant jasmine rice or the best calamari in Nassau. Our favorite main courses are the cannelloni with lobster sauce and any of the grilled seafood dishes, which emerge just right — still juicy, not dried out.

If the smell of cigar smoke doesn't thrill you, steer clear of the second-floor veranda, where patrons puffing stogies and sipping pre- and post-dinner drinks fill the small tables. Happy hour runs from 5 to 7 p.m., and the restaurant has live jazz a couple of nights a week.

See map p. 148. Bank Lane at Bay Street, near Parliament Square. ☎ *242-356-7012. Reservations recommended. Lunch main courses: $14–$20; dinner main courses: $16–$35. AE, DISC, MC, V. Open: Tues–Sat noon to 3 p.m. and 6–10 p.m.*

Café Skan's
$ Downtown Nassau   BAHAMIAN/AMERICAN

Good, filling food that's easy on the wallet keeps this bustling cafe packed. Located across from the Straw Market, this establishment is more coffee shop than cafe. The food is just as substantial as what you'd get at a regular restaurant, although you can also drop in for lighter fare, such as sandwiches and burgers. Bahamians pile in here early in the morning to devour dishes like their mamas made for them, including corned beef and grits, *chicken souse* (chicken parts and vegetables in a seasoned broth), stew fish, and broiled grouper with johnnycake. Of course, you can have "the usual" — a stack of pancakes, fluffy omelets, and French toast. The chefs turn out savory conch fritters or conch chowder, Bahamian bean soup with dumplings, and rib-sticking pork chops. Everything is accompanied by generous side dishes, like peas and rice or macaroni and cheese. The cuisine has no pretense: It's just good, honest, straightforward food.

See map p. 148. Bay Street at Market Plaza, across the street from the Straw Market. ☎ *242-322-2486. Reservations not accepted. Breakfast: $4–$9; sandwiches: $6–$12; main-course platters: $6–$20. MC, V. Open: Mon–Thurs 7:30 a.m.–5 p.m.; Fri–Sat 7:30 a.m.–6 p.m.; Sun 7:30 a.m.–4 p.m.*

Nassau and Paradise Island Dining

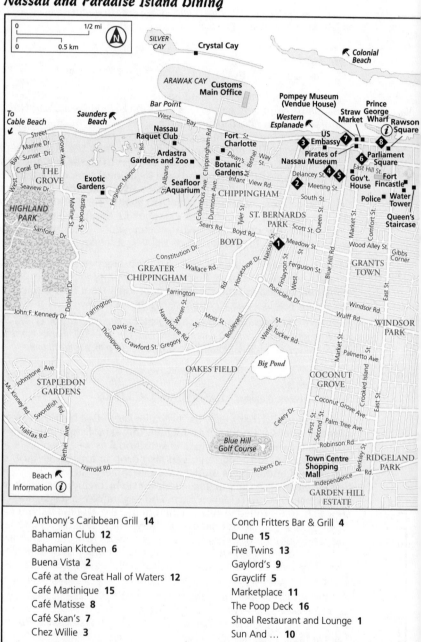

Anthony's Caribbean Grill **14**
Bahamian Club **12**
Bahamian Kitchen **6**
Buena Vista **2**
Café at the Great Hall of Waters **12**
Café Martinique **15**
Café Matisse **8**
Café Skan's **7**
Chez Willie **3**

Conch Fritters Bar & Grill **4**
Dune **15**
Five Twins **13**
Gaylord's **9**
Graycliff **5**
Marketplace **11**
The Poop Deck **16**
Shoal Restaurant and Lounge **1**
Sun And ... **10**

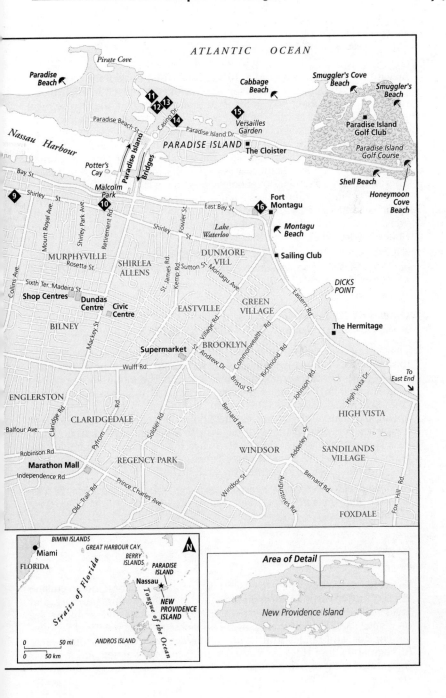

ATLANTIC OCEAN

Pirate Cove

Paradise Beach

Cabbage Beach

Smuggler's Cove Beach

Smuggler's Beach

11 12 13

Paradise Beach St

Casino Dr.

14

Paradise Island Dr.

15

Versailles Garden

Paradise Island Golf Club

Paradise Island Golf Course

Nassau Harbour

PARADISE ISLAND ▪ The Cloister

Shell Beach

Honeymoon Cove Beach

Bay St.

Potter's Cay

Paradise Island Bridges

Malcolm Park

10

9 Shirley St.

East Bay St.

16 Fort Montagu

Mount Royal Ave.

Shirley Park Ave.

Retirement Rd.

Shirley St.

Fowler St.

Lake Waterloo

Montagu Beach

Sailing Club

MURPHYVILLE

Rosetta St.

SHIRLEA ALLENS

St. James Rd.

Kemp Rd.

Sutton St.

DUNMORE VILL

Montagu Ave.

DICKS POINT

Collins Ave.

Sixth Ter. Madeira St.

Shop Centres

Dundas Centre

Civic Centre

EASTVILLE

GREEN VILLAGE

Eastern Rd.

To East End

BILNEY

Mackey St.

Village Rd.

BROOKLYN

Commonwealth Rd.

Richmond Rd.

The Hermitage

Supermarket

St. Andrew Dr.

Bristol St.

Johnson Rd.

High Vista Dr.

Wulff Rd.

Bernard Rd.

HIGH VISTA

ENGLERSTON

Claridge Rd.

CLARIDGEDALE

Soldier Rd.

Pyfrom Rd.

WINDSOR

Adderley St.

SANDILANDS VILLAGE

Balfour Ave.

Robinson Rd.

Marathon Mall

Independence Rd.

REGENCY PARK

Old Trail Rd.

Prince Charles Ave.

Windsor St.

Augustines Rd.

Bernard Rd.

Fox Hill Rd.

FOXDALE

BIMINI ISLANDS

GREAT HARBOUR CAY

BERRY ISLANDS

N

Miami

FLORIDA

Straits of Florida

PARADISE ISLAND

Nassau

NEW PROVIDENCE ISLAND

Tongue of the Ocean

ANDROS ISLAND

0   50 mi
0   50 km

Area of Detail

New Providence Island

Chez Willie
$$$$ **Nassau** FRENCH/BAHAMIAN

Elegant Nassau is recaptured at this charmer that evokes the days when the Duke and Duchess of Windsor were ruling the roost. On a fair night, opt for alfresco dining as you listen to piano music and admire the regal statuary in the courtyard. The host is Willie Armstrong, and his romantic spot is worth a journey into Nassau (take a taxi at night). Chefs imaginatively prepare tiptop foodstuffs or else follow classic recipes — perhaps delicate stone-crab claws in a Dijon mustard sauce or a fresh Bahamian tuna and crab mousse. Main courses are well-executed, including lobster Thermidor and a sautéed Dover sole in a tarragon-laced tomato sauce. The typical Bahamian grouper gets a fancy touch, encased in puff pastry with crabmeat and served with a creamy coconut sauce. Other classics are beef Wellington, a delicate chateaubriand, and a roast rack of lamb — the Duke's favorite dishes from the '40s.

See map p. 148. West Bay Street. ☎ *242-322-5364. Reservations recommended. Jacket preferred for men. Main courses: $30–$52; fixed-price menu for two: $60–$100 per person. AE, DISC, MC, V. Open: Daily 6:30–10 p.m.*

Conch Fritters Bar & Grill
$–$$ **Downtown Nassau** BAHAMIAN/AMERICAN

This casual bar and grill is the best place in the center of Nassau for you to sample conch in many variations, including not only the best conch fritters in town but also cracked conch, which is the mollusk's version of breaded veal cutlet. This is the first local restaurant you notice when coming in from Cable Beach to Nassau, and the eatery enjoys a mixed following of locals and visitors. If you don't like conch, try the excellent crispy fried chicken or that Florida favorite from the '50s — surf and turf. This is one of the places that offers guava duff, a famous Bahamian specialty, for dessert. The bright décor is enlivened by plants and wood parrots, and live music is presented on most nights.

See map p. 148. Marlborough Street, opposite the British Colonial Hilton. ☎ *242-323-8801. Burgers, sandwiches, and platters: $12–$38. AE, MC, V. Open: Daily 11 a.m.–11 p.m.*

Gaylord's
$$ **Nassau** INDIAN

For a change of pace, come to Gaylord's for some of the best Indian cuisine in Nassau. This restaurant is in a distinctive 19th-century building, and inside, silk drapes the ceilings, decorative brass plates and sculpture are on display, and Indian music plays. The menu includes plenty of vegetarian choices, and ranges from mild, creamy *kormas* (balls of ground meat or vegetables in a thick, seasoned sauce) to bold curries and *tandoori* (marinated meat or fish cooked in a clay oven) main courses. Along with lamb, beef, chicken, and fish, you're likely to find the inevitable conch worked into the selections. Tandoori conch was a first for us, and it's a tasty way to prepare this mollusk. Vegetable *samosas* (pastries filled with curried vegetables or meat) make good starters. We can make a meal just out of the freshly baked breads alone, especially when they're filled with flavored onions or cheese. For dessert, try the carrot pudding.

See map p. 148. Dowdeswell Street, in front of Princess Margaret Hospital. ☎ 242-356-3004. Reservations recommended. Main courses: $14–$35; vegetarian dinner: $23. AE, MC, V. Open: Mon–Sat noon to 3 p.m. and daily 6:30–11 p.m.

Graycliff
$$$$$ Nassau   CONTINENTAL

Opposite Government House, Graycliff is in the most atmospheric mansion in Nassau and is far more elegant than Buena Vista. This restaurant — where you should dress in your most formal resort wear — is no longer "the tops" in The Bahamas, a position it held for years. Sun and . . . , for example, offers even better food. But for the allure of yesterday, Graycliff still ranks high. You can order a drink on the balcony bar or ask for a table on the cool terrace, while listening to the soft piano tunes of Coward, Gershwin, and Cole Porter. The cuisine is basically the type that pleased gourmets in decades past before the "revolution" came: perfectly grilled and choice steaks, lobster Graycliff in a white-wine medora sauce, plump juicy pheasant in a pineapple sauce, and grouper in a Dijon mustard sauce. It's all served up in an antique-filled setting with elegant china and old English silverware. Graycliff continues to attract diners whose big night out involves the consumption of Iranian caviar, fine brandy, a Grand Marnier soufflé, Cuban cigars, and a selection from a *carte* of some 175,000 wine bottles.

See map p. 148. West Hill Street and Blue Hill Road, across from Government House. ☎ 242-322-2796. Reservations required. Jackets advised for men for dinner. Lunch main courses: $22–$32; dinner main courses: $38–$52. AE, MC, V. Open: Mon–Fri noon to 3 p.m. and daily 6:30–10 p.m.

The Poop Deck
$$–$$$ Nassau   BAHAMIAN/SEAFOOD

Even if this place didn't serve good food (which it does!), we'd still hang out here at night. We're drawn to its open-air, waterside location with a panoramic view of the marina — which lights up at night near the bridge to Paradise Island. In such a setting, only a nautical atmosphere with seafaring artifacts will do. The food is straightforward and prepared with fresh ingredients — perfect for The Poop Deck's beer-drinking, cigarette-smoking, sports-loving devotees. We recommend the crab-stuffed mushrooms to start, and as an entree, the Bahamian steamed chicken, flavored with tomatoes, onions, and sweet peppers in the Creole style, and accompanied with mango salsa and sweet-potato fish cakes. The cracked lobster, which is batter-coated and sautéed, lures in many a diner. The burgers and sandwiches make a satisfying lunch. The chef's version of the celebrated guava duff is the best we've sampled in New Providence.

To sit at one of the best tables (at the edge of the balcony), get here just before noon for lunch or 5 p.m. for dinner. Don't come alone, though, because single diners aren't seated at these front tables.

See map p. 148. East Bay Street, next to Nassau Yacht Haven. ☎ *242-393-8175. Reservations recommended. Lunch main courses: $10–$25; dinner main courses: $18–$29. AE, DC, DISC, MC, V. Open: Daily noon to 4:30 p.m. and 5–10:30 p.m.*

Shoal Restaurant and Lounge
$–$$ **Nassau   BAHAMIAN**

This restaurant is one we return to again and again, although its food is only slightly better than the grub served at other local favorites, such as Conch Fritters or Café Skan's. At times, the chefs at all these local dives seem to use the same recipes handed down from generations. We like to go truly Bahamian here and drop in for breakfast with friends to sample *boil fish,* cooked with salt pork, onions, and green peppers. This dish is always served with johnnycake. Chicken souse is a real morning eye-opener, but it may be strictly for devotees, not for the faint of heart. We asked our waiter what it's made with. He advised, "You wouldn't want to know. Just eat and enjoy." When we go to this no-frills restaurant at night, we order the crawfish salad or the steamed conch. Of course, the menu always features steak and lobster, too. Dishes come with fried plantains and mounds of peas and rice. Once very scarce on menus, guava duff is now almost a mandatory offering at every restaurant, and a sublime version is offered here as well. The restaurant will provide transportation to and from your hotel. You'll need all the help you can get returning to your hotel if you down several of the bartender's lethal Bahama Mamas.

See map p. 148. Nassau Street, near the College of the Bahamas. ☎ *242-323-4400. Main courses: $9.50–$17. AE, DISC, MC, V. Open: Fri 7:30 a.m.–6 p.m.; Sat 6–11 p.m.; Sun–Thurs 7:30 a.m.–11 p.m.*

Sun and . . .
$$$–$$$$ **Nassau   CONTINENTAL**

Nassau's finest fare, even better than that of Graycliff or Buena Vista, is served by candlelight on a patio by a rock pool. This world-class restaurant is a classic citadel of refined cuisine and service offered with an overlay of English colonial charm. An Iberian-style courtyard, complete with fountains and a drawbridge, sets the romantic aura. Chefs prepare the exceptional ingredients with a finely honed technique. We can't predict what will be on the menu when you visit, but if we awarded stars for grand cuisine, we'd give them to the chef's smoked moulard duck breasts or the duck-stuffed ravioli with porcini mushrooms. Focus on the absolutely sensational boiled lobster or the classic roast spring lamb, which is almost melt-in-your-mouth tender. The soufflés are incomparable. Most diners opt for the Grand Marnier soufflé, but our favorite is the soufflé with rum raisins and Black Label Bacardi.

See map p. 148. Lakeview Road off Shirley Street. ☎ *242-393-1205. Reservations recommended. Jackets requested for men. Main courses: $32–$48. AE, DISC, MC, V. Open: Tues–Sun 6:30– 9 p.m. Closed Aug–Sept.*

Checking Out Paradise Island's Best Restaurants

Anthony's Caribbean Grill
$$ Paradise Island   AMERICAN/CARIBBEAN

Near the Atlantis Resort and Comfort Suites, this laid-back tropical spot offers a pleasant alternative to hotel dining rooms. Brightly decorated with Bahamian artwork, Anthony's features an extensive menu that includes familiar but well-prepared dishes that never achieve greatness but are full of flavor, seasoning, and spice. For a taste of the islands, we go for the peppery jerk chicken on a bed of multicolored pasta, known as "Rasta pasta." Named after the music of The Bahamas, the 20-ounce Junkanoo steak with well-seasoned vegetables is only for the trencherman. The ribs sizzle in their salsa laced with coconut and mango. But in general, this restaurant is like an upscale TGI Fridays, serving the usual array of pizzas (though some are studded with lobster), burgers, and fried chicken. The bartender is known for his 48-ounce sparklers, with rum, vodka, amaretto, and fruit punch. "With two of these," the bartender assured us, "we'll carry you out on a stretcher."

See map p. 148. Casino Drive, across from Comfort Suites. ☎ *242-363-3152. Lunch platters: $8–$15; dinner: $11–$39. AE, DISC, MC, V. Open: Daily 7:30 a.m.–11 p.m.*

Bahamian Club
$$$$ Paradise Island   FRENCH/INTERNATIONAL

Within the sprawling mega-resort of the Atlantis, this restaurant is a rather chic dining room imbued with the aura of the days of British colonialism. No place in either New Providence or Paradise Island serves such good cuts of meat, especially T-bone steaks and perfectly roasted prime rib. Diners come here in search of robust flavors. The menu features classics such as broiled lobster, Dover sole, and salmon steak. You may begin your meal with a fresh jumbo shrimp cocktail or a salad of baby spinach leaves. Even though the restaurant imports its main ingredients, they don't taste that way after the skilled chefs work their magic in the kitchen.

See map p. 148. In the Coral Towers of the Atlantis Resort. ☎ *242-363-3000. Reservations required. Main courses: $38–$50. AE, DC, DISC, MC, V. Open: Wed–Mon 6–11 p.m.*

Café at the Great Hall Of Waters
$$$$$ **Paradise Island**   **INTERNATIONAL**

This restaurant gives you a splashy look at the water wonderland of the Atlantis Resort, even if you're not a guest of the hotel. Paradise Island has better restaurants, notably Five Twins (reviewed later in this chapter), but none are this dramatic. You feel like a scuba diver as you look through gigantic picture windows that display the illuminated "ruins" of the lost city of Atlantis. Everywhere you look, rainbow-hued fish swim past stone "archaeological" remains, and rows of lobsters parade through the sand. The restaurant offers a kids' menu, and little ones love taking walks along the aquarium walls between courses. In such a setting, the food becomes almost secondary, although it's quite good. Lobster is a specialty, but you can also order well-prepared versions of crab legs or grilled salmon. The chefs import top-quality ingredients, such as lamb, and work their magic with it. Desserts are uniformly luscious.

See map p. 148. In the Royal Towers of the Atlantis Resort. ☎ *242-363-3000. Reservations required. Main courses: $30–$50. AE, DC, MC, V. Open: Thurs–Mon 7–11 a.m., 11:30 a.m.–2:30 p.m., and 6–10 p.m.*

Café Martinique
$$$$$ **Paradise Island**   **FRENCH**

The most elegant and upscale restaurant on Paradise Island lies adjacent to the Marina Village restaurant and shopping compound that's associated with the Atlantis Paradise Island. This mixture of *haute* Paris with a French Colonial twist is enormously appealing. A wrought-iron "birdcage" elevator hauls you and your party upstairs to the tastefully posh dining area, where masses of flowers, trolleys laden with cheeses and dessert, and the cuisine of superchef Jean-Georges Vongerichten await your pleasure. This is one of the very few dining areas at Atlantis where men are asked to wear jackets. Begin with such delectable items as foie gras, caviar, or smoked salmon. The main courses are limited, but each dish is sublime, especially the lobster Thermidor and the Dole sole meunière. The chefs are known for their grills, everything from prime rib for two to a succulent veal chop.

See map p. 148. In the Marina Village at the Atlantis Paradise Island, Casino Drive. ☎ *242-363-3000. Reservations required. Main courses: $31–$75. AE, DC, DISC, MC, V. Open hours vary with the season and occupancy levels of the hotel, but usually daily 6–11 p.m.*

Dune
$$$$ **Paradise Island**   **INTERNATIONAL**

One of the most sophisticated and cutting-edge restaurants on Paradise Island is in the west wing of the lobby level of the Ocean Club. It has a charcoal gray and black décor that looks like it was plucked directly from a chic enclave in Milan; a sweeping view of the ocean; a teakwood floor that evokes a yacht's; and very attentive service. Near the restaurant's entrance is a thriving herb garden from which many of the culinary flavorings are derived. The chefs here invariably select the very finest ingredients, which are then handled with a razor-sharp technique. Every dish has a special something, such as shrimp dusted with orange powder and served with artichokes and arugula. Other splendid choices are tuna spring rolls with soybean salsa, or chicken-and-coconut milk soup served with shiitake cakes. The goat cheese-and-watermelon salad is an unexpected delight. Filet of grouper — that standard throughout The Bahamas — is at its savory best here, served with a zesty tomato sauce.

See map p. 148. In the One&Only Ocean Club. ☎ *242-363-2501, ext. 64739. Reservations required. Main courses lunch: $12–$25; dinner: $22–$50. AE, DC, DISC, MC, V. Daily 7–11 a.m., noon to 3 p.m., and 6–10:30 p.m.*

Five Twins
$$$$$ Paradise Island ASIAN/SEAFOOD

Save this dining mecca for a special evening. While a singer croons smooth melodies, you can eat by candlelight on fine china, either inside or outside on a terrace that overlooks the marina. Attracting high rollers from the nearby casino, this restaurant is the best in the Atlantis's massive gambling-and-entertainment complex. The Thai-Japanese-Indonesian cuisine is contemporary Pacific Rim with a European flair. Color, texture, artistic presentation and, of course, flavor play major roles in each dish, whether you choose freshly caught grouper, snapper, shrimp, or lobster. You can start with nuanced chilled oysters with apple slaw or a pepper-cured salmon with vegetable tempura. The restaurant also features a sushi bar as well as a separate upscale rum-and-cigar lounge. After dinner, a DJ spins party tunes from a booth suspended above the dance floor. Children under age 12 aren't allowed in the restaurant.

See map p. 148. In the Casino complex of the Atlantis Resort. ☎ *242-363-3000. Reservations recommended. Main courses: $40–$60. AE, MC, V. Open: Daily 6–10:30 p.m., with a sushi and satay bar open daily 6:30–11 p.m.*

Marketplace
$$$$ Paradise Island INTERNATIONAL

Decorated with old vases and terra-cotta tiles, this large buffet-style restaurant is reminiscent of a sprawling market. The food is fresh, but it's a mass feeding station. You go here to fill up, not to find food as good as that at Conch Fritters Bar & Grill — still, this is the finest buffet on Paradise Island. Before you start loading your plate, browse the various cooking stations and do some strategic planning. From fresh fruit to omelets, you can make breakfast as light or as heavy as you want. At lunch and dinner, you can find everything from fresh seafood and made-to-order pastas to freshly carved roast beef and lamb. No intimate affair, this place seats some 400 diners. Sit inside or on the patio overlooking a lagoon.

See map p. 148. In the Royal Towers of the Atlantis Resort. ☎ *242-363-3000. Reservations recommended. Full buffets: $24–$51. AE, DC, MC, V. Open: Daily 7–11 a.m., noon to 3 p.m., and 5:30–10 p.m.*

Dining at Cable Beach's Best Restaurants

The Black Angus Grill
$$$$ **Cable Beach STEAK**

The casino crowd flocks to this popular restaurant. Beef is the star of the show, but poultry and seafood play supporting roles. Because Bahamian cattle farms don't exist, the restaurant imports frozen meat. The meat is always juicy, however, and the chef knows how particular some carnivores are. So, rare means rare, medium-rare means medium-rare, and you won't see any pink if you ask for your meat well-done, whether you order prime rib, filet mignon, or a T-bone steak. If you want both seafood and meat, you can order the surf and turf — the lobster tail is sweet and plump. Another good choice is the chicken carbonara (made with Parmesan cheese, bacon, garlic, and white wine).

See map p. 157. On the second level of the casino complex of the Wyndham Nassau Resort & Crystal Palace Casino. ☎ *242-327-6200. Main courses: $26–$55. AE, DC, DISC, MC, V. Open: Daily 6–11 p.m.*

Café Johnny Canoe
$–$$ **Cable Beach BAHAMIAN/INTERNATIONAL**

This brightly decorated eatery is so wild and festive that at first, you may think it's just a tourist trap. It's obviously geared toward visitors, but the island cuisine is very authentic and full of regional flavor. Enjoy familiar favorites such as light pancakes and fluffy omelets, or on Saturday and Sunday, try old-fashioned Bahamian recipes, including tuna and grits, boil fish, or stewed conch (each served with johnnycakes). For substantial Bahamian fare, you can devour the classic cracked conch with peas and rice or enjoy the grilled mahimahi with macaroni and cheese. The icing on the cake, so to speak, is the guava duff for dessert. On Friday at 8 p.m., a Junkanoo band performs, turning the place into a carnival.

See map p. 157. West Bay Street, in front of the Nassau Beach Hotel. ☎ *242-327-3373. Breakfast: $6–$14; salads, sandwiches, and lunch and dinner platters $10–$30. DISC, MC, V. Open: Sun–Thurs 7:30 a.m.–11 p.m.; Fri–Sat 7:30 a.m.–midnight.*

Sole Mare
$$$$ **Cable Beach NORTHERN ITALIAN**

Overlooking the ocean from the second level of the casino complex in the Wyndham Nassau Resort & Crystal Palace Casino, Sole Mare is one of the most elegant choices in Cable Beach. Guests enjoy admirable Northern Italian cuisine served at candlelit tables with soft guitar music playing in the background. Some claim "you can't eat good Italian in The Bahamas," but Sole Mare proves them wrong with such standout dishes as pasta with lobster and shrimp sautéed in garlic olive oil and white wine. The veal

Cable Beach Dining

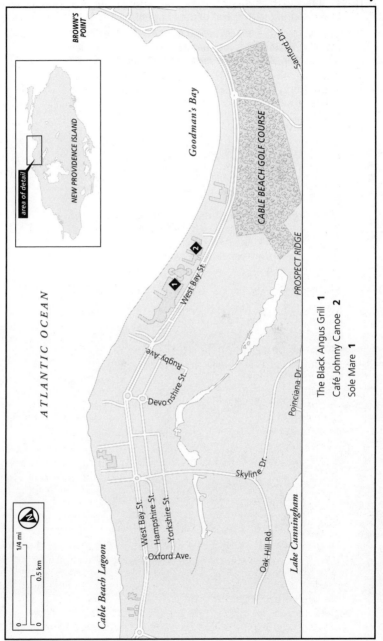

The Black Angus Grill **1**

Café Johnny Canoe **2**

Sole Mare **1**

sautéed with endive, capers, and white wine makes another enticing choice, along with the al dente cappellini with a zesty tomato sauce.

See map p. 157. In the Wyndham Nassau Resort & Crystal Palace Casino. ☎ *242-327-6200. Reservations required. Jackets preferred for men. Main courses: $35–$70. AE, DC, DISC, MC, V. Open: Tues–Sat 6–11 p.m. (hours may vary; call ahead).*

Chapter 13

Having Fun On and Off the Beach in New Providence

● ●

In This Chapter

▶ Catching some rays on New Providence's best beaches

▶ Enjoying the island's watersports

▶ Exploring land attractions, shopping, and nightlife

▶ Taking two great day trips

● ●

*N*ew Providence offers more action, both wet and dry, than anywhere else in The Bahamas. Watersports — from scuba diving and snorkeling to Jet-Skiing and parasailing — keep vacationers entertained when they aren't playing golf or tennis, horseback riding, mountain biking, or just strolling the streets of downtown Nassau. In this chapter, we present the hottest nightlife, the widest selection of duty-free shops and designer boutiques, and the best human-made attractions — from botanical gardens to intriguing museums.

Combing the Beaches

Although mega-resorts discourage non-guests from relaxing on their beaches, you can find plenty of unmarked, unnamed public beaches on New Providence and Paradise Island.

Beaches that are absolutely accessible to the public are

✔ **Cabbage Beach:** On Paradise Island, this beach is a real showcase. Its broad, white sands stretch for at least 3km (2 miles). Casuarines, palms, and sea grapes border it. This beach draws crowds in winter, but you can find a little more elbow room by walking to the northwestern stretch of the beach. You can reach Paradise Island from downtown Nassau by walking over the bridge, taking a taxi, or boarding a ferry at Prince George Dock. Cabbage Beach doesn't have public bathroom facilities, but you can patronize one of the handful of bars and restaurants nearby and use its facilities. Technically, you are a customer even if you buy only one soft drink.

Fun in New Providence

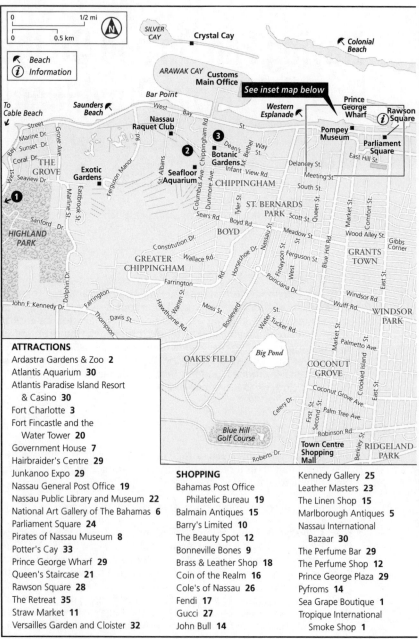

ATTRACTIONS
Ardastra Gardens & Zoo **2**
Atlantis Aquarium **30**
Atlantis Paradise Island Resort
  & Casino **30**
Fort Charlotte **3**
Fort Fincastle and the
  Water Tower **20**
Government House **7**
Hairbraider's Centre **29**
Junkanoo Expo **29**
Nassau General Post Office **19**
Nassau Public Library and Museum **22**
National Art Gallery of The Bahamas **6**
Parliament Square **24**
Pirates of Nassau Museum **8**
Potter's Cay **33**
Prince George Wharf **29**
Queen's Staircase **21**
Rawson Square **28**
The Retreat **35**
Straw Market **11**
Versailles Garden and Cloister **32**

SHOPPING
Bahamas Post Office
  Philatelic Bureau **19**
Balmain Antiques **15**
Barry's Limited **10**
The Beauty Spot **12**
Bonneville Bones **9**
Brass & Leather Shop **18**
Coin of the Realm **16**
Cole's of Nassau **26**
Fendi **17**
Gucci **27**
John Bull **14**

Kennedy Gallery **25**
Leather Masters **23**
The Linen Shop **15**
Marlborough Antiques **5**
Nassau International
  Bazaar **30**
The Perfume Bar **29**
The Perfume Shop **12**
Prince George Plaza **29**
Pyfroms **14**
Sea Grape Boutique **1**
Tropique International
  Smoke Shop **1**

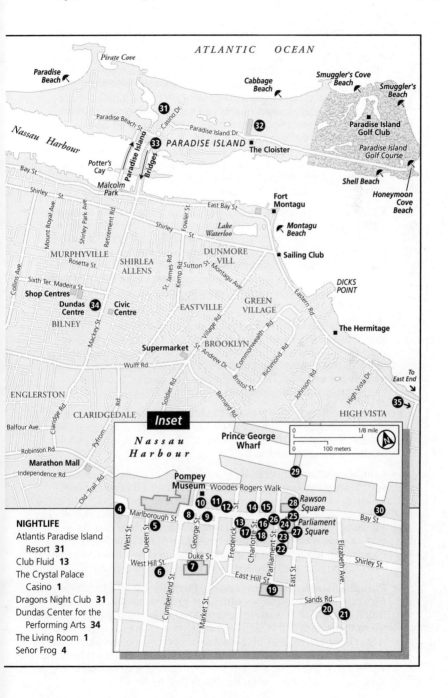

NIGHTLIFE

Atlantis Paradise Island Resort **31**

Club Fluid **13**

The Crystal Palace Casino **1**

Dragons Night Club **31**

Dundas Center for the Performing Arts **34**

The Living Room **1**

Señor Frog **4**

✔ **Cable Beach:** The name "Cable Beach" refers to a string of resorts and beaches that lie in the center of New Providence's northern coast. This beachfront is the most popular area in The Bahamas. It offers 7km (4 miles) of soft, white sand, and the hotels that line the waterfront offer diverse restaurants, snack bars, and watersports. Calypso music floats to the sand from hotel pool patios, where vacationers play musical chairs and see how low they can limbo. Vendors wind their way between sunblock-slathered bodies. Some sell armloads of shell jewelry, T-shirts, beach cover-ups, and fresh coconuts. Others offer their hair-braiding services or sign up visitors for water-skiing, Jet-Skiing, and banana-boat rides. Kiosks advertise parasailing, scuba diving, and snorkeling trips, as well as party cruises to offshore islands.

Waters can be rough and reefy, but a little farther along the shore, they can be calm and clear. Because guests of the resorts use their hotel facilities, no public restrooms are available here. (If you're not a guest of the hotel, you're not supposed to use the facilities.) The Cable Beach resorts begin 5km (3 miles) west of downtown Nassau. Even though resorts line much of this long swath of beach, the public can access various sections of the beach without crossing private hotel grounds.

✔ **Caves Beach:** On the north shore, past the Cable Beach properties, Caves Beach lies some 11km (7 miles) west of Nassau. It stands near Rock Point, right before the turnoff along Blake Road that leads to the airport. Most visitors don't know of this place, so it's usually not crowded. This beach has soft sands. No toilets or changing facilities are available here.

✔ **Delaporte Beach:** Just west of the busiest section of Cable Beach, Delaporte Beach is another public-access beach where you can escape the crowds. It opens onto clear waters and boasts white sands, although it has no toilets or changing facilities.

✔ **Goodman's Bay:** This public beach is east of Cable Beach on the way toward the center of Nassau. Goodman's Bay and Saunders Beach (see review later in this section) often host local fundraising cookouts where vendors sell fish, chicken, conch, peas and rice, or macaroni and cheese. People swim and socialize to blaring reggae and calypso music. To find out when one of these beach parties is happening, ask the staff at your hotel or pick up a local newspaper. This beach has a playground, plus toilets.

✔ **Paradise Beach:** This gem is one of Paradise Island's best beaches. *Chikees* (thatched huts) — which are great when you've had too much sun — dot this white sandy beach. It lies at the far western tip of the island, and is largely populated with guests of the Atlantis. If you're not a resident of the Atlantis, getting access to the beach is difficult. If you're staying at a hotel in Nassau and want to come to Paradise Island for a day at the beach, you're better off going to Cabbage Beach (see earlier review in this section).

✔ **Saunders Beach:** This beach, located east of Cable Beach, is where many islanders go on the weekends. To reach it, take West Bay Street from Nassau in the direction of Coral Island. This beach lies across from Fort Charlotte, just west of Arawak Cay. Like Goodman's Bay (see review earlier in this section), it often hosts fun local fundraising cookouts that are open to the public. This beach doesn't have any public facilities.

✔ **Western Esplanade (also called Junkanoo Beach):** If you're staying at a hotel in downtown Nassau, such as the British Colonial, this is a good nearby beach to visit. It's a narrow strip of sand and has a snack bar, changing facilities, and toilets.

Playing in the Surf

Most water action jumps off from **Cable Beach, Paradise Beach,** and **Prince George Dock** in downtown Nassau. For a change of scenery, many folks board tour boats to **Blue Lagoon Island** and **Rose Island,** two popular cays just offshore.

Jet-Skiing, parasailing, banana-boat rides, water-skiing, and windsurfing are available on the beaches in front of Cable Beach and Paradise Island hotels. In many cases, however, independent vendors who aren't affiliated with the hotels run these sports, which means that the resorts aren't responsible for any problems that may arise.

Snorkeling and parasailing

If you want shallow diving and snorkeling without having to go out on a boat, New Providence Island offers dozens of possibilities. Our favorite spot is **Love Beach,** near the Compass Point hotel. Also attracting snorkelers are such scenic areas as **Rose Island Reefs, Booby Rock Channel,** and **Gambier Deep Reef,** plus some underwater wrecks lying in shallow water.

In the western part of the island, the nature reserve at offshore **Gouldings Reef Cay** offers some of the best snorkeling on the island, and it's never crowded. You can see some of the most majestic elkhorn coral in all of The Bahamas.

Excursions by boat take you to the best and most dramatic snorkeling sites — sites that are more impressive than what you can do yourself off the coast. **Barefoot Sailing Cruises** (☎ 242-393-0820; www.barefoot sailingcruises.com) is based at **Bayshore Marina,** on East Bay Street near the Paradise Island bridge. Their 12m (41-ft.) sailboat takes no more than 16 passengers; their 17m (56-ft.) sailboat holds a maximum of 30, and their 20m (65-ft.) catamaran accommodates 65. The size and type of boat that you sail on depends on the number of people booked on any given day. A half-day snorkel sail to **Atoll Island** or **Spruce Cay** runs

$55 per person, including beverages and snacks; the full-day trip costs $89 with lunch.

Another good choice is **Flying Cloud** (☎ 242-393-4430), which is based at the ferry terminal on Paradise Island. This 17m (57-ft.) catamaran takes a maximum of 50 passengers. Snorkeling cruises go to **Rose Island** for a half-day of fun that costs $55 per person; a two-and-half-hour sunset cruise costs $50 per person. Snorkel gear and lessons, if necessary, are included in the price, along with transportation to and from your accommodations.

Parasailing is another exhilarating sport. You're strapped to a parachute that's tied with a long leash to a boat. As the boat takes off, you float gently into the air as if you're flying. Independent operators along Cable Beach and Paradise Island Beach charge about $40 for eight to ten minutes in the sky.

Scuba diving

If you visit any of the Out Islands, you may want to save your underwater scuba time for those less-visited reefs. The waters around New Providence offer excellent dive sites, but too many scuba divers may be admiring all the tropical fish, huge sponges, and varied coral reefs around the dramatic caves, cliffs, ocean holes, ledges, and wrecks.

On New Providence Island, **Southwest Reef** lures scuba divers with its giant coral heads that stand in anywhere from 4 to 8m (12–25 ft.) of water, with staghorn corals and elkhorn along with rainbow-hued fish.

Another great dive site is **Shark Wall,** lying 16km (10 miles) off the coast, along with such sites as **Razorback, Booby Rock Reef,** and **Rose Island Reef.** Dive outfitters can also lead you to the many old **shipwrecks** off the coast, along with caves and cliffs. Wrecks include *Mahoney* and *Alcora,* and the wreck used in the James Bond film, *Never Say Never Again.* Divers also explore the airplane propeller used in another Bond film, *Thunderball.*

Neophytes can take a quickie "resort course," also known as a beginner's class (about $89). Full-certification courses run anywhere from $499 to $695. Plan to pay about $89 for a two-tank dive, $55 to $65 for a night dive, and $110 to $130 for a shark dive. Most operators sell you a videotape of your aqua-action for about $50, and they transport you to and from your hotel.

With more than three decades of experience, **Bahama Divers** (☎ 242-393-5644), at the Nassau Yacht Haven by the bottom of the Paradise Island bridge, is Nassau's oldest and most reliable company.

Even if you're not a scuba diver, you and your kids can still breathe underwater. Try helmet diving with **Hartley's Undersea Walk** (☎ 242-393-8234; www.underseawalk.com) at the **Nassau Yacht Haven** on East

Bay Street. During this three-and-a-half-hour excursion (about $75), you take a 30-minute boat ride out to a reef. After donning a lead and glass helmet, you descend a ladder into 4 to 5m (12–15 ft.) of water. Air is pumped into the helmet through a long tube. You can keep your glasses on or your contact lenses in, because your face and hair stay completely dry. Following the instructions of your guide, you spend about 20 minutes wandering in slow motion around the ocean floor, past crayon-colored sea plants, corals, and fish. To secure your reservation, arrive 30 minutes before your scheduled departure time.

Climbing Aboard

You can experience Bahamian waters and marine life firsthand without getting wet. But remember that these are Atlantic waters, not the tranquil Caribbean Sea, and the waves can be rough at times, causing seasickness for those who aren't used to it.

Sailing

For the best sailing charter to some of the Out Islands, try **Amarok Sailing Charters** (☎ 719-379-4605 or 242-477-4471). The crewed 12m (41-ft.) Amarok ketch carries up to six passengers and specializes in six-day trips to the Exumas, which are about five hours from Nassau. The trip costs from $1,800 per couple. You can read more about the Exumas in Chapter 24.

For a shorter sailing adventure, **Barefoot Sailing Cruises** (☎ 242-393-0820) offers a two-hour champagne sunset cruise ($39, including cold hors d'oeuvres). You sail through Nassau Harbour, under the bridges, into Montagu Bay, by the cruise ships, and maybe along the northern coast of Paradise Island. You can munch cheese and crackers as you sip your bubbly, and you don't need to dress up — many passengers wear shorts. The price includes ground transportation. Depending on the number of vacationers booked, you may cruise on a 12m (41-ft.) sailboat carrying no more than 16 passengers or a 16m (54-ft.) sailboat taking a maximum of 30.

Flying Cloud (☎ 242-393-4430) carries up to 50 passengers on its 17m (57-ft.) catamaran. Depending on the time of year that you go, the two-and-a-half-hour evening cruise takes in the setting sun ($45, including hot and cold hors d'oeuvres). During the three-hour dinner cruise ($50), you can chow down on soup, salad, fish, beef, rice, vegetables, and dessert, served with wine. All rates cover transportation to and from your hotel.

When comparing Barefoot Sailing Cruises and Flying Cloud, we find cruises aboard Barefoot more adventurous and fun, especially when the passengers are few. For a real sailing experience, book on a sailboat instead of the larger catamaran. If the catamarans are crowded, you may feel like you're riding on a cattle boat, especially with all the eating and drinking. On a sailboat, the atmosphere is more romantic, and the night is yours.

Another option is **Majestic Tours Ltd.** (☎ 242-322-2606), which books three-hour cruises on two of the biggest catamarans in the Atlantic. These tours offer views of the water, sun, sand, and outlying reefs. The downside of these cruise boats is the large number of passengers aboard. The upside is that they're affordable and the most professionally run. The *Yellow Bird* carries up to 250 passengers and departs from Prince George's Dock; ask for the exact departure point when you make your reservation. The cost is $25 per adult, $12 for children under 10; snorkeling equipment is $12 extra. The outfitter has another boat, the *Robinson Crusoe,* which holds 350 passengers. On Wednesday, Friday, and Sunday, cruises run from 10 a.m. to 4:30 p.m.; adults cost $50 per person and children 11 and under are half price. Sunset dinner cruises are on Tuesday and Friday from 7 to 10 p.m.; adults cost $55 per person and children are half price.

Dolphin diversions and other ocean adventures

Are dolphins really smiling? Why is their skin so warm and smooth? Can they understand each other's chatter? Find out the answers to these questions and many more during a **Dolphin Encounter** on **Blue Lagoon Island** (☎ 242-363-1003). This popular activity is often booked well in advance.

The Close Encounter program ($85) enables you to stand in shallow water and pet the dolphins, and the Swim with the Dolphins program ($165) lets you delve deeper. Both sessions last about three hours, including the boat ride to and from Blue Lagoon, a part of Salt Cay, which is about 5km (3 miles) northeast of Paradise Island.

Several tour operators take visitors to and from Blue Lagoon Island, but you can't book a Dolphin Encounter through all of them.

Some marine studies show that contrary to popular belief, dolphins don't like being touched by humans. So you can decide whether you want to interact with an animal that may not be enjoying your company.

Enjoying semi-submarine rides

To see coral reefs, you can take a ride in a semi-submarine. Contact **Seaworld Explorer** (☎ 242-356-2548) to board its 45-passenger semi-submersible observatory. The trip begins with a 15-minute catamaran ride and narrated tour along Nassau's coastline. Then you spend about an hour in the "sub." The vessel doesn't actually dive, but it does have windows that are about 3m (10 ft.) below the surface of the ocean, so you get close-up views of fish, coral, and a shipwreck. This 90-minute excursion takes you to **Sea Gardens Marine Park** and costs $37 for adults and $19 for children ages 3 to 12. You can arrange transportation between your hotel and the trip's starting point — Bay Street and Elizabeth Avenue in downtown Nassau — for an additional $3 each way.

Fishing for fun

Bahamian waters are thick with game fish, and some travelers spend every day of their vacations casting lines. The best time to fish for wahoo is from November to February; for blue marlin, June and July; and for bonito and blackfin tuna, May to August. For a half-day charter for two to six anglers, you can spend anywhere from $400 to $600 or, for a full day, $800 and up. If you want to join a group for a half-day (usually in the morning), you spend about $70 per person. Two of New Providence's best companies are **Born Free Charters** (☎ **242-363-4144;** www.born freefishing.com) and **Nassau Yacht Haven** (☎ **242-393-8173;** www. nassauyachthaven.com).

Exploring on Dry Land

Wandering the historic streets of Nassau is an adventure in itself. Seeing the sights from a horse-drawn carriage makes you feel as if you've been transported into the past. From impressive old forts, small museums, and attractive pink-and-white government buildings to manicured gardens, aquariums, and a zoo, New Providence and Paradise Island can keep you busy.

To get around New Providence, you can rent a car, take taxis, or hop aboard the far cheaper *jitneys* (public buses or vans that run in front of Cable Beach hotels and throughout Nassau). These vans may take a while, but they eventually get you within shouting distance of the attractions in this area. Jitney routes are often roundabout, but you're treated to impromptu tours of neighborhoods that you may otherwise miss.

To get to Paradise Island, you can take a taxi across the bridge from Nassau or you can walk. After you're there, you can take shuttle buses around the island or hoof it.

The following attractions are the best that New Providence offers.

Ardastra Gardens & Zoo
Nassau

The gardens here are a treat for the eyes, but the animals are the real draw. You see creatures great and small, from iguanas, *hutias* (indigenous rodents), and peacocks to monkeys, lemurs, and various felines. You can even stroke a tame boa constrictor or get your photo snapped with a colorful macaw on your shoulder.

The zoo is known for its marching flamingos performances. The fun begins when the leggy pink birds trot en masse into the arena. Like a drill sergeant, their trainer shouts commands, and the flamingos all stop, abruptly change direction, or stretch out their wings. The trainers summon audience members to join the flock in hilarious poses. After the performance, you can ask the flamingos for their autographs as they gather by the lake with the wild ducks and Australian black swans. Allow about 90 minutes for the show, which hits the stage three times a day.

See map p. 160. West Bay Street and Chippingham Road, near Ft. Charlotte. ☎ *242-323-5806.* www.ardastra.com. *From Cable Beach, take bus #10 that travels along West Bay Street; or you can take a brief taxi ride. Admission: $12 for adults, $6 for children. Open: Daily 9 a.m.–4:30 p.m.*

Atlantis Aquarium
Paradise Island

The world's largest tropical aquarium exhibits some 50,000 sharks, stingrays, turtles, and other fish and sea creatures collected from around the planet. Plan to spend about 90 minutes here.

If you want to slide down the waterfall on the "Mayan temple" through a clear tube that cuts through a shark tank, you have to book a room at the Atlantis Resort or one of its sibling properties (the Ocean Club or neighboring Comfort Suites). Only guests of these hotels can ride down the water slides, swim in the elaborate pools, and enjoy the many other outdoor aquatic attractions.

Both guests and non-guests, however, can walk through the acrylic underwater tube, looking up to see hammerheads that seem to swim past palm trees through the sky above you. In the dim passageways of "The Dig," colorful fish swarm around streets and statues evocative of Atlantis.

Feedings of the giant green moray eels occur twice a day; before you visit, check the times. At the touch tank, children get a kick out of handling the spiky sea urchins, large conch shells, soft starfish, and surprisingly heavy sea cucumbers.

See map p. 160. Royal Towers, Atlantis Resort. ☎ *800-ATLANTIS or 242-363-3000. Admission: $25 for adults, $13 for children 12 and under. Tours last one hour and occur daily 10 a.m.– 6 p.m.*

Atlantis Paradise Island Resort & Casino
Paradise Island

Gambling is the main event here, but there's so much to see at the entertainment complex of this mega-resort. Although most casinos keep the outdoors outdoors, the unusual design of this huge casino allows sunshine to stream in through skylights. Designer boutiques, watering holes, restaurants — all on the expensive side — and plenty of gaping vacationers surround the casino.

See map p. 160. Casino Drive, Paradise Island, just across the bridge. ☎ *800-ATLANTIS or 242-363-3000. Admission: Free. Open: Daily 24 hours.*

Fort Charlotte
Nassau

If you have the time or desire to see only one fort in New Providence, make it Fort Charlotte. With a commanding view of the harbor, it was built in 1788 by Lord Dunmore, the royal governor, and named for Queen Charlotte, the wife of King George III. Tour guides tell visitors all about the moat, drawbridge, cannons, underground passages, and dungeons, but relate no stories of battles because the fort never saw one. You aren't charged for admission, but your guide expects a tip. You can combine a visit here with a trip to nearby **Ardastra Gardens & Zoo** and **Arawak Cay** (where local chefs whip up Bahamian favorites in small, no-frills restaurants).

See map p. 160. West Bay Street and Chippingham Road, about a mile west of downtown Nassau. No phone. Admission: Free. Open: Daily 8 a.m.–4 p.m.

Fort Fincastle and the Water Tower
Nassau

Like Fort Charlotte, Nassau's other major fort, Fincastle never saw a battle. It was a lighthouse until 1816 when it was turned into a signal tower, 61m (200 ft.) above the sea. Its 38m-tall (126-ft.) Water Tower, which you can reach by taking an elevator to the observation platform, gives you the most panoramic view of New Providence. The fort is named in honor of Lord Dunmore, the royal governor who ordered its construction in 1793. His second title was Viscount Fincastle.

Young men hang out here, insisting that you go on a guided tour, but you can easily see the remains and enjoy the view on your own. These would-be tour guides are hard to shake off, however.

See map p. 160. Bennett's Hill, Elizabeth Avenue, just south of Shirley Street. Admission for Water Tower: $1. Open: Mon–Sat 8 a.m.–5 p.m.

Hairbraider's Centre
Nassau

Whether you want a single beaded plait, cornrows in an intricate design, or many itty-bitty loose braids with colorful rubber bands, this open-air pavilion is the place to go. Depending on what style you want, the cost ranges from $3 to more than $100, and styling can take anywhere from minutes to hours to complete. At one time, hairbraiders roamed the shores of Cable Beach and Paradise Island in search of customers. Although you still may find some of these nimble-fingered women hawking their services on the sand, the government set up the Hairbraider's Centre to cut down on beach vendors. Normally, you can find braiders here Monday through Saturday between 9 a.m. and 3:30 or 4 p.m. A few braiders may show up on a Sunday if they need money and some cruise ships are in port.

Agree on a price and style before your Bahamian beautician touches your tresses. Put plenty of sunblock on your newly exposed scalp to avoid a wicked sunburn.

See map p. 160. Prince George Dock, near Rawson Square, downtown Nassau.

Historic Nassau

Set aside a couple of hours for some good old-fashioned Nassau street-walking. You won't even get arrested. As you wander through the capital, you'll see that the past is well preserved. The best time for an amble is after 10 a.m. and before 4 p.m., Monday through Saturday. Many stores and museums close on Sunday, and on Saturday, the streets are congested because that's when the Changing of the Guard takes place at Government House. Try to find out from the staff at your hotel when the fewest cruise ships are in port, because those passengers really clog the center of town.

A good place to begin your tour is **Rawson Square,** which links **Bay Street,** the main thoroughfare, with **Prince George Wharf,** also known as **Prince George Dock,** where the cruise ships dock. Horse-drawn carriages — each carrying up to three passengers — wait here to give leisurely tours. You can also see a statue of former shopkeeper Sir Milo Butler, the country's first native Bahamian — and first post-independence — governor. On the northern side of the square, the **Ministry of Tourism Information Booth** doles out helpful maps and brochures. Across the way is **Parliament Square,** with its statue of a young Queen Victoria and its pink, white-trimmed Georgian-style government buildings that date back to the late 1700s and early 1800s.

Nassau Public Library and Museum, on Bank Lane, is an octagonal build-ing, which has been here since around 1797, and was once the Nassau Gaol (in other words, the local slammer). Shelves of books line the small prison cells. History buffs can check out the time-worn prints and colonial docu-ments in the little museum. Stamp collectors head for the **Nassau General Post Office** at the end of Parliament Street. You can then walk northeast to the foot of **Queen's Staircase.** These 65 steps lead to **Fort Fincastle** and the **Water Tower,** both of which offer views of Nassau and the harbor.

To the west, at Duke and George streets, stands the pink-and-white **Government House.** Since 1801, this house has been the official resi-dence of the governor-general, the queen's representative. A statue of Christopher Columbus stands midway up the front steps. The stately white columns and wide circular driveway make this mansion the perfect setting for the dignified **Changing of the Guard Ceremony** that takes place outside every other Saturday at 10 a.m. The real crowd-pleaser of this event is the **Royal Bahamas Police Force Band.** The music is at least as colorful as the uniforms: stark-white tunics, navy trousers with bright red stripes, and white pitch helmets with crimson bands.

If you're into antiques, walk north (back toward Bay Street) to the re-stored **Balcony House,** located at Market Street and Trinity Place. This

18th-century, two-story house with a balcony is Nassau's oldest wooden residential building. Furniture from the early 1800s through the 1940s decorates the rooms, and most visitors rave about the handsome mahogany staircase that was salvaged from a wrecked ship during the 1800s. You can spend a half-hour here. A donation is expected.

Finally, stroll over to the open-air **Straw Market** at Market Street, where vendors sell items such as shell jewelry, clothing made from African and Indonesian fabrics, woodcarvings, sun hats, baskets, place mats, and bags woven from straw. East of the Straw Market is the waterfront **Woodes Rodgers Walk,** which is lined by mail boats, sponge boats, and vendors hawking fruit, vegetables, fish, and conch. Continue your stroll until you reach the imposing cruise ships docked back at Prince George Wharf.

Junkanoo Expo
Nassau

Unless you're vacationing during Christmas or New Year's, you'll miss the beloved **Junkanoo Festival.** This country's answer to Carnival and Mardi Gras begins with a parade in the wee hours of Boxing Day (Dec 26) and New Year's Day. If your visit doesn't coincide with the real deal, the Junkanoo Expo, which is housed in an old Customs shed, is the next-best thing. With a little imagination, you can picture the colorful costumes and whimsical masks on dancers and musicians as they parade down Bay Street. You can also watch the video of last year's bash. Some of the handcrafted costumes on display take months to create.

See map p. 160. At the entrance to Prince George Dock. ☎ *242-323-3182. Admission: Free. Open: Daily 9 a.m.–6 p.m.*

National Art Gallery of The Bahamas
Nassau

At long last, The Bahamas has a national gallery to showcase its talented artists. In a restored historic building in the center of Nassau, the gallery displays Bahamian art, past and present. Bahamian art, as an entity, has existed for only 50 years. Museum curators claim that the current collection is only the nucleus of a long-range strategy to beef up the number of works. Most paintings in the exhibit are divided into a historical and a contemporary collection. The collection honors pioneering Bahamian artists as well as younger and more modern painters. Even though some paintings fall into the realm of primitive or even native art, many are quite sophisticated — especially Amos Ferguson's *Snowbirds.* In this painting, Ferguson used house paint on cardboard to create a remarkable portrait.

See map p. 160. Villa Doyle, West Hill Street. ☎ *242-328-5800. Admission: $3 for adults, $2 for seniors and students, $1 for children 14 and under. Tues–Sat 11 a.m.–4 p.m.*

Amos Ferguson: The painting painter

The Bahamas' best known artist, Amos Ferguson, used to be a house painter. Born on Exuma in 1920, he once ran a small farm and helped with his father's carpentry business. When he later moved to Nassau, he took up house painting. Using house paint instead of oil or acrylic, he started creating striking color-rich "naive" pictures. Many vacationers got to know his early work through a Nassau Straw Market vendor named Bea, who eventually became his wife.

During the 1980s, Ferguson tumbled onto the international art scene. His often whimsical works — still created with house paint — are now owned by collectors around the world. His thought-provoking themes revolve around biblical and historical images, nature and folklore, and the masks, costumes, and music of the Bahamian Junkanoo festival.

Pirates of Nassau Museum
Nassau

You need half an hour for the self-guided tour through this museum that brings Nassau's buccaneering days to life. During the 18th century, pirates ruled the waves around New Providence as they grew rich from the goods they pillaged from merchant ships. You can go below deck on a replica of a pirate ship, *Revenge,* where you can view the kitchen area, hammocks, cannons, and animals, such as goats, chickens in crates, and, of course, rats. Battles rage through the special effects of sounds and lights, and the dungeon feels damp and creepy. You can hear pirates planning their next attack and smell the sea air. Kids of all ages enjoy the wax figures and the re-created ship and buildings, including the favorite pirate hangout: the tavern. Exhibits tell the story of Woodes Rodgers, who the English crown shipped here to clean up the pirate pandemonium.

See map p. 160. Corner of King and George streets, a block south of the Straw Market.
☎ *242-356-3759. Admission: $12 adults, $6 children 3–18, free 2 and under. Open: Mon–Sat 9 a.m.–6 p.m.; Sun 9 a.m.–12:30 p.m.*

Potter's Cay
Nassau

In the islands, the local market is an integral part of daily life. Already visited the Straw Market? Fine, but that overcrowded bazaar is for tourists. On the other hand, Potter's Cay, located beneath the original Paradise Island bridge, is for Bahamians. This place is an ideal spot for watching sloops from the Out Islands bring in huge mounds of glistening fish and conch. Seeing restaurant chefs buying fresh seafood straight off the boats isn't unusual.

You can even take notes for your own kitchen while a fisherman prepares conch salad that couldn't be any fresher: He bores a hole into the shell, extracts the unfortunate conch, skins it, dices it, marinates it in lime juice, and seasons it with onions and peppers. In the stalls that line the water's edge, vendors sell this zesty salad along with conch fritters, conch chowder, and fresh herbs. You also find pineapples (many from Eleuthera), bananas, papayas, limes, and other just-plucked fruit.

Vendors here don't appreciate having their photographs taken, especially if you're not purchasing anything. Point a camera in their direction, and they make their objections abundantly clear. As colorful as this site can be, abstain from capturing it on film, unless you have a very long lens or a 007-style camera hidden in your sunglasses.

See map p. 160. Located directly under the bridge that links Nassau and Paradise Island.

Queen's Staircase
Nassau

During the 1790s, enslaved men cut 65 steps out of solid limestone to form a staircase leading from old Nassau to the top of Fort Fincastle. Later, this 31m (102-ft.) staircase was named in honor of the 65-year reign of Queen Victoria.

At the bottom of the stairs, guides wait to present the history of the staircase. Their recitations are so well memorized that some of them sound like robotic recordings. At the top, you can easily walk to Fort Fincastle and the Water Tower.

See map p. 160. Across Shirley Street, toward the rise away from the harbor, and near Princess Margaret Hospital in downtown Nassau.

The Retreat
Nassau

You can visit the Botanical Gardens, but the 4.5 hectares (11 acres) of this National Trust property are better maintained. Two hundred species of rare and exotic palms from around the world, other unusual trees, and delicate native orchids fill these flourishing grounds.

The Retreat is the place for birders to see and hear all kinds of feathered friends, such as banana quits, northern mockingbirds, black-and-white warblers, and red-legged tanagers.

You can take a half-hour tour on Tuesday, Wednesday, or Thursday at noon, or visit on your own. The Retreat is about a 20- to 30-minute taxi ride from Cable Beach, depending on traffic. If you don't mind a longer trip, you can also take a public bus from the hotel areas.

See map p. 160. Village Road, across from Queens College, just east of downtown Nassau. ☎ 242-393-1317. Admission: $2 for adults, $1 for children. Open: Mon–Fri 9 a.m.–5 p.m.

Versailles Gardens and Cloister
Paradise Island

Europe is literally transported to The Bahamas in these gardens. This 12th-century cloister was originally built by Augustinian monks in southwestern France and was reassembled here, stone by stone. But the reassembly of the complicated monument didn't follow most conventional construction methods. Huntington Hartford, the A&P grocery heir, purchased the cloister from the estate of William Randolph Hearst at San Simeon in California. Unfortunately, after Hearst bought the cloister, it was hastily dismantled in France for shipment to America, but the parts weren't numbered — and they all arrived unlabeled on Paradise Island. The monument puzzle remained unsolved until artist and sculptor Jean Castre-Manne set about to reassemble it, piece by piece. It took him two years, and what you see today presumably bears some similarity to the original. Tropical flowers and classical statues fill the gardens, which extend over the rise to Nassau Harbour. Although the monument remains a timeless beauty, recent buildings have encroached on either side, marring Huntington Hartford's original vision.

See map p. 160. Adjacent to the Ocean Club Resort, Paradise Island. Admission: Free.

Walking tours
Nassau

Goombay Guided Walking Tours, arranged by the Ministry of Tourism, leave from the Tourist Information Booth on Rawson Square daily. Tours last for one hour and include descriptions of some of the city's most venerable buildings, with commentaries on Nassau's history, customs, and traditions.

See map p. 160. Tourist Information Booth on Rawson Square in Nassau. ☎ 242-323-3102. Admission: $12 for all ages. Open: Daily 9 a.m.–2 p.m. Tour schedule varies; advance reservations required.

Keeping Active

Most of the sports action in and around New Providence is linked to the Atlantic. But when you're ready to dry off, you have plenty of choices.

Biking

A half-day bicycle tour with **Bahamas Outdoors Ltd.** (☎ 242-362-1574; www.bahamasoutdoors.com; about $59) takes you on a 5km (3-mile) bike ride along some scenic forest and shoreline trails in the Coral Harbour area on the southwestern coast of New Providence. You pass along a trail with a scenic backdrop of mangrove creeks and pine forests and can take time off for a kayak trip to a shallow for snorkeling.

Use these handy Post-It® Flags to mark your favorite pages.

Do anything.
Just add
Dummies.

Bell Channel Inn

"A world of detailed and authoritative information."
—U.S. News & World Report

Visit us at www.dummies.com

- ✔ **Read more than 2,500 articles adapted from our best selling books**
- ✔ **Sign up for free Dummies eTips newsletters**
- ✔ **Enter to win sweepstakes**

Some of the major hotels on Paradise Beach and Cable Beach rent bikes to their guests. You can bike along Cable Beach or the beachfront at Paradise Island, but Nassau traffic is too congested.

Golfing

New Providence courses frequently host international tournaments. At the 18-hole **Cable Beach Golf Course** (☎ 242-327-1741), the oldest course in The Bahamas, greens fees run $140 with carts included. This course is the most convenient for many vacationers because it's just across the road from the main Cable Beach hotels. **Ocean Club Golf Club** on Paradise Island Drive (☎ 242-363-6682), at the east end of the island, is an 18-hole championship golf course designed by Tom Weiskopf. This course overlooks both the Atlantic Ocean and Nassau Harbour. Attracting every caliber of golfer, the par-72 course is famous for its Hole 17, which plays entirely along the scenic Snorkelers Cove. Greens fees, including cart, are $250 per player, and rental clubs and shoes are available.

Gyms and spas

Many of the large hotels have exercise rooms for guests to use. Some also offer spa facilities, including **Sandals Royal Bahamian** and the **Crystal Palace Casino** complex, both on Cable Beach; and **Atlantis Paradise Island Resort & Casino** and **One&Only Ocean Club,** both on Paradise Island. If your hotel doesn't have a gym or spa, or if you need more extensive equipment or pampering to keep up your routine, check out **Windermere Spa & Salon** (☎ 242-393-0033) at the Harbour Bay Shopping Centre on East Bay Street in Nassau.

Horseback rides

Small groups of riders spend 90 minutes riding along wooded and beachside trails through **Happy Trails Stables** (☎ 242-362-1820; www. bhahamahorse.com). The $95 price tag includes transportation between your hotel and the stables. The stables are in the Coral Harbour area in southwestern New Providence, about 20 minutes from Cable Beach and 45 minutes from Paradise Island. You have to make reservations for these guided rides, which go out twice a day.

Tennis

Among hotels with tennis courts — some lit for night play — are the **Radisson, Sandals,** and **Nassau Beach Hotel** on Cable Beach, and the **Atlantis** and **One&Only Ocean Club** on Paradise Island. Some hotels allow in-house guests to play for free, but other hotels charge a small hourly fee. If your hotel doesn't have courts, you can arrange to play elsewhere, usually for $5 to $7 an hour, plus about $6 for racquet rental.

Shopping the Local Stores

You can find a variety of bargains in Nassau, including Swiss watches, Japanese cameras, French perfumes, Irish crystal and linens, and British china.

You don't have to pay import duties on 11 categories of luxury goods, including china, crystal, fine linens, jewelry, leather goods, photography equipment, watches, fragrances, and other merchandise. Antiques, of course, are exempt from import duty worldwide. But even though prices are duty-free, you can still end up spending more on an item in The Bahamas than you would back in your hometown. It's a tricky situation.

If you're contemplating a major purchase, such as a good Swiss watch or expensive perfume, do some research in your hometown discount outlets before making a serious purchase in The Bahamas. Although the alleged 30- to 50-percent discount off stateside prices may apply on some purchases, that's not true in most cases. We discovered that certain cameras and electronic equipment are listed in The Bahamas at, say, 20 percent or more below the manufacturer's "suggested retail price." That sounds good, except the manufacturer's "suggested retail price" may be a lot higher than what you'd pay in your hometown. You aren't getting the discount you think you are. Some shoppers even take along department-store catalogs from the States to determine whether the items they're considering are indeed a bargain.

Mostly European, American, and Asian imports fill vacationers' shopping bags. Bahamian-made goods are much scarcer. Even at Nassau's **Straw Market,** you may be surprised at the number of items made in China, Indonesia, and Kenya. But at this open-air market, you also find plenty of locally produced straw goods, along with Bahamian sauces and seasonings, perfumes, woodcarvings, shell jewelry, dolls, and art.

Be prepared for persistent vendors. Someone may slip a necklace around your neck in an attempt to convince you that you can't live without it. In addition to the large Bay Street Straw Market, you find similar setups across from the Radisson and Wyndham hotels on Cable Beach.

Pay the first price you're quoted, and the vendor will look at you as if you have three eyes. Bargaining is a way of life here. Don't be afraid to turn your back on something you really want. Chances are, the previously stubborn vendor will call after you with a suddenly reduced price that's "only for you."

Although bargaining is *expected* at straw and produce markets, it isn't welcome at all in most stores. At glitzy boutiques, such as the ones at Atlantis Paradise Island Resort & Casino, salespeople give you a price and stand firm.

Antiques

Marlborough Antiques (corner of Queen and Marlborough streets; ☎ 242-328-0502) carries the type of antiques you'd expect to find in a shop in London: antique books, antique maps and engravings, English silver (both sterling and plate), and unusual table settings (fish knives and so on). Among the store's most appealing objects is its collection of antique photographs of the islands. Works by Bahamian artists Brent Malone and Maxwell Taylor are also on display.

Art

Although many locals come to **Kennedy Gallery** (on Parliament Street; ☎ 242-325-7662) for custom framing, the gallery also sells original artwork by well-known Bahamian artists, including limited-edition prints, handicrafts, pottery, and sculpture.

Brass and copper

With two branches on Charlotte Street, the **Brass and Leather Shop** located at 12 Charlotte St., between Bay and Shirley streets (☎ 242-322-3806) offers English brass, handbags, luggage, briefcases, attachés, and personal accessories. Shop number two, located at Marathon Mall on Marathon Road, sells handbags, belts, scarves, ties, and small leather goods from such famous designers as Furla, Bottega Veneta, Pierre Balmain, and others. If you look and select carefully, you can find some good buys here.

Cigars

Many cigar aficionados come to the **Tropique International Smoke Shop** (in Wyndham Nassau Resort & Crystal Palace Casino, West Bay Street; ☎ 242-327-7292) to indulge their passion for Cubans, which are handpicked and imported by Bahamian merchants. The staff at this outlet trained in Havana, so they know their cigars.

Remember, the United States prohibits the importation of Cuban cigars because of the trade embargo. If you buy them, you're supposed to enjoy them in The Bahamas.

Coins and stamps

At the **Bahamas Post Office Philatelic Bureau** (in the General Post Office at the top of Parliament Street on East Hill Street; ☎ 242-322-1112), you find beautiful Bahamian stamps slated to become collector's items. One of the most sought-after stamps has a seashell motif.

Coin of the Realm (Charlotte Street, just off Bay Street; ☎ 242-322-4497) is a family-run shop located in a lovely building hewn out of solid limestone over 200 years ago. The shop offers not only fine jewelry, but also mint and used Bahamian and British postage stamps and rare (and not-so-rare) Bahamian silver and gold coins. It also sells old and modern Bahamian paper currency.

Fashion

One of Nassau's more formal and elegant clothing stores, **Barry's Limited** (Bay and George streets; ☎ 242-322-3118) sells garments made from lamb's wool and English cashmere. Elegant sportswear (including Korean-made guayabera shirts) and suits are sold here. Most of the clothes are for men, but women often stop in for a look at the fancy handmade Irish linen handkerchiefs and the stylish cuff links, studs, and other accessories. **Bonneville Bones** (Bay Street; ☎ 242-328-0804) is the best men's store we've found in Nassau. You can find everything from standard T-shirts and designer jeans to suits here. **Cole's of Nassau** (Parliament Street; ☎ 242-322-8393) offers the most extensive selection of designer fashions in Nassau. Women can buy everything from swimwear and formal gowns to sportswear and hosiery. Cole's also sells gift items, sterling-silver designer and costume jewelry, hats, shoes, bags, scarves, and belts.

Fendi (Charlotte Street at Bay Street; ☎ 242-322-6300) is Nassau's only outlet for the well-crafted, Italian-inspired accessories endorsed by this famous leather-goods company. With handbags, luggage, shoes, watches, cologne, wallets, and portfolios to choose from, the selection may well solve some of your gift-giving quandaries.

Handicrafts

Sea Grape Boutique (West Bay Road, next to Travelers Rest; ☎ 242-327-5113) is the finest gift shop on New Providence, with a fascinating inventory of exotic decorative items. It includes jewelry crafted from fossilized coral (sometimes with sharks' teeth embedded inside), beadwork from Guatemala, Haitian paintings, silver from India, hairbrushes shaped like parrots, and clothing that's well-suited to the sometimes steamy climate of The Bahamas. A second branch of this outfit, **Sea Grape, Too,** is located in the Radisson Hotel's Mall, on Cable Beach (☎ 242-327-5113).

Jewelry

The jewelry department at **John Bull** (corner of Bay and Charlotte streets; ☎ 242-322-4253) offers classic selections from Tiffany & Co.; cultured pearls from Mikimoto; the creations of David Yurman, Stephen Lagos, Carrera y Carrera, and Sea Life by Kanbana; Greek and Roman coin jewelry; and Spanish gold and silver pieces. John Bull is the best name in the business. The store also features a wide selection of watches, cameras, perfumes (including Estée Lauder, Chanel, and Calvin Klein at discount prices — though you should check carefully to make sure that you're getting a bargain), cosmetics, leather goods, and accessories. This store is one of the best places in The Bahamas to buy a Gucci or Cartier watch. The outlet has been the authorized agent for Rolex in The Bahamas for 30 years, and the store itself has been doing business since 1929.

Leather

In addition to the stores mentioned in this section, another good store for leather goods is the **Brass and Leather Shop,** which we describe in the "Brass and copper" section earlier in this chapter.

Gucci (Saffrey Square on Bay Street; ☎ 242-325-0561), is the best place to buy leather goods in Nassau. The wide selection includes handbags, wallets, luggage, briefcases, gift items, scarves, ties, casual clothes, evening wear for men and women, umbrellas, shoes, sandals, watches, and perfume, all by Gucci of Italy.

The well-known retail outlet **Leather Masters** (Parliament Street; ☎ 242-322-7597) carries an internationally known collection of leather bags, luggage, and accessories by Ted Lapidus, Lanvin, and Lancel of Paris; Etienne Aigner of Germany; and i Santi of Italy. Leather Masters also carries luggage by Piel and Marroquinera of Colombia; leather wallets by Bosca; and pens, cigarette lighters, and watches by Colibri. The store also sells silk scarves, neckties, and cigar accessories.

Linens

The Linen Shop (Ironmongery Building on Bay Street, near Charlotte Street; ☎ 242-322-4266) is the best outlet for linens in Nassau. It sells beautifully embroidered bed linens, Irish handkerchiefs, hand-embroidered women's blouses, and tablecloths. Look also for the most exquisite children's clothing and christening gowns in town.

Maps

Balmain Antiques (second floor of Mason's Building on Bay Street, near Charlotte Street; ☎ 242-323-7421) offers a wide and varied assortment of 19th-century etchings, engravings, and maps, many of them antique and all reasonably priced. Other outlets have minor displays of these collectibles, but this outlet has the finest. Some items are 400 years old. Discussing your interests with Mr. Ramsey, the owner, is usually best so that he can direct you to the proper drawers. His specialties include The Bahamas, America during the Civil War, and black history. He also has a collection of historical military items.

Markets

The **Nassau International Bazaar** (from Bay Street down to the waterfront, near Prince George Wharf) consists of some 30 shops selling international goods in a new arcade. The $1.8-million complex sells goods from around the globe. With cobbled alleyways and garretted storefronts, the area looks like a European village, making it a pleasant place for browsing.

Prince George Plaza (Bay Street) is popular with cruise-ship passengers. Many fine shops, such as Gucci, are located here. When you get tired of shopping, you can eat at one of the several nearby restaurants and cafes.

The **Straw Market** occupies a tent on Bay Street, opposite the intersection of Bay Street with George Street. Hours of the Straw Market are daily from 7 a.m. to around 8 p.m., although each individual vendor (there are around 200 of them) sets his or her own hours. Merchandise includes hats, weavings, baskets, valises, and more, all woven from reeds, straw, and grasses.

Perfumes and cosmetics

Nassau has several good perfume outlets that also stock a lot of nonperfume merchandise.

- ✔ **The Beauty Spot:** The largest cosmetic shop in The Bahamas, this outlet sells duty-free cosmetics by Lancôme, Chanel, Yves Saint Laurent, Elizabeth Arden, Estée Lauder, Clinique, Prescriptives, and Biotherm, among others. It also operates facial salons. Bay and Frederick streets; ☎ **242-322-5930.**

- ✔ **Bonneville Bones:** This store carries a wide selection of duty-free fragrances and cosmetics. It's known for the quality of its goods and service. Bay and George streets; ☎ **242-322-2095.**

- ✔ **The Perfume Bar:** This little gem has exclusive rights to market Boucheron and Sublime in The Bahamas. It also stocks the Clarins line (but not exclusively). Bay Street; ☎ **242-322-7216.**

- ✔ **The Perfume Shop:** In the heart of Nassau, within walking distance of the cruise ships, The Perfume Shop offers duty-free savings on world-famous perfumes. Treat yourself to a bottle of Eternity, Giorgio, Poison, Lalique, Shalimar, or Chanel. Those are just a few of the scents for women. For men, the selection includes Drakkar Noir, Polo, and Obsession. Corner of Bay and Frederick streets; ☎ **242-322-2375.**

Steel drums

If you fall under the Junkanoo spell and want to take home some steel drums, visit **Pyfroms** (Bay Street; ☎ **242-322-2603**). The drums will be useful if island fever overtakes you after you return home.

Living It Up After Dark

Nassau, Cable Beach, and Paradise Island were designed for party time. After dark, the bars at the larger hotels and at plenty of restaurants are packed. Vacationers and residents bump hips on the crowded dance floors of local nightclubs. For many visitors, the casinos are the focal point of nightlife — and for some, day life as well.

The newer of New Providence's dynamic duo, the casino complex at **Atlantis Paradise Island Resort** (☎ 242-363-3000) is the largest in the Caribbean. Craps tables, baccarat, blackjack, roulette, Caribbean stud poker, and more than 1,000 slot machines give you plenty of excuses to try your luck. Tables are open from 10 a.m. to 4 a.m. daily, and the one-arm bandits are ready round-the-clock. Also on-site and drawing a party crowd is **Dragons Night Club,** open from 9 p.m. to 1 a.m.

The **Crystal Palace Casino** (☎ 242-327-6200) lies between the Wyndham Nassau and Radisson resorts on Cable Beach. Tables are open from 10 a.m. to 4 a.m. during the week, and 24 hours a day on weekends. Slot machines, of course, are willing to eat your coins anytime, day or night.

If you're craving a real slice of local life, find out what's happening at the **Dundas Center for the Performing Arts** (on Mackey Street in Nassau; ☎ 242-393-3728). These plays and musicals, put on by local or foreign performers, give you a taste of Nassau's artsy scene.

Club Fluid, West Bay Street, near the corner of Frederick Street (☎ 242-356-4691), is set within a two-story building in downtown Nassau. This basement-level nightclub features a baby-blue and white interior, dozens of mirrors, two bars, and a dance floor. It attracts an animated crowd of local residents, ranging in age from about 20 to 45, who appreciate the reggae, soca, hip-hop, and R&B music. It opens Wednesday to Saturday from 9 p.m. to 2 a.m., with a cover ranging from $12 to $20.

Señor Frog, West Bay Street, near the British Colonial Hilton (☎ 242-323-1777), is a hard-to-hate bar, restaurant, cafe, and taco joint that manages to satirize itself. The interior is deliberately and somewhat claustrophobically overcrowded with references to Latino music, frogs, *faux* palm trees, and battered wooden tables that have hosted all kinds of food and beverage service — from midday salsa and chips to "Let's sample all of the best margaritas available on this menu" contests conducted informally among heavy-drinking cruise-ship drop-ins. Expect merengue music (especially on weekends, when tables are pushed aside to form an ersatz dance floor); a color scheme of orange, brown, and terra cotta; and a menu loaded with, among other choices, burgers, fajitas, and tacos.

The Living Room, in the Nassau Beach Hotel, West Bay Street (☎ 242-327-7711), is located on the cellar level of the also-recommended hotel and is an earth-toned, stone-trimmed bar and disco that has welcomed during its long and suds-soaked life celebrities such as Diana Ross and Lenny Kravitz. Outfitted with low-slung sofas and armchairs in a style you may associate with someone's private living room, it has a convivial bar area and a dance floor which can, as evenings progress, become animated and a lot of fun. Open Tuesday to Sunday 9 a.m. to 4 p.m.

Entrance is free for guests of the Nassau Beach Hotel, with a cover charge of between $10 and $15 per person for everyone else.

Going Beyond Nassau

Tour operators take vacationers to the two most popular offshore cays, activity-packed **Blue Lagoon Island** and the more tranquil **Rose Island.** You decide whether you want to be in a small, personalized group or part of a huge crowd that descends on one of these peaceful islands.

Trip #1: Rose Island respite

Remote **Rose Island** is a sliver of land poking up out of the sea northeast of the Prince George waterfront docks of Nassau. Shelling is one of the lures of this little islet. If you want to escape the crowds of Nassau, you can take a boat, the *Robinson Crusoe,* which leaves Wednesday, Friday, and Sunday at 10 a.m. from Nassau and returns at 4:30 p.m. The cost is $50, $25 for children ages 2 to 11, and free for kids under 5. You can relax in a hammock, snorkel among the coral reefs, and enjoy the white sand beach before and after your sizzling barbecue lunch with unlimited white wine (included in the price). Bookings for this island retreat trip are available through **Majestic Tours** (☎ **242-322-2606;** www.majestic holidays.com).

Trip #2: A sail to Exuma

If you want to see the Exuma island chain on a daylong excursion, try the **Fantastic Exuma Powerboat Adventure.** The boat departs Nassau Harbour at 9 a.m. and arrives in the Exuma Cays about an hour later. Stops include snorkeling at a private cay (Ship Channel), a visit with the iguanas on Allan's Cay, feeding stingrays along the shore, and a barbecue lunch. A full bar is available all day, and the drinks are free. The cost is $190, or $120 for children 2 to 12. Transportation from a participant's hotel to the port of embarkation is included in the price. The experience comes to a conclusion around 5pm. For more information and prices, contact **Powerboat Adventures** (☎ **242-393-7116;** www.powerboat adventures.com).

Part IV
Grand Bahama

The 5th Wave

By Rich Tennant

In this part . . .

*1*f Grand Bahama — a low-key yet high-impact island —
appeals to you, this part introduces you to the best ways
you can make the most of your stay. You can use the advice
about arriving and about exploring the island to help familiar-
ize yourself with the lay of the land.

We help you find accommodations that fit your style and your
budget. Whether you want a meal at the water's edge or in a
British-style pub, we give you Grand Bahama's best bets. We
also offer plenty of suggestions on how to spend your days
and nights, from savoring a beachside nature preserve to
rolling the dice.

Chapter 14

Settling into Grand Bahama

In This Chapter

▶ Knowing what to expect when you get to Grand Bahama
▶ Getting around Grand Bahama

*G*rand Bahama was the dream of Virginian financier Wallace Groves, who envisioned it as a miniature Miami Beach. Today, with its high-rise hotels, golf courses, marinas, international bazaars for shopping, bevy of Continental restaurants, and golden-sand beaches, that dream has been realized. Grand Bahama is the second-most popular tourist destination in The Bahamas, rivaled only by Nassau and Paradise Island. It's the northernmost and the fourth-largest landmass in The Bahamas, stretching for 188km (73 miles).

Both **Freeport** and **Lucaya** lack the upscale chicness of Paradise Island or even Nassau, but they do have fabulous beaches. The affordable hotels and restaurants make Freeport and Lucaya the preferred destinations for middle-class families (as opposed to the high rollers who are attracted to Cable Beach and Paradise Island). Lucaya was developed about a decade later than Freeport, but today the tourist facilities of the two major resort areas have more or less merged into an indistinguishable whole.

Grand Bahama is so big that many areas remain unspoiled, especially in the **West End** or the **East End,** which host very few resorts or restaurants. You can also get close to nature at the Rand Memorial Nature Centre and the Garden of the Groves. And the Lucayan National Park, with its underwater caves, forest trails, and a secluded beach, is another major attraction for adventurous travelers.

Arriving at the Airport

Although some people arrive in cruise ships, most visitors swoop down on Grand Bahama in planes. Getting through **Freeport International Airport** (☎ 242-352-2052) is generally quite easy. Upon your arrival, you're launched into your vacation with the sound of live calypso or reggae music.

Navigating your way through passport control and Customs

With your passport (or birth certificate and photo ID), return airline ticket, and a completed Immigration Arrival/Departure Card, get in the shortest visitors' line. Hold on to your copy of the immigration card because you need to present it before leaving The Bahamas.

The well-marked airport is easy to navigate. You collect your baggage and declare that you haven't brought in any contraband. Customs officials may or may not open your luggage to confirm your claim. You can then pick up maps and helpful brochures at the tourist information desk, get some extra cash in U.S. dollars from an ATM, and head for the exit.

Getting from the airport to your hotel

Metered taxis greet each flight, ready to whisk vacationers off to hotels. (The cabdriver lobby is powerful enough to ban buses at the airport, so you have to rely on a taxi.) Depending on where you are going, the cost ranges from $11 to $20. Downtown Freeport is only a five-minute ride from the airport; Lucaya, the beach resort area, is a ten-minute ride.

If your vacation package includes hotel transfers, present your voucher to the driver of a van that's clearly marked to go to your hotel. If you want to explore Grand Bahama at your own pace, you can pick up a rental car at the airport (see "Getting Around Grand Bahama" later in this chapter).

Cruising into Grand Bahama

Freeport is a popular port of call for major cruise ships. If you opt for one of these floating resorts, expect limited time ashore.

On Grand Bahama Island, your cruise ship will dock at a dull industrial-looking wasteland on the western part of the island, far removed from the center of all the action at Freeport or Lucaya. For shopping, sightseeing, the best beaches, or gambling, you must take a $10 taxi ride over to the resort areas. Taxis await all arriving cruise ships.

Island hopping

If you want to visit some other islands while on Grand Bahama, you can do so aboard **Major's Airlines**, a small commuter-type airline that flies out of Freeport International Airport (☎ 242-352-5778). This Major's offers regular flights to Bimini for $140 round-trip; to Abaco for $160 round-trip; to Andros for $220 round-trip; and to Eleuthera for $230 round-trip. Most of its carriers transport 9 to 15 passengers. Flights aren't available every day, so call for schedules, reservations, and other information.

Choosing Your Location

Because Freeport is a 15-minute bus ride from the beach, Lucaya has become much more popular, and has all but put Freeport out of business. At press time, the focal point of Freeport, the mammoth **Crowne Plaza Golf Resort & Casino,** lies rotting in the sun waiting for a developer with millions to take it over. But there are still a few hotels in Freeport, some less expensive than those in Lucaya.

Freeport's once-great shopping mecca, the International Bazaar is looking a little tired these days, and the **Port Lucaya Marketplace** is giving it a run for its money. Many of the major stores at the International Bazaar also opened branches at the Port Lucaya Marketplace, charging the same prices for the same kinds of merchandise.

Although both Freeport and Lucaya have plenty of good places to leave your money, we prefer leaving our money at Port Lucaya because of its gingerbread-trimmed, wooden buildings and the live music heard most evenings in **Count Basie Square.**

Even if you stay in Freeport, you can still sample Lucaya's attractions — buses, minivans, and taxis connect these resort areas. Neither area is far from Grand Bahama's golf courses, horse stables, and natural attractions, such as **Garden of the Groves, Rand Memorial Nature Center,** and **Lucayan National Park.** Check out Chapter 3 for more background info on — and a map of — this location.

Getting Around Grand Bahama

Whether you board a bus, catch a taxi, mount a motor scooter, pedal a bike, or walk, getting to the most interesting parts of this island is relatively easy. For the most flexibility, you can rent a car, although you don't need one to get around.

Exploring by foot

Nearly devoid of hills, Grand Bahama Island is good for long strolls because outside Freeport and Lucaya, it's largely undeveloped. Flourishing botanical gardens and nature reserves, such as **Lucayan National Park** and **Bahamas National Trust Rand Nature Centre,** are prime locales for hoofing it. For guided nature hikes, contact **Kayak Nature Tours** (☎ **242-373-2485**). If human-made wonders are more to your liking, the International Bazaar and its surroundings in Freeport and the Port Lucaya Marketplace and its Lucaya seaside neighborhood are best for a shopper's stroll.

Taking a bus

Grand Bahama's public bus service, run by privately licensed minivans, makes getting around Freeport and Lucaya almost hassle-free. You typically wait five to seven minutes at any given stop. Sometimes vans sit longer because drivers often don't leave until they have a minimum number of passengers. The fare is $1 for adults and 50¢ for children, and drivers request exact change, either in U.S. or Bahamian money. When you board, tell the driver your destination.

Taking a taxi

The majority of taxis are limousines. The government sets fares and requires cabs to have working meters, but many drivers don't turn them on for routine trips; instead, they quote you a flat fare. If you're not sure what the approximate cost of a taxi ride should be, ask someone at your hotel desk before you leave. One or two passengers pay $3 for the first kilometer (¾ mile) and 40¢ for each additional half-kilometer (¼ mile). Each additional passenger over the age of 3 costs a flat fee of $2, and for each piece of luggage beyond two, the driver collects 50¢. Taxis wait outside hotels, restaurants, and attractions and cruise the streets, where you can flag them down. Two reliable companies to call are **Freeport Taxi** (☎ **242-352-6666**) and **G.B. Taxi Union** (☎ **242-352-7101**).

Driving around

Unlike Nassau, driving on Grand Bahama, with its long, broad roads, is easy. A car comes in handy if you'd rather not rely on taxis and mini-vans. Much of the island is undeveloped, so heavy traffic isn't a problem, and you can easily find places to park. Like the British, islanders drive on the left.

You can find car-rental companies around Freeport International Airport. Cars begin at $50 a day, jeeps at $70, and vans at $120. Availability varies, so if you haven't made a reservation before you arrive, you may have to call around until you find the size or type of car that you want. The major companies are **Avis** (☎ **242-352-7666**), **Dollar** (☎ **242-352-9325**), and **Hertz** (☎ **242-352-9250**).

Other fun ways to get around

Mopeds and **minibikes** may seem like an ideal way to get around Grand Bahama. But if you're used to driving on the right side of the road, a miscalculation while riding a moped on the left here can end up being painful. If you're willing to risk it, plan on spending about $15 for the first hour, plus $5 for each additional hour, or $40 to $55 a day. You need to have a valid driver's license and leave your credit card or $100 cash as a deposit. Wearing helmets — provided with each rental — is mandatory. You can make arrangements to rent through your hotel or at one of the scooter rental shops you see near gas stations and other spots along the road. If you arrive on Grand Bahama by cruise ship, you can rent motor scooters at Freeport Harbour.

Grand Bahama's pancake-flat topography makes **bicycling** an attractive option. As you're whizzing by (riding on the left side of the road), the breeze can mask the sun's power, so be sure to slather on plenty of sunblock. Wearing a brimmed hat is also a good idea. Some hotels offer complimentary bikes, while other accommodations, along with roadside bike-rental outfits, let you rent one for $15 to $20 a day. See Chapter 17 for more on biking and other activities in Grand Bahama.

WHEN IS JUNKANOO ?

Fast Facts: Grand Bahama

American Express

The Scotiabank ATM accepts American Express cards. For any other services, however, contact the office on New Providence, because there is no Amex representative on Grand Bahama.

ATMs

The international ATMs at Bank of Nova Scotia branches dispense both Bahamian and U.S. currency. This bank also operates two ATMs that dispense only U.S. dollars at Crowne Plaza Resort & Casino in Freeport. For 24-hour access to your funds, head to the ATMs at the Royal Bank of Canada, located at East Mall Drive and Explorers Way or Boulevard Service Station on Sunrise Highway; these machines offer only Bahamian currency. Bank of Nova Scotia and Royal Bank of Canada ATMs accept MasterCard, Visa, and any credit or bank card linked to the PLUS or Cirrus network. The Scotiabank ATM also accepts cards on the Novus network, along with American Express.

Baby Sitting

Hotel staff can help you make arrangements to hire an experienced sitter.

Doctors

See "Hospitals."

Emergencies

For an **ambulance**, call ☎ 242-352-2689. For **police**, call ☎ 919. Other potentially useful numbers are the Bahamas Air Sea Rescue Association (BASRA), at ☎ 242-352-9246; the Fire Brigade, at ☎ 242-352-8888; and the National Park Service, at ☎ 242-352-5438.

Hospitals

Government-run Rand Memorial Hospital (☎ 242-352-6735) is on East Atlantic Drive. For information about a clinic close to your hotel, call the hospital or ask the staff at your accommodations. Before you leave home, check your health insurance to see whether you're covered while traveling abroad. If you're not, you may want to purchase a traveler's insurance plan with emergency medical expense coverage (see Chapter 9 for details).

Information

You can find tourist information desks at the airport, the International Bazaar, Port Lucaya Marketplace, and the larger hotels, or contact the Grand Bahama Island Tourism Board at ☎ 242-352-8044 or 242-352-6909.

Internet Access

Visit the Cyberclub at Seventeen Center (☎ 242-351-4560; cyberclub@grand bahama.net). It's open Monday through Saturday from 9 a.m. to 7 p.m.

Newspapers and Magazines

To keep abreast of island happenings, including fundraising beach cookouts, plays, and other events, check out *Freeport News,* the local daily. You can also get *The Tribune* and *The Nassau Guardian,* both published in Nassau, here. *What-to-Do* and *Island Scene* are free magazines geared toward vacationers; they're full of dining and shopping tips, as well as information about Grand Bahama attractions. You can find them at hotels, shops, and tourist offices.

Pharmacies

Try the Sunrise Medical Center (☎ 242-373-3333) on Sunrise Highway in Freeport or Lucayan Medical East (☎ 242-373-7400) on East Sunrise Highway in Lucaya.

Police

In an emergency, call ☎ **919.**

Post Office

Located in downtown Freeport on Explorer's Way (☎ 242-352-9371), the post office is open Monday through Friday from 9 a.m. to 5:30 p.m.

Restrooms

Public toilets are available at the airport and at the International Bazaar, as well as the Port Lucaya Marketplace. Except for Xanadu Beach at Lucaya, don't expect any of the other more remote beaches on island to have public toilets.

Safety

Freeport and Lucaya are usually safe, as long as you take the same precautions you would anywhere else in the world: Don't venture into deserted areas alone, especially at night, and be discreet with your money, jewelry, and other valuables. Traveling by the island's privately run minivans is safe.

Taxis

Although all taxis have meters, many drivers don't use them. Rates for two passengers are $3 for the first kilometer (¾ mile), plus 40¢ for each additional half-kilometer (¼ mile); additional passengers over age 3 cost a flat fee of $2. If you have more than two pieces of luggage, each additional piece costs 50¢. Taxis are easy to come by, but if you'd like to call one, try Freeport Taxi (☎ 242-352-6666) or G.B. Taxi Union (☎ 242-352-7101).

Chapter 15

Staying in Style in Grand Bahama

. . . .

In This Chapter

▶ Deciding where to stay
▶ Evaluating the top choices

. . . .

*I*n this chapter, we describe the accommodations that appeal to most first-time visitors. We considered locations, amenities, quality of service, architecture, and proximity to Grand Bahama's best attractions.

Surveying the Scene

Here you have a choice of more than 4,000 bedrooms or suites, ranging from simple double bedrooms common to most American roadside motels to one- or two-bedroom condo units of timeshares, some of which may be someone else's vacation home when she is off island.

Of course, you have your choice of sprawling resorts, just as you do on Paradise Island (prices, however, are cheaper on Grand Bahama). Many of these resorts offer various meal plans. The cost is usually less expensive if you book in on half-board terms (that is, breakfast and dinner), leaving you free to have lunch somewhere else during your exploration of the island.

If you want a beachfront location, opt for Lucaya. If gambling and shopping are more important to you, a hotel in Freeport may be just fine. For escapists, you can find some resorts in the distant East End, away from everything but those white sandy beaches.

Rack rates are for two people spending one night during the high season of winter and spring, unless we indicate otherwise. *Rack rates* simply mean published rates, but you can often do better (see Chapter 7 for details). Room rates at all-inclusive resorts include not only all meals and beverages, but also tips, taxes, transportation to and from the airport, and most activities and entertainment.

Grand Bahama Island abounds in package deals appealing to honey-mooners, golfers, gamblers, scuba divers, and others. The best deals are offered from mid-April to mid-December.

The Best Accommodations

Here are our top hotel picks on Grand Bahama Island.

Best Western Castaways Resort & Suites
$$ Freeport

The 118-room Castaways is a modest and unassuming hotel despite its excellent position adjacent to the International Bazaar and the casino. Guests stay here because of its location and low price. The hotel isn't on the beach, but a free shuttle can take you to nearby Williams Town Beach or Xanadu Beach. Gardens surround the four-story hotel, and the hotel has a pagoda roof and an indoor/outdoor garden lobby with shops, a game room, and tour desks. Rooms are a basic motel style, and the best units are on the ground. The hotel has a large, unheated freshwater pool with a wide terrace and a pool bar that offers sandwiches and cool drinks. The Flamingo Restaurant features unremarkable Bahamian and American dishes. The Yellow Bird Show Club stays open until 3 a.m. and features limbo dancers and fire-eaters Monday through Saturday. A children's playground adjoins the pool.

See map p. 194. East Mall Drive. ☎ *800-WESTERN or 242-352-6682. Fax: 242-352-5087.* www.bestwestern.com. *Rack rates: $125 double, $155 suite. Children under 12 stay free in parent's room. AE, MC, V.*

Island Palm Resort
$ Freeport

Set within the commercial heart of Freeport, this 143-unit three-story motel consists of four buildings separated by parking lots and greenery. Within an easy walk from virtually everything in town, and 2km (1¼ miles) from the International Bazaar, it offers good value in no-frills, eminently serviceable rooms with well-kept bathrooms equipped with shower/tub combinations. Complimentary shuttle-bus service ferries anybody who's interested to nearby Williamstown Beach (also called Island Seas Beach), where you can use the beachfront facilities (including jet skis and snorkeling equipment) of its sibling resort, a timeshare unit known as Island Sea.

See map p. 194. E. Mall Drive (P.O. Box F-44881), Freeport. ☎ *242-352-6648. Fax: 242-352-6640.* http://islandpalm.tripod.com. *Rack rates: $85 double. Extra person $15. AE, DISC, MC, V.*

Pelican Bay at Lucaya
$$–$$$ Lucaya

On a peninsula jutting into a series of inland waterways, this hotel has more architectural charm than any other on the island, evoking a Danish seaside village. Located next door to the Underwater Explorers Society (UNEXSO), the 69-unit Pelican Bay attracts scuba divers. Lucaya's finest beach is across the road. Town house–style buildings, trimmed with white latticework and gingerbread, are painted in earth tones. Each large unit has a wet bar and bathrobes. Balconies offer vistas of the marina, waterway, whirlpool, or two large, unheated freshwater pools. For the breeziest stay, request one of the end rooms that offer cross-ventilation. The older rooms look out on the marina, while the newer deluxe units overlook the bay.

If you dine at the **Ferry House Restaurant,** which is just a brief stroll away, you can charge the excellent meals to your room. Along the marina, a passageway leads directly to Port Lucaya Marketplace and the watersports vendors. Don't take this route if you've had a few Goombay Smashes or Bahama Mamas; the walkway has no outer wall or railing, so you could fall right into the water.

See map p. 194. Royal Palm Way, by Port Lucaya Marketplace and UNEXSO, the dive operator. ☎ *800-600-9192 or 242-373-9550. Fax: 242-373-9551.* www.pelicanbay hotel.com. *Rack rates: $145–$200 double, $250 suite. Rates include breakfast. AE, MC, V.*

Port Lucaya Resort and Yacht Club
$$ Lucaya

With its own 50-slip marina, this 163-room hotel and yacht club attracts boaters and shoppers. Despite being adjacent to Port Lucaya Marketplace, the resort is surprisingly tranquil and has a secluded feel. Buildings one through six are the quietest because they're removed from the music and bustle of the marketplace. Deluxe rooms overlook the marina, and the tidy, well-maintained bathrooms have adequate shelf space. An Olympic-size, unheated freshwater pool is set off by a whirlpool, and you can sip a drink from the poolside Tiki Bar. Plenty of watersports are at or near the hotel, and you can reach the beach by walking across the road and through the huge Lucayan resort. If you're traveling with children, consider dropping them off at Our Lucaya's Camp Lucaya (see the review of the Westin & Sheraton at Our Lucaya later in this section). The **Trade Winds Café,** Port Lucaya Resort's main restaurant, serves standard fare at breakfast and dinner, but you can find far better and more varied dining options at the nearby marketplace.

See map p. 194. Next to Port Lucaya Marketplace. ☎ *800-582-2921 or 242-373-6618. Fax: 242-373-6652.* www.portlucayaresort.com. *Rack rates: $100–$145 double, $175–$250 suite. AE, DISC, MC, V.*

Ritz Beach Resort
$$ Lucaya

Enveloped by semitropical gardens, the Ritz (not related to the other fabled hotel chain) is adjacent to the **Pirates of The Bahamas Theme Park.**

The origins of this resort date back to 1995. The resort is made up of two buildings, and it also embraces a 50-room complex called Coral Suites. All

Grand Bahama Accommodations

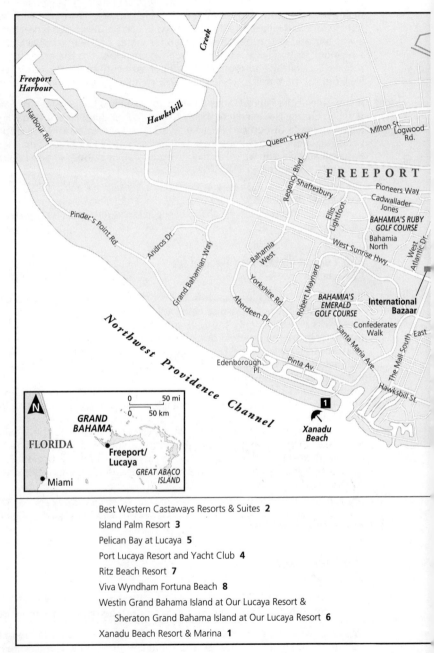

Best Western Castaways Resorts & Suites **2**
Island Palm Resort **3**
Pelican Bay at Lucaya **5**
Port Lucaya Resort and Yacht Club **4**
Ritz Beach Resort **7**
Viva Wyndham Fortuna Beach **8**
Westin Grand Bahama Island at Our Lucaya Resort &
Sheraton Grand Bahama Island at Our Lucaya Resort **6**
Xanadu Beach Resort & Marina **1**

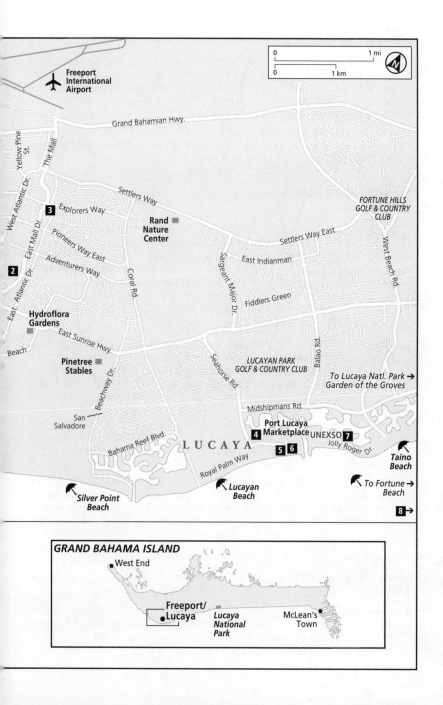

Freeport International Airport

Grand Bahamian Hwy.

Yellow-Pine St.

The Mall

West Atlantic Dr.

East Mall Dr.

East Atlantic Dr.

Settlers Way

3 Explorers Way

Pioneers Way East

Adventurers Way

2

Hydroflora Gardens

East Sunrise Hwy.

Beach

Pinetree Stables

Beachway Dr.

Coral Rd.

Rand Nature Center

Settlers Way East

East Indianman

Sargeant Major Dr.

Fiddlers Green

FORTUNE HILLS GOLF & COUNTRY CLUB

West Beach Rd.

LUCAYAN PARK GOLF & COUNTRY CLUB

Balao Rd.

To Lucaya Natl. Park →
Garden of the Groves

Seahorse Rd.

San Salvadore

Bahama Reef Blvd.

L U C A Y A

Midshipmans Rd.

Port Lucaya Marketplace

4

UNEXSO **7**

Jolly Roger Dr.

5 6

Royal Palm Way

Taíno Beach

Silver Point Beach

Lucayan Beach

To Fortune →
Beach

8 →

0   1 mi
0   1 km

GRAND BAHAMA ISLAND

West End

Freeport/
Lucaya

Lucaya National Park

McLean's Town

the bedrooms are in concrete coral buildings, and your options range from efficiency and studio units to one-bedroom suites to elaborate villa and penthouse accommodations. The bedrooms are spacious and well furnished.

Your amenities depend on how much you want to pay. Penthouses are located on the third and fourth levels; one multilevel studio penthouse comes with its own sun deck and private pool. The hotel's eating facilities are actually at the Taino Beach Vacation Club, where guests can patronize two international restaurants and five bars. The Ritz also has a pool bar.

See map p. 194. Jolly Roger Drive, Taino Beach. ☎ *242-373-9354. Fax: 242-373-4421.* www.timetravelcorp.com. *Rack rates: $199 efficiency, $299 studio, $499 penthouse. Children 12 and under stay free in parent's room. AE, MC, V.*

Viva Wyndham Fortuna Beach
$$$$ Lucaya

Evoking an Italian version of a Club Med, this property sits on 11 hectares (26 acres) in front of one of the island's best white sand beaches. Although the Viva Wyndham welcomes families and hosts a children's program, most vacationers here are young couples. This European-owned resort has a definite Italian accent. You hear more *ciaos* than hellos. Guests play bocce ball on the beach and dine on Italian and some Bahamian cuisine. Because of its strong Continental overlay, the cuisine is better here than at your typical Grand Bahama hotel.

Not far from the **Bahamas National Trust Rand Memorial Nature Centre** and **Lucayan National Park,** this beach resort has a one-size-fits-all price tag. You don't need to dig into your pocket for food, drinks, nightly entertainment, or most activities, although you have to pay extra for scuba diving, fishing, water-skiing, and horseback riding. Six kilometers (4 miles) from Lucaya and 10km (6 miles) from Freeport, this resort is an attractive getaway. More than half the comfortable rooms have views of the water while the others overlook the gardens. If you want accommodations in an isolated setting, you won't mind staying here and having to rent a car to explore the rest of the island.

See map p. 194. Doubloon Road and Churchill Drive, 6km (4 miles) east of Lucaya. ☎ *242-373-4000. Fax: 242-373-5594.* www.wyndham.com. *Rack rates: $124 double. Rates include all meals and most activities. Children under 11 stay free in parent's room. AE, DC, MC, V.*

Westin Grand Bahama Island at Our Lucaya Resort & Sheraton Grand Bahama Island at Our Lucaya Resort
$$$–$$$$ Lucaya

This massive $400-million resort, one of the largest in The Bahamas and by far the finest, most appealing, and best-accessorized on Grand Bahama Island, is firmly anchored beside one of the best white sandy beaches in The Bahamas — Lucayan Beach.

The first of the resort's three sections was completed in 1998 as the **Sheraton Grand Bahama Island at Our Lucaya Resort.** With a vague South Beach Art Deco design, it's laid out like a massive, open-sided, stone-trimmed hexagon, with about half of the rooms facing the beach and the swimming pool, the other half facing the gardens. The 513-room resort is contemporary but relaxed, drawing a high percentage of families. Bedrooms are whimsical and fun, thanks to fabrics you'd expect on a loud Hawaiian shirt from the Elvis era.

In 2000, two newer, more upscale, and more cutting-edge subdivisions of Our Lucaya were opened next door. The smaller and somewhat more private of the two is **Westin Lighthouse Pointe,** a 322-unit, low-rise condo and timeshare complex that focuses specifically on an adult clientele. Its larger counterpart, and the one we find the most appealing, is the 536-unit **Westin Breakers Cay,** a ten-story, white-sided tower whose edges curve sinuously in a postmodern S-curve beside the beach. Each of this complex's three subsections, along with a convention center and well-equipped health, spa, and exercise facility, stretch like pearls in a necklace along a narrow strip of beachfront. Also on-site, within a two-story compound flanking the sea, is The Lanai, which comprises 23 sprawling two-bedroom suites, each furnished in colonial Caribbean style. The complex contains an impressive diversity of restaurants, each designed with a different theme and ambience. Each of the subdivisions has a swimming pool. The Sheraton at Our Lucaya's pool seems to flow around a replica of a 19th-century sugar mill, complete with an aqueduct worthy of the ancient Romans. And the Westin at Our Lucaya is separated from the powder-white sands of Lucaya Beach by a trio of lap pools, each 15m (49 ft.) long and 1.2m (4 ft.) deep, whose edges replicate the sinuous S-shape of the hotel's footprint.

A spa and fitness center, a quartet of tennis courts, a convention center, a state-of-the-art casino (The Isle of Capri — at press time the only functioning casino on Grand Bahama Island), and an upscale shopping mall have been added in recent years, and there's an increasing emphasis on golf, thanks to the opening of the Reef Course (p. 222).

Children aged 2 to 12 can be amused and entertained throughout daylight hours every day at The Bahamas' best-run children's venue, Camp Lucaya.

See map p. 194. Royal Palm Way, across from Port Lucaya Marketplace. ☎ *800-OUR-LUCAYA or 242-373-1333. Sheraton fax: 242-373-8804. Westin fax: 242-350-5060.* www. ourlucaya.com. *Rack rates: Sheraton $129–$199 double, including all meals and activities; Westin Lighthouse Point or Breakers Cay $199–$259 double; Sheraton or Westin $460–$750 suite. AE, DC, DISC, MC, V.*

Xanadu Beach Resort & Marina
$$$ **Xanadu Beach**

Permeated with one of the most quirky and idiosyncratic histories of any hotel in The Bahamas, this 186-room hotel is radically different from the way it was when it housed the reclusive billionaire Howard Hughes. Despite storm damages in 2004 and 2005 and all kinds of setbacks, Xanadu is back, soaring triumphantly above a scrub-dotted landscape that's criss-crossed with canals and upscale villas. Despite negative fortunes and a hotel scene that has shifted to an increasing degree away from Freeport and toward Port Lucaya, Xanadu has hung on, struggling to provide service and comfort to visitors. Much of the allure of Xanadu today is the result of the hard work and devotion of the Donato family. It benefited in 2005 from a big influx of cash that reconfigured the lobby area into a fantasy of the Spanish baroque. Regrettably, however, there's a sense that this place is still barely clinging to economic viability. Damage to the roofline and some of the balustrades remain in need of repair. Bedrooms, however, are comfortable and the nearby beach is sandy, inviting, and alluring, even though many of the beachfront structures need rebuilding.

See map p. 194. P.O. Box F-42438, Freeport. ☎ *242-352-6783. Fax: 242-352-6299.* www. xanadubeachhotel.com. *Rack rates: $145–$245 double,$245–$450 suite. AE, DC, MC, V.*

Chapter 16

Dining Out in Grand Bahama

In This Chapter

▶ Finding the best food beyond your hotel dining room
▶ Discovering restaurants with island ambience

*M*ost restaurants in Freeport and Lucaya don't give your wallet as much of a workout as those in Nassau and Paradise Island. You don't have as many dining options either, but from fast food to fine food, the choices of locales and cuisine are plentiful enough. Menus spotlight locally caught seafood and typical Bahamian dishes, but you also find the usual array of international fare. Restaurants import nearly all food-stuffs, especially meats, fruits, and vegetables.

Have a casual lunch at a waterside cafe, followed by an elegant candlelit dinner at a hotel. Or try an unassuming, family-run spot that specializes in Bahamian favorites. Islanders head to the rustic restaurants and bars in the **West End** for the freshest — and cheapest — snapper, jack fish, grouper, conch, and other local seafood. Sunday night is party night in the West End. The trip is a 40km (25-mile) drive from Freeport by taxi or rental car.

The **East End** begins east of the Lucayan National Park, 45km (28 miles) east of Freeport/Lucaya at the settlement of High Rock. Only the adventurous escape the resort-studded Freeport/Lucaya area and venture into this sparsely inhabited section for lunch while they're driving around the island. Don't expect any fancy dining — just some local eateries serving Bahamian favorites with homemade goodness. And, yes, a view of the sea.

Getting a Taste for Grand Bahama

Grand Bahama chefs aim for international appeal, turning out the usual array of food to please everybody: pasta, barbecued ribs, burgers, even quesadillas, souvlaki, sushi, or Wiener schnitzels. Early-bird specials and festive happy hours with discounted drinks lure patrons to various spots. Some Freeport and Lucaya restaurants open only for dinner, and some close between meals; so even when reservations aren't necessary, you may want to call before going out of your way.

See the Introduction at the beginning of the book for an explanation of the price categories used in this chapter. For details about Bahamian specialties, turn to Chapter 2.

Dining at Grand Bahama's Best Restaurants

Beckey's Restaurant & Lounge
$–$$ Freeport BAHAMIAN

Beckey's culinary creations make you think that you've stumbled into a Bahamian home. No matter what time of day you get to this friendly dining spot, you can order fluffy pancakes, scrambled eggs, or local breakfast favorites, such as stew fish or *boil fish* (fish cooked with salt pork, onions, and green peppers) with grits. For lunch or dinner, the steamed snapper, pan-fried grouper, or cracked conch are island favorites that are prepared with zest. We prefer the local specialties instead of the regular American-style food. The bartender makes a Beckey's Special, a lips-to-hips concoction of coconut rum and vanilla ice cream with a splash of brandy. During happy hour, complimentary conch fritters come with the two-for-one mixed drinks. Beckey's is just across from Hydroflora Garden, about a five-minute drive from the International Bazaar.

See map p. 202. East Sunrise Highway at East Beach Drive. ☎ *242-352-5247. Breakfast: $5–$11. Main courses: $7–$25. AE, MC, V. Open: Daily 7 a.m.–10 p.m.*

Bishop's Restaurant
$ East End BAHAMIAN

For down-home dishes, known mainly by locals, this establishment is an East End favorite. The restaurant opens onto views of the sea. Far from the high-rise hotels, this little restaurant and lounge is reminiscent of The Bahamas of the 1920s and '30s. It serves some of the best cracked conch we've sampled on Grand Bahama Island; the cooks roll the conch in a light batter and fry it in piping-hot oil so that its crust is slightly crunchy. Another favorite that's always on the menu is fried grouper with classic peas and rice. Or, for a savory dish, order the chicken barbecued in zesty sauce.

See map p. 202. High Rock. ☎ *242-353-4515. Main courses: $10–$18. AE, MC, V. Open: Daily 9 a.m.–7 p.m.*

China Temple
$ International Bazaar CHINESE

This Chinese joint also offers takeout. Over the years, this food has proved to be the dining bargain of the bazaar. The menu is familiar and standard: chop suey, chow mein, and sweet-and-sour dishes. The food's certainly not gourmet Asian fare, but it's cheap and it may hit the spot when you crave something different.

See map p. 202. International Bazaar. ☎ *242-352-5610. Lunch main courses: $7–$9; dinner main courses: $10–$14. AE, MC, V. Open: Mon–Sat 10:30 a.m.–10 p.m.*

Churchill's
$$$$ Lucaya AMERICAN

One of the island's most elegant and formal restaurants is imbued with a vague sense of the faded grandeur of what used to be known as the British Empire. Surpassed only by the Ferry House and Luciano's, both of which are recommended below, Churchill's lures diners from other parts of Grand Bahama Island to a dining room that opens onto the lobby of the Westin Hotel at Our Lucaya. The venue includes a British-colonial bar with dark wood floor and trim, potted plants, ceiling fans, a grand piano, and big-windowed views over the sea. This is the island's best chophouse, featuring both succulent steaks flown over from the mainland and locally caught seafood. The manor-house setting is an appropriate foil for the finely honed service and top-quality ingredients, deftly prepared. Regrettably, it's open less frequently than we'd like, sometimes operating only on weekends, and only at dinner, during low and shoulder season.

See map p. 202. At the Westin & Sheraton at Our Lucaya Resorts, Royal Palm Way. ☎ *242-373-1333. Reservations required. Main courses: $26–$65. AE, DC, DISC, MC, V. Usually Mon–Sat 6–11pm, but during off season, hours vary according to occupancy levels of the hotel.*

Fatman's Nephew
$–$$ Lucaya BAHAMIAN

The next generation carries on the culinary tradition of the late Fatman, a chef whose Grand Bahama restaurant once had countless loyalists. At this newer location overlooking the Port Lucaya Marketplace Marina, the focus is on seafood. You can sample various grilled or spicy Cajun-style fish or try local favorites, such as cracked conch. On most days, you encounter at least eight kinds of game fish, including wahoo and kingfish. The menu features other island dishes, too, like curried chicken, daily specials, burgers, and steaks. Sometimes an especially authentic dish appears on the menu, such as Bahamian-style shark soup made from the flesh of hammerheads. Not every dish wins an award, but the place is an enduring favorite. The casual atmosphere is idyllic for having drinks and appetizers on the breezy terrace above the water.

See map p. 202. Port Lucaya Marketplace. ☎ *242-373-8520. Main courses: $10–$38. AE, DISC, MC, V. Open: Mon–Fri 5–11 p.m.*

Ferry House
$–$$ Lucaya INTERNATIONAL

A short stroll from Port Lucaya Marketplace, the Ferry House sits in a tranquil spot away from the crush of shops and hotels. The huge windows of

Grand Bahama Dining

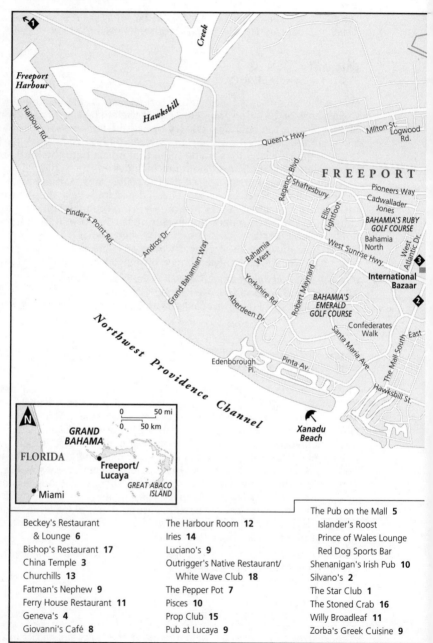

Beckey's Restaurant
  & Lounge **6**
Bishop's Restaurant **17**
China Temple **3**
Churchills **13**
Fatman's Nephew **9**
Ferry House Restaurant **11**
Geneva's **4**
Giovanni's Café **8**

The Harbour Room **12**
Iries **14**
Luciano's **9**
Outrigger's Native Restaurant/
  White Wave Club **18**
The Pepper Pot **7**
Pisces **10**
Prop Club **15**
Pub at Lucaya **9**

The Pub on the Mall **5**
  Islander's Roost
  Prince of Wales Lounge
  Red Dog Sports Bar
Shenanigan's Irish Pub **10**
Silvano's **2**
The Star Club **1**
The Stoned Crab **16**
Willy Broadleaf **11**
Zorba's Greek Cuisine **9**

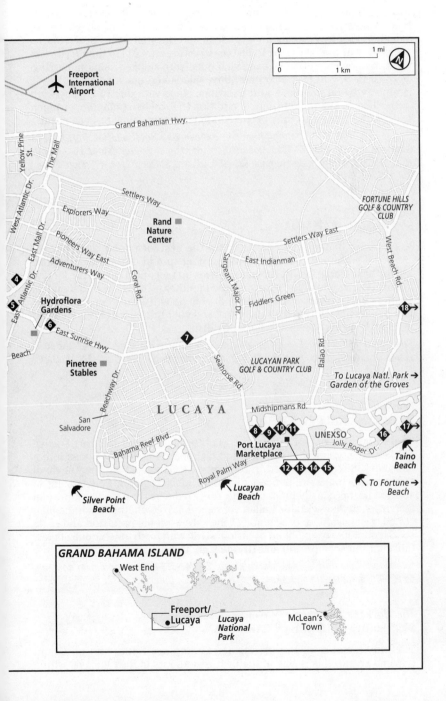

Freeport International Airport

Grand Bahamian Hwy.

Yellow Pine St.

The Mall

West Atlantic Dr.

East Atlantic Dr.

East Mall Dr.

Settlers Way

Explorers Way

Pioneers Way East

Adventurers Way

Rand Nature Center

FORTUNE HILLS GOLF & COUNTRY CLUB

Settlers Way East

East Indianman

West Beach Rd.

Sargeant Major Dr.

Fiddlers Green

4

5

Hydroflora Gardens

6

East Sunrise Hwy.

Coral Rd.

7

Beach

Pinetree Stables

LUCAYAN PARK GOLF & COUNTRY CLUB

18

Balao Rd.

To Lucaya Natl. Park →
Garden of the Groves

L U C A Y A

Seahorse Rd.

Midshipmans Rd.

San Salvador

Beachway Dr.

Bahama Reef Blvd.

8 9 10 11

UNEXSO

16

17

Port Lucaya Marketplace

Jolly Roger Dr.

Taino Beach

12 13 14 15

To Fortune →
Beach

Silver Point Beach

Royal Palm Way

Lucayan Beach

0   1 mi
0   1 km

GRAND BAHAMA ISLAND

West End

Freeport/
Lucaya

Lucaya National Park

McLean's Town

this dockside restaurant are always flung open, offering views of pleasure boats and ferries. The menu changes frequently, depending on what fresh fish and other ingredients are available, and the staff bakes bread on the premises. For breakfast, the Danish pastries are a treat. For lunch, you can have an open-faced Danish sandwich piled with smoked salmon, herring, or roast beef. You may also find filling salads and quesadillas. Icelandic lamb may be on the menu at dinnertime, along with duck à l'orange and butterflied or coconut shrimp. In addition to local fish (snapper, grouper, and dolphin), the chef may prepare imported trout, tuna, or even sushi.

See map p. 202. Bell Channel, near the Pelican Bay Hotel and the Port Lucaya Marketplace. ☎ *242-373-1595. Reservations recommended for dinner. Lunch platters: $15–$23; dinner main courses: $30–$50. AE, MC, V. Open: Mon–Fri noon–2 p.m.; Tues–Sun 6–9 p.m.*

Geneva's
$ Freeport   BAHAMIAN

Ask a native Bahamian where to go for the best local food, and chances are you'll end up at this unassuming dining spot in downtown Freeport. Run by an amiable family, Geneva's serves up hefty portions of the kind of home cooking you'd get from your own mother — if she were Bahamian. Tender conch comes cracked, stewed, or in a savory chowder. Order your grouper steamed, broiled, or pan-fried, and your thick pork chops steamed or fried. Peas and rice is the best side dish.

See map p. 202. Kipling Lane, The Mall at West Sunrise Highway. ☎ *242-352-5085. Lunch sandwiches and platters: $6–$12; main courses: $9–$25. DISC, MC, V. Open: Daily 7 a.m.–11 p.m.*

Giovanni's Café
$ Lucaya   ITALIAN/SEAFOOD

Tucked away in one of the pedestrian thoroughfares of the Port Lucaya Marketplace, you find a yellow-sided clapboard house that opens into a charming 38-seat Italian trattoria. The chefs (including head chef Giovanni Colo) serve Italian-influenced dishes of local seafood, specializing in seafood pasta (usually prepared only for two diners) and lobster. Giovanni stamps each dish with his Italian verve and flavor, whether it's Bahamian conch, local seafood, or scampi. Dishes show off his precision and rock-solid technique, exemplified by sirloin steak with fresh mushrooms, delectable shrimp scampi, and an extremely good spaghetti carbonara.

See map p. 202. Port Lucaya Marketplace. ☎ *242-373-9107. Lunch main courses: $9.50–$15; dinner main courses: $13–$38. AE, MC, V. Open: Mon–Sat 8 a.m.–10 p.m.*

The Harbour Room
$$$ Lucaya   EUROPEAN/CARIBBEAN

The only member of the prestigious Chaine des Rotisseurs on Grand Bahama Island, this is one of the best restaurants in Port Lucaya, with a definite Continental flair; a creative kitchen; a polite, hardworking staff; and a sense of *Gemütlichkeit* in the tropics. Tucked away into one corner, the lavish bar area features esoteric liquors and liqueurs and an upscale and stylish décor that you may have expected in a chic hideaway in Berlin. The dining room is simpler. Designed as a foil for the cuisine, and not an architectural statement in its own right, it's outfitted with dark wood trim and the kind of nautical décor that's especially charming when the Atlantic winds outside blow hard and cold. Its owners are not shy about publicizing their culinary ambitions. They serve one of the few white (as in New England) styles of conch chowder we've seen in The Bahamas. Jumbo cheeseburgers are appropriately juicy, but more appealing may be the Delmonico steaks, veal chops with Provençal herbs, or shrimp Alfredo with marinara-flavored pasta. Chilean sea bass poached in chardonnay-flavored butter sauce is a specialty, as is something known as "lobster St-Jacques," wherein chunks of lobster are spooned over a bed of garlic-flavored mashed potatoes, covered with cheese, and broiled.

See map p. 202. In the Port Lucaya Marketplace. ☎ *242-374-4466. Reservations recommended. Main courses: $23–$34. Children's platters $5–$9. AE, MC, V. Open: Wed–Sat 5–11 p.m.; Sun 11 a.m.–4:30 p.m. and 6–11 p.m.*

Iries
$$$ Lucaya CARIBBEAN

This is one of the newest restaurants at the Westin & Sheraton Hotels at Our Lucaya, and as such, a team of food and beverage experts threw tons of money and research into the appropriate blend of Caribbean tradition and postmodern sales and marketing. The result reminds you of the dining room of a massive colonial Caribbean manor house, replete with replicas of pineapples (the region's traditional symbol of hospitality), Rastafarian-inspired paintings, and the kind of elaborately carved mahogany furniture that may have graced the home of a 19th-century Caribbean planter. You get an airy sense of spaciousness and old-fashioned, 19th-century dignity and restraint. Menu items include lobster and grilled corn bisque, cracked conch with spicy pick-a-pepper sauce and sweet-potato wedges, grilled sirloin steak with cumin and thyme, Caribbean-inspired shrimp scampi, blackened grouper with fire-roasted peppers and pineapple sauce, and tamarind-glazed hen. On your way in, check out the Bahamian Junkanoo costume on display. It's one of the most elaborate, most outrageous, and most costly examples of its kind. Replete with sequins and mystical references, it's something of which the Bahamian staff here is genuinely proud.

See map p. 202. The Westin & Sheraton at Our Lucaya Resort, Royal Palm Way. ☎ *242-373-1333. Main courses: $25–$48. AE, MC, V. Open: Sat–Wed 6–11 p.m., but hours vary according to the season and occupancy levels of the hotel.*

Luciano's
$$$–$$$$ Lucaya CONTINENTAL

This elegant restaurant overlooks the Port Lucaya Marketplace Marina and has a certain Continental charm. Whet your appetite with a seafood crepe, garlic-infused escargot, or chilled melon with port. Inspired by classical European recipes with some local flair thrown in, the seafood and meat courses are uniformly excellent. We recommend the Bahamian grouper filet with toasted almonds and lemon butter. Flambéed with cognac, the scampi is another palate pleaser. The duckling breast comes in a green peppercorn sauce, and the rack of lamb (served for two) is carved table-side. Dessert brings a velvety smooth crème brûlée, pears over vanilla ice cream topped with raspberry sauce, and crepes, among other treats.

See map p. 202. Port Lucaya Marketplace. ☎ *242-373-9100.* www.portlucaya. com/lucianos. *Reservations required. Main courses: $27–$44. AE, MC, V. Open: Mon–Sat 5:30–10 p.m. (last seating).*

Outrigger's Native Restaurant/White Wave Club
$ **Smith's Point   BAHAMIAN**

Cement-sided and simple, with a large deck extending out toward the sea, this restaurant was here long before the construction of the nearby Port Lucayan Marketplace, which lies only four blocks away. The restaurant area is the domain of Gretchen Wilson, whose kitchens produce a rotating series of dishes that include such lip-smacking dishes as lobster tails, minced lobster, steamed or cracked conch, pork chops, chicken, fish, and shrimp, usually served with peas 'n' rice and macaroni. Every Wednesday night, from 5 p.m. to 2 a.m., the restaurant is the venue for Outrigger's Famous Wednesday Night Fish Fry, when as many as a thousand diners will line up for platters of fried or steamed fish, priced at $10 to $15 each. A DJ and dancers round out the experience. Almost as well-attended are the establishment's Bonfire Nights, where set-price all-you-can eat barbe-cued dinners go for $30 per person every Tuesday and Thursday evening (you can also order à la carte). If you're not looking for a meal, at any time of the week you may consider stepping into the nearby ramshackle bar, the White Wave Club.

See map p. 202. Smith's Point. ☎ *242-373-4811. Main courses: $10–$16. No credit cards. Open: Sun–Fri 4–10 p.m.; Sat 1–9 p.m.*

The Pepper Pot
$ **Freeport   BAHAMIAN**

This restaurant may be the only place on Grand Bahama that specializes in Bahamian takeout food. Find this establishment in a tiny shopping mall after about a five-minute drive east of the International Bazaar. You can order the best guava duff on the island, a savory conch chowder, the stan-dard fish and pork chops, chicken souse (an acquired taste), cracked conch, sandwiches and hamburgers, and an array of daily specials.

See map p. 202. East Sunrise Highway (at Coral Road). ☎ *242-373-7655. Breakfast: $3–$6; main courses: $11–$15; vegetarian plates: $5–$6. No credit cards. Open: Daily 24 hours.*

Pisces
$–$$ Lucaya   BAHAMIAN/INTERNATIONAL

This restaurant is our favorite among the many in the Port Lucaya Marketplace, and we're seconded by a healthy mix of locals and yacht owners who pack the place every weekend. Decorated with Tiffany-style lamps and captain's chairs, it boasts the most charming wait staff on Grand Bahama Island. Lunches are relatively simple affairs, with fish and chips, sandwiches, and salads. You can order pizzas anytime, and they're available in 21 varieties, including one with conch, lobster, shrimp, and chicken. Dinners are more elaborate and better tasting, and you have a choice of curries (including a version with conch); lobster in cream, wine, and herb sauce; all kinds of fish and shellfish; and several kinds of delicious pasta dishes.

See map p. 202. Port Lucaya Marketplace. ☎ *242-373-5192. Reservations recommended. Pizzas: $12–$28; dinner main courses: $9–$30. AE, DISC, MC, V. Open: Mon–Sat 5 p.m.–1:30 a.m.*

Prop Club
$$ Lucaya   AMERICAN/INTERNATIONAL

This is one of our favorite informal restaurants in the Our Lucaya/Port Lucaya compound. Set within its own low-slung building on the grounds of the Westin & Sheraton hotels, it's the kind of place that raffish-looking crew members from any of the chartered yachts moored at anchor nearby search out specifically during their time in port. And despite its location on the grounds of the most upscale resort on Grand Bahama Island, it manages to remain fun, funky, and laid-back, with a bemused humor at its own Rastafarian references. Looking for a bar, a cafe, a restaurant, a dance hall, or a pickup joint? This place can (and has been) all things to all kinds of people. It evokes a battered airplane hangar where mail planes may have been repaired during World War II. Many of the industrial parts hanging from the ceiling, including a collection of semi-antique airplane propellers and ship hulls, evoke a less high-tech age, when an airplane engine may actually have been repaired by a pilot wielding a monkey wrench, grease, and copper wire. When the weather's right (which is most of the time), large doors open to bring the outdoors inside, and the party overflows onto the beach. The all-Bahamian staff is good-looking, the drinks are stiff, the music is fine, and the place can be a lot of fun. Dig into a "mountain of ribs," or else savor the crab cakes (which actually contain a lot of crab, not just stuffing). Ever had a grilled margarita chicken sandwich? You can order one here, along with juicy oversize burgers, fajitas, spicy conch chowder, and the like. Many dishes are at the lower end of the price scale, making this restaurant an affordable choice.

See map p. 202. At the Westin & Sheraton at Our Lucaya Resorts, Royal Palm Way. ☎ *242-373-1333. Main courses: $12–$32. AE, DC, MC, V. Open: Restaurant daily 11:30 a.m.–10 p.m.; bar Sun–Thurs 11:30 a.m.–1 a.m., Fri–Sat noon–2 a.m.*

The Pub on the Mall

No matter what type of food you're in the mood for, chances are you can find it at one of the four watering holes under one roof at the **Pub on the Mall** (located at The Mall and Ranfurly Circus, opposite the International Bazaar). A meal usually costs $21, including soup or access to the salad bar, but not dessert; or you can order bar food for $5 per platter.

Inexpensive pub fare, from fish and chips to T-bone steak and lamb, draws diners to **Prince of Wales Lounge** (☎ 242-352-2700; open Mon–Sat noon–1 a.m.). Arrive between 5 and 7 p.m., and you can feast on salad, one of two main courses, dessert, and coffee, all for only about $8. Thirsty? Try a potent Pub Special: coconut rum, tequila, cherry brandy, pineapple juice, orange juice, grenadine, and bitters served in a pint mug.

Sit on the balcony at **Islander's Roost** (☎ 242-352-5110; reservations recommended; open Mon–Sat 5:30–11 p.m.). The steak, prime rib, and fish here are nothing special, but the frozen daiquiris are sumptuous, and the tropical décor puts you in a vacation mood.

A huge satellite TV broadcasting American and European sports dominates the **Red Dog Sports Bar** (☎ 242-352-2700; open daily noon–midnight). If you need energy for all that rootin', hootin', and hollerin', order chicken and fries, fish and chips, or other pub grub, washed down with a brew or two.

Pub at Lucaya
$–$$ Lucaya   ENGLISH/BAHAMIAN

By day, you can dine on typical English pub grub. Along with fish and chips, you can find dependable chicken and asparagus pie, shepherd's pie, and steak-and-ale pie. Fat burgers add an American twist to the menu. At dinner, Bahamian dishes rule, including grilled fish or cracked conch served with a heaping mound of peas and rice. Dine inside or alfresco, overlooking the water. Although you shouldn't feel any discomfort here, opt for a Painkiller, a rum-filled cocktail that can leave you smashed.

See map p. 202. Port Lucaya Marketplace. ☎ *242-373-8450. Main courses: $13–$40; sandwiches and burgers: $8–$11. AE, MC, V. Open: Daily 11 a.m.–11 p.m. (bar until 1 a.m.).*

Shenanigan's Irish Pub
$–$$$ Lucaya   CONTINENTAL

Dark and beer-stained from the thousands of pints of Guinness, Harp, and Killian's that have been served and spilled here, this pub is the premier Boston Irish hangout on Grand Bahama Island. Many visitors come just to soak up the suds — sometimes for hours at a time — and perhaps eventually order some food. If you get hungry, you can order surf and turf, French-style rack of lamb for two, seafood Newburg, and several preparations of

chicken. Don't expect more than comfort food, but it's satisfying and affordable (unless you order the expensive steak-and-lobster combo).

See map p. 202. Port Lucaya Marketplace. ☎ *242-373-4734. Main courses: $10–$45.
AE, DISC, MC, V. Open: Mon–Thurs 5 p.m.–midnight; Fri–Sat 5 p.m.–2 a.m.*

Silvano's
$–$$ Freeport   ITALIAN

The only authentic Italian dining spot in Freeport, this 80-seat restaurant
serves a fine, but not exceptional, cuisine. The standard repertoire from
Mama's kitchen is presented here with quality ingredients, most often
shipped in from the United States. The grilled veal steak is our favorite,
although the homemade pastas are also alluring. The pastas are served
with a wide variety of freshly made sauces. The chef also works his magic
with fresh shrimp. Service is polite and helpful.

See map p. 202. Ranfurly Circus. ☎ *242-352-5111. Reservations recommended. Lunch
main courses: $7–$14; dinner main courses: $15–$42. AE, DISC, MC, V. Open: Daily
noon–3 p.m. and 5:30–11 p.m.*

The Star Club
$ West End   BAHAMIAN

Among the unassuming places to chew and sip in the West End — about a
45-minute drive from downtown Freeport — The Star Club is the one with
the most character. Opened in 1946 as Grand Bahama's first hotel, this colonial wooden and concrete two-story building sits on the waterfront. In its
heyday, it welcomed such guests as Ernest Hemingway, Sidney Poitier, and
Martin Luther King, Jr. When other nightspots close, The Star Club is still
a happening place because it's open nearly 24 hours a day. After partying
elsewhere on the island, many locals head here to listen to music (recorded
or the occasional live band), play pool, and watch the sun rise.

Conch in all its incarnations, fried chicken, burgers, and fish and chips are
on the menu, along with peas and rice. The cook will fill you up with a satisfying meal or snack, but you won't be on the phone to the editors of
Gourmet magazine. When the weather cooperates, you can watch men prepare fresh conch salad out front at a waterside stand. The owner here
claims that it's common knowledge that The Star Club's conch salad is the
best on the island. We agree. The bartender won't divulge the secret recipe
for his club's legendary Bahama Mamas, but these drinks keep folks
coming back for more.

See map p. 202. Bayshore Road. ☎ *242-346-6207. Main courses: $10–$16. No credit
cards. Food served daily 10 a.m.–2 a.m.*

The Stoned Crab
$$$ Lucaya   SEAFOOD

The most romantic restaurant on the island, The Stoned Crab sits beneath
a soaring pyramid-shaped roof at the edge of the beach. You can eat inside,

but the best seats in the house are on the alfresco patio. The stone crab claws here are some of the sweetest you'll ever taste, and the fish — try the wahoo, yellowfin tuna, or swordfish — are also beautifully prepared. Other good selections are the crab-and-avocado cocktail and the broiled seafood platter that's aromatically seasoned with oregano, garlic, and white wine. For guests not wanting to eat fish, the restaurant offers a number of Continental dishes nightly, including chicken parmigiana. If you're not the designated driver, be sure to order a Stoned Crab (a potent rum and fruit juice cocktail) or an Irish coffee. Because the seafood is freshly caught, not everything on the menu is always available.

See map p. 202. Taino Beach. ☎ *242-373-1442. Reservations strongly recommended. Main courses: $22–$45. AE, MC, V. Open: Tues–Sun 11 a.m.–3 p.m.*

Willy Broadleaf
$$ Lucaya   INTERNATIONAL/BUFFET

At the first-class Westin & Sheraton at Our Lucaya, you're treated to one of the most lavish buffet dinners in the entire Bahamian chain. The chefs conceive of their offering as a giant spread of exotic dishes based on recipes from around the globe. The décor fits the cuisine, evoking a courtyard patio in Mexico, a marketplace in old Cairo, the dining hall of an Indian maharajah, and even an African village. From India comes tandoori chicken, from Greece moussaka. Another tasty treat is a sausage made from wild boar. Expect freshly made salads, hot and cold dishes, and luscious desserts.

See map p. 202. The Westin & Sheraton at Our Lucaya, Royal Palm Way. ☎ *242-373-1333. Buffet: $12 for cold foods, $20 for hot and cold food. AE, DC, DISC, MC, V. Open: Daily 6:30–11 p.m.*

Zorba's Greek Cuisine
$–$$ Lucaya   GREEK/BAHAMIAN

First thing in the morning, locals line up for the Bahamian breakfasts served at this casual dining spot. From chicken souse to corned beef and grits, all the island eye-openers are on the menu. Eggs and fluffy Greek pastries snag less daring early risers. Lunch may be a fat gyro or a souvlaki kebab. Dinner can begin with a Greek salad and then move on to moussaka, with baklava for a sweet finish. You can eat inside or enjoy your meal alfresco. We can't pretend the food here is like a trip to the Greek isles, but it's satisfying in every way.

See map p. 202. Port Lucaya Marketplace. ☎ *242-373-6137. Lunch main courses: $4–$15; dinner main courses: $14–$28. AE, DISC, MC, V. Open: Daily 7 a.m–11 p.m.*

Chapter 17

Having Fun On and Off the Beach in Grand Bahama

*F*rom booze cruises and snorkeling excursions to fishing trips and kayak paddles, Grand Bahama keeps water lovers busy. The variety of beaches rimming the island allows devotees to spend their entire vacations sun-worshipping. Landlubbers can enjoy excellent golf, tennis, horseback riding, hiking, biking, shopping, and sightseeing. Compared with Nassau and Paradise Island, Grand Bahama may not be party central after dark, but you can find more than enough nightspots for drinking, dancing, and romancing.

Combing the Beaches

White sandy beaches hug Grand Bahama's southern shores, some 97km (60 miles) of strands. Footprints are few and far between on most of these shores. The busiest and best beaches are in **Lucaya,** the island's watersports mecca, where you find the cluster of resort hotels. Freeport hotels, built inland, shuttle their guests to nearby sandy shores. **Xanadu Beach,** located at a resort near Freeport, is a favorite for guests with beachless accommodations and cruise-ship passengers. This beach can be crowded at times in winter, but it boasts gorgeous, soft, white powdery sands that open onto tranquil waters. The beach, which stretches for 1.5km (1 mile), has a backdrop of coconut palms and Australian pines. Here you find some of the best watersports on the island, including snorkeling, boating, Jet-Skiing, and parasailing. On weekends, residents head to the sands at **William's Town,** east of Xanadu Beach and south of Freeport. Many visitors get their first glimpses of golden **Taino Beach,** just east of Lucaya, when they stop by The Stoned Crab restaurant for a meal (see Chapter 16). Parasailing, Jet-Skiing, and banana-boat rides at Taino Beach keep vacationers active.

Fun in Grand Bahama

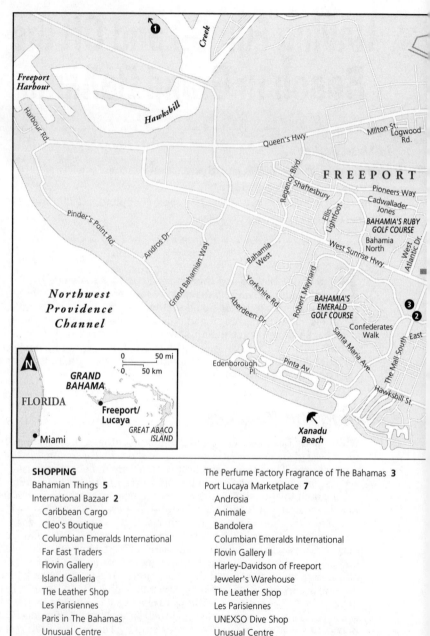

SHOPPING

Bahamian Things **5**

International Bazaar **2**
- Caribbean Cargo
- Cleo's Boutique
- Columbian Emeralds International
- Far East Traders
- Flovin Gallery
- Island Galleria
- The Leather Shop
- Les Parisiennes
- Paris in The Bahamas
- Unusual Centre

The Perfume Factory Fragrance of The Bahamas **3**

Port Lucaya Marketplace **7**
- Androsia
- Animale
- Bandolera
- Columbian Emeralds International
- Flovin Gallery II
- Harley-Davidson of Freeport
- Jeweler's Warehouse
- The Leather Shop
- Les Parisiennes
- UNEXSO Dive Shop
- Unusual Centre

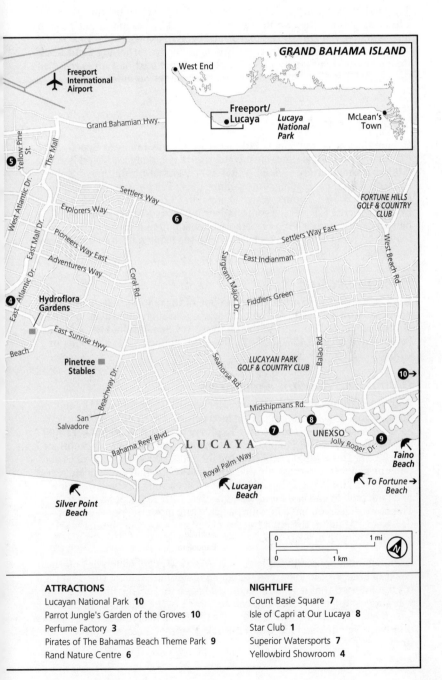

ATTRACTIONS

Lucayan National Park **10**
Parrot Jungle's Garden of the Groves **10**
Perfume Factory **3**
Pirates of The Bahamas Beach Theme Park **9**
Rand Nature Centre **6**

NIGHTLIFE

Count Basie Square **7**
Isle of Capri at Our Lucaya **8**
Star Club **1**
Superior Watersports **7**
Yellowbird Showroom **4**

The farther east you go, the less crowded the beaches become. You hit **Churchill Beach**, then **Smith's Point**, followed by **Fortune Beach** (where an all-inclusive resort draws many Europeans), and **Barbary Beach.** About a 20-minute drive from the hotels in Lucaya, stunning **Gold Rock Beach** slumbers at **Lucayan National Park.** One part of it lures residents for weekend picnics, while other sections remain secluded.

Playing in the Surf

Ocean Motion Water Sports Ltd., Sea Horse Lane, Lucayan Beach (☎ 242-374-2425), is the largest watersports company on Grand Bahama. It offers a wide variety of daily activities — weather permitting — from 9 a.m. to 5 p.m. Parasailing, for example, costs $50 per person; snorkeling trips cost $35 for 1½ hours; water-skiing costs $25 per 3km (2-mile) pull; Hobie Cats cost $20 per person; windsurfing costs $30 per hour; and banana-boating costs $10 per person for a 3km (2-mile) ride. Call for information on other activities, including deep-sea fishing, bottom-fishing, and kayaking.

Banana-boating

You can join a row of other riders on one of these long, yellow inflated boats for a bouncy trip. As the boat snakes through the waves, you get splashed, so hold on tight to the handles! Try **Sea Affairs Ltd.** at Xanadu Beach, Lucaya (☎ 242-352-2887). Rides generally cost $10 for kids or adults.

Diving and dolphin encounters

Both the National Association of Underwater Instructors (NAUI) and the Professional Association of Diving Instructors (PADI) hold diving certification classes at the **Underwater Explorer's Society (UNEXSO; ☎ 800-992-DIVE** or 242-373-1244; www.unexso.com), Port Lucaya Marketplace, which offer three full days of training for $400. UNEXSO is one of Grand Bahama's oldest and most reliable companies. The half-day quickie resort course ($75) includes a shallow reef dive. Dives start at about $25 for a one-tank plunge and $50 for a two-tank dive, with all necessary gear. The more dives you have in your package, the more the per-dive cost decreases. At night, the colors of the ocean are especially intense. A UNEXSO night dive costs $35.

A goal of most scuba divers is to visit *Theo's Wreck,* which lies off the coast of Freeport. In 1982, the Bahamian government sank this 70m (230-ft.) freighter so that it would become a haven for marine life. Their plan was successful, and today you can see some of the most varied marine life off island, ranging from moray eels to sea turtles, at the wreck. Other popular dive sites include **Golden Rock, Pygmy Caves,** and **Silver Point Reef.**

Bahamian-owned **Caribbean Divers,** at the Bell Channel Inn, opposite Port Lucaya (☎ 242-373-9111), is another good outfitter. Its certification courses begin at $350, and its resort course runs $89. Prices begin at $35 for a one-tank dive and $64 for a two-tank dive, including equipment. Caribbean Divers also offers night dives for $60 and shark dives starting at around $100. You can rent underwater cameras for $40. For the optimal experience underwater, the company limits groups to a maximum of 18 divers.

Another outfitter is **Xanadu Undersea Adventures** at Xanadu Beach Resort (☎ **800-327-8150** or 242-352-3811; www.xanadudive.com). Certification courses begin at $450, and resort courses run $40 to $280. You can have your dive videotaped for $35 or rent your own underwater camera for $25 to $30, plus film. Dives begin at $40 for one tank and $70 for two tanks. Ask about shark dives for $40 and night dives for $20.

If you want to dive with dolphins, you can do so through UNEXSO's **The Dolphin Experience.** For the **Close Encounter** ($69 for adults, free for children age 7 and younger), a ferry takes you from Port Lucaya Marketplace to Sanctuary Bay, 3km (2 miles) away. Atlantic bottlenose dolphins nuzzle your dangling legs as you sit on a partially submerged dock. Participants stand waist-deep in the water and pet some of these powerful creatures. The butter-smooth skin of these amiable mammals feels amazingly soft and warm. While small groups take turns going into the water, an expert tells you all about the origins, behaviors, likes, and dislikes of the dolphins. You spend only about 15 minutes body-to-body with the dolphins.

If you want more time up close and personal, opt for the **Swim with the Dolphins** program ($149). When you're underwater, you can hear their clicks and clucks as they converse with each other. Contact UNEXSO for more information.

No matter which dolphin program you choose, reserve as far in advance as possible.

UNEXSO, which pioneered shark diving ($100) in The Bahamas, schools you on proper human-shark interaction and takes all kinds of precautions to ensure your safety.

You can have your shark dive videotaped for $30 and up. If you'd rather snap shots yourself, you can rent underwater cameras from UNEXSO for $10 and up.

Jet-Skiing and water-skiing

Some people object to Jet Skis, which zoom across the waves like aquatic motorcycles, saying they're at odds with Grand Bahama's tranquillity and calm waters. However, if you're interested in this adventure, **Sea Affairs Ltd.,** at Xanadu Beach (☎ 242-352-2887) can arrange it for you. The rental costs $30 for 15 minutes or $50 for 30 minutes.

If water-skiing is more to your liking, you can also book with **Sea Affairs Ltd.**, at a price of $20 per person for a 2.4km (1½-mile) ride.

Kayaking

To explore Grand Bahama's more pristine corners, you can rent Funyaks through **Paradise Watersports** at Xanadu Beach (☎ 242-352-2887). Rentals cost $9 for 30 minutes or $14 for an hour, plus a $10 deposit.

You can also combine a kayak trip with a guided nature walk: Make a reservation with **Grand Bahama Nature Tours** (☎ 242-373-2485; www. grandbahamanaturetours.com), run by Bahamian-German husband-wife team Ed and Erika Gates. You spend 90 minutes of this six-hour adventure paddling double kayaks along a tidal creek and through a mangrove forest with branches that create a shady canopy. As fish dart by, you can spot egrets, greenback herons, and other seabirds. A trek through **Lucayan National Park** introduces you to ancient Lucayan Indian caves, and you're treated to a picnic lunch on **Gold Rock Beach,** where you can swim. The excursion costs $79 for adults, and is free for kids age 10 and under (half price for children 11–16). Kayak Nature Tours provides air-conditioned transportation to and from your hotel, complete with drivers who provide a running narration about Bahamian history, lore, and sights. The ride is about 40 minutes from the International Bazaar and 30 minutes from Port Lucaya Marketplace. Kayak Nature Tours also hosts trips to nearby islands. (See "Going Beyond Grand Bahama," later in this chapter.)

Parasailing

Parasailing involves being strapped into a harness that's attached to a parachute on one end and a boat on the other. When the boat takes off, away you go, up toward the clouds. The people, ocean, and beach below shrink to toy-size. Although you're airborne for only about five minutes, the thrill lasts much longer in your memory. Contact **Reef Tours** at the Port Lucaya Dock (☎ 242-373-5880). A ride costs $50 per person.

Snorkeling

The waters around Grand Bahama are clear and ideal for snorkelers, who can spot such varied marine life as sea turtles, moray eels, and horse-eyed jacks. Ben's Cave is a favorite. This panoramic cavern is part of the Lucayan Cave system. The coral beds at Silver Point Reef and Gold Rock also draw snorkelers. Most hotels either host their own snorkeling excursions or can help you make arrangements for trips elsewhere. **Reef Tours** (☎ 242-373-5880) runs one-hour-and-45-minute excursions that cost $35 for adults and $16 for children.

Climbing Aboard

You can find plenty of opportunities to explore sea life without getting wet.

Parrot Jungle's Garden of the Groves
Lucaya

This attractive 5-hectare (12-acre) oasis has a pond full of alligators as well as a petting zoo with Vietnamese potbellied pigs, Pygmy goats, and a cockatoo. Macaws on perches welcome visitors, and you can spot an iguana, a peacock, ducks, and raccoons. Allow at least 45 minutes to see the animals and to wander across footbridges and along paths past waterfalls, fruit trees, flowers, and lacy ferns. You can spend a few quiet moments in the historic chapel that sits on a rise overlooking the garden. Built with native stone, the chapel is topped by a Spanish tile roof. The garden — 25 minutes from the International Bazaar and 15 minutes from the Port Lucaya Marketplace — honors American financier and developer Wallace Groves, who founded Freeport with his wife, Georgette.

See map p. 212. On Magellan Drive, off Midshipman Road, Lucaya. ☎ *242-373-5668 or 242-373-1456. Admission: $9.95 adults, $6.95 ages 3–10, free for children under 3. Open: Daily 9:30 a.m.–4 p.m.*

Perfume Factory
Freeport

Touring the fragrance laboratory housed in a replica of a 19th-century Bahamian mansion takes a mere five minutes. You can discover how the company produces perfumes, colognes, and lotions from tropical ingredients. You're then invited to purchase some. But most people find the mix-your-own sessions here the best reason to visit. Be prepared for an olfactory workout. For $30, you can sniff honeysuckle, lavender, gardenia, jasmine, cinnamon, ginger, and an array of other aromas to decide which two or three essential oils to combine into your own signature creation. You can name your concoction and have it bottled and labeled. Choosing your special scent can take anywhere from 15 minutes to a half-hour.

See map p. 212. Behind International Bazaar. ☎ *242-352-9391. Admission: Free. Open: Mon–Fri 9:30 a.m.–5:30 p.m.; Sat noon–4 p.m.*

Pirates of The Bahamas Beach Theme Park
Taino Beach

Islanders think of this amusement park as their Disney World. This theme park is one of the largest watersports centers in The Bahamas, featuring pools for diving and swimming, along with an array of activities, such as parasailing, banana-boating, snorkeling, kayaking, paddle-boating, and Jet-Skiing. Children have their own Captain Kidd's Camp with a supervised playground. Something's always happening here, including beach or bonfire parties. The park doesn't charge a general admission fee, but you're charged for some of the attractions, such as the 18-hole minigolf course ($6 per person). Bonfire Party Night on Tuesday, Thursday, and Sunday lasts from 6 p.m. to midnight. The price — adults $50, children $20 — includes free transportation from your hotel, live entertainment, and an all-you-can-eat buffet dinner. A restaurant and bar are housed in a wooden structure that evokes a Spanish galleon.

See map p. 212. Jolly Roger Drive. ☎ *242-373-8456. Admission: Free. Open: Mon–Fri 8 a.m.–4 p.m.; Thurs–Sun 2–10:30 p.m.*

Rand Nature Centre
Freeport

Nature buffs, especially bird lovers, need at least two hours to appreciate this 40-hectare (100-acre) reserve run by the Bahamas National Trust, a nonprofit conservation association. Named in honor of philanthropist James H. Rand, this slice of wild Grand Bahama is 3km (2 miles) from the International Bazaar and less than 6km (3½ miles) from Port Lucaya Marketplace. One of the highlights is a pond studded with a flock of pink flamingos, The Bahamas' national bird. You can get a close-up look at this endangered species, so bring your camera. Other feathered friends you may spot are a red-legged thrush, a banana quit, or a Cuban emerald hummingbird. A pair of binoculars comes in handy, especially for the two-hour guided bird walk that's held the first Saturday of each month, starting at 8 a.m. A variety of orchids is among more than 100 different types of plants here. Several species of Bahamian boa constrictors reside in the exhibit room, along with other indigenous and imported creatures.

See map p. 212. East Settler's Way, less than a half-kilometer east of Coral Road. ☎ *242-352-5438. Admission: $5 adults, $3 children 5–12, free for ages 5 and younger. Open: Mon–Fri 9 a.m.–4 p.m.*

Guided tours

Several tour companies offer informative tours of Grand Bahama Island. One reliable company is **H. Forbes Charter Services Ltd.,** The Mall at West Sunrise Highway, Freeport (☎ **242-352-9311;** www.forbescharter. com). From its headquarters at the International Bazaar, this company offers half- and full-day bus tours. The most popular option is the half-day Super Combination Tour, priced at $25 per adult and $20 per child under 12. The tour includes guided visits to the botanical gardens, drive-through tours of residential areas and the island's commercial center, and stops at the island's deepwater harbor. The tour also includes shopping and a visit to a wholesale liquor store. Tours depart Monday through Saturday at 9 a.m. and 1 p.m.; the tour lasts 3½ hours.

If you're a nature lover, escape from the casinos and take a bush-and-sea safari with **East End Adventures** (☎ **242-373-6662**). The safari takes you through dense pine forests and along deserted beaches, and you go inland on hikes to such sites as *blue holes* (natural pools where fresh water floats on top of salt water), mangrove swamps, and underground caverns. You may even figure out how to crack conch. You eat a native lunch on a serene beach in Lightbourne's Cay, a remote islet in the East End. Most of the tour is laid-back; you can snorkel in blue holes or shell hunt. The company conducts safaris daily between 8 a.m. and 5:30 p.m. The cost is $110 for adults and $55 for kids ages 2 to 12.

Trekking to the "Wild" West End

Rent a car or hire a taxi and head to **West End,** which is about 45 minutes from downtown Freeport. Fishing boats recline along the one narrow road that parallels the coastline. This tranquil fishing community is the place to go when you're in the mood to have a few drinks or swap a tale or two with locals, or when you have a taste for fresh home-style seafood. Small roadside kitchens move snapper, jack fish, and grouper from the ocean to the frying pan in record time.

Once the capital of Grand Bahama, West End is inhabited by descendants of the first settlers of the island. Freeport and Lucaya may be new compared to Nassau, but other parts of Grand Bahama were developed long before its modern resort areas. West End is the site of the island's annual Junkanoo parades on Independence Day (July 10) and Boxing Day (Dec 26). On your way to West End, you pass other old seaside settlements — some dilapidated, and some in colorful ruins. Many of the tiny houses are painted bright blues, yellows, and greens. You may also come upon a *blue hole* (a natural pool where fresh water floats on top of saltwater). When the tide is right, many locals swim in these pools.

Keeping Active

Beaches are paramount on Grand Bahama, but you can find much more to island life than making waves. Visitors have many options for staying active on solid ground.

Biking

A guided bike trip is an ideal way to see parts of Grand Bahama that most visitors miss. Starting at **Barbary Reach,** you can pedal a mountain bike along the southern coast parallel to the beach. Stop for a snack, lunch, and a dip. Finally, you reach **Lucayan National Park,** some 12 (1? miles) away. Explore the caves where the Indians buried their dead in the days when Grand Bahama was theirs. Crabs here have been known to come up though holes in the ground carrying bits of bones once used by the Lucayans. **Kayak Nature Tours (☎ 242-373-2485),** the company that sponsors these trips, transports you home to your hotel by van, so you don't have to exhaust yourself in the heat cycling back. The cost is $79 for adults, half price for children ages 10 to 16. All equipment, sustenance, and round-trip transportation from your hotel are included.

Golfing

Grand Bahama is home to more golf courses than any other Bahamian island. Open to the public throughout the year, the golf courses host a variety of international tournaments. No need to worry if you don't feel like lugging your own clubs — you can rent clubs from any Freeport or Lucaya pro shop.

The ultimate in relaxation

The ideal place to relieve the stress of everyday life can be found at the **Westin & Sheraton at Our Lucaya's Senses Spa**. The spa boasts an exercise facility with health checks, personal trainers, and yoga classes. A cafe serves fresh, natural food and elixirs. During one of their signature treatments, the Total Senses Massage, two massage therapists work in sync to relieve your tension. Throughout the Salt Glo body polish treatment, a therapist buffs away dead-skin cells and polishes your skin with natural elements from The Bahamas. Note that residents of either the Westin or Sheraton can use the health and exercise facilities without charge, but that spa, health, massage, and beauty treatments must be scheduled in advance and require payment of additional fees. See Chapter 15 for more information on the hotels.

Fortune Hills Golf & Country Club, Richmond Park, Lucaya (☎ 242-373-2222), was originally intended to be an 18-hole course, but the back 9 were never completed. You can replay the front 9 for 18 holes and a total of 6,916 yards from the blue tees. Par is 72. Greens fees cost $31 for 9 holes, $43 for 18. Electric two-seater carts cost $43 for 9 and $55 for 18 holes. Club rental costs $18 for 18 holes and $14 for 9 holes.

The best-kept course on Grand Bahama is the **Lucayan Golf Course**, Lucaya Beach at Our Lucaya (☎ 242-373-1333). Made over after hurricane Jeanne of 2004, this beautiful course is defined as a traditional golf layout with rows of pine trees separating the fairways. Greens are fast, with a couple of par fives more than 500 yards long, totaling 6,824 yards from the blue tees and 6,488 from the whites. Par is 72. Greens fees are $120 for 18 holes, including a mandatory shared golf cart.

Its slightly older sibling golf course, with an entirely separate clubhouse and staff, is **The Reef Course**, Royal Palm Way, at Our Lucaya (☎ 242-373-1333; www.ourlucaya.com/reef_course.asp). Designed by Robert Trent Jones, Jr., who called it "a bit like a Scottish course but a lot warmer," it features a wide-open layout without any rows of trees to separate its fairways, but lots of water traps — similar to a links course in the north of Britain. It requires skill, patience, and precise shot-making to avoid its numerous lakes. You'll find water on 13 of the 18 holes and various types of long grass swaying in the trade winds. The course boasts 6,920 yards of links-style playing grounds.

At either of the above-mentioned golf courses, residents of either the Westin or Sheraton Hotels, with which the courses are associated, pay between $84 and $120 for 18 holes, depending on the season. Nonresidents are charged between $98 and $140 for 18 holes. Use of an electric-powered golf cart is included in those rates.

Hiking and birding

Early freed slaves carved out the **Heritage Trail** as they made their way from one part of the roadless island to the other. This 13km (8-mile) trek, which runs parallel to the beach, takes you to flourishing Lucayan National Park. At the park, you can spot birds and explore old caves that the island's Native Americans once used for fishing, collecting fresh water, and burying their dead. But the best part of this all-day excursion is the picnic lunch on a dune, shaded by casuarinas overlooking the beach, and, of course, the swim afterward. You won't have to hike back to your starting point because **Kayak Nature Tours (☎ 242-373-2485)** provides transportation. The cost of the tour is $69 per person. This company also takes vacationers on early morning bird-watching tours that include snacks and transportation to and from hotels.

Horseback riding

Take a ride with **Pinetree Stables (☎ 242-373-3600)**, Beachway Drive, along a wooded trail through a mangrove swamp to a golden sand beach. These stables are conveniently located halfway between the International Bazaar and the Port Lucaya Marketplace. The two-hour ride costs $75 per person. Groups of up to ten people go out with two guides per trip twice a day, Tuesday through Sunday. Make reservations as far in advance as you can, especially in the summer.

Tennis

In Freeport, most visitors play tennis at the nine hard-surface courts at **Crowne Plaza Golf Resort & Casino (☎ 242-352-9661)**. The cost is $10 an hour for guests and $12 for non-guests. Six courts have lights for night play (for an extra $12). In Lucaya, **The Westin & Sheraton at Our Lucaya (☎ 242-373-1333)** has four courts, each available for $12 to $18 an hour for guests and non-guests alike. You can rent racquets (for $5) and balls ($3) and take lessons ($55 per hour) at either of these hotels.

Shopping the Local Stores

If you're in the market for watches, leather, crystal, china, perfume, or gemstone and 14-carat gold jewelry, European and American imports can be considerably less expensive here than at home. Of course, list prices prevail, and knowing what these prices are back home is always good so that you can determine whether you're indeed getting a bargain.

Not a whole lot in the stores is actually produced in The Bahamas — that is, beyond some clothing, lotions, fragrances, crafts, and straw goods. Many of the items at the island's straw markets come from elsewhere, including all those colorful, flowing Indonesian fabrics that are so popular for women's wear.

Port Lucaya Marketplace is an open-air shopping and dining complex that sprawls along the waterfront in Lucaya. Fire-engine red British telephone booths stand near pastel shingle-roofed buildings festooned with bougainvillea. Many restaurants are on second-story balconies overlooking the channel. Nearly 100 pubs, restaurants, and boutiques draw both visitors and residents. Some afternoons and most evenings, live music spills from the bandstand in the lacy harborside gazebo at **Count Basie Square.**

At the older **International Bazaar** in Freeport, the shops, eateries, and architecture take visitors around the world. You enter through a towering *torii* archway, a symbol of welcome in Japan. Designed in the 1960s, the place now has a somewhat seedy feel. In many cases, merchandise and food are only loosely related to the countries represented by the architecture of the section where they're sold. But strolling along the maze of slender, meandering walkways is still amusing. Turn a corner, and your surroundings suddenly change from Tokyo to the Left Bank of Paris, from Latin America to Africa, from East India to Hong Kong. You may have a hard time comparison shopping because figuring out how to get back to a place you came from can be tricky. For the most part, prices here are good — in many cases 20 to 40 percent lower than in the United States.

Behind the entrance to the International Bazaar, the **Straw Market** is packed with stalls where vendors call out to passersby, "It doesn't cost anything to look!" Baskets, wide-brimmed hats, bags, place mats, and dolls are among the most popular straw goods. Tables are also piled high with T-shirts, beach towels, shell jewelry, magnets, mugs, and mahogany African-style Bahamian woodcarvings. The **International Arcade,** which links the bazaar with the Casino at Bahamia, houses branches of glitzy stores, such as Parfum de Paris, Columbian Emeralds, and the Leather Shop. Here, you can also find artisans in booths, including glass blowers and jewelry designers.

International Bazaar

Here are some worthwhile shops found at the bazaar.

[SEE LEO'S STUDIO IN PORT LUCAYA

Art

Flovin Gallery (☎ 242-352-7564) sells original Bahamian and international art, frames, lithographs, posters, and Bahamian-made Christmas ornaments and decorated coral. It also offers handmade Bahamian dolls, coral jewelry, and other gift items. There's another branch at **Port Lucaya Marketplace.**

Crystal and china

Island Galleria (☎ 242-352-8194) boasts an awesome collection of crystal. The store includes works of utilitarian art in china and crystal by Waterford, Aynsley, Lenox, Dansk, Belleek, and Swarovski. The store can pack and ship anything you buy. Another branch is located in Port Lucaya Marketplace (☎ 242-373-4512).

Fashion

Cleo's Boutique (☎ 242-352-3340) offers apparel from evening wear to lingerie, as well as everything in between. A warm and inviting destination, Cleo's prides itself on capturing the Caribbean woman in all her moods. You can also find a wide array of costume jewelry beginning at $25 per piece.

Far East Traders (☎ 242-352-9280) sells Asian linens, hand-embroidered dresses and blouses, silk robes, lace parasols, smoking jackets, and kimonos. A branch is located inside the Island Galleria at Port Lucaya Marketplace.

Paris in The Bahamas (☎ 242-352-5380) contains the biggest selection of luxury goods under one roof in the International Bazaar. The staff wears couture black dresses, and everywhere there's a sense of French glamour and conspicuous consumption. The store offers both Gucci and Versace leather goods for men and women; crystal from Lalique, Baccarat, Daum, Kosta Boda, and Orrefors; and a huge collection of cosmetics and perfumes.

Gifts

Caribbean Cargo (☎ 242-352-2929) is one of the island's best gift shops, specializing in such items as picture frames, candles, clocks, and clothes.

Unusual Centre (☎ 242-373-7333) is exactly what its name suggests. Where else can you find a wide array of items made of eel skin or goods made from exotic feathers, such as peacock? Another branch is located at Port Lucaya Marketplace (☎ 242-352-5994).

In addition to these gift shops in the bazaar, **Bahamian Things,** 15B Poplar Crescent (☎ 242-352-9550), sells an array of locally handcrafted items, including books on The Bahamas, Abaco ceramics, woodwork, and even handmade Christmas decorations.

Jewelry

Colombian Emeralds International (☎ 242-352-5464) is a branch of the world's foremost emerald jeweler, offering a wide array of precious gemstone jewelry and one of the island's best watch collections. Careful shoppers will find significant savings over U.S. prices. The outlet offers certified appraisals and free 90-day insurance. Two branches are also located in Port Lucaya Marketplace (☎ 242-373-8400).

Leather

The Leather Shop (☎ 242-352-5491) is another good outlet, carrying a much more limited Fendi line but also many other designers, including

Land and HCL. Additional leather goods include shoes and gift items. Other locations include Port Lucaya Marketplace (☎ 242-373-2323) and **Regent's Centre** (☎ 242-352-2895).

Perfume

Les Parisiennes (☎ 242-352-5380) offers a wide range of perfumes, including the latest from Paris. It also sells Lancôme cosmetics and skin-care products. You'll find a branch at Port Lucaya Marketplace (☎ 242-373-2974).

The Perfume Factory Fragrance of The Bahamas (☎ 242-352-9391) is the top fragrance producer in the country. The shop is housed in a model of an 1800s mansion, and visitors can go inside to hear a five-minute commentary and to see the mixing of fragrant oils. A "mixology" department lets you create your own fragrance from a selection of oils. The shop's well-known products include Island Promises, Goombay, Paradise, and Pink Pearl (which has conch pearls in the bottle). The shop also sells Guanahani, a fragrance created to commemorate the 500th anniversary of Columbus's first landfall in the New World. ("Guanahani" was the Indian name for the southern Bahamian island of San Salvador, traditionally believed to be the site of Columbus's landing.) Other perfumes and colognes include Sand, the number-one Bahamian-made men's fragrance in the country.

Port Lucaya Marketplace

The following are some of the highlights of the marketplace.

Androsia (☎ 242-373-8387) is the Port Lucaya outlet of the famous batik house of Andros Island. Its designs and colors capture the spirit of The Bahamas. Fabrics are handmade on the island of Andros. The store sells quality cotton resort wear, including simple skirts, tops, jackets, and shorts for women, and it also offers a colorful line of children's clothes.

Animale (☎ 242-374-2066) attracts fashionistas who would define this as a hot boutique with the kind of clingy sophisticated tropical fashion that makes any reasonably shaped woman look good. Come here for long cotton dresses that make the female form look more-than-usually provocative, and fashion accessories such as oversize straw hats, chunky necklaces, and animal-print scarves.

Bandolera (☎ 242-373-7691) carries a collection of chic women's clothing that's many, many cuts above the usual run of T-shirts and tank tops. The staff can be rather haughty here, however.

Colombian Emeralds International (☎ 242-373-8400) is a branch of the world's foremost emerald jeweler offering a wide array of precious gemstone jewelry and one of the island's best watch collections. Careful shoppers will find significant savings over U.S. prices. The outlet offers certified appraisals and free 90-day insurance.

Flovin Gallery II (☎ 242-373-8388) is a branch of the art gallery that's located in the International Bazaar. It sells a collection of oil paintings (both Bahamian and international), along with lithographs and posters. In its limited field, it's the best in the business. It also features a number of gift items, such as handmade Bahamian dolls and decorated corals.

Harley-Davidson of Freeport (☎ 242-373-8269) is one of only two registered and licensed Harley outlets in The Bahamas. You can special-order a motorcycle if you feel flush with funds from a casino. Or you can content yourself with T-shirts, leather vests, belts, caps, sunglasses, and gift items.

Jeweler's Warehouse (☎ 242-373-8401) is a place for bargain hunters looking for good buys on discounted, closeout 14-karat gold and gemstone jewelry. Discounts can be up to 50 percent, but the quality of many of these items remains high. You can get guarantees and certified appraisals.

UNEXSO Dive Shop (☎ 242-373-1250) is the premier dive shop of The Bahamas. It sells everything related to the water: swimsuits, wet suits, underwater cameras and video equipment, shades, hats, souvenirs, and state-of-the-art diving equipment.

Living It Up After Dark

At press time, Grand Bahama maintained only one casino, the **Isle of Capri** at the Westin & Sheraton at Our Lucaya Resorts, Royal Palm Way (☎ 242-373-1333). It's set within its own free-standing building on the resort grounds. Outfitted in a neutrally modern, not-particularly-ostentatious design, it contains a crescent-shaped bar, a restaurant, and games that include baccarat, Caribbean stud poker, blackjack, roulette, and some 400 slot machines. It's open daily from 10 a.m. to 2 a.m. or later; entrance is free.

For an evening with island appeal, try the **Yellowbird Showroom** at **Best Western Castaways Resort,** East Mall Drive, Freeport (☎ 242-352-6682). Fire eaters, calypso singers, and limbo dancers put on a festive show Monday through Saturday from 9 to 11 p.m. ($20 per person, including one drink; or $32 per person for the show, dinner, and drinks). About a 45-minute drive from Freeport, **West End** is a local after-hours target, particularly **The Star Club** (☎ 242-346-6207), which usually stays open until dawn. Where Grand Bahama's local nightclubs leave off, hotel and restaurant bars and lounges pick up the slack, with crowded dance floors.

In Port Lucaya Marketplace's waterfront **Count Basie Square,** live music pumps from the gazebo almost every night, starting around 7:30 p.m. You may hear calypso played on steel drums, a reggae band, a Junkanoo troupe, or a gospel group. Some say that the idea for the marketplace

---

Bahamian theater

If you're visiting The Bahamas between September and June, call the 450-seat **Regency Theater,** West Sunrise Highway (☎ 242-352-5533), and ask if any shows are running. This is the home of two nonprofit companies, The Freeport Players' Guild and the equally talented Grand Bahama Players. You could see anything from reprises of such Broadway and West End (London) blockbusters as *Oliver!* to contemporary works by Bahamian and Caribbean playwrights. Tickets cost from $15 to $20.

---

itself originated with the Count, the legendary American jazz pianist and bandleader who spent his last years on Grand Bahama. Most of Port Lucaya's stores close after dark, but the marketplace still throbs with activity under the stars. The bars and restaurants surrounding the square are serious hangout spots for both residents and visitors.

If you didn't get enough of the waters surrounding Grand Bahama during the day, make a reservation for a moonlight dinner cruise with **Superior Watersports** (☎ 242-373-7863). You can feast on steak and lobster on a fun-filled 22m (72-ft.) catamaran. Cruises run Monday, Wednesday, and Friday from 6 to 9 p.m. and depart from Port Lucaya Marketplace; the cost is $59 for adults and $39 for children.

Going Beyond Grand Bahama

Whether you're a novice or an experienced kayaker, one of the following excursions can introduce you to another side of The Bahamas.

Trip #1: Kayak and snorkel adventure to Peterson Cay

You can go from Grand Bahama, one of the country's largest islands, to one of its smallest, by kayak. Nearby uninhabited **Peterson Cay** is an itty-bitty national park on a reef. After you reach this pristine slip of land edged by a luscious beach, Freeport and Lucaya seem like Las Vegas. You can go on this excursion with **Kayak Nature Tours** (☎ 242-373-2485). When you arrive at the tour's starting point — about a 25-minute drive from Freeport — you paddle for about 30 minutes to the cay. For about 90 minutes, you can snorkel around the island with the colorful fish and marine life. A trip with Kayak Nature Tours costs $69 per person. The company keeps snorkel groups to a maximum of ten people, even when more participants are in the total group of kayakers. The company provides all the necessary gear, and your driver entertains you with a running narration about Grand Bahama as you're transported to and from your hotel.

Trip #2: Kayak trip to Indian Cay

Another kayak adventure offered by **Kayak Nature Tours** (☎ 242-373-2485) costs $89 per person and takes seven hours. This trip combines a kayak adventure with a snorkeling tour and is excellent for first-time snorkelers or more experienced adventurers. The tour begins with sightseeing in the old hamlet of West End, site of the first settlement on Grand Bahama Island. Then guests go by kayak to **Indian Cay,** one of the most remote of all the islands in the North Bahamas. According to legend, Ponce de León discovered this cay and named it *La Vieja* (The Old One) after an old Lucayan woman he found there. Upon seeing her, he knew at once that he hadn't found the Fountain of Youth he so eagerly sought. Participants take a short nature walk across this tiny cay that time forgot, then later, back on "mainland" Grand Bahama, explore underwater trails at Old Bahama Bay Resort. At the resort, visitors are served lunch on a private beach.

Part V
The Abacos: Prime Out Islands

AFTER SAILING AROUND ELBOW CAY, DERK AND HEATHER HEAD FOR THE INTERESTING GROTTOS OF NOSE CAY.

In this part . . .

We explore The Abacos, which lie north of New
Providence. You discover what makes the most popular of these serene landfalls special, whether you're considering an inn at a marina in Marsh Harbour, a small beach hotel
on Elbow Cay, an upscale yacht club on Green Turtle Cay, or
a modern resort on Treasure Cay. In this part, we give you
plenty of suggestions for having fun in the sun and sampling
everything from conch fritters to lobster. Most importantly,
you find out the best ways to travel among these small,
scenic cays by air, land, and sea.

Chapter 18

Marsh Harbour and Great Abaco Island

. . . .

In This Chapter
▶ Getting around Marsh Harbour
▶ Finding Marsh Harbour's best accommodations and restaurants
▶ Exploring the island's best beaches, watersports, and attractions

. . . .

*A*fter New Providence Island (where you find Nassau and Paradise Island) and Grand Bahama Island (home to Freeport and Lucaya), the "prime" grouping of islands is the Abaco archipelago. The island chain is the most visited of the Out Islands, and it's a prime destination for boaters and fishermen.

When people speak of **"the Abacos,"** they're referring to a boomerang-shaped archipelago of mostly minor cays, lying in the northeastern part of the island nation. The Abacos begin at tiny Walker's Cay in the north and stretch for 209km (130 miles) in a southwesterly direction. Most of these cays are uninhabited.

As the center of Abaconian commerce, **Marsh Harbour** is the best refueling stop in all the Out Islands, with the largest range of facilities, including marinas, shopping centers, banks, and pharmacies. Even though Marsh Harbour is large enough to boast a Pizza Hut, it's still small enough to walk around; it has only one traffic light. However, the town lacks the quaint New England charm of New Plymouth (see Chapter 20) or the allure of Hope Town (see Chapter 19).

Marsh Harbour is also the major transportation hub of the Abacos, with its airport functioning as the main arrival point for most visitors — at least those who didn't sail in on a boat.

Arriving at the Airport

Regardless of where you're going in the Abacos, Marsh Harbour is the easiest town to reach. Minor airstrips are in the Abacos, including

Treasure Cay (see Chapter 21), but Marsh Harbour offers the most convenient flights servicing the Abaco chain.

The airport is a ten-minute drive south of Marsh Harbour. Upon arrival, you'll find restrooms, phones, and a little snack bar, along with taxis waiting to take you where you want to go. There are no car-rental agencies at the airport; you have to make arrangements after you reach Marsh Harbour.

Choosing Your Location

Marsh Harbour is at the crook of the bend in the archipelago (just opposite of Elbow Cay). **Treasure Cay** lies to the north, a distance of 45km (28 miles) from Marsh Harbour, and you reach it by taking a badly paved road.

If you're an adventurer, you'll want to drive 40km (25 miles) farther north to **Little Abaco Island.** Birders come here to look for the West Indian red-bellied woodpecker, and sometimes you can still see wild horses. On the way to Little Abaco, you pass the Treasure Cay airport and the dock where visitors take a ferry to **Green Turtle Cay.** The last town on **Great Abaco Island** is a hamlet called **Cooper's Town.** After that, you can take a causeway that links Great and Little Abaco islands.

Little Abaco's small settlements are hardly worth a stopover — you can take in Cedar Harbor (with a few good beaches) and Mount Hope, which you reach after another 8km (5 miles) and is mainly known for its drugstore and grocery. A drive 8km (5 miles) to the northwest delivers you to the hamlet of **Fox Town,** which may be the end of your tour, with its post office and police station. The actual end of the line is another 3km (2 miles) ahead when you come to **Crown Haven.** After this point, you have to turn around and go back south to Marsh Harbour.

Although there are tiny harbors of no importance in Great Abaco, when locals refer to "the harbor," they mean the yacht-filled Marsh Harbour in the center of the Abacos. Marsh Harbour opens onto the Sea of Abaco. To better understand the geography of the Abacos, refer to the map "The Abaco Islands" in Chapter 3.

Where you stay in the Abacos — Marsh Harbour, Elbow Cay, Green Turtle Cay, or Treasure Cay — depends on your tastes and interest. Before you make a decision, go through all four of these island chapters to see which one appeals to you, because each island of the Abacos has its devotees as well as its detractors. For example, Green Turtle Cay may draw a snobby yachting crowd who may not be charmed at all by the more middlebrow allures of Marsh Harbour.

Marsh Harbour

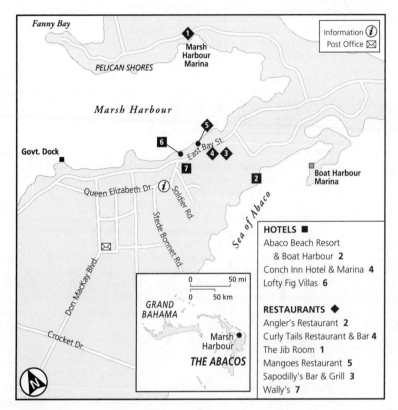

Fanny Bay

Information ⓘ
Post Office ✉

Marsh Harbour Marina ❶

PELICAN SHORES

Marsh Harbour

❺

6

East Bay St.

❹ ❸

Govt. Dock

7

2

Queen Elizabeth Dr. ⓘ

Soldier Rd.

Boat Harbour Marina

Stede Bonnet Rd.

Sea of Abaco

Don Mackay Blvd.

✉

Crocket Dr.

0   50 mi

0   50 km

GRAND BAHAMA

Marsh • Harbour

THE ABACOS

HOTELS ■
Abaco Beach Resort
   & Boat Harbour **2**
Conch Inn Hotel & Marina **4**
Lofty Fig Villas **6**

RESTAURANTS ◆
Angler's Restaurant **2**
Curly Tails Restaurant & Bar **4**
The Jib Room **1**
Mangoes Restaurant **5**
Sapodilly's Bar & Grill **3**
Wally's **7**

Getting Around Marsh Harbour and Great Abaco

In many of the smaller islands of the Abacos, including Treasure Cay and Green Turtle Cay (see Chapters 21 and 20, respectively), you can manage without a car. If you plan to stay in Marsh Harbour and visit one of the offshore islands, such as Elbow Cay (reached by ferryboat; see Chapter 19), you still don't need a car. But if you want to explore "mainland" Great Abaco Island, including points south such as **Bahamas National Trust Sanctuary,** you need a car.

✔ **Hoofing it:** Marsh Harbour is a small town, and you can get around on foot, but you won't really find that much to see. We suggest saving your legs for a day trip to Elbow Cay (see Chapter 19), where you can walk endlessly along its beaches of golden sand.

✔ **Driving around:** You don't need a car to get around the town itself, but if you want to explore the rest of the island on your own, you can rent a car, usually for $70 to $80 a day or $350 to $400 per week (be prepared for bad roads, though). In Marsh Harbour, call **A&P Rentals** (☎ **242-367-2655**), Don MacKay Boulevard, to find out whether any vehicles are available.

✔ **Pedaling around: Rental Wheels of Abaco** (☎ **242-367-4643**), Queen Elizabeth Drive, rents bikes for $10 a day or $45 a week and mopeds for $45 a day or $200 a week. The best place to go biking is the long road heading south from Marsh Harbour. Along the way, you may want to stop at a secluded beach to beat the heat of the day.

✔ **Taking a taxi:** Unmetered taxis, which you often have to share with other passengers, meet all arriving flights. They can take you to your hotel if it's on the Abaco "mainland"; otherwise, they can drop you at a dock where you can hop aboard a water taxi to one of the neighboring offshore islands, such as Green Turtle Cay or Elbow Cay. Most visitors use a combination taxi and water-taxi ride to reach the most popular hotels. From Marsh Harbour Airport to Hope Town on Elbow Cay, the cost is about $12 for the transfer. You can also make arrangements for a taxi tour of Great or Little Abaco. These tours, however, are expensive, and you don't really see that much. Sightseeing on foot in one of the Loyalist settlements, such as New Plymouth, is better. Taxis are independently owned and operated, so there's no central number to call. But you can easily find a taxi at the airport. If you need one otherwise, you can ask the staff at your hotel to summon one for you.

✔ **Boarding a boat:** Because Marsh Harbour is the boating capital of The Bahamas, some Bahamians use boats more frequently than a car to get around. **Albury's Ferry Service** (☎ **242-367-3147**) can take you to the most interesting offshore islands, including Elbow Cay and Great Guana Cay.

Staying in Style

Abaco Beach Resort & Boat Harbour
$$$–$$$$ **Marsh Harbour**

This 82-room beachfront resort — the biggest and best in Marsh Harbour — is a good choice, especially if you're serious about diving or fishing. This property extends over a sprawling acreage at the edge of town and meets up with a small beach. The business has several different faces: the hotel, with its handsomely furnished rooms that overlook the Sea of Abaco; the well-managed restaurant and bar; the Boat Harbour Marina, which has slips for 180 boats and full docking facilities; and a full-fledged dive shop. The beach here is small and gravel studded and isn't reason enough to check in. But it is private, reserved only for residents of the hotel. The bedrooms are better equipped than the ones at its rival, Conch Inn Hotel (see next review). At the Abaco Beach Resort, the rooms are air-conditioned and include a TV and extras, such as a minibar, hair dryer, and safe. **Angler's Restaurant** is one of Marsh Harbour's best (see the review in the "Dining Out" section later in the chapter). A swim-up bar and beachfront bar serve light snacks and grog. Two tennis courts, a fitness center, a sauna, and massage services are on-site. Staff can also arrange boat rentals for you at the marina.

See map p. 235. The Sea of Abaco. ☎ *800-753-9259 or 242-367-4154. Fax: 242-367-2158.* www.abacoresort.com. *Rack rates: $240–$365 double, $480 one-bedroom suite. AE, DISC, MC, V.*

Conch Inn Hotel & Marina
$$ **Marsh Harbour**

Slightly downscale from the Abaco Beach Resort & Boat Harbour (see previous review), this little nine-room inn lies at the southeastern edge of the harbor. One of the world's largest yacht-chartering companies, The Moorings, leases this casual, one-story hotel on a long-term basis. A number of sandy beaches are within driving distance. Its small motel-style bedrooms have two double beds, and you can get rollaways if you have extra occupants. All units overlook the yachts bobbing in the nearby marina. A freshwater pool, fringed with palm trees, and a nearby branch of the Dive Abaco scuba facility are on the premises. The on-site restaurant and bar is **Curly Tails** (see the review in the "Dining Out" section later in this chapter).

See map p. 235. East Bay Street. ☎ *242-367-4000. Fax: 242-367-4004. Rack rates: $120 double. Extra person $20. AE, MC, V.*

Dolphin Beach Resort
$$$ **Great Guana Cay**

Even better than any of the accommodations of Marsh Harbour is an escape to the offshore **Great Guana Cay** and this ten-room charmer (for more details on this cay, refer to "Going Beyond Marsh Harbour and Great Abaco" later in this chapter). Set directly astride one of the best beaches in The Bahamas, and a 15-minute walk north of Guana Cay's largest settlement (Guana Village), this resort offers informal but very comfortable lodgings. Four of the units are in the main house and have queen-size beds, ceiling fans, small refrigerators, and microwaves; three of them contain private screened-in decks with teakwood furniture. The oceanfront cottages, which accommodate between two and four guests, have queen-size beds, ceiling fans, air-conditioning, and kitchenettes. The showers are outside but are secluded and screened by island flora. The place is private, intimate, and laid-back. The on-site restaurant, **The Landing,** offers a "conch crawl," which is a Bahamian take on a lobster tank. **Nippers,** a beachfront bar and grill, is a five-minute walk away. A saltwater pool is on-site, and guests can also get bikes, kayaks, and snorkeling gear from the hotel.

Outside Guana Village. ☎ *800-222-2646* or 242-365-5137. www.dolphinbeach resort.com. *Rack rates: $200–$290 double, $350–$440 cottage. MC, V.*

Lofty Fig Villas
$$ Marsh Harbour

This family-owned, six-unit bungalow colony overlooks the harbor. It doesn't have the services of a resort like Abaco Beach, but it's good for families and self-sufficient types. Built in 1970, the villas stand in a tropical landscape with a freshwater pool and a gazebo where you can barbecue. Rooms have one queen-size bed and a queen-size sofabed, a dining area, a kitchen, and a private screened-in porch. The hotel provides maid service Monday through Saturday. The hotel is about a ten-minute walk from a supermarket and shops, and you can find restaurants and bars just across the street. You can also find marinas, a dive shop, and boat rentals close by. From the Lofty Fig, you have to walk, bike, or drive a half-kilometer (1 mile) east to a point near the Marsh Harbour ferryboat docks for access to a sandy beach and a snorkeling site. (Many visitors opt to go to Great Guana Cay for their day at the beach.)

See map p. 235. East Bay Street. ☎ *and fax 242-367-2681. Rack rates: $130 daily or $845 weekly for two. Extra person $20. MC, V.*

Nettie's Different of Abaco
$$$ Casuarina Point

A wide deck and a garden surround this 20-room, family-managed bonefishing club, which is set within the hamlet of **Casuarina Point,** 29km (18 miles) south of Marsh Harbour. This ecologically conscious place was built at the edge of a saltwater marsh favored by a variety of birds, wild hogs, and iguana; it's a good choice for bird-watchers and superb for bonefishing enthusiasts. It's not luxurious, but it's a peaceful place near good snorkeling and virgin beaches. The hotel is closely associated with several bonefishing guides in the neighborhood, any of whom can arrange full-day fishing excursions costing from $375 per couple. (This cost doesn't include all equipment. Be sure that you understand the arrangements thoroughly before you commit yourself.) Each of the small to midsize bedrooms has a screened-in porch, a ceiling fan, a small bathroom, and simple furnishings; eight rooms have air-conditioning. During your stay, you're in the midst of a close-knit, isolated community that's firmly committed to preserving the local environment and heritage. You can even visit a living museum that takes you back through 100 years of the island's history. The hotel also has a bar and restaurant where the staff can recite a selection of simple Bahamian fare to you before you sit down for your meal. The food is quite good. Non-guests can drop in for meals.

Casuarina Point. ☎ *877-505-1850* or 242-366-2150. Fax: 242-327-8152. www. differentofabaco.com. *Rack rates: $200 double, from $1,300 per week. AE, MC, V.*

Dining Out

Angler's Restaurant
$$ Marsh Harbour   BAHAMIAN/SEAFOOD

Angler's is the main restaurant of Marsh Harbour's major resort (Abaco Beach Resort & Boat Harbour; see our review in the "Staying in Style" section earlier in this chapter). The place is open and airy, overlooking the Sea of Abaco. Within a few steps of your seat, dock pilings rise from the water, and yachts and fishing boats come and go. The menu changes daily, but it always features fresh seafood — which the chef prepares with finesse — along with a well-chosen selection of meat and poultry dishes. Begin with spicy lobster bisque, a timbale of grilled vegetables, or perhaps crab Rangoon, served on bean-sprout slaw with a pineapple-coconut sauce. Main dishes dance with flavor, notably the lobster stir in a mango chile sauce and the guava-glazed charred lamb chops. We also recommend the freshly-caught red snapper, prepared with just the right infusion of fresh basil.

See map p. 235. In the Abaco Beach Resort & Boat Harbour. ☎ 242-367-2158. Reservations recommended for dinner. Main courses: $6–$29. AE, DISC, MC, V. Open: Daily 7:30 a.m.–2:30 p.m. and 6–9:30 p.m.

Curly Tails Restaurant & Bar
$–$$ Marsh Harbour   BAHAMIAN

Only the Angler's Restaurant (see our earlier review in this chapter) is more sophisticated than this winning choice. Located at the Conch Inn Hotel & Marina, Curly Tails attracts a lot of yachties and visiting professional athletes. The cooks use local ingredients, such as freshly caught grouper and snapper, whenever they can. They also seem to know every conceivable way to prepare conch. The regulars don't even consult the menu; they just ask, "What's good?" Diners also look for daily specials, such as curried or steamed chicken. Fish and seafood are always on the menu. If you're frittering away a few hours, drop in for a rum-based drink.

A taste of the Abacos

In Marsh Harbour, conch salad is sold right on the docks. "It'll make a man out of you," one local vendor tells everybody, even if the person is a woman. If you stick around long enough, you'll see Billy Thompson coming by in his little truck. He's said to make the world's best homemade soursop-and-mango ice cream. If you want to go really casual, try **Island Bakery,** Don MacKay Boulevard (☎ 242-367-2129), which has the best Bahamian bread and cinnamon rolls on the island, often emerging fresh from the oven. You can even pick up the makings for a picnic.

The bar, set beneath an octagonal gazebo near the piers, is a fine place to meet people.

See map p. 235. At the Conch Inn (The Moorings), East Bay Street. ☎ *242-367-4444. Lunch salads, sandwiches, and platters: $6–$14; dinner main courses $18–$28. MC, V. Open: Daily 7 a.m.–10:30 p.m.*

The Jib Room
$–$$ **Marsh Harbour   BAHAMIAN/AMERICAN**

This funky restaurant/bar is a hangout for local residents and boat owners who savor its welcoming spirit. If you want the house-special cocktail, a Bilge Burner, get ready for a head-spinning combination of apricot brandy, rum, coconut milk, and vodka. Saturday night brings Jib's steak barbecue, when the staff serves up as many as 300 steaks. The only other dinner nights are Wednesday and Thursday, when grilled baby back ribs may be the featured dish of the day. Other choices include a seafood platter, New York strip steak, and broiled lobster — and yes, you've had it all before in better versions, but dishes are well prepared. Go for the convivial atmosphere rather than the food.

See map p. 235. Marsh Harbour Marina, Pelican Shores. ☎ *242-367-2700. Lunch platters: $8.50–$12; fixed-price dinner: $20–$25. MC, V. Open: Wed–Sat 11:30 a.m.– 2:30 p.m.; Wed–Thurs and Sat 8–11 p.m.*

Mangoes Restaurant
$–$$ **Marsh Harbour   BAHAMIAN/AMERICAN**

Set near the harborfront in one of the town's most distinctive buildings, Mangoes is the best — and certainly the most popular — restaurant on the island, drawing both yachties and locals. It boasts a cedar-topped bar and a cathedral ceiling that soars above a deck jutting out over the water. The chefs try a little harder here, offering a typical menu but adding a hint of island spirit. They dress up grilled grouper with a bit of mango and tomatoes, and cracked conch makes an appearance as well. Your best bet, as is the case in nearly all Bahamian restaurants, is the fresh catch of the day. At lunch, you can sample their locally famous "conch burger."

See map p. 235. Front Street. ☎ *242-367-2366. Reservations recommended. Lunch: $12–$15; dinner main courses: $18–$35. MC, V. Open: Mon–Sat 11:30 a.m.–2:30 a.m.; daily 10 p.m.–midnight.*

Mother Merle's Fishnet
$ **Dundas Town   BAHAMIAN**

Mother Merle's Fishnet prepares many of the meals eaten aboard the yachts and sailing crafts in the nearby harbor. The restaurant doesn't have a dining room on the premises, so you'll have to eat your meal elsewhere, but the well-prepared food makes up for this limitation. The setting is a cement house on the town's main street. Inside, you find the gentle but aging matriarch Merle Williams, who's assisted by her able-bodied daughters, Angela and Shirley. As Mother Merle tells it, all Bahamian women are

The premier yachting event

In July, Marsh Harbour hosts **Regatta Time in Abaco,** attracting sailboats and their crews from around the world. Every year, the event is held sometime between Independence Day in the United States and Independence Day in The Bahamas (in other words, between July 4 and July 10). Many of the yachties participating in this event stay at the Green Turtle Club. For event registration forms and more information, visit www.go-abacos.com/regatta/rtia-regatta.html.

good cooks, and you may very well believe her words when you taste her family's three different preparations of chicken, all secret family recipes. Locals swear that Mother Merle makes the best cracked conch in the Abacos, and she's also known for her different preparations of grouper.

Dundas Town, the hamlet that adjoins Marsh Harbour, lying directly north of the center. ☎ *242-367-2770. Main courses: $9–$17. No credit cards. Open: Tues–Sat 6–10:30 p.m.*

Sapodilly's Bar & Grill
$ Marsh Harbour   BAHAMIAN

One of Marsh Harbour's better restaurants occupies an open-air pavilion across the road from the harborfront in an area of town known as "the tourist strip." Even if you eventually head into the high-raftered interior dining room, take time out for a drink or two on the covered open-air deck, surrounded by vibrant Junkanoo colors and a crowd of local hipsters, yacht owners, marina workers, and businessmen visiting from other parts of The Bahamas. Lunch may consist of grilled fish sandwiches, burgers, salads, and quiche. Dinners are more elaborate, with 12-ounce New York strip steaks, flavor-filled shrimp kebabs in teriyaki sauce, and zesty curried filets of grouper. Live music plays every Friday and Saturday from 8 to 11 p.m.

See map p. 235. East Bay Street. ☎ *242-367-3498. Reservations recommended. Lunch platters and sandwiches: $8–$13; dinner main courses: $18–$26. MC, V. Open: Daily 11:30 a.m.–3 p.m. and 6–10 p.m.*

Wally's
$$ Marsh Harbour   BAHAMIAN/INTERNATIONAL

This eatery sits across the street from the water and occupies a tidy pink colonial villa on a lawn dotted with hibiscus. It has an outdoor terrace, a boutique, and an indoor bar and dining area filled with Haitian paintings. The house drink is a Wally's Special, which contains four kinds of rum and a medley of fruit juices. The chef prepares the best Bahamian cracked conch at Marsh Harbour, as well as tender filet mignon, lamb chops, tarragon chicken, and an excellent version of smothered grouper. Main dishes come with a generous house salad and vegetables. The place really hops at lunchtime, when things can get very busy as hungry diners devour dolphinfish burgers, several kinds of chicken platters, and well-stuffed sandwiches.

See map p. 235. East Bay Street. ☎ *242-367-2074. Reservations recommended for dinner. Lunch sandwiches and platters: $9–$15; dinner main courses: $27–$30. AE, DISC, MC, V. Open: Mon–Sat 11:30 a.m.–3 p.m., Fri–Sat 6–9 p.m. Closed six weeks during Sept–Oct.*

Enjoying the Sand and Surf

Exploring almost-deserted beaches and sailing to nearby islands, such as Elbow Cay, are part of the fun of any visit to Great Abaco Island.

Combing the beaches

Of the major towns of the Out Islands, Marsh Harbour has one of the least appealing sets of beaches. You can opt for any of a trio of private beaches, but none is very enticing, and all carry the stigma of not really wanting outsiders. The easiest of these three beaches to visit is the one at the Abaco Beach Resort, but it's small, not really fabulous and, again, private. Buy a drink for a local at the hotel bar and you're in, but that is a somewhat uncomfortable arrangement, at best.

Most beachgoers get into their cars and head south of Marsh Harbour. After 15 to 20 minutes of southbound driving, starting at points south of Little Harbour, lots of good beaches begin to appear. The beaches in the vicinity of the hamlet of **Casuarina Point** benefit from some battered, all-Bahamian restaurants in the vicinity.

Some swimmers heading south from Marsh Harbour go eastward from the main highway whenever an offshoot road appears, usually at points near Little Harbour or at points south of Little Harbour. Other times, they simply stop their cars wherever they feel like it.

None of the beaches of Great Abaco Island has facilities or lifeguards. Guard your valuables and be safe.

Playing in the surf

Divers swim to the **Abacos Train Wreck,** which you can explore in 4.5 to 6m (15–20 ft.) of water; the wreck consists of two almost-intact locomotives lying on their sides. Yet another wreck nearby, the *Adirondack,* lies in shallow water some 3 to 7.5m (10–25 ft.) deep. Many divers also come here to explore the government-protected **Sea Preserve and Fowl Cay Land,** which teems with multi-colored sea life in shallow reefs.

One of the best places to snorkel, with a colorful offshore reef, moray eels, and a plethora of beautiful rainbow-hued fish, is **Mermaid Reef.** It lies on a narrow, scrub-covered peninsula known as **Pelican Shore,** which forms the northernmost edge of Marsh Harbour's harborfront. You can drive to a point near the origin of Pelican Shore, trek across a stretch of scrub and sand, and then swim out to Mermaid Reef. Alternatively, some hardy locals sometimes swim from central Marsh Harbour across the harbor, walk across the very narrow sands of Pelican Shore, and then swim once again the short distance to Mermaid Reef.

Dive Abaco, at the Conch Inn Hotel & Marina (☎ **800-247-5338** in the U.S. or 242-367-2787; www.diveabaco.com), provides services as simple as renting snorkeling gear or as in-depth as offering full dive trips to tunnels and caverns in the world's third-longest barrier reef. Uncertified novice divers can take all-inclusive resort courses for $150. Two-tank dives, including tanks and weights for certified divers, are $80. Snorkeling is $50. Trips depart daily at 9:30 a.m., and demand dictates afternoon trips. **Sea Horse Boat Rentals,** at the Abaco Beach Resort & Boat Harbour (☎ **242-367-2513**), also rents snorkeling gear.

Climbing aboard

Because the Abacos are the boating capital of The Bahamas, many visitors arrive for only one purpose: to charter a boat and go sailing.

Ask about the depth of the harbor before you rent and, even more importantly, before you attempt to navigate your way in or out of Marsh Harbour, because Hurricane Floyd changed the configuration of the channel. People with yachts that have deep drafts have reported trouble getting in and out of the port.

If you want to try *bareboating* in The Bahamas — boating without a captain or crew — **Abaco Bahamas Charters** (☎ **800-626-5690** or 242-366-0151; www.abacocharters.com), can set you up. Weekly charters with a choice of boats begin at $1,625, with a $1,500 deposit required. Only experienced sailors can rent.

The Moorings (☎ **888-952-8420** or 242-367-4000) is one of the leading charter sailboat outfitters in the world. It operates from an eagle's nest perch behind the Conch Inn Hotel & Marina, overlooking a labyrinth of piers and wharves — at least 80 berths, with more on the way — where hundreds of upscale watercrafts are tied up (many of them for rent). With one of its vessels, you can enjoy short sails between the islands, stopping at white sandy beaches and snug anchorages. Yacht rentals generally range from $455 to $1,280 a day, with a skipper costing another $144 per day, and an onboard cook (if you want one) priced at an additional $122 per day.

For the more casual boater, **Sea Horse Boat Rentals,** at the Abaco Beach Resort (☎ **242-367-2513**), offers some of the best rentals. A 5.5m (18-ft.) Boston Whaler rents for $170 per day; a 6.5m (22-ft.) Privateer rents for $200 per day. You can also rent other vessels, and all boats are equipped with a Bimini top, coolers, a compass, and a swimming platform, along with life jackets, a paddle, docking lines, and other equipment.

Exploring on Dry Land

In monuments or sightseeing attractions, Nassau doesn't fear competition from little Marsh Harbour, which some regard as a mere refueling stopover. However, Marsh Harbour is the best center for exploring the nature-created sights of Great Abaco Island, which consists of both Great Abaco and Little Abaco.

A fully graded and tarred main highway links all the settlements on the "mainland" with such colorfully named hamlets as Fire Road, Mango Hill, Coopers Town, Joe Creek, Red Bays, Snake Cay, Little Harbour, Sandy Point, Cherokee Sound and, our favorite, Hole in the Wall, which lies at the "bottom" of Great Abaco. (See "The Abaco Islands" map in Chapter 3 to help you visualize the area.)

Driving south for 40km (25 miles) from Marsh Harbour along the **Great Abaco Highway,** you come first to **Cherokee Sound,** with a population of 150. Cherokee Sound is located at the end of a peninsula that juts out into Cherokee Sound. Residents are descendants of Loyalists who fled the mainland U.S. in 1783 and remained faithful to the British Crown.

These people faced an inhospitable land, and for two centuries have tried making a living as best they can. The men dive for lobsters or go out at night "sharking." They sell the jaws of the sharks in Marsh Harbour. They also hunt down tiniki crabs as well as pigeon and wild boar in the remote pinelands of the Abacos.

From Cherokee, you can head north to **Little Harbour,** a settlement about 12km (8 miles) south. While in Little Harbour, visit **Pete Johnston's Foundry** (☎ 242-367-2720). In the Abaco gift and souvenir shops, you'll see a remarkable book, *Artist on His Island,* detailing the true-life adventures of Randolph and Margot Johnston, who lived a Swiss Family Robinson–type adventure with their three sons. Arriving on this southerly point of the Abacos aboard their old Bahamian schooner, the *Langosta,* they lived in one of the natural caves on the island until they eventually erected a thatched dwelling for themselves in 1951. The Johnstons, including son Pete, have achieved international fame as artists and sculptors — though they still live at Little Harbour, a cay shaped like a circle, with a white sand beach running along most of it.

Pete Johnston, using an old "lost-wax" method, casts his bronze sculptures, many of which are in prestigious galleries today. Margot Johnson creates porcelain figurines of island life — birds, fish, boats, and fishers. She also works in glazed metals. They welcome visitors at their studio daily from 10 to 11 a.m. and from 2 to 3 p.m. Their art comes in a wide price range.

Before leaving the foundry, you can stop in for a drink at laid-back **Pete's Pub.** This rustic pub is beloved by yachties throughout the Abacos. The artwork is intriguing, and the beer is cold. The pub was constructed in part by the timbers of the *Langosta*. In the evening, Pete Johnson may sing a medley of sea chanties, accompanying himself on his guitar.

After leaving Cherokee and Little Harbour, you can return to the Great Abaco Highway, heading south once again to reach the little fishing village of **Casuarina Point,** west of Cherokee Sound. Here you find a lovely stretch of golden sands and some jade-colored boneflats.

If you keep going south, you come to **Crossing Rocks,** a little fishing village 64km (40 miles) south of Marsh Harbour, noted for its kilometer-long beach of golden sand. The hamlet where locals barely eke out a living takes its name from the isthmus where Great Abaco Island narrows to its thinnest point.

If you continue traveling south, you come to a fork in the road: The southern road goes to the **Abaco National Park** (also called Bahamas National Trust Sanctuary) and the aptly named **Hole in the Wall,** which is the end of the line for Great Abaco.

Protected by the government, the 8,296-hectare (20,500-acre) Abaco National Park, established in 1994, sprawls across the southeastern portion of Grand Abaco Island. Some 2,023 hectares (5,000 acres) of it is pine forest, with a lot of wetlands that are home to native bird life, including the endangered Bahama parrot. Hardwood forests, sand dunes, and mangrove flats fill the area. Rangers under the sponsorship of the **Bahamas National Trust** (☎ 242-393-1317), which operates occasional tours of the sanctuary, protect this area.

Touring on your own can be extremely difficult, and any private outfitters in the area aren't very well organized. An exception is **Ron and Erin Lowe-Pagliaro** (www.abacooutback.com), who offer sea-kayaking, snorkeling, land tours, and birding excursions. A half-day kayak trip costs $55 per adult or $35 for children 11 and under; a full day costs $85 for adults and $45 for children. They also offer a tour 2½ hours south of Marsh Harbour through the Abaco National Park to Hole in the Wall; the cost is $95 per adult or $55 per child. Contact them via their Web site.

Living It Up After Dark

The most popular gathering spot in Marsh Harbour is the **Sand Bar** at the Abaco Beach Resort & Boat Harbour (☎ 242-367-2158), opening onto the Sea of Abaco. The yachting crowd, often from Miami, hangs out here, swapping tall tales of the sea while downing lethal rum punches. Another good hangout is at **Wally's,** East Bay Street (☎ 242-367-2074), the second-most frequented place to hang out. You can enjoy Wally's special punch on an outdoor terrace or inside a cozy bar. On Wednesday and Saturday, live entertainment often performs. **Sapodilly's Bar & Grill** (☎ 242-367-3498), East Bay Street, attracts an interesting blend of locals and visitors, some of whom play at its pool table, others preferring to mix and mingle at the bar.

Going Beyond Marsh Harbour and Great Abaco

The greatest day trip is to Hope Town on **Elbow Cay** (see Chapter 19). **Great Guana Cay** is less known but is also an intriguing jaunt by ferry from Marsh Harbour.

Great Guana, on the east side of the island chain, stretches 4km (7 miles) from tip to tip and lies between Green Turtle Cay and Man-O-War Cay. It's the longest of the Abaco cays. The beachfront runs the length of the cay and is spectacular — one of the loveliest in The Bahamas. The reef fishing is superb, and bonefish are plentiful in the shallow bays.

The settlement stretches along the beach at the head of palm-fringed **Kidd's Cove,** named after the pirate. The ruins of an old sisal mill near the western end of the island make for an interesting detour. The island has about 150 residents, most of them descendants of Loyalists who left Virginia and the Carolinas to settle in this remote place.

As in similar settlements in New Plymouth and Man-O-War Cay, houses here resemble those of old New England. Over the years, the traditional pursuits of the islanders have been boatbuilding, carpentry, farming, and fishing. It doesn't take long to explore the village because it has only two small stores, a one-room schoolhouse, and an Anglican church.

Albury's Ferry Service, Marsh Harbour (☎ 242-365-6010), runs three ferries per day to Great Guana Cay. A round-trip ticket costs $15; one-way is $10.

Instead of driving around the island, most people get around in small boats. On the cay, you can charter a boat for a half-day or a full day (or a month, for that matter). One company to try is **Seagull Fishing Charters** (☎ 242-366-0266) in Hope Town. Carrying up to six passengers in a 9.4m (31-ft.) Stapleton, Seagull offers sailings from Elbow Cay to Lubbers Quarters for $490 for four hours; from Marsh Harbour to Man-O-War for $530 for four hours, and from Marsh Harbour or Elbow Cay to Guana Cay for $590 for four hours.

If you want to stay at this remote location, **Dolphin Beach Resort** is a good hotel. (See the listing in the "Staying in Style" section earlier in this chapter.) Most visitors come just for the day, returning to Marsh Harbour for the night.

For fun on the beach, head for **Nipper's Beach Bar & Grill** (☎ 242-365-5143), a dive where visitors hang out with the locals. Right on the sands, you sit in split-level gazebos and take in the most stunning seascape in the Abacos, with a snorkeling reef just 11m (36 ft.) offshore. Burgers and well-stuffed sandwiches satisfy your hunger at lunch. But the best time to go is on a Sunday afternoon for a pig roast. One guest supposedly consumed five "Nipper Trippers" — the bartender's specialty, a mix of five different rums along with tropical juices — and lived to tell about it.

Fast Facts: Marsh Harbour and Great Abaco

ATMs

You find few ATMs in the Out Islands. If you must have cash on your Out Island trip, make arrangements before you leave Nassau or Freeport; we counted just seven ATMs in the entire chain of Out Islands, including the one at the post office in Marsh Harbour.

Emergencies

Call ☎ **919** for medical, dental, or hospital emergency. To report a fire call ☎ **411.**

Hospitals

The best medical clinic in the Abacos is the Government Clinic, Queen Elizabeth Drive (☎ 242-367-2510). Hours are Monday through Friday from 9 a.m. to 5 p.m.

Information

Contact the Abaco Tourist Office at Queen Elizabeth Drive in the commercial heart of town (☎ 242-367-3067). The office is open Monday through Friday from 9 a.m. to 5:30 p.m.

Internet Access

Check with your hotel to see whether it provides Internet access.

Pharmacies

Go to the Chemist Shop Pharmacy, Don MacKay Boulevard (☎ 242-367-3106). It's open Monday through Saturday from 8:30 a.m. to 5:30 p.m.

Police

Call the police at ☎ **242-367-2560.** The station is located in the center of town near Marsh Harbour's sole traffic light.

Post Office

The Marsh Harbour Post Office is on Don MacKay Boulevard (☎ 242-367-2571).

Safety

More crime occurs in Marsh Harbour than anywhere else in the Abacos, but taking the same precautions that you would take at home should be enough to protect you and your belongings. Keep valuables in a safe place and don't go into deserted, unfamiliar areas alone at night.

Taxis

Taxis meet incoming flights at the Marsh Harbour airport. During your stay, the staff at your hotel can call one for you whenever you need one.

Chapter 19

Elbow Cay

*V*isit Elbow Cay and you risk coming back year after year, as so many Canadians, Americans, and Europeans who now own vacation homes do. The main settlement is Hope Town, a charming Cape Cod–like village with narrow paved streets, saltbox cottages, little clapboard houses with white picket fences around flowering gardens, and a red-and-white striped lighthouse.

Autumn is quiet in these parts, so some hotels and restaurants close in September and October. Elbow Cay isn't a bustling island with big resorts, so you find few places that have TVs or even phones in the rooms.

Arriving in Elbow Cay

Anyone can board a plane and get off in a vacation spot, but you have to be determined to have an out-of-the-ordinary beach vacation to choose an island like Elbow Cay. Not only do you have to board a plane — or two — but you also have to take a taxi, a ferry, and a shuttle van to get to your hotel. That is, unless you sail in on a boat.

The best way to get to Elbow Cay is to fly into **Marsh Harbour** (see Chapter 18), home of the Abacos' main airport. From here, you take a taxi to the dock to catch the ferry across Whale Cay Channel to **Hope Town,** about 20 minutes away ($10 one-way, same-day round-trip $15). Service is three times a day.

You need to coordinate your flight arrival and departure with the ferry schedule. Ask the staff at your hotel for details or call **Albury's Ferry Service** (☎ 242-365-6010). If you contact your hotel, your hotel staff can meet you at the ferry dock.

Elbow Cay

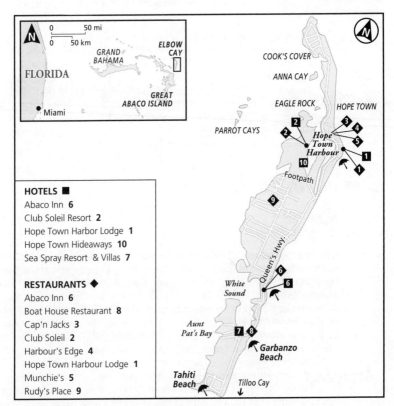

HOTELS ■
Abaco Inn **6**
Club Soleil Resort **2**
Hope Town Harbor Lodge **1**
Hope Town Hideaways **10**
Sea Spray Resort & Villas **7**

RESTAURANTS ◆
Abaco Inn **6**
Boat House Restaurant **8**
Cap'n Jacks **3**
Club Soleil **2**
Harbour's Edge **4**
Hope Town Harbour Lodge **1**
Munchie's **5**
Rudy's Place **9**

Choosing Your Location

Elbow Cay's long and secluded white sand shores, some backed by
sandy dunes, are serious contenders for The Bahamas' most stunning
locales. Elbow Cay is practically divided by White Sound, a small, tranquil body of water. Accommodations are on or near sandy shores in
Hope Town and White Sound, but because the hotels are small and few
in number, beaches remain virtually vacant.

Getting Around Elbow Cay

Many visitors rent boats to get around the island, explore nearby cays,
and go on fishing and snorkeling trips. Even if you're not interested in
playing sea captain, you can still move easily around Elbow Cay.

✔ **Hoofing it:** The quiet, narrow streets of Hope Town are reserved for pedestrians, and you can walk to many other parts of tiny Elbow Cay.

✔ **Wheeling around:** You can't rent a car on Elbow Cay, but that isn't a problem. Hope Town, the scenic seaside village, bans all motor vehicles. If you want a golf cart delivered to your hotel, call **Island Cart Rental** (☎ **242-366-0448;** www.islandcarrentals.com); these gas or electric carts go for $40 to $45 a day or $240 to $270 week. Hotels provide shuttle vans to and from town. Some dining rooms offer pickup and drop-off service at dinnertime, if you call ahead. Bicycles — often free for hotel guests — are available at or near most accommodations.

Staying in Style

Abaco Inn
$$ White Sound

This sophisticated, 22-unit adult retreat — popular with honeymooners — faces a white sandy beach on White Sound. The inn stands at the narrowest point in Elbow Cay. On the east side, the more turbulent surf of the ocean washes in. Up the shore is a secluded beach where some buffs sun in the nude, which is technically illegal in The Bahamas. More of a resort than its chief rivals, Hope Town Harbour Lodge and Club Soleil Resort, Abaco Inn offers you a choice of eight luxury villa suites with sunrise and sunset sea views or a series of simply but comfortably furnished guest cottages fronting either the Atlantic or White Sound. Shaded by sea grape and palm trees, hammocks wide enough for two hang outside cottages. A stone fireplace keeps the lounge in the main house cozy. Yachties favor the bar or the on-site restaurant, one of the island's finest. (See the review in the "Dining out" section later in this chapter.) Vans periodically take guests to and from Hope Town. Bicycles are complimentary, and many people rent boats.

See map p. 249. Three kilometers (2 miles) south of Hope Town. ☎ *800-468-8799 or 242-366-0133. Fax: 242-366-0113.* www.abacoinn.com. *Rack rates: $126–$1,240 double. AE, DISC, MC, V.*

Club Soleil Resort
$$ Hope Town

This colorfully landscaped seven-room hotel, with the popular seafood restaurant **Club Soleil** (reviewed in this chapter's "Dining Out" section), is across Hope Town Harbour. The accommodations aren't as fine as those at Abaco Inn (see previous review), but they're comfortable and far more tranquil because of the secluded property near the lighthouse on the western edge of Hope Town. You reach the resort by boat — either one you rent and moor at the hotel's marina or else a hotel boat that's sent to bring you over. At the resort, you find several lovely golden sand beaches and an on-site saltwater pool. The midsize accommodations feature a clean-cut, tasteful décor. Bedrooms have amenities such as private balconies that open onto the water and cedar-lined closets for storing your belongings. You don't have a phone, but you get a TV with VCR. In addition, the staff can arrange all sorts of watersports.

See map p. 249. Near the lighthouse at Hope Town Harbour. ☎ *888-291-5428 or 242-366-0003. Fax: 242-366-0254.* www.clubsoleil.com. *Rack rates: $130–$150 double, $140 triple, $150 quad, $160 two-bedroom apt. AE, MC, V. Closed Sept.*

Hope Town Harbour Lodge
$$–$$$ Hope Town

This Hope Town landmark sits on a narrow bluff between the harbor, with its red-and-white striped lighthouse, and the ocean, with its white sand beach. Snorkeling is idyllic at the reef just offshore, where spotting turtles and dolphins along with all kinds of crayon-colored fish is the norm.

Some of the 19 cheerfully decorated guest rooms have decks overlooking the pool and the ocean. Book one of these units, located across the road from the main building, if you want a minifridge and, more importantly, if you don't want to climb many stairs. Other rooms in the main building are smaller and have views of the town and harbor. A few paces down the road from the main building is the historic **Butterfly House** — one of the oldest surviving homes in Hope Town. The hotel owners transformed it into a two-bedroom, two-bathroom, two-deck vacation cottage with a full kitchen. As many as six people can stay here comfortably. You can dine by the saltwater pool, on the terrace high above Hope Town Harbor, or in the more formal wood-paneled restaurant. (See the listing later in this chapter's "Dining Out" section.) The staff can arrange boat rentals and watersports for you.

See map p. 249. Between Hope Town Harbour and the beach in Hope Town. ☎ *866-611-9791 or 242-366-0095. Fax: 242-366-0286.* www.hopetownlodge.com. *Rack rates: $150–$175 double, $400–$525 Butterfly House for four–six people. MC, V.*

Hope Town Hideaways
$$$ Hope Town

Staying in Hope Town Hideaways is like living in your own second home in The Bahamas. These five gingerbread-trimmed villas lie across the harbor from where the ferryboats from Marsh Harbour arrive. The villas, tucked away on 4.5 hectares (11 acres) of grounds, live up to their name. The accommodations are part of a larger complex of privately owned homes, surrounded by grounds handsomely landscaped with orange trees, mangoes, and flamboyant bougainvillea. One or two couples — the maximum is six guests — can sleep comfortably in the units, each with a large kitchen, dining room, living area with two single daybeds, and two bedrooms with queen-size beds. Furnishings are custom built. You're not on the beach, but you can enjoy the freshwater pool.

See map p. 249. Near the lighthouse, on a 12-slip marina. ☎ **242-366-0224.** *Fax: 242-366-0434.* www.hopetown.com. *Rack rates: $400 cottage for up to four guests. DISC, MC, V.*

Sea Spray Resort & Villas
$$–$$$ White Sound

These villas are on 2.4 hectares (6 acres) of landscaped grounds 6km (3½ miles) south of Hope Town near the southernmost tip of Elbow Cay. With its jagged limestone coast, the beach at this hotel may not be good for swimming, but surfers have a ball in the rolling waves. Fortunately, a good sandy beach is just a five-minute walk away, and either an energizing hike or an invigorating bike ride can take you to beautiful, secluded Tahiti Beach. Sea Spray's five oceanside and harborside cottages range from one-bedroom, one-bathroom to two-bedroom, two-bathroom. All have decks, barbecue pits, air-conditioned bedrooms, and ceiling fans. Kitchens are fully equipped, but you don't need to cook because you can find a good restaurant, the **Boat House** (reviewed later in the "Dining Out" section), right on the premises. Unlike some homelike accommodations that have limited housekeeping service, these villas come with daily maid service. Grounds are handsomely landscaped, and the waterfront swimming pool is a relaxing spot. Most guests rent boats here at the 60-slip marina.

See map p. 249. About 5km (3 miles) south of Hope Town. ☎ **242-366-0065.** *Fax: 242-366-0383.* www.seasprayresort.com. *Rack rates: $180–$260 one-bedroom unit; $350 two-bedroom unit, $430 three-bedroom unit. AE, MC, V.*

Dining Out

You can find a decent variety of culinary offerings on Elbow Cay, from Bahamian favorites to gourmet international dishes. Most restaurants serve variations of rum punch, and nearly every menu has both Key lime pie and coconut pie.

You don't need to dress up at most restaurants here — shorts and a T-shirt are fine. However, **Abaco Inn, Club Soleil,** and **Hope Town Harbour Lodge** have the most upscale dining, so casual resort clothes are more appropriate. Several restaurants provide complimentary transportation to and from your hotel.

Abaco Inn
$$$–$$$$ White Sound BAHAMIAN/INTERNATIONAL

This beachside inn offers Elbow Cay's best food, served in a semi-elegant alfresco setting. The finest tables are outside on the bluff overlooking the water. The breakfast menu may include a colorful frittata. Lobster salad and pasta dishes are the best choices at lunchtime. Before dinner, guests gather on the deck for drinks; we recommend the Bahama Breeze (Bacardi Gold, coconut rum, banana rum, apricot brandy, and fruit punch). The evening menu frequently changes, but may include coconut-crusted grouper or tender New Zealand lamb chops, followed by a smooth crème brûlée.

See map p. 249. Three kilometers (2 miles) south of Hope Town. ☎ *242-366-0133. Reservations recommended for dinner. Lunch sandwiches, salads, and platters: $8–$12; main courses: $15–$32. AE, DISC, MC, V. Open: Daily 8–10:30 a.m., noon–3 p.m., and 6:30–9:30 p.m. Call to arrange complimentary transportation to and from the inn.*

Boat House Restaurant
$$–$$$ White Sound   BAHAMIAN/INTERNATIONAL

You can dine inside, but why would you want to when you can also sit outside on the deck overlooking the marina? For dinner, top billing goes to the chef's signature calypso grouper — a filet sautéed in lemon and lime juices with a medley of herbs, then broiled with Nassau Royale (a Bahamian liqueur) and served with freshly toasted almonds and mixed vegetables. Lobster here comes any way you like it. For more variety, try the seafood platter, which includes lobster tail, grouper, and savory conch. On Monday nights, catch the Bahamian barbecue buffet, complete with local specialties such as cracked conch, grouper fingers, savory barbecued chicken or ribs, johnnycake, peas and rice, and coconut pie. After your plate is full, you can feast to the sounds of live Bahamian music.

See map p. 249. 6km (3-1/2 miles) south of Hope Town, at the Sea Spray Resort. ☎ *242-366-0065. Reservations recommended at night. Main courses: $15–$30. MC, V. Open: Daily 8a.m.–6 p.m. and 6:30–11 p.m. Call to arrange complimentary transportation to and from Sea Spray Resort.*

Cap'n Jacks
$ Hope Town   BAHAMIAN

Depending on when you come, you may find turtle burgers or crawfish on the menu at this casual alfresco dining spot at the edge of the harbor. Any time of year, the grouper and conch are well prepared and are the freshest food on the menu. Landlubbers gravitate toward the more routine fried chicken and burgers. The Key lime pie and the chocolate silk pie are justifiably popular dessert choices. Try Cap'n Jacks's version of the omnipresent Goombay Smash. Come on Wednesday or Friday between 8 and 11 p.m. for live local music.

See map p. 249. On Hope Town Harbour. ☎ *242-366-0247. Main courses: $8.25–$22. MC, V. Open: Mon–Sat 8 a.m.–9 p.m.*

Club Soleil
$$$ Hope Town   SEAFOOD

Windows around this breezy wood-paneled dining room at the edge of the harbor make you feel as if you're on a boat. You look out to Hope Town, just across the water. Vernon Malone (brother of Rudy Malone, owner of this hotel and restaurant) depicted a miniature version of town in the restaurant's driftwood wall sculpture. Sunday brunch is the big deal here, with the eggs Benedict getting rave reviews from us. Dinner may be poached salmon or a seafood platter, with Key lime pie for dessert. The chefs competently prepare all dishes with imported ingredients and turn out a very tempting menu, although one that doesn't reach the level of the Abaco Inn. For a cocktail, try a Tropical Shock, made from dark, light, and coconut rum with fruit juices.

Make reservations through your hotel or Vernon's Store in Hope Town. If you don't have your own boat, arrange to be picked up at the post office dock in town and ferried across.

See map p. 249. Near the lighthouse at Hope Town Harbour. ☎ 242-366-0003. Reservations recommended for dinner and Sunday brunch. Main courses: $16–$26. MC, V. Open: Tues–Sat 7–10 a.m. and 5:30–10 p.m.; Sun 11:30 a.m.–1:30p.m.

Harbour's Edge
$$–$$$$ Hope Town   BAHAMIAN

Harbour's Edge is almost always busy, if "busy" is an adjective you can use to describe sleepy Elbow Cay. The deck is topped with wooden picnic tables that give you a front-row seat for viewing the candy-cane lighthouse and the boat-packed harbor. At lunch, patrons eagerly gobble up the *gullywings* (chicken wings), conch chowder, crawfish salad, and fish sandwiches. Chefs prepare dinners of grilled, blackened, or fried grouper, as well as steamed or grilled Bahamian crawfish. With afternoon happy hours, a Saturday-night DJ, and the island's only pool table, this place is a lively hangout for a loud, young crowd. Try an Over the Edge, the restaurant's signature drink, made with banana rum and fruit juices.

See map p. 249. Just north of the public dock in Hope Town. ☎ 242-366-0087. Lunch main courses $9–$18; dinner main courses: $15–$38. MC, V. Open: Wed–Mon 11:30 a.m.–11 p.m.; bar Wed–Mon 10 a.m.–2 a.m. Closed mid-Sept to mid-Oct.

Hope Town Harbour Lodge
$$$–$$$$ Hope Town   BAHAMIAN/INTERNATIONAL

Lunch by the pool that overlooks a sandy beach is a special affair at the Hope Town Harbour Lodge. Popular midday treats are the curried tuna, the curried lobster, and the grouper Rueben. You eat dinner either in the dining room, with its pickled wood-paneled walls, or on the terrace above the harbor. Consider tasting the Chinese-style grouper spring rolls with a mustard-laced chutney or the peppered filet mignon. The menu is hardly inventive, but the staff properly seasons and prepares dishes well.

See map p. 249. Between the beach and Hope Town Harbour in Hope Town. ☎ 242-366-0095. Reservations recommended for dinner. Lunch main courses: $7–$12; dinner main courses: $20–$38. MC, V. Open: Daily 11:30 a.m.–3 p.m.; Tues–Sun 6:30–8 p.m.

Munchie's
$ Hope Town   BAHAMIAN

Bahamian-born, European-trained Norris Smith spent years as the acclaimed chef at Hope Town Harbour Lodge before opening this snack stand in 1993. He now whips up the island's best burgers and sandwiches made from turkey, beef, conch, or grouper, along with peas and rice, macaroni and cheese, and other local favorites that have brought him a loyal following among both residents and repeat visitors. Take your food with you to the beach or relax at one of the umbrella-shaded tables.

See map p. 249. On Back Street, across from Vernon's Store. ☎ *242-366-0423. Main courses: $8–$10. Open: Mon–Sat 10 a.m.–10 p.m. Closed mid-Sept to mid-Oct.*

Rudy's Place
$$ Just outside Hope Town   BAHAMIAN

At Rudy's, you feel as if you've been invited to dine with friends, because this rustic restaurant is in a former private residence. The hearty meals include the island's best conch fritters, soup (maybe potato, lima bean, or broccoli), a fresh salad, freshly baked warm bread, and dessert (try the "chocolate suicide" cake). Your main course could be New York strip steak or lamb chops with mint jelly. The most justifiably popular choice is the crawfish; the chef removes the meat from the shell, lightly batters and fries it, places it back in the shell, and then bakes it with Parmesan cheese. The wine list offers a good selection of French, German, Portuguese, and American vintages.

 Don't be surprised if your waiter is a child — the son or daughter of one of the other workers. When you call to make a reservation, you can arrange complimentary transportation to and from your hotel.

See map p. 249. Center Line Road. ☎ *242-366-0062. Reservations recommended. Fixed-price dinner: $20–$30. MC, V. Open: Mon–Sat 6:30–9 p.m. Closed Sept–Oct.*

Exploring the Sand and Surf

Exploring empty beaches and sailing to nearby cays are activities central to any Elbow Cay vacation. On dry land, the small harborside village known as **Hope Town** is the place to wander.

Combing the beaches

In Hope Town, you'll find sandy beaches right at your doorstep, and beaches in the south are only about a 15-minute ride away. Near Sea Spray Resort in White Sound, **Garbanzo Beach** lures many surfers. Isolated **Tahiti Beach,** at the southern end of the island (a little more than a half-kilometer, or 1 mile, from Sea Spray), got its name from its thick wall of palms. At low tide, the shelling can be excellent along this gorgeous curve of sand, and these shallow waters make for good bone-fishing, too. Across the water, you can see uninhabited **Tilloo Cay** and the thrashing waves of the Atlantic in the distance.

Tahiti Beach is about a ten-minute bike ride from Sea Spray and about 20 minutes from Abaco Inn, both in the White Sound area. To get here, you may have to walk your bike up and down a few of the small but rocky rises.

Along the way, you pass sea grape trees, fluffy long-needled pines, and other varied roadside vegetation. Turn left when you come to the first major left (by the house on the bluff). Turn right when you see two stone pillars. Go downhill and turn left at the end of the road at the wire fences. Take this path to the end. Walk along the dense palm grove to the beach. Because you're heading for the shore, which is public, ignore the PRIVATE — NO TRESPASSING signs.

Pencil-thin Tilloo Cay and the tiny **Pelican Cays** lie to the south of Elbow Cay. Their irresistible deserted beaches make them excellent targets for a day's sail. The waters around Tilloo Cay, packed with grouper and conch, are particularly good for both fishing and swimming. In the **Pelican Cays Land and Sea Park, Sandy Cay Reef** is one of the most colorful dive sites around. The area is protected, so line fishing, spear fishing, crawfishing, and shelling are all taboo.

Playing in the surf

In the Abacos, Elbow Cay is one of the best places for snorkeling. A favorite strip of beach for snorkelers is **Mermaid Beach,** with a colorful reef that teems with moray eels and various tropical fish. The beach is at **Mermaid Reef,** 3km (2 miles) north of Hope Town on the eastern side of the island. If you need snorkeling equipment, check with your hotel — most have snorkel gear on hand to rent or lend to guests who don't bring their own. Otherwise, contact **Sea Horse Boat Rentals** (☎ 242-367-2513; www.seahorseboatrentals.com).

Through scuba-outfitter **Froggies Out Island Adventures** (☎ 242-366-0431; www.froggiesabaco.com), two-tank dives start at $95, plus equipment. Resort courses run $145, and certification courses are $500. Half-day snorkel boat trips start at $45, and you can spend plenty of time — as much as two hours — in the water.

The waves and breezes at **Garbanzo Beach,** in the White Sound area, make it prime hang-ten territory. If you don't bring your own surfboard, the staff at nearby **Sea Spray Resort** (☎ 242-366-0065) can help you get one.

Climbing aboard

The waters off the coast of Elbow Cay are a popular spot for boating and fishing. Head down to the marina if you want to join in the fun.

For boat rentals, starting at about $100 a day for a 5m (17-ft.) Boston Whaler, call **Island Marine** (☎ **242-366-0282**; www.islandmarine.com), near Hope Town, or **Sea Horse Boat Rentals** (☎ **242-367-2513**; www.seahorseboatrentals.com) in Marsh Harbour. Ask about recommendations for local fishing guides.

If you want to forego the 20-minute ferry ride to Elbow Cay after you arrive at the airport in Marsh Harbour, you can rent a boat to get here on your own and then use the boat for your entire vacation. At **The Moorings** (☎ **888-952-8420** or 242-367-4000; www.moorings.com), rates start at around $455 a day for an 11m (36-ft.) monohull boat that can carry a maximum of six people.

Exploring on Dry Land

No cars are allowed in the heart of Hope Town. Bikers and pedestrians have these narrow paved streets to themselves. What you do find are some harborside restaurants and pastel-painted saltbox cottages with purple and orange bougainvillea tumbling over stone and picket fences. Amid the usual island fare at the handful of souvenir shops, you see resort wear made out of *Androsia,* the fabric produced on the Bahamian island of Andros.

Stores in Hope Town are shut tight on Sunday, and the various churches — surprising in number for such a tiny village — are in full swing. You may happen upon the outdoor Catholic service held in waterfront **Jarret Park Playground,** next to the main dock.

To find out why "Malone" is such a common surname, stop by the **Wyannie Malone Museum** (officially open most days from 10 a.m. to noon but unofficially open "whenever"). This small collection of island lore pays tribute to the South Carolinian widow and mother of four who founded Hope Town around 1783. Like other parts of the Abacos, including Green Turtle Cay and Man-O-War Cay, Elbow Cay was settled by European Americans loyal to the British Crown. Unwilling to face the outcome of the American Revolution, they began new lives in The Bahamas.

The most photographed site in the Out Islands is Hope Town's red-and-white striped **lighthouse** at the edge of the Hope Town Harbour. Before the lighthouse was erected in 1838, many of Hope Town's residents made a good living luring ships toward shore to be wrecked on the treacherous reefs and rocks, turning the salvaged cargoes into cash. To protect their livelihood, some people tried in vain to destroy this beacon while it was being built. Today, you can climb to the top of the 40m (130-ft.) tower for panoramic views of Hope Town Harbour and town. Most weekdays between 10 a.m. and 4 p.m., the lighthouse keeper is happy to give you a peek. The lighthouse is within walking distance of Club Soleil and Hope Town Hideaways. If you're staying elsewhere, you can make arrangements through your hotel for a visit.

Living It Up After Dark

On Saturday nights, a young party crowd gathers at **Harbour's Edge** (☎ **242-366-0087**), a Hope Town bar and restaurant that has the island's only pool table. On Monday nights, Bahamian barbecues draw many people to **Sea Spray Resort** (☎ **242-366-0065**), about 5km (3 miles) from Hope Town. The food is as good as the low prices, and you can hear live music. Other evenings, people hang out at the bars of hotels and restaurants — or they turn in early to rest up for yet another day of exploring.

Going Beyond Elbow Cay

Spend a day scuba diving, snorkeling, and island hopping with **Froggies Out Island Adventures** (☎ **242-366-0431;** www.froggiesabaco.com). You have easy access in and out of the water from this company's double-deck 11 and 17m (35- or 55-ft.) yachts, which come complete with bathrooms. While you sit on the top deck or in the shade down below, your boat may pass a pod of dolphins. You stop at **Fowl Cay Land,** filled with caves and 17m (55-ft.) pillars of coral. If you're snorkeling, you may not be able to swim in and out of the grottoes, but you can see plenty of fish, including frown-faced groupers and other colorful marine life. You may even spot sharks.

You also stop at **Great Guana Cay,** a pretty island that's even quieter than Elbow Cay, for lunch at a restaurant, and then you head to **Man-O-War Cay** to roam around the handsome old shipbuilding village. (For more details about Man-O-War Cay, see Chapter 21.) Nature walks and beachcombing are part of this excursion. Adult snorkelers are $55 and children are $40. Prices for certified divers start at $75.

Fast Facts: Elbow Cay

American Express and ATMs

No Amex services or ATMs are available on Elbow Cay. You can access your cash at an ATM in Marsh Harbour.

Emergencies

Call the police at ☎ 242-367-2560.

Hospitals

You need to head to the medical center in Marsh Harbour, a 20-minute boat ride away. In an emergency, contact the staff of your hotel.

Information

Contact the Abaco Tourist Office in Marsh Harbour at ☎ 242-367-3067.

Internet Access

Check with your hotel for Internet access. No cybercafes are located on Elbow Cay.

Pharmacies

Some hotels and shops in Hope Town carry over-the-counter medications and toilet articles, but the best and most fully stocked pharmacy in the Out Islands is the Chemist

Shop Pharmacy (☎ 242-367-3106), located on Don MacKay Boulevard in Marsh Harbour (20 minutes by ferry from Elbow Cay). It's open Monday through Saturday from 8:30 a.m. to 5:30 p.m.

Police

See "Emergencies."

Post Office

At the end of the "post office dock" (the main public dock in Hope Town), the post office (☎ 242-366-0098) is open weekdays from 9 a.m. to 5 p.m. but is closed for lunch, usually between 1:30 and 2:30 p.m.

Safety

Elbow Cay is a very safe island. Remember to take the same precautions that you would whether you're at home or on vacation: Keep valuables in a safe place and don't go into deserted, unfamiliar areas alone at night.

Taxis

Taxis meet incoming flights at the Marsh Harbour airport, and they greet arriving ferries as well. During your stay, the staff at your hotel can call one for you whenever you need one.

Chapter 20

Green Turtle Cay

In This Chapter

▶ Navigating Green Turtle Cay
▶ Finding Green Turtle Cay's best accommodations and restaurants
▶ Enjoying the beaches, watersports, and land-based attractions

Green Turtle Cay is about 5km (3 miles) west of Great Abaco Island, the "mainland." The beach-rimmed coastline of this 5.6km-long (3½-mile), .8km-wide (½-mile) island dips in and out of bays and sounds. Most vacationers get around by boat — usually on a rented craft. If you don't charter your own boat, you can easily join fishing, snorkeling, or diving excursions.

One of the best ways to spend a day is to explore deserted beaches on nearby uninhabited islets. On some trips, your captain may spear a few lobsters, catch some fish, and grill them for you right on shore.

Coral colonies starting in relatively shallow water make for exceptional snorkeling, and diving is good here as well. Anglers and boaters flock to Green Turtle Cay, especially during the spring and summer. The fewest visitors check in to hotels in the fall.

Arriving in Green Turtle Cay

Fly to **Treasure Cay Airport** (see Chapter 21), where a taxi can take you to the ferry dock for departures to Green Turtle Cay. At the dock, you may have to wait a while for the ferry. Green Turtle Cay is about a 15- to

---

A tip on tipping

As your taxi pulls up to the ferry dock on the Treasure Cay side, chances are young boys will be waiting to load your bags onto the boat, whether you need help or not. This is The Bahamas' equivalent of kids shoveling snow or mowing lawns for pocket money. Be as gracious and as generous as you can.

Green Turtle Cay

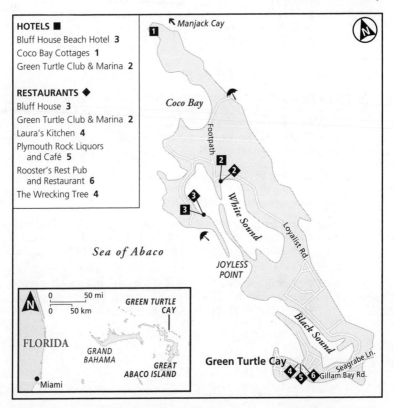

HOTELS ■
Bluff House Beach Hotel **3**
Coco Bay Cottages **1**
Green Turtle Club & Marina **2**

RESTAURANTS ◆
Bluff House **3**
Green Turtle Club & Marina **2**
Laura's Kitchen **4**
Plymouth Rock Liquors
   and Café **5**
Rooster's Rest Pub
   and Restaurant **6**
The Wrecking Tree **4**

Manjack Cay

Coco Bay

Footpath

White Sound

Loyalist Rd.

Sea of Abaco

JOYLESS POINT

Black Sound

0   50 mi
0   50 km

GREEN TURTLE CAY

FLORIDA

GRAND BAHAMA

GREAT ABACO ISLAND

Miami

Green Turtle Cay

Seagrabe Ln.

Gillam Bay Rd.

20-minute ride from the dock. The ferry takes you directly to the **Green Turtle Club,** if you're staying there, or to **New Plymouth.** This land-and-sea transfer costs $16 per person round-trip.

Treasure Cay Airport is one of three airports in the Abacos, so be sure that you book the right destination. If you fly into Marsh Harbour, you have to take a 45-minute taxi ride for $80 or more to the Green Turtle Cay ferry dock. Before making your airline reservations, check the ferry schedule with your hotel to be certain that your flight doesn't arrive too late or too early.

Choosing Your Location

The island's two main resorts are on the water in the north. **Bluff House** borders both a quiet sandy bay and a marina, and the **Green Turtle Club,** a short walk from a good beach, sprawls along a marina. If you're vacationing with friends or family, consider renting a beachside cottage. If you seek historic charm, head for the **New Plymouth Inn,** located in New Plymouth, the New England–style, 18th-century village at the southern end of the island.

Getting Around Green Turtle Cay

Although you can walk to many parts of Green Turtle Cay, water is the most common mode of transportation. Some hotels provide water transport to town or to weekly hotel parties. Many vacationers rent boats (see "Exploring the Sand and Surf" later in this chapter), but if you prefer not to, you have other options for getting around.

- ✔ **Hoofing it:** Most of the island is accessible on foot. The virtually car-free streets of New Plymouth, a quiet 18th-century seaside village, are prime walking territory.

- ✔ **Going by golf cart:** On Green Turtle Cay, golf carts stand in for rental cars. **D & P Rentals** (☎ **242-365-4655**), at the Green Turtle Club Marina, lets you use one of theirs at $45 for eight hours or $60 per day.

- ✔ **Pedaling around:** You can bike all over the island. Cycling is especially scenic in historic New Plymouth. For $14 a day, **Brendal's Dive Center** (☎ **242-365-4411**), at the Green Turtle Club Marina, rents cruisers and ten-speeds.

Staying in Style

Green Turtle Cay has only two large places to stay. And what goes for "large" here is still fewer than 35 rooms. Although some units are plush, don't count on finding a TV or phone in yours. Like the other Abaco Islands, Green Turtle Cay is for vacationers who want a retreat. If you're expecting a large, amenity-studded resort, you'll be disappointed.

Bluff House Beach Hotel
$$–$$$ Between White Sound Harbour and Sea of Abaco

With a popular, elegant restaurant, Bluff House sits on the highest spot on the island, which is only 24m (80 ft.). The marina hugs one side of the property while a cozy beach borders another. The view of the water from the main house and the pool deck is panoramic. Originally built as a private house during the 1950s, Bluff House grew over the years as the owners added rooms for visiting friends. Today guests — often honeymooners — stay in 30 units, ranging from ordinary hotel rooms to plush three-bedroom villas. The décor is as varied as the accommodations, with hardwood, tiled, or carpeted floors, Oriental rugs, and antique floral patterns in some rooms, and airy wicker furniture in others. Spacious, split-level suites with balconies overlook the ocean. Guests receive complimentary use of snorkel gear, and the staff can make arrangements for other water-sports. (If you swim out to the rocky ledge around the corner, you can find some good snorkeling.) A shuttle bus transports guests to New Plymouth, in the southern part of the island, three times a week.

Wooden boardwalks and stairs lead up and down the hilly grounds. Don't think about taking high heels to this terrain; if you have any trouble walking, don't even consider Bluff House.

See map p. 261. Northern end of the island between White Sound Harbour and Sea of Abaco. ☎ *800-745-4911 or 242-365-4247. Fax: 242-365-4248.* www.bluffhouse. com. *Rack rates: $150–$180 double, $225–$265 one-bedroom villa. AE, MC, V.*

Coco Bay Cottages
$$$ At the Sea of Abaco

On the north end of Green Turtle Cay, at a point where 152m (500 ft.) of land separates the Atlantic Ocean from the Sea of Abaco, this four-unit cottage complex opens onto a beach on the Atlantic side of the island and another sandy beach on the more tranquil bay. These accommodations are ideal for guests who want to anchor in for a while (literally — lots of folks arrive by private boat, which you can moor here for free; otherwise you can come directly by water taxi from the airport dock). Done in a refreshing style of Caribbean furnishings and pastel colors, the oceanfront property occupies 2 hectares (5 acres) dotted with some 50 tropical fruit trees. Each cottage has two bedrooms, a living room, a dining room, and a fully equipped kitchen with a microwave. Rebuilt in 1988 and renovated in 1996, the spacious cottages have improved over the years. Linens and kitchen utensils are provided (you can also stock up on groceries at three shops in New Plymouth), and ceiling fans and trade winds cool the rooms.

See map p. 261. In the north near the Sea of Abaco. ☎ *800-752-0166 or 242-365-5464. Fax: 242-365-5465.* www.cocobaycottages.com. *Rack rates: $600 daily or $4,000 weekly. MC, V.*

Green Turtle Club & Marina
$$$ White Sound Harbour

Although it's the fanciest hotel in the Abacos, the Green Turtle Club is far from stuffy. A lively crowd gathers in the clubhouse lounge most nights for conversation, backgammon, and predinner cocktails. Yachting flags hang from the ceiling beams, and business cards and dollar bills scrawled with names paper the walls. During the coolest time of year, a fire often roars in the hearth in this cozy lounge. With plenty of fishermen and boaters arriving, spring and summer are the most popular — and most expensive — seasons here. The 34 rooms and villas vary in size, view, and décor and are spread out along the marina and near a pool. In your room, you're likely to find a Queen-Anne dresser and four-poster mahogany bed, an Oriental throw rug and vase, an oak floor and wood-trimmed door, a snazzy bathroom with a dressing area, and a patio. Some of the deluxe rooms even have

TVs. Calm **Coco Bay Beach** is about a five-minute walk from here, and the rougher ocean beach is just ten minutes away. Talk to the staff to arrange a variety of watersports. Once a day, a shuttle bus takes guests into town.

See map p. 261. Northern end of the island in White Sound Harbour. ☎ *800-963-5450 or 242-365-4271. Fax: 242-365-4272.* www.greenturtleclub.com. *Rack rates: $180–$295 double, $395 suite, $470 villa. MAP $41 adults, $26 children. AE, MC, V.*

Dining Out

The hotel restaurants are the fanciest — and, of course, the most expensive — places to dine. They all have just one seating for dinner, so be sure to make reservations. Folks tend to dress up for dinner at **Bluff House** and **Green Turtle Club & Marina.** Although this practice may mean shirts with collars for men, neither restaurant requires jackets or ties. In New Plymouth, you can find several casual, local restaurants to try. Lobster season is during August and September.

Bluff House
$$ Between White Sound Harbour and Sea of Abaco
BAHAMIAN/CONTINENTAL

At this hilltop hotel restaurant, dinner is served on a deck overlooking the harbor. Thursday — with a barbecue buffet and a live band — is a big night. On Tuesday nights a one-man band usually performs. Other evenings are more subdued, with guests sharing boating, fishing, and diving stories over first-rate food at candlelit tables. The house drink is a rum–and–fruit juice concoction called the Tranquil Turtle. One night you may order the prime rib or lobster, while another evening you can sample the roast lamb wrapped in bacon with honey-rosemary glaze. Or try the crispy duck breast with a grapefruit and Grand Marnier sauce. Many of the homemade desserts come from local recipes. The chef can handle special requests, such as dishes for vegetarians or diabetics.

See map p. 261. In the north between White Sound Harbour and Sea of Abaco. ☎ *242-365-4247. Reservations required (call by 5 p.m.). Complete dinner: $35. AE, MC, V. Open: Daily 11:30 a.m. until closing (bar 6:30–11 p.m.).*

Green Turtle Club & Marina
$$$–$$$$ White Sound Harbour   AMERICAN/BAHAMIAN

Breakfast and lunch are casual here, served on a screened-in patio shadowed by a buttonwood tree. Dinner is in the elegant dining room, and women dress up and men wear shirts with collars. Guests often gather for drinks and to swap tales in the bar, and then a staff member escorts them to candlelit tables with high-backed Queen Anne chairs in the dining room. The menu changes daily, but whether you're having New York strip steak, ginger lobster medallions, or broiled grouper in guava sauce, your meal is served on fine china. A well-prepared vegetarian dish is always available.

The cuisine is invariably excellent. The Green Turtle Club offers musical entertainment three times a week; Wednesday is the most popular night.

See map p. 261. In the north, in White Sound Harbour. ☎ 242-365-4271. Reservations required. Main courses: $19–$30. AE, MC, V. Open: Daily 10 a.m.–6 p.m.

Laura's Kitchen
$$ New Plymouth   BAHAMIAN

Cozy, family-run Laura's Kitchen may not win awards for its simple décor, but this handsome old cottage is a good place to find Bahamian favorites. The menu includes good-tasting dishes, such as cracked conch, tasty grouper, fried shrimp, lobster, fried chicken, and steak. Although vacationers often visit, Laura's has a loyal local following as well.

See map p. 261. King Street, near the ferry dock. ☎ 242-365-4287. Reservations recommended for dinner. Lunch main courses: $4–$10; dinner main courses: $13–$25. MC, V. Open: Mon–Sat 11 a.m.–3 p.m. and 6–9 p.m.; Sun 5:30–8 p.m. Closed Sept and Dec 25.

Plymouth Rock Liquors and Café
$ New Plymouth   BAHAMIAN

Plymouth Rock may be a liquor store, but with counter and takeout service for breakfast and lunch, this establishment is more than that. For breakfast, you can order eggs or *chicken souse* (a hot and spicy souplike Bahamian specialty). For lunch, try a conch burger, cracked conch platter, or a more prosaic hamburger. For dessert, many patrons choose the apple turnovers or the hummingbird cake (sweetened with banana and pineapple). Alongside shelves packed with alcohol (the store has 60 types of rum for sale), you can also browse through a mega-selection of hot sauces from The Bahamas and elsewhere. When you're through feeding your body, you can tend to your spirit at the art gallery next door.

See map p. 261. Parliament Street, next to Barclay's Bank. ☎ 242-365-4234. Menu items: $4–$10. DISC, MC, V. Cafe open: Mon–Sat 9 a.m.–3:30 p.m.

Rooster's Rest Pub and Restaurant
$ Just outside New Plymouth   BAHAMIAN

Rooster's Rest is best known for the live reggae and calypso music that turns it into party central on Friday and Saturday nights. But it's also a good place to sample generous portions of the usual local suspects: fried grouper, cracked conch, peas and rice, and, of course, a Goombay Smash or two.

See map p. 261. Gilliam's Bay Road, across from The Bahamas Telephone Company and the school. ☎ 242-365-4066. Reservations recommended for dinner. Lunch burgers and snacks: $8–$12; dinner main courses: $10–$20. MC, V. Open: Mon–Sat 11:30 a.m.–9:30 p.m.

The Wrecking Tree
$ New Plymouth   BAHAMIAN

A large, shady cedar tree grows up through the front porch of this popular eatery. Some people say that The Wrecking Tree got its name because
19th-century wrecking vessels brought their salvage to this spot, but many
residents can tell you the true origin: People used to sit under the tree and
drink until they got "wrecked." Stop here for pastries, cool drinks, or a
Bahamian meal. Start off with zesty conch fritters, and then try the fish,
conch, pork chops, ribs, turtle steak, or crawfish.

See map p. 261. Bay Street. ☎ *242-365-4263. Complete dinner: $13–$15. No credit
cards accepted. Open: Mon–Sat 11 a.m.–9 p.m.*

Exploring the Sand and Surf

Along with sampling Green Turtle Cay's aquatic activities, you can visit a
museum and wander the streets of New Plymouth, the historic waterfront village.

Combing the beaches

About a ten-minute walk from Bluff House and five minutes from the
Green Turtle Club, **Coco Bay** is one of the most beautiful crescents in
The Bahamas. Shaded by casuarina pine trees and lapped by lazy waves,
this long beach is often empty. The rougher **Ocean Beach,** about a ten-
minute stroll from either Bluff House or the Green Turtle Club, is another
stunner. Frothy waves thrash the stark white sand, which is set off by
the intense blue of the Atlantic.

You can take a boat trip to one of the nearby uninhabited islands that
are ringed with even more pristine beaches. On **Manjack Cay,** for example, the expanse of sugar-white sand seems to go on forever, and the
shallow, clear water is a brilliant shade of turquoise. There's no regular
service from the ferry dock; negotiate with one of the local boatmen or
hook up with one of the trips offered by **Captain Ray** (☎ **916-933-3766**).

Playing in the surf

With one of the world's largest barrier reefs, the Abacos offer some of
The Bahamas' best and least crowded snorkeling and diving sites, with
plenty of variety. You can get an eyeful of reefs starting at depths of just
1.5m (5 ft.) and ranging to 18m (60 ft.) and more. Like sheets on a clothes-
line, sprawling schools of fish billow by coral caverns, huge tube and
barrel sponges, and fields of elk and staghorn coral. Sea turtles and large
groupers are common sights. In fact, the waters are so clear that you can
often see farther than 30m (100 ft.).

Scuba divers can poke around the wreck of the ***San Jacinto,*** an American
steamship that was built in 1847 and sank two decades ago. At this site,

you can feed the resident bright green moray eel. Plan to spend about $135 for a scuba resort course, $500 for full certification, $55 for a one-tank dive, or $75 for a two-tank dive.

If you like small groups and big fun, try **Brendal's Dive Center** (☎ 242-365-4411; www.brendal.com) at the Green Turtle Club Marina. Whether you're an experienced diver or snorkeler or you're just getting your feet wet, the personal attention you get makes the difference here. Originally from Acklins, a small Bahamian island to the south, the dive company has more than two decades of underwater experience. A special treat for snorkelers is the wild dolphin encounter trip ($75 per person), which includes stops at undisturbed islands. This company also rents kayaks ($10 per hour/$190 per week for singles; $12 per hour/$250 per week for doubles). You can also hook up with **Green Turtle Divers** (☎ 242-365-4271).

Climbing aboard

If you've had enough of sitting on the beach and relaxing, you can explore the ocean. From boat rentals to fishing expeditions, Green Turtle Cay offers an array of offshore activities.

Based at the Green Turtle Club Marina, **Brendal's Dive Center** (☎ 242-365-4411) can take you on a group sunset cruise (complete with rum punch) on an 8.8m (29-ft.) sailboat for $60 per person (up to eight passengers). If you'd prefer to see the coral without getting wet, book one of Brendal's glass-bottom boat trips ($50 per person).

Contact **Donny's Boat Rentals,** in Black Sound (☎ 242-365-4119), for speedboats. This company rents Whaler and Mako motorboats starting at $70 a day. Or you can try **Reef Rentals,** directly across from the ferry dock in New Plymouth (☎ 242-365-4145). This fleet includes a sleek motorboat made on Man-O-War Cay, the nearby island long known for its excellent boatbuilding. Rentals start at $265 for three days for a 5.7m (19-ft.) Wellcraft boat.

Reserving a boat when you make your hotel and airline reservations is a good idea, particularly during the busy spring and summer.

Some of America's most devoted anglers arrive here just to fish the coast off this cay. You find giant game fish as well as tropical fish in these waters, including a few dolphinfish, yellowfin tuna, and even the big game wahoo.

Fishing charters run from $130 to $235 for a half-day and $240 to $350 for a full day. You can make arrangements through your hotel. The annual **Green Turtle Club Fishing Tournament** (☎ 800-688-4752 or 242-365-4271) was on hold at press time, but call for information to see whether it's on when you visit in May.

Exploring on Dry Land

Walking in New Plymouth is journeying back in time. To get a taste of how Green Turtle Cay and the rest of the Abacos came to be, poke around the **Albert Lowe Museum** (☎ 242-365-4094), on Parliament Street in New Plymouth. Housed in a charming old cottage, the museum was founded in 1976 by acclaimed local artist Alton Lowe, who named the place after his father, Albert, a direct descendant of one of the European-American families who settled the island. Albert was an avid model shipbuilder; you can see some of his mini-schooners on display, along with paintings by Alton (whose prints are for sale), timeworn photographs, and other historical artifacts, some dating back to the 18th century. Admission is $5 for adults and $2.50 for students; children 5 and under are free. The museum is usually open Monday through Saturday from 9 a.m. to 4 p.m. and closed for lunch between 11:45 a.m. and 1 p.m.

Across from New Plymouth Inn on Parliament Street, the **Memorial Sculpture Garden** honors residents of the Abacos, both living and dead. What blooms in this garden are busts of island notables on stone pedestals. Read about some of the American Loyalists who came to The Bahamas from New England and the Carolinas. Statues are also dedicated to their descendants and to those people who were enslaved in these islands. You can see everyone from Albert Lowe to African-Bahamian Jeanne I. Thompson, the second woman to practice law in The Bahamas. This garden is laid out in the pattern of the British flag.

Living It Up After Dark

On Friday and Saturday nights, a mostly young, local crowd parties to reggae and calypso music at **Rooster's Rest Pub and Restaurant** (☎ 242-365-4066) on Gilliam's Bay Road, just outside New Plymouth. During the week, the island's calypso-reggae band, the Gully Roosters, plays at the **Green Turtle Club** (☎ 800-688-4752 or 242-365-4271) one night and at **Bluff House** (☎ 242-365-4247) another night. Both "venues" are on the northern end of the island.

Those fruity, rum-based cocktails known as Goombay Smashes are all over Green Turtle Cay. But **Miss Emily's Blue Bee Bar** (☎ 242-365-4181), located on Victoria Street in New Plymouth is supposedly the birthplace of this beloved, much-imitated drink. Of course, the original recipe, created by the late Miss Emily, is a well-kept secret. Everyone from Bahamian prime ministers to international TV stars has entered this tiny, unassuming hangout. Miss Emily's is open Monday through Friday from 11 a.m. until "whenever."

Going Beyond Green Turtle Cay

One of the island's best aquatic adventures is a day sail with **Brendal's Dive Center** (☎ 242-365-4411), located at the Green Turtle Club Marina. Whether you're a snorkeler or a scuba diver, the highlight is hand-feeding graceful stingrays. Because you're giving them snacks, they aren't interested in nibbling on you. If you don't know how to snorkel or scuba dive, Brendal's is a good place to learn.

On the trip, you stop at a secluded beach on an island so small that you can circle it on foot in 20 minutes. After catching some fish or lobster, your captain grills it right on the beach and serves it along with conch salad, homemade bread, and a green salad. The weather, sea conditions, and your preferences determine exactly where else you go. Brendal manages to strike that rare balance between pure professionalism and laid-back flexibility, so you can design almost any trip you want.

For the most relaxing, intimate scuba or snorkeling excursion, make a special request for the sailboat that carries a minimum of four and a maximum of eight passengers. Otherwise, you'll probably travel in a motorboat that holds up to 24 divers (although that many divers are rarely on board).

Fast Facts: Green Turtle Cay

American Express and ATMs

No Amex services or ATMs are available on Green Turtle Cay. You can access your cash at an ATM in Marsh Harbour.

Emergencies

Call ☎ 911 for fire emergencies.

Hospitals

Contact the government clinic (☎ 242-365-4028), an eye-catching pink-and-white building in New Plymouth.

Information

For visitor-related information, contact the Abaco Tourist Office (☎ 242-367-3067).

Internet Access

Resorts generally offer Internet access. Green Turtle Cay doesn't have any cybercafes.

Pharmacies

The only pharmacy in the Out Islands is the Chemist Shop Pharmacy (☎ 242-367-3106), located on Don MacKay Boulevard in Marsh Harbour. It's open Monday through Saturday from 8:30 a.m. to 5:30 p.m.

Police

Call ☎ 242-365-4450.

Post Office

Open Monday through Friday 9 a.m. to 5 p.m., the post office (☎ 242-365-4242) is on Parliament Street in New Plymouth.

Safety

Green Turtle Cay is a very safe island. However, you still need to take the same precautions that you should take anywhere you go: Keep valuables in a safe place and don't go into deserted, unfamiliar areas alone at night.

Taxis

Taxis meet incoming flights at the Treasure Cay Airport, and they greet arriving ferries as well. During your stay, the staff at your hotel can call a taxi for you whenever you want.

Chapter 21

Treasure Cay

● ●

In This Chapter
▶ Traveling on Treasure Cay
▶ Reviewing Treasure Cay's accommodations and restaurants
▶ Enjoying watersports and land-based attractions

● ●

*A*ttractive condos and villas, a championship golf course, a marina, and a golden sand beach draw visitors to **Treasure Cay,** especially in winter.

Treasure Cay is a resort area, not an island — at least not anymore (see the sidebar "When an island isn't an island" later in this chapter). This resort area looks and feels like the planned vacation community that it is — a bit sterile for our tastes. Don't be surprised if your stay makes you forget that you're in The Bahamas.

Not much existed here before Treasure Cay was born in the 1960s, so don't expect to find any historic sites or long-standing communities full of local color. The good news is that you can sail to nearby islands — Green Turtle Cay, Man-O-War Cay, and Elbow Cay — to visit three of The Bahamas' oldest and most charming villages.

Arriving at the Airport

Treasure Cay International Airport (☎ 242-365-0605) is one of the three airports in the Abacos. Taxis meet arriving flights, and they charge about $15 for one or two people for the 10- to 15-minute ride to the Treasure Cay resorts.

Choosing Your Location

You have a choice of two settings: either at a 150-slip marina, one of the best boat hangouts in the islands; or on a 5.6km (3½-mile) beach of stark white sand and calm, clear water.

Most vacationers rent golf carts or bikes to get to local restaurants and to explore their surroundings. The marina and golf course are close to both hotels. At the shopping center near the marina, you find the bank, post office, grocery store, and car rental and sports shops, along with two souvenir stores.

Getting Around Treasure Cay

Renting a car isn't necessary. To get where you're going, you can walk, bike, rent a golf cart, or take a taxi. Some restaurants outside the resort even send a shuttle to pick you up from your hotel.

- ✔ **Taking a taxi:** Except for moving between the airport or ferry dock and your hotel, you won't need a cab. For details about taxi fares, call the **Treasure Cay Airport Taxi Stand** (☎ 242-365-8661). For that special occasion when you need airport pickups or a trip to dinner in style, call **Elegante Limo Service** (☎ 242-365-8248 or 242-365-8053; $115 an hour for up to ten passengers); this company also rents golf carts.

- ✔ **Driving around:** The only real reason to rent a car is for the 35-minute drive to Marsh Harbour to catch the ferries to Elbow Cay and Man-O-War Cay, two offshore islands. (See the "Going Beyond Treasure Cay" section later in this chapter.) If you decide you want to do so, you can rent a car for $70 a day at the **Cornish Car Rental,** Treasure Cay Airport (☎ 242-365-8623). A more scenic way to get to these islands is to rent or charter a boat from Treasure Cay. (See recommendations later in this chapter.)

- ✔ **Wheeling around on a bicycle or golf cart:** Through **Wendell's Bicycle Rentals** (☎ 242-365-8687), across from the bank in the Treasure Cay shopping center, you can rent beach cruisers (single-gear bikes with wide wheels) or mountain bikes for $7 a day or $41 a week. Four-seater electric golf carts go for $40 a day or $245 a week through Wendell's or **Claridge Golf Carts** (☎ 242-365-8248 or 242-365-8053), just outside town.

Staying in Style

The two hotels here offer a variety of accommodations, from standard rooms and suites to apartments and villas.

Rooms can be scarce in May when the place is packed with fishing fanatics angling for fame in the **Treasure Cay Billfish Championship.**

In addition to the cay's two main hotels, you can also arrange condo rentals. The best agency for this service is **Bahama Beach Club** (☎ 800-563-0014 in the U.S. or Canada). A three-night minimum stay is required, and prices are $315 per night for a two-bedroom unit, $350 per night for a three-bedroom unit, and $400 per night for a four-bedroom unit.

Treasure Cay

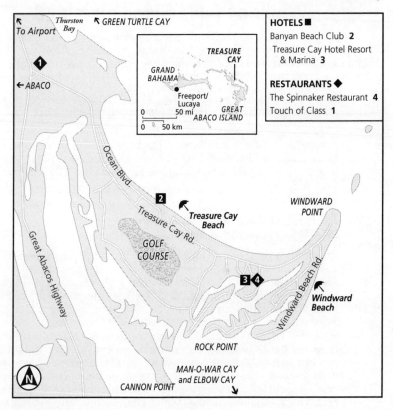

HOTELS ■
Banyan Beach Club **2**
Treasure Cay Hotel Resort
& Marina **3**

RESTAURANTS ◆
The Spinnaker Restaurant **4**
Touch of Class **1**

Banyan Beach Club
$$$ Treasure Cay Beach

Banyan Beach Club offers 21 spacious condos (ideal for families) in a prime location — right on the beach that's widely known as one of the best in The Bahamas because of its gentle curve, white sand, and turquoise water. Some of these one- and two-bedroom units have an additional sleeping area: a loft with two twin beds, which you reach by a spiral or ladder-style staircase. Queen-size beds are in downstairs rooms. Patios or balconies have expansive views. The one-bedroom units face the swimming pool, while the larger apartments, with two or three bathrooms, overlook the beach. All units come with kitchens complete with a dishwasher, microwave, blender, and coffeemaker. The upstairs apartments in both shingle-roof buildings have high-angled ceilings. Guests get acquainted at the Monday night cocktail parties or over hamburgers and hot dogs at the beach bar and grill. Treasure Cay's golf course is within strolling distance, but most people get there on the golf carts they rent to cruise the resort. You can easily arrange watersports at the Treasure Cay Marina.

When an island isn't an island

Cay is pronounced "key" in The Bahamas, and it means "a little island." So how come Treasure Cay, on the east coast of Great Abaco, is part of the "mainland"? Well, Treasure Cay used to be a separate chunk of land, known as Lovel's Island, at least as far back as the 1780s. Eventually, landfill erased the sliver of Carleton Creek that ran between Treasure Cay and Great Abaco.

See map p. 273. Less than a kilometer (about a half-mile) north of Treasure Cay Hotel Resort & Marina. ☎ *888-625-3060 or 242-365-8111. Fax: 242-365-8112.* www.banyan beach.com. *Rack rates: $175–$250 one-bedroom units, $235–$350 two-bedroom units. AE, MC, V.*

Treasure Cay Hotel Resort & Marina
$$$–$$$$ Treasure Cay Marina

One of the biggest of the Out Island resorts, this property attracts boaters, golfers, fishermen, and divers, as well as escapists seeking a remote retreat. Guests appreciate the *House and Garden*–style architecture, the spectacular beachfront, and the marina facilities. Simply furnished in tropical motifs, most accommodations overlook the dozens of sailing crafts moored in Treasure Cay Marina. The deluxe suites are very attractive, with fully equipped kitchens and two bathrooms. Renowned architect Dick Wilson designed the 18-hole golf course. Tennis courts are lit for night play, and you can rent watersports equipment. Guests sometimes rent electric golf carts (around $35 per day) or bikes to explore the far-flung palm and casuarina groves of the sprawling property. For a full review of the resort's restaurant, **The Spinnaker,** see the "Dining Out" section later in this chapter.

See map p. 273. Treasure Cay Marina. ☎ *800-327-1584 or 954-525-7711 for reservations, or 242-365-8801.* www.treasurecay.com. *Rack rates: $140–$240 double, $280 suite. Full board $20 extra per person. AE, DISC, MC, V.*

Dining Out

Many vacationers to Treasure Cay stay in accommodations with kitchens or kitchenettes. However, if you know you're never going to feel like putting fire to a pan, consider purchasing your hotel's meal plan or dine at nearby local restaurants, some of which provide transportation.

You can find rather standard food at the **Beach Bar & Grill** at the Banyan Beach Club (☎ 242-365-8111), which opens daily from 11:30 a.m. to 6 p.m. Platters of food cost from $4 to $8. Another eatery worth considering is the roadside **Coconut's** on Queen's Highway (☎ 242-365-8885), which serves typically Bahamian fare, such as grouper and conch along with a few Italian specialties. Main courses range from $12 to $25, and it's open daily from 6 to 9:30 p.m.

The Spinnaker Restaurant
$$$ Treasure Cay Marina   AMERICAN/BAHAMIAN

Serving reliable seafood, steak, pasta, and Bahamian specialties, this resort restaurant at the Treasure Cay Marina has a prime waterside spot. For lunch, the cracked conch makes a good choice. At night, the portions of meat and potatoes or fresh fish (prepared in a variety of ways, from steamed to blackened) are generous. Guests of the Banyan Beach Club, less than a kilometer (about a half-mile) away, usually arrive by golf cart.

See map p. 273. On the water in Treasure Cay Marina. ☎ 242-365-8469. Reservations suggested for dinner. Main courses: $17–$30. MC, V. Open: Daily 7 a.m.–10 p.m. Limited hours in autumn and early winter.

Touch of Class
$$-$$$ North of Treasure Cay resort   BAHAMIAN

Call ahead to have this popular local eatery send a courtesy van to pick you up at your hotel. Touch of Class is the spot when you're ready to try some real Bahamian food, such as fried freshly caught grouper filet with a sauce of tomatoes, sweet peppers, and onions; or tender cracked conch served with a mound of peas and rice. If you can't decide, try the seafood plate, which offers a sampling of grouper, lobster, and conch. Both the Key lime pie and the banana cream pie are luscious desserts.

See map p. 273. On Queen's Highway, a ten-minute drive from Treasure Cay resort. ☎ 242-365-8195. Main courses: $15–$33. MC, V. Open: Nightly 6–9 p.m.

Exploring the Sand and Surf

Highlighted by the Treasure Cay Billfish Championship each spring, watersports in Treasure Cay mean big fun. Golfers don't have to head to Nassau or Freeport for a great game. Treasure Cay may be far less developed than the more popular islands, but its golf course is a big draw.

Combing the beaches

If you desire a beach with some of the softest, whitest sand you can imagine, and water in some of the most amazing shades of blue and green, then **Treasure Cay Beach** is for you. What's especially alluring about this beach is that — unlike eye-catching strands on busier, more built-up islands — this shore is never crowded because it extends for 5.5km (2½ miles).

Playing in the surf

Treasure Cay's excellent boating, fishing, scuba diving, and snorkeling make it tempting to spend most of your time in the water.

Certified divers can hook up with **Treasure Divers** (☎ 242-365-8582; www.treasure-divers.com). A shorter one-tank dive goes for $83 and a longer two-tank dive for $83. **J.I.C. Boat Rentals** (☎ 242-365-8582; www.richsrentals.com) can book you on a snorkel sail ($35 per person with a six-person minimum) or on a beach snorkel trip ($68 per person), after which the freshly caught grouper and lobster are grilled right on the beach.

Climbing aboard

Treasure Cay makes a good starting point for exploring the Abacos by sea. At **Rich's Boat Rentals** (☎ 242-365-8465; www.richsrentals.com), boats ranging from 6 to 8m (21–27 ft.) start at around $130 a day. A guided charter starts at about $250 for a half-day or $400 for a full day. With 7 to 8m (24–26 ft.) fully equipped boats, **J.I.C. Boat Rentals** (☎ 242-365-8582) is another good outfit.

Treasure Cay's surrounding waters offer some of the country's best fishing, including **deep-sea, sea-bottom,** and **drift fishing.** Off the coast, fishermen pursue barracuda, grouper, yellowtail, snapper, tuna, marlin, dolphinfish, and wahoo. The cay's own bonefish flats are just a short boat ride from the Treasure Cay Marina. Charters start at $425 for a half-day and $550 for a full day. Make arrangements through your hotel, **Treasure Cay Marina** (☎ 242-365-8250), Rich's Boat Rentals, or J.I.C. Boat Rentals.

Exploring on Dry Land

If you prefer to stick to dry land, check out the following options.

The **Treasure Cay Golf Club** (☎ 242-365-8535) at the Treasure Cay Resort & Marina offers one of the best courses in The Bahamas. The course is a 72-par 18-holer. Greens fees run $63 for 18 holes or $58 for 9. Reserving tee times is necessary from October to June.

Treasure Cay Hotel Resort & Marina (☎ 242-365-8250) offers six tennis courts — three clay surfaces ($16 per hour) and three hard surfaces ($14 per hour) — all lit for night play. Check with the hotel to make arrangements to play.

Living It Up After Dark

Fishermen, yachties, and hotel guests head for the **Tipsy Seagull Bar** at the Treasure Cay Hotel Resort & Marina (☎ 242-365-8535), which presents live music in winter (only on Fri and Sat nights in the off season). When a fishing tournament is on island, this bar is jampacked. The setting is an A-frame, and the décor is nautical memorabilia. Bar patrons who want to hang out can order such treats as pizza and lobster from the resort's adjoining restaurant, The Spinnaker. Happy hour is nightly from 5 to 7 p.m. The bar closes in autumn, in the early winter months, and during other slow periods.

Going Beyond Treasure Cay

You can get some local flavor and a blast from the past if you sail off to one, two, or three of the Abacos' nearby historic villages.

Trip #1: Green Turtle Cay

A brief ferry ride takes you across the water to Green Turtle Cay, one of the prettiest islands in The Bahamas. The hamlet of **New Plymouth** may make you think that you landed in Cape Cod because it shares a similar architectural heritage with that New England summer haunt. White picket fences enclose the front yards of the small clapboard houses. In this subtropical village, these buildings are trimmed in pastel pinks, blues, and greens and are shaded by bushy palm trees. Once the most prosperous settlement in the Abacos, New Plymouth was founded by British Loyalists who fled the U.S. after the American Revolution. Stroll around the quiet streets, sip a Goombay Smash, stop for a meal, and visit the art and maritime museum.

The ferry from Treasure Cay to Green Turtle Cay runs several times a day. To get to the ferry dock from the Treasure Cay Hotel, you have to take a 15-minute taxi ride to the departure dock. This ride costs $15 for one or two passengers. Before long, the ferry pulls up to New Plymouth (about $11 round-trip for adults and $7 for children). For more details about hotels, restaurants, sights, and activities on Green Turtle Cay, check out Chapter 20.

Trip #2: Elbow Cay and Man-O-War Cay

Elbow Cay and Man-O-War Cay, two nearby islands, make wonderful boating targets. The red-and-white striped lighthouse in Elbow Cay's **Hope Town Harbour,** in Hope Town, is the most photographed man-made attraction in the Out Islands. Sandy dunes back some of the broad, quiet beaches on this long, slim island. Saltbox houses with picket fences make this another contender for a Cape Cod fishing village look-alike. Take a load off at one of the harborside bars and restaurants.

To reach Man-O-War Cay from Hope Town, you must return to Marsh Harbour, where you can catch a ride aboard **Albury's Ferry Service** (☎ 242-367-3147). Ferries leave daily at 10:30 a.m., 4 p.m., and 5:30 p.m.; the cost is $15 per passenger. Once you arrive at Man-O-War Cay, you can wander through its trim streets lined with brightly painted cottages. You'll notice something different right away: Unlike most of The Bahamas (where the majority of residents are of African ancestry), nearly everyone here is a direct descendant of one European American couple who settled the island in the 1820s.

In The Bahamas, you can expect to find at least one small bar for every small church, but not on Man-O-War Cay. You'll see cozy houses of worship, but you won't find any bars or liquor stores at all. Folks on this uncrowded island take their religion very seriously. Don't risk offending anyone by publicly sipping any beer or other alcohol you may have brought along or by walking around in your bathing suit or other skimpy attire.

Residents and visitors celebrate Man-O-War Cay's boat-building history at the waterfront **Sail Shop** (☎ **242-365-6014**), which offers colorful bags handmade from the canvas once used for all those sails. The shop is open Monday through Friday from 8 a.m. to 5 p.m. and until 4 p.m. on Saturday.

To strike out on your own or for a guided charter, contact **Rich's Boat Rentals** (☎ **242-365-8465**) or **J.I.C. Boat Rentals** (☎ **242-365-8582**). A trip from Treasure Cay to Man-O-War Cay (45 minutes on a good day) takes about an hour on the water. A trip from Treasure Cay to Elbow Cay takes about ten minutes more.

For a different kind of scenic adventure, you can also rent a car in Treasure Cay (from $75 per day), drive 35 minutes to Marsh Harbour, and then take the 20-minute ferry ride (through Albury's Ferry Service) to Elbow Cay or Man-O-War Cay. To either island, the fare is $8 each way or $15 same-day round-trip for adults; and $8 one-way or $6 same-day round-trip for children ages 6 to 12. Your time is limited by the ferry schedule, however, so you'll probably make it to only one of the two islands. (For information about Elbow Cay's hotels, restaurants, and sightseeing opportunities, see Chapter 19.)

Fast Facts: Treasure Cay

American Express and ATMs

No Amex services or ATMs are available on Treasure Cay. You can access your cash at an ATM in Marsh Harbour.

Emergencies/Police

Call ☎ 242-365-8048.

Hospital

If health problems arise, contact the Corbett Medical Center (☎ 242-365-8288), behind the Treasure Cay administration building and near the marina.

Information

For visitor-related information, contact the Abaco Tourist Office (☎ 242-367-3067).

Internet Access

Resorts generally offer Internet access; check with your hotel. No cybercafes are available on Treasure Cay.

Pharmacy

For prescriptions and other drug-store needs, go to The Hair Depot, in the National Insurance Building in the hamlet of Coopers Town, directly north of Treasure Cay.

Post Office

In the Treasure Cay shopping center near the marina, the post office (☎ 242-365-8230) is open Monday through Friday from 9 a.m. to 4 p.m.

Safety

Although Treasure Cay is a safe resort, don't forget to take the same precautions that you should whether you're at home or on vacation: Keep valuables in a safe place and don't go into deserted, unfamiliar areas alone at night.

Taxis

Taxis meet incoming flights at the airport. During your stay, staff at your hotel can call one for you whenever the need arises.

Part VI
The Out Islands

Tragically, Doug had just completed the vocabulary portion of his SAT exam before setting sail that day.

In this part . . .

We journey to four of The Bahamas' most appealing Out Islands. This section reviews one of the most intriguing of all Bahamian islands — actually a series of islands — called Eleuthera. A slender wisp of an island, visitors go to Eleuthera mainly for its offshore Harbour Island. Harbour Island is known for its attractive 18th-century harborside houses and its small hotels overlooking a pink-sand beach. The island of Exuma is sailing heaven, and avid scuba divers flock to San Salvador.

In this part, you find all the information that you need for a great trip to the Out Islands. We include tips on how to get there, what to see and do when you're there, and where you can find the best accommodations and food and the liveliest nightlife.

Chapter 22

Harbour Island

In This Chapter

▶ Getting around Harbour Island
▶ Reviewing Harbour Island's best accommodations and restaurants
▶ Exploring the best beaches, watersports, and historic attractions

*I*f you're looking for a small, sophisticated hotel on a never-crowded sandy shore, head to **Harbour Island.** This little cay off northern Eleuthera is home to The Bahamas' coziest collection of distinctive oceanfront accommodations. This sandy stretch is *pink.* Mother Nature created this stunning pastel hue over the eons by pulverizing coral and shells. Scoop up a handful of the speckled sand, and you'll see what we mean.

Arriving in Harbour Island

Harbour Island, 2.4km (1½ miles) off the coast of Eleuthera (see Chapter 23), is one of those special places that requires a bit of work and patience to reach. If you come by air, you need to fly into the small, unassuming **North Eleuthera Airport** (from Miami, Ft. Lauderdale, or Nassau). Then you take a five-minute taxi ride to the dock (about $4 per person) and a ten-minute ferry ride to Harbour Island's **Government Dock** ($5 per person). Next, unless you're staying at The Landing, which is just across the road, you take a short taxi ride to your hotel ($4 per person).

Another way you can get to Harbour Island is to board a speedy 177-passenger catamaran in Nassau. Just contact **Bahamas Fast Ferry** (☎ **242-323-2166;** www.bahamasferries.com). You begin this two-hour trip at the **Potters Cay Dock,** which is under the bridge leading from Paradise Island to downtown Nassau. The fare for one of these daily excursions is $110 round-trip or $65 one-way for adults; and $70 round-trip or $45 one-way for children ages 2 to 11. The ferry also pulls up to Harbour Island's Government Dock, where taxis wait to take you to your hotel.

Harbour Island

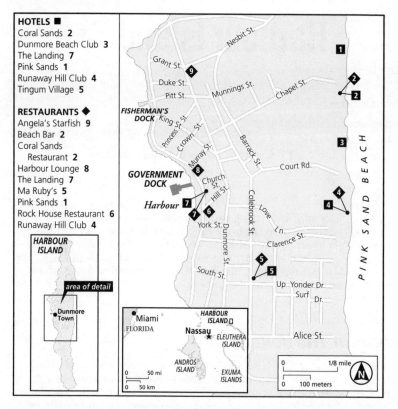

HOTELS ■
Coral Sands **2**
Dunmore Beach Club **3**
The Landing **7**
Pink Sands **1**
Runaway Hill Club **4**
Tingum Village **5**

RESTAURANTS ◆
Angela's Starfish **9**
Beach Bar **2**
Coral Sands
  Restaurant **2**
Harbour Lounge **8**
The Landing **7**
Ma Ruby's **5**
Pink Sands **1**
Rock House Restaurant **6**
Runaway Hill Club **4**

Choosing Your Location

If Harbour Island (called "Briland" by locals) had only the beautiful beach and the great hotels, it still would be a top-notch vacation choice. But this island also offers the well-preserved 17th-century **Dunmore Town,** the first capital of The Bahamas. Dunmore Town is within walking distance (or biking and golf-cart reach) of all accommodations. The western shore offers panoramic sunsets, and **Pink Sand Beach** along the eastern coast is the only place to be at sunrise.

What little after-dark action the island does have "jumps up" on weekends at or close to the hotels.

Getting Around Harbour Island

Harbour Island is very small — just 5km (3 miles) long and less than a kilometer (½-mile) wide — so you can get where you need to go easily. Here's a closer look at transportation choices.

✔ **Taking a taxi:** The island is so small that you really need a cab only when arriving and leaving with luggage. Taxis wait for incoming ferries at Government Dock, and the staff at your hotel can call a cab for you whenever you need one.

✔ **Hoofing it:** On this compact island, Dunmore Town (which is ideal for strolling), restaurants, nightspots, and most other places are within walking distance of the hotels. The best place to go for a leisurely walk is the 5km (3-mile) Pink Sand Beach along the eastern shore.

✔ **Wheeling around:** You don't see many cars on Harbour Island's nearly deserted roads. If you do feel the need to move faster than your feet can carry you, call **Michael's Cycles** (☎ **242-333-2384**), on Colebrook Street. You can choose among bicycles ($12 per day), two-seater scooters ($30 per day), and four-person golf carts ($48 per day).

Staying in Style

Most hotels in Harbour Island are expensive. Some daily rates appear high — until you notice that the rates include breakfast and dinner.

If you stay in a moderately priced or inexpensive hotel, you can still treat yourself to the fancy resorts and restaurants by dining at them now and then, and you always have access to that dreamy pink beach. See the Harbour Island map in this chapter for more information on the island's accommodations.

No matter your location, you receive as much — or as little — personal attention as you want. Your accommodations may even have an honor bar, where you just sign for whatever drinks you fix yourself.

 Most hotels and restaurants close during parts of September, October, and November. Also, because most of the resorts are on a bluff high above the sand, stairs lead from them down to the coast.

Coral Sands
$$$ On the beach

You can sleep especially well at this sprawling 39-room beach resort where the owner, who also owns a Connecticut-based bedding company, replaced all the mattresses with the company's super-durable, super-comfortable brand. Coral Sands, which dates back to the 1960s, exchanged its former retro look for a totally fresh face. Done in tones of pink and turquoise, guest rooms are decorated with wicker furniture and attractive artwork. Some units contain balconies or patios. The rooms have various sizes and views, but all are in buildings surrounded by greenery. In the newest of these blocks of buildings, four oceanfront one-bedroom apartments with wraparound decks can be turned into two- or three-bedroom units by adding adjoining rooms.

A favorite spot is the spacious **Beach Bar,** on a deck hanging high over the pink shore. Lunches and light suppers are served here. You can have elegant dinners at **Coral Sands Restaurant,** located on a broad veranda in the main building.

See map p. 284. Chapel Street. ☎ *800-468-2799 or 242-333-2350. Fax: 242-333-2368.* www.coralsands.com. *Rack rates: $285–$385 double, from $560 two-bedroom suite. AE, MC, V.*

Dunmore Beach Club
$$$$$ **On the beach**

On a bluff above the pink sand beach, this 15-room inn is the quintessential elegant hideaway, with 3 hectares (8 acres) of lush, well-manicured grounds. The comfortable "rooms," simply decorated in tranquil colors, are scattered cottages with private patios that have views of the water. The bathrooms in ten of the rooms contain hot tubs that are large enough for romantic trysts, and the shower stalls are spacious as well. A tennis court is on-site, and rates include three top-notch meals a day. A stairway connects the hotel to the beach.

If you'd rather have a root canal than wear a jacket or a cocktail dress to dinner, don't check in here. Dunmore Beach Club isn't the only Harbour Island hotel where guests dress up at night, but it is a bit on the stuffy side. This hotel was once the hangout of the Duke and Duchess of Windsor and their friends, and a subdued, slightly stiff atmosphere of the private club it once was still lingers.

See map p. 284. Colebrook Street, eastern coast. ☎ *800-891-3100 or 242-333-2200. Fax: 242-333-2429.* www.dunmorebeach.com. *Rack rates: $499–$599 double, $669–$789 suite. Rates include breakfast, lunch, and dinner. MC, V. Closed Sept–Oct.*

The Landing
$$$–$$$$ **Dunmore Town**

This intimate inn is understated, tasteful, and lovely, giving you a touch of class like Dunmore Beach Club but for less money. Set in buildings that have stood here since the early 1800s, this small inn is located in the heart of historic Dunmore Town. Its owner is India Hicks, the daughter of the famed London decorator David Hicks, and a bridesmaid to Lady Diana during her wedding to Prince Charles. The seven guest rooms are decorated plantation-style, with mahogany-stained four-poster beds and hardwood floors. Some rooms have broad verandas and ceiling fans, and most of them look out to the harbor across the road. The restaurant is reason enough to stay here. (See a review of this restaurant in the "Dining Out" section later in this chapter.) To reach the beach, you have to go all the way across Harbour Island — however, this feat is hardly a difficult one. If you're traveling with children, ask for a room with an extra single bed.

See map p. 284. Bay Street, across from Government Dock. ☎ *242-333-2707. Fax: 242-333-2650.* www.harbourislandlanding.com. *Rack rates: $240–$345 double. Rates include breakfast. MC, V.*

Pink Sands
$$$$$ On the beach

This 25-room inn, set on 8 hectares (20 acres) adjacent to the beach, is the epitome of Out Island chic. It's a classier joint than even the Dunmore Beach Club, its chief rival. You won't find a better hideaway or honeymoon retreat in all The Bahamas. The Pink Sands is also less snobbish and a lot hipper than the Dunmore. Jamaican-born Chris Blackwell, who brought Bob Marley to world attention, took over Pink Sands in 1992 and transformed it from a hurricane-ravaged inn into the pocket of posh that it is today.

The airy, spacious bedrooms have either an ocean or a garden view. Smaller units contain Art Deco touches straight out of Miami's South Beach; larger, more expensive units feature Indonesian (especially Balinese) furnishings and art, as well as huge decks. All rooms have kitchenettes or kitchens, central air-conditioning, pressurized water systems, walk-in closets, satellite TV, CD players and a CD selection, wet bars, private patios with teak furnishings, and beautifully tiled bathrooms. The rooms also have dataports, and the staff can supply you with fax machines and cellphones, if you need them.

When not on the beach, guests head for the swimming pool, the tennis courts (one is lit for night play), the exercise room, or the library. You can have breakfast and dinner surrounded by leafy greenery on the main dining terrace. (The daily rates include a full breakfast and the four-course candlelit evening meal.) The beachside **Blue Bar** serves lunch and hosts the Saturday night Bahamian barbecues. For a few extra bucks, you can even order room service, an alien concept at most Out Island hotels.

See map p. 284. Chapel Street. ☎ *800-OUTPOST (800-688-7678) or 242-333-2030. Fax: 242-333-2060.* www.islandoutpost.com. *Rack rates: $750–$850 one-bedroom cottage, from $1,300 two-bedroom cottage. Rates include breakfast and dinner. AE, MC, V.*

Runaway Hill Club
$$$$ On the beach

Guests who first meet at Runaway Hill often book their next vacations together here the following year. Because this inn has only ten rooms (most with patios or balconies), everyone quickly gets to know each other. Set on a rise high above the swimming pool and beach (accessible by staircase), the main building was once a private home. With its individually and beautifully decorated rooms, it looks as if it still is. Our favorite place to sleep is the huge downstairs room with ceramic floor tiles in an intricate pink pattern and a spacious bathroom with twin sinks. The more modern rooms, in a separate hilltop villa, are more similar in size and décor. No matter where you stay, you find artfully arranged furnishings and well-maintained private bathrooms. Guests dress up for the elegant candlelit dinners here, joined by those lucky non-guests who've managed to reserve tables as well. The friendly staff is always on hand to help make arrangements for watersports and other activities.

See map p. 284. Colebrook Street, Central Harbour Island. ☎ *242-333-2150. Fax: 242-333-2420.* www.runawayhill.com. *Rack rates: $375–$425 double. MAP $120 extra per person. MC, V. No children under 18 accepted. Closed Sept to mid-Nov.*

Tingum Village
$ Southern Harbour Island

You won't find anything fancy about Tingum Village, and with just 19 rooms in cottages with large terraces, "village" is certainly a misnomer. However, the village's proximity to the island's beach (a four-minute walk away), its excellent Bahamian restaurant, **Ma Ruby's** (see our review in the "Dining Out" section below), and the friendliness of the staff, all make up for the lack of bells and whistles common at pricier Harbour Island hotels. A local family runs this quiet, low-key establishment. The hotel feels more like the "real" Bahamas than most of the island's more polished but foreign-owned and managed accommodations. The neat, clean rooms look out to a grassy expanse edged by palms, hibiscus, and other vegetation. If you want a hot tub in your room, book one of the two suites.

See map p. 284. Colebrook Street. ☎ *242-333-2161. Fax: 242-333-2161. Rack rates: $135 double, $140 triple, $300 cottage. MC, V.*

Dining Out

For such a small island, a surprising selection of first-rate dining rooms, most of them at hotels, awaits you.

Dinner reservations are crucial, and you may need to make yours in the morning. Vacationers tend to dress up for dinner, especially at the more expensive resorts during the winter season. On the other hand, local spots featuring home-style Bahamian cooking are casual affairs. The majority of restaurants close between meals, and some restaurants also close completely for varying periods of time between September and November.

Angela's Starfish
$–$$ Just outside Dunmore Town   BAHAMIAN

For more than a quarter century, this family-run restaurant has been churning out Bahamian dishes that keep folks streaming through the doors. Sit inside, where the casual décor has nautical touches, or on the palm-shaded lawn overlooking the water and mainland Eleuthera. At night, tiny bulbs hidden inside conch shells illuminate the tables. The honey-brown cracked conch is the perfect combination of crispy on the outside and tender on the inside. You can order fish, chicken, and pork chops, all served with mounds of peas and rice and all of which are also well pre-pared. Key lime and coconut pie are the featured desserts.

You're welcomed here as long as you heed the sign that requests that patrons refrain from swearing and wearing bare-backed clothing.

See map p. 284. At the top of the hill at Dunmore and Grant streets. ☎ *242-333-2253. Breakfast: $6–$12; lunch: $5–$10; dinner main courses: $13–$25. No credit cards. Open: Daily 7:30 a.m.–8:30 p.m.*

Beach Bar
$$–$$$ Northern Harbour Island   BAHAMIAN/INTERNATIONAL

At the Coral Sands resort, this casual restaurant and bar has a long lunch hour and is one of the most popular places along this broad strip of pink sands. You can sit at tables on a sunny deck hanging high above the rosy sand — the spot is perfect for a long, tall rum punch. You can order an early lunch or a very late lunch. Begin with conch fritters, the conch salad, the conch chowder, or the cracked conch. Main courses focus on sand-wiches; one is made with rock lobster, and another with roast beef. If you like something more substantial, order the grilled New York strip steak or the catch of the day cooked to your specifications.

See map p. 284. Chapel Street, at the Coral Sands hotel. ☎ *242-333-2350. Sandwiches: $12–$18; main courses: $16–$19. AE, MC, V. Open: Daily 11:30 a.m.– 4 p.m.*

Coral Sands Restaurant
$$$ Northern Harbour Island   BAHAMIAN/INTERNATIONAL

If you prefer more elegant dining, stick around for dinner at this hotel's more formal restaurant. This establishment is Harbour Island's only ocean-front bar and restaurant. If the weather's right, everybody tries to get a table on the breeze-swept terrace overlooking the pink sands and the ocean.

Signature dishes include white conch chowder and lobster served with asiago cheese and a sauvignon blanc white sauce. Taste these dishes and you'll know at once why this dining room is one of the island's finest. Most diners wisely opt for one of the delectable fish dishes, including herb-crusted grouper or filet of snapper with fresh citrus chunks and a pinot sauce. Meat dishes, all imported, range from a tender prime Angus beef sirloin steak to New Zealand lamb chops. For dessert, you can finish off with a yummy chocolate torte.

See map p. 284. Chapel Street, at the Coral Sands hotel. ☎ 242-333-2350. Reservations required. Main courses: $25–$34. AE, MC, V. Open: Daily 7–8:30 p.m.

Harbour Lounge
$$$–$$$$ Dunmore Town   BAHAMIAN

Arrive early to stake out a spot on the terrace so you can watch the sun slide into the harbor while you sip a Bahama Mama. Because you're right on Bay Street, the main thoroughfare, this restaurant is also the place to see and be seen. Along the water across the street, vendors sell straw goods, fruit, and vegetables. After dinner, a very local crowd gathers at the bar. Specialties include the blackened grouper, garlic shrimp with pasta, lobster, cracked conch, and Key lime pie. The food is some of the most satisfying and authentic on the island.

See map p. 284. Bay Street, in front of Government Dock. ☎ 242-333-2031. Reservations recommended for dinner. Lunch: salads, sandwiches, and platters $10–$22; dinner main courses: $10–$38. MC, V. Open: Tues–Sun lunch 11:30 a.m.– 3 p.m., dinner 6–9:15 p.m.

The Landing
$$$$$ Dunmore Town   INTERNATIONAL

The cozy atmosphere of this intimate restaurant makes it clear that the owners enjoy their hands-on involvement. Dating back to 1800, this handsome building is part of The Landing hotel, which has a handful of guest rooms. Both dinner and Sunday brunch are special events here. You can dine in the bright yellow and white dining room or in the garden. Linens and fine china dress the tables, where you sit in saddle-back chairs. The restaurant always features a first-rate chef whose cooking pays tribute to the aristocratic credentials of the place. For your evening meal, you can choose among rock Cornish hen, cappellini with lobster, and Angus beef. The golden-brown, pan-fried grouper with mashed potatoes, eggplant, and green salsa is another bestseller. Dessert offerings may include ice cream, sorbet, and rich but surprisingly light chocolate cake, followed by various gourmet coffees.

See map p. 284. Bay Street, across from Government Dock. ☎ 242-333-2707. Reservations recommended for dinner. Lunch main courses: $12–$22; dinner main courses: $35–$42. AE, MC, V. Open: Sun 8 a.m.–11 p.m.; Mon–Tues and Thurs–Sat 6:30–10:30 p.m.

Ma Ruby's
$-$$ Southern Harbour Island BAHAMIAN

Matriarch Ma Ruby is known for her cheeseburgers, which Jimmy Buffett — Mr. "Cheeseburger in Paradise" himself — ranked as among the ten best in the world. But we'd come back on another day and sample her conch burger, which we feel is worthy of an award as well — that and her hearty, flavorful Bahamian meals, such as conch fritters, stewed grouper, and baked chicken. Main dishes are accompanied by Ma Ruby's peas and rice. For dessert, try the Key lime pie or cheesecake. You dine on a court-yard patio by a grassy garden enclosed by palm trees.

If you want to use a credit card to purchase your meal, the restaurant requires a minimum charge of $65.

See map p. 284. Colebrook Street, at Tingum Village. ☎ *242-333-2161. Reservations not required. Breakfast: $6–$14; lunch: $8–$12; dinner main courses: $18–$26; set price four-course meal: $28–$35. MC, V. Open: Daily 8:30 a.m.–2 p.m. and 6–9:30 p.m.*

Pink Sands
$$$$$ Northern Harbour Island INTERNATIONAL

The four-course dinner menu is prix fixe at this snazzy beach resort that attracts celebrities. You can dine on a garden patio where the candlelit teak tables are tucked away into private leafy corners. Chefs sometimes jazz up the mainly European gourmet food with Caribbean and Asian influences. You can begin with leek and potato soup with smoked mahimahi or a savory tiger shrimp bisque with cognac. Your main course may be filet of grouper with saffron-scented risotto, grilled beef tenderloin with roasted portobello mushrooms and braised potatoes, or salmon baked in an herb crust and served with tomato-scallion *beurre blanc* (white butter). The mango cream pie is a luscious dessert. A lengthy wine list features excellent choices from France, South Africa, Australia, Chile, and the United States.

See map p. 284. Chapel Street, eastern coast. ☎ *242-333-2030. Reservations required. Three-course dinner: $70. AE, MC, V. Open to non-guests for dinner only, daily 11:30 a.m.–3:30 p.m. and 7–9 p.m.*

Rock House Restaurant
$$$ Dunmore Town INTERNATIONAL

This restaurant feels like a hip *bodega* in Miami. It has lots of varnished mahogany, pale yellow walls, spinning ceiling fans and, in addition to the table groupings for groups of two and four diners, a very large "chef's table" with 16 chairs (reputedly among the furnishings in Washington, D.C.'s White House before a long-ago refurbishment). Lunches are charm-ing but rather simple affairs, with dishes such as burgers, rock lobster salad sandwiches, and conch chowders. Dinners are more elaborate and more of a showcase for the chef. The best menu items include "Ying-yang" soup, crafted from roasted red and yellow peppers with smoked mozzarella and chile oil; chicken with Asian noodles and a tahini-flavored aioli; crab cakes served with a confit of sweet peppers and béarnaise sauce; grilled lobster tail with clarified butter; and tiger-shrimp spaghetti with local goat cheese, peppers, and parsley. Especially flavorful is a crispy pan-fried chicken breast with a citrus-flavored herb sauce.

See map p. 284. In the Rock House Hotel, at Bay and Hill streets. ☎ 242-333-2053. Reservations recommended. Lunch main courses: $15–$24; dinner main courses: $36–$55; Fri night buffet: $35 per person. AE, MC, V. Open: Daily 6–11 p.m.

Runaway Hill Club
$$$$$ On the beach   CONTINENTAL

To see the daily prix-fixe menu, stop by in the morning to read what's on the old brass music stand by the entrance to the inn. Showing up early helps you for two reasons: First, dinner reservations go quickly at Runaway Hill. Second, this wonderfully decorated former home overlooking the ocean is gorgeous by daylight. See it and you just may want to book a room here for your next vacation. At night, the small, elegant dining room glows with candlelight. The chef turns out cuisine with skill and a certain flair, although it doesn't ever rise to spectacular heights. Your four-course meal may include lobster bisque followed by seafood pasta with scampi, pork tenderloin, rack of veal, or veal piccata. Dessert options may include chocolate pie with walnuts or an imaginative strawberry creation.

The restaurant has just one seating (8 p.m.), following cocktails (7:30 p.m.), so tables are at a premium. Men wear shirts with collars, and women really dress up.

See map p. 284. Colebrook Street, central Harbour Island. ☎ 242-333-2150. Reservations required. Complete four-course dinner: $60. AE, MC, V. Open: Mon–Sat 8 p.m. Closed Sept to mid-Nov. No children.

Enjoying the Sand and Surf

Fishing (especially bonefishing), scuba diving, and snorkeling are the main aquatic diversions. Relaxing on the beach, wandering around historic Dunmore Town, and socializing with residents round out the roster of activities.

Combing the beach

Pink Sand Beach is truly amazing. Nearly five exquisite kilometers (3 miles) of mostly unpopulated pink sand run along the eastern coast of the island. Take a stroll or plan a picnic here, and don't forget to watch the sunrise — it's spectacular. Sunbathing along this calm strand is best in the morning.

Playing in the surf

You may not be able to see forever in these waters, but on a clear day, visibility is often as good as 61m (200 ft.). This area boasts a diversity of dive sites.

In **Current Cut,** between Eleuthera and Current Island, experienced scuba divers can drift dive at exhilarating speeds with the current that rushes through an underwater chasm. The current carries divers between the rock walls for about a kilometer (a half-mile), along with a blizzard of reef fish, stingrays, and even some mako sharks. Another exceptional dive site is the wreck of a 60m (197-ft.) **steel freighter** that sank in 1917.

For both scuba and snorkeling trips, the place to go is **Valentine's Dive Center** (☎ 242-333-2080; www.valentinesdive.com), on the harbor side of the island in the heart of Dunmore Town. A scuba resort course costs $85. A one-tank dive for certified divers runs $40, and a two-tank trip is $120. Half-day snorkeling sails cost $40 per person.

For an unusual adventure, certified divers can try **reef running,** a ride on an underwater scooter ($120). Decked out in your scuba gear, you cover much more marine territory than you do with regular diving.

Climbing aboard

You can rent a motorboat through **Michael's Cycles** (☎ 242-333-2384 or 242-464-0994) on Colebrook Street near Seagrapes nightclub. Plan to spend about $65 for a half-day or $75 for a full day on a 4m (13-ft.) boat and $125 for a half-day or $175 for a full day on a 5m (17-ft.) boat. Kayaks here go for $40 a day.

You can make arrangements for fishing guides and charters through your hotel or by contacting **Valentine's Dive Center** (☎ 242-333-2080), on the harbor side of the island in Dunmore Town. Deep-sea fishing trips start at $550 for a half-day or $750 for a full day.

Exploring on Dry Land

Dunmore Town, located on the harbor side of Harbour Island, was named for the 18th-century royal governor of The Bahamas who helped develop it and who had a summer home here. You can walk around these narrow, virtually car-free lanes in less than 20 minutes, or you can stroll slowly to savor the sight of the old gingerbread cottages that line the waterfront. Overhung with orange, purple, and pink bougainvillea, white picket fences enclose these wooden houses painted pastel blue, green, and lilac. Wind chimes tinkle in front of shuttered windows, and coconut palms and wispy casuarina pines shade grassy yards.

Americans and Canadians own some of these houses, which have whimsical names, such as "Up Yonder" and "Beside the Point," instead of house numbers. You can rent a few of these houses when you vacation here. One of the oldest, **Loyalist Cottage,** was built in 1797. It survives from the days when the original settlers, loyal to the British Crown, left the American colonies after the Revolutionary War. The porches along the harbor make for prime sunset watching. Lucky for you, some porches aren't connected to private homes. The terrace at Harbour Lounge Bar and Restaurant is an idyllic perch. Just across the road from Loyalist Cottage, you can browse through straw goods, T-shirts, fruits, and vegetables at the vendors' stalls.

On Sundays, residents dressed to kill stand in sociable clusters outside churches before and after services. Two of The Bahamas' first churches are in Dunmore Town and are still going strong: **St. John's,** The Bahamas' oldest Anglican church, established in 1768; and **Wesley Methodist Church,** built in 1846.

Spend some time wandering the streets — some hilly, some flat — away from the heart of town. You can see roosters doing their jerky marches through front yards and horses grazing in small fields. You'll find unassuming but perfectly good Bahamian restaurants, bars, and nightclubs in this locals' area.

A Shopper's Guide to Harbour Island

Dunmore Town is no Nassau, but you can find several stores carrying items that are worth a look, such as local artists' works, Androsia resort wear (made from the colorful batik fabric created on the Bahamian island of Andros), and handicrafts like music boxes in the shape of Harbour Island cottages and one-of-a-kind toothbrushes.

The standout boutique is **Miss Mae Tea Room and Fine Things** (☎ 242-333-2002), on Dunmore Street. Among the ever-changing, always-artful, mostly imported merchandise, you may find Haitian-style paintings, silver jewelry from Bali, local painted boxes, antique chests, gourmet wine vinegar from France, and Italian olive oil.

Blue Rooster (☎ 242-333-2240), in the center of town, offers what may be the most upscale and stylish collection of men's and women's clothing and (casual) evening wear on the island. Come here for something sporty to wear to a posh hotel's dining room, especially if the button-down look appeals to you. **The Shop at The Landing** (☎ 242-333-2707), at The Landing Resort, usually wins as the most stylish clothing store on the island. It focuses on fashionable sportswear and clothes that you can wear to a casual island cocktail party, a posh brunch, or a buffet dinner aboard a yacht.

You may also want to check out **Princess Street Gallery** (☎ 242-333-2788), where Charles Carey restored an ancestral home and uses it to display works by local artists.

A few vendors sell fruit, vegetables, T-shirts, and straw goods (baskets, bags, hats, place mats) along **Bay Street,** at the edge of the harbor. You can hone your bargaining skills at this open-air mini-marketplace.

Living It Up After Dark

During the week, life after dark means hanging out at hotel and restaurant bars. Some resorts offer live music with dinner two evenings a week. The other nightspots see most of their action on weekends. The youngest, liveliest local crowd gravitates toward **Seagrapes** (no phone), a large club at Colebrook and Gibson streets. On Friday or Saturday, you're likely to catch a live band here, but the dance floor is packed even when a DJ reigns.

The poolroom at the **Vic-Hum Club** (☎ 242-333-2161), on Barrack Street, is another popular haunt. Calypso, American pop, and R&B pumps from the speakers, and classic record album sleeves decorate the walls and ceilings. Ask the owner to show you "the world's largest coconut," which measures some 84cm (33 in.) around.

Pool, satellite TV sports, and periodic live music entertain patrons at hilltop **Gusty's** (☎ 242-333-2165), on Coconut Grove Avenue in the north. Get here early enough and nab the perfect perch for sunset watching.

Fast Facts: Harbour Island

American Express and ATMs

No Amex services are available on Harbour Island. An ATM is available at Royal Bank of Canada (☎ 242-333-2250), on Dunmore Street.

Emergencies

Call the police at ☎ **242-333-2111** or contact the Harbour Island Medical Clinic at ☎ **242-333-2227**.

Information

In the unlikely event that your request stumps the staff at your hotel, try the Harbour Island Tourist Office (☎ 242-333-2621), on Dunmore Street.

Internet Access

Resorts usually offer Internet access. Arthur's Bakery, located in the center of town, has also installed Internet service. You can use its computer or bring your own laptop for a fee of $10 for 15 minutes. Hours are Monday through Saturday from 8 a.m. to 2 p.m.

Police

Call ☎ **242-333-2111**. The police station is on Gaol Alley between Dunmore and Colebrook streets.

Pharmacy

You can get prescriptions filled at Briland's Pharmacy (☎ 242-333-3427), located at Johnson's Plaza, Dunmore Street. Hours are Monday through Saturday from 9 a.m. to 5 p.m.

Post Office

The post office (☎ 242-333-2111) is on Gaol Alley, and it's open Monday through Friday from 9 a.m. to 5:30 p.m.

Chapter 23

Eleuthera

. . . .

In This Chapter

▶ Getting around Eleuthera
▶ Reviewing Eleuthera's best accommodations and restaurants
▶ Enjoying the island's beaches, watersports, and land attractions

. . . .

*V*isitors flock to Harbour Island, a small island off the coast of Eleuthera, to be coddled in comfort, but adventurous travelers head for "mainland" Eleuthera. Although Harbour Island is flourishing, the great heyday of tourism for mainland Eleuthera has dwindled since The Bahamas became independent. Many embittered locals blame the late Prime Minister Lynden Pindling for discouraging foreign investment.

At one time, some of the best-known names in the world visited Eleuthera. If celebs come today, they visit Harbour Island, not the mainland. However, Eleuthera's natural attractions, which made it alluring in the first place, are still here to welcome you.

Arriving at the Airports

Eleuthera has two main airports. **North Eleuthera Airport** (☎ 242-335-1242) serves the northern part of the island along with the two major offshore cays, Harbour Island and Spanish Wells. **Governor's Harbour Airport** (☎ 242-332-2321) serves the center of the island. A third airport at Rock Sound no longer receives as many flights as it used to and is used mostly by local residents.

When you make your reservations, be sure that your flight will arrive at the appropriate airport; one visitor flew into Rock Sound Airport only to face a $100 taxi ride and a water-taxi trip before reaching his final destination of Harbour Island in the north.

Bahamasair (☎ 800-222-4262; www.bahamasair.com) offers daily flights between Nassau and the three airports in Eleuthera. In addition, several commuter airlines fly from the Florida mainland with either non-stop or one-stop service. Many private flights use the North Eleuthera Airport, with its 1,371m (4,500-ft.) paved runway. This airport is an official Bahamian port of entry, and a Customs and Immigration official is on hand.

Eleuthera

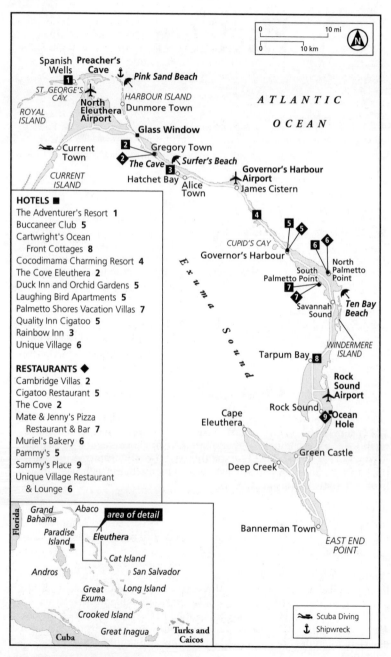

HOTELS ■
The Adventurer's Resort **1**
Buccaneer Club **5**
Cartwright's Ocean
  Front Cottages **8**
Cocodimama Charming Resort **4**
The Cove Eleuthera **2**
Duck Inn and Orchid Gardens **5**
Laughing Bird Apartments **5**
Palmetto Shores Vacation Villas **7**
Quality Inn Cigatoo **5**
Rainbow Inn **3**
Unique Village **6**

RESTAURANTS ◆
Cambridge Villas **2**
Cigatoo Restaurant **5**
The Cove **2**
Mate & Jenny's Pizza
  Restaurant & Bar **7**
Muriel's Bakery **6**
Pammy's **5**
Sammy's Place **9**
Unique Village Restaurant
  & Lounge **6**

Spanish Wells
Preacher's Cave
Pink Sand Beach
ST. GEORGE'S CAY
ROYAL ISLAND
North Eleuthera Airport
HARBOUR ISLAND
Dunmore Town
ATLANTIC OCEAN
Glass Window
Current Town
Gregory Town
The Cave
Surfer's Beach
CURRENT ISLAND
Hatchet Bay
Alice Town
Governor's Harbour Airport
James Cistern
CUPID'S CAY
Governor's Harbour
North Palmetto Point
South Palmetto Point
Ten Bay Beach
Savannah Sound
Exuma Sound
WINDERMERE ISLAND
Tarpum Bay
Rock Sound Airport
Cape Eleuthera
Rock Sound
Ocean Hole
Green Castle
Deep Creek
Bannerman Town
EAST END POINT

Florida
Grand Bahama
Abaco
area of detail
Paradise Island
Eleuthera
Cat Island
Andros
San Salvador
Great Exuma
Long Island
Crooked Island
Great Inagua
Turks and Caicos
Cuba

≈ Scuba Diving
⚓ Shipwreck

USAir Express (☎ 800-428-4322; www.usairways.com) operates flights to two of Eleuthera's airports directly from the mainland of Florida. Flights depart once a day from Miami and fly nonstop to North Eleuthera and then continue on, after briefly unloading passengers and baggage, to Governor's Harbour. Small carriers include **Twin Air** (☎ 954-359-8266; www.flytwinair.com), which flies from Ft. Lauderdale three times a week to Rock Sound and Governor's Harbour and four times a week to North Eleuthera.

An inter-island link, **Bahamas Fast Ferries** (☎ 242-323-2166; www.ferry bahamas.com), originates in Potter's Cay, beneath the Paradise Island Bridge. From there, it leaves at regular intervals for Harbour Island, North Eleuthera, and Governor's Harbour. Round-trip fares are $110 for adults and $70 for children under 12.

Choosing Your Location

The very lack of accommodations will make the location decision for you. In days of yore, **Rock Sound,** with its fabled Windermere Club or Cotton Bay Club, was far chicer than today's Harbour Island. Chartered planes carrying CEOs landed several times a day, but those days are now memories. Except for private villas, Rock Sound is devoid of rentals.

As you leave Rock Sound heading north of its airport, you come to **Tarpum Bay,** where you find only a handful of simple inns. North of here, the settlement of **Palmetto Point** has a cluster of other modest villas. In the middle of the island farther north, **Governor's Harbour** — or at least its economy — never recovered from the day a hurricane washed away Club Med. However, a number of offbeat accommodations, such as Duck Inn and Orchid Gardens, are far superior to any place south of Governor's Harbour.

As you move north into **Hatchet Bay** and **Gregory Town,** you come upon some other modest digs. Although simple, the little mom-and-pop places are clean, comfortable, well maintained, and affordable. Check them out.

Getting Around Eleuthera

It's virtually impossible to get lost on Eleuthera — only one road meanders along the entire length of its snake-shaped form, and you stray from it very rarely.

  ✔ **Taking a taxi:** Most visitors take a taxi only when they arrive at one of the local airports or when they have to return to that airport to go home. Taxis meet all incoming flights and are also available at ferry docks. Because cabbies are independent operators on Eleuthera, you can't call one central number. If you need to call a taxi, your hotel staff can summon one for you, but you may have to wait a while, so plan ahead.

✔ **Hoofing it:** You can easily traverse all the settlements — really, hamlets, in most cases — on foot. With little traffic on the island, walking is an enjoyable experience here.

✔ **Wheeling around:** You don't find any American car-rental agencies on the island. Usually, your hotel staff can arrange for a car rental (prices are from $80 a day). Often, we've ended up with someone's private car. The best bet for car rentals is the North Eleuthera-based **Fine Threads Taxi, Rental Cars & Tours** (☎ **242-359-7780** or 242-335-1556). Here, owner Frederick Neely (nicknamed "Fine Threads" because of his well-tailored clothes) either rents you a car or takes you on a private island tour. An eight-hour experience for 2 or 3 people costs $200; 8 to 12 people, $300. Tours usually begin at 9 a.m. and take in a series of bars, restaurants, and geological or historical attractions in Rock Sound, Lower Bogue, Palmetto Point, and Gregory Town. If you negotiate with your driver, you may also visit Preacher's Cave.

✔ **Sailing on a ferry:** For information about how to reach Harbour Island from Eleuthera, refer to Chapter 22. To reach the other off-shore island, Spanish Wells, take the convenient "on demand" ferry service (☎ **242-554-6268**) to North Eleuthera. A ferry runs between Gene's Bay in North Eleuthera to the main pier at Spanish Wells. The ferries depart whenever passengers show up, and the cost is $8 per person round-trip or $4 one-way.

Staying in Style

Because all the luxury properties on Eleuthera have gone belly-up, nearly every place you stay on the mainland is affordable. If you like to spend big bucks, you can always sail over to Harbour Island. Otherwise, you can expect a reasonably priced vacation.

Although we personally like Eleuthera in the late summer and fall when most visitors have departed, not all inns and hotels are likely to be open, especially in late September, October, and November. If business is slow, hoteliers simply close their doors.

Don't come expecting a lot of personal attention. Eleuthera caters to self-sufficient types. We often met the hotel owner when checking into a rental and didn't see him or her again until we paid the bill.

The Adventurer's Resort
$ Spanish Wells

This hotel is the most appealing and recommendable spot in Spanish Wells — not that there is much competition. It occupies a two-story, pale lavender-colored building in a well-tended garden about a half-kilometer

(⅓ mile) west of the town center. The resort doesn't have an on-site restaurant or bar, but a staff member can direct you to nearby eateries and to the beach, which lies about a kilometer away. The 18 small bedrooms have simple, durable furniture with tropical upholstery; six of the units are apartments with kitchenettes. All accommodations are equipped with air-conditioning and TV but no phone. The resort provides maid service when you rent a regular double room but not when you rent an apartment.

See map p. 298. Harbourfront. ☎ *242-333-4883. Fax: 242-333-5073.* www.bahamas vg.com/adventurers.html. *Rack rates: $75 double, $110 one-bedroom apt with kitchenette, $165 two-bedroom apt with kitchenette. MC, V.*

Buccaneer Club
$ Governor's Harbour

This three-story, five-room farmhouse, built more than a century ago, offers views of the harbor. Today, it sports yellow-painted plank siding, white trim, and an old-fashioned design. The beach lies within a ten-minute stroll, although the house has a small saltwater pool on-site. Bedrooms are comfortable, unpretentious, well maintained, and outfitted with simple but colorful furniture. Rooms have air-conditioning but no TVs or phones. Your host and hostess are Michelle and Dwight Johnson, an Indian/Bahamian entrepreneurial team who foster a calm, quiet atmosphere. The Johnsons prepare lunch and dinner and serve it daily in an airy annex with island murals. Tasty specialties include Bahamian and American standbys: steaks, burgers, club sandwiches, cracked conch, grilled grouper with lemon butter sauce, and chili.

See map p. 298. Haynes Drive at Buccaneer Drive. ☎ *242-332-2000. Fax: 242-332-2888. Rack rates: $113 double. DISC, MC, V.*

Cartwright's Ocean Front Cottages
$ Tarpum Bay

Cartwright's is a cluster of three simple cottages right by the sea, with fishing, snorkeling, and swimming at your door. This spot is one of the few places where you can sit on your patio and watch the sunset. The small cottages are fully furnished, with utensils, stove, refrigerator, pots, and pans. The inn also provides maid service. You're within walking distance of local stores and restaurants. Rooms are air-conditioned but contain no phones. Regular hotel services are skimpy, although laundry service is available, as well as baby sitting, if arranged in advance.

See map p. 298. Bay Street. ☎ *242-334-4215. Rack rates: $100 one-bedroom cottage, $150 two-bedroom cottage, $180 three-bedroom cottage. No credit cards.*

Cocodimama Charming Resort
$$$ Governor's Harbour

This charmingly named and private hideaway is set by the water 9.5km (6 miles) north of Governor's Harbour. Built in a modern Bahamian style with verandas, the 12-room property opens onto a beach where you can enjoy such sports as kayaking, Hobie Catting, snorkeling, and windsurfing. Scuba-diving trips and deep-sea fishing can also be arranged. The spacious and handsomely furnished bedrooms are spread over a trio of pastel-painted cottages in a tropical garden. The accommodations are furnished with teak from Bali and Italian ceramics. Each unit is a suite unto itself with a hammock-hung patio. Some of the bedrooms have a comfortable sofa that can be used as a third bed. The owners of the hotel are expatriates from Italy, and the menu reflects their origin, though it includes many Bahamian dishes as well.

See map p. 298. Alabaster Bay (P.O. Box 122). ☎ *242-332-3150. Fax 242-332-3155.* www.cocodimama.com. *Rack rates: $185–$230 double. MAP (breakfast and dinner) $60 per person, free for children under 9. MC, V. Closed Sept 4–Nov 22.*

The Cove Eleuthera
$$ Gregory Town

On a pink sandy cove 2.5km (1½ miles) northwest of Gregory Town and 5km (3 miles) southeast of the Glass Window, this 26-room resort is set on 11 hectares (27 acres) partially planted with pineapples; it consists of a main clubhouse and eight tropical-style bungalows, each containing four units, nestled on the oceanside. All the rooms are imbued with island charm. Each one has tile floors and a porch, with no TVs or phones to distract you. All accommodations, each with a spacious living area, are equipped with a bathroom that includes a shower stall.

The restaurant (see listing later in the "Dining Out" section) serves three meals a day, and the lounge and poolside patio are open daily for drinks and informal meals. Kayaks, bicycles, two tennis courts, and a small freshwater pool compete with hammocks for your time. There's fabulous snorkeling right off the sands here, with colorful fish darting in and out of the offshore reefs.

See map p. 298. Queen's Highway. ☎ *800-552-5960 in the U.S. and Canada, or 242-335-5142. Fax: 242-335-5338.* www.thecoveeleuthera.com. *Rack rates: $195–$245 double, $345 one-bedroom suite. MC, V.*

Duck Inn and Orchid Gardens
$$$ Governor's Harbour

The accommodations you rent here are larger, plusher, more historic, and more charming than what you'd expect in a conventional hotel. The complex consists of three clapboard-sided houses, each built between 80 and 175 years ago, and each almost adjacent to another, midway up a hillside overlooking the sea. All units come with kitchenettes, air-conditioning, and TV, but no phone. Nassau-born John (J. J.) Duckworth and his Michigan-born wife, Katie, along with their son John Lucas, are your hosts. They spend much of their time nurturing a sprawling collection of beautiful orchids that they cultivate for export to Europe and the U.S. The collection of orchids, some 4,000 strong, is one of the largest in North America.

See map p. 298. Queen's Highway. ☎ *242-332-2608.* www.duckinncottages.com. *Rack rates: $150 double, $300 for cottages. AE, DISC, MC, V.*

Laughing Bird Apartments
$ **Governor's Harbour**

These four simple apartments lie near the edge of Governor's Harbour on a beach in the center of Eleuthera, and they're a good bet if you want to settle in for a week or so. Efficiencies come with a living/dining/sleeping area and a separate kitchen. Apartments face the beach on an acre of landscaped property. The units are bright, clean, and airy, and they have air-conditioning and TV but no phone. The staff offers bike rentals, tables and chairs for outdoor eating, and a garden barbecue. The staff can also make arrangements for water-skiing, surfing, fishing, sailing, tennis, golf, and snorkeling.

See map p. 298. Haynes Avenue and Birdie Street. ☎ *800-688-4752 in the U.S. or 242-332-2012. Fax: 242-332-2358. Rack rates: $95–$105 double. DISC, MC, V.*

Palmetto Shores Vacation Villas
$$ **Palmetto Point**

These accommodations are a good choice if you want your own apartment and value independence and privacy over hotel services. Asa Bethel rents 12 villas that are suitable for two to four guests. Units are a plain Bahamian-style, with living rooms, kitchens, and wraparound balconies that open directly onto your own private beach. Furnishings are simple but reasonably comfortable. Rooms have air-conditioning and TV/VCRs, and the villas lie within walking distance of local shops and tennis courts. The staff can help arrange car rentals, snorkeling, and deep-sea fishing, and can also provide free Sunflower sailboats.

See map p. 298. Palmetto Point. ☎ *888-688-4752 in the U.S. or 242-332-1305. Rack rates: $100–$120 one-, two-, and three-bedroom villas. Extra person $30 winter. MC, V.*

Quality Inn Cigatoo
$$ **Governor's Harbour**

This 22-room inn is on a hill and offers panoramic views of the ocean. Owners Franco and Katherine Ostini, two world travelers, try to bring some of the polish of Europe to the laid-back aura of Eleuthera. Nothing much happens here; you create your own amusement. You can lounge in a deck chair by the freshwater pool or take in a view of the tropical gardens. A good sandy beach, ideal for both beachcombing and swimming, is only a five-minute walk away.

Although comfortable and well maintained, the décor of the bedrooms wouldn't seem out of place in Miami in the 1960s. Built around the pool, the bedrooms open onto ocean or garden views. Each has a private balcony with chairs. If you're just passing through, consider a stopover here for lunch, because the Bahamian-style food is good.

See map p. 298. Haynes Avenue. ☎ *242-332-3060. Fax 242-332-3061. Rack rates: $113–$129 double. MC, V.*

Rainbow Inn
$$ Hatchet Bay

Three kilometers (2 miles) north of Alice Town and near a sandy beach, the Rainbow Inn is a venerable survivor in an area where many competitors have failed. Quirky and appealing to guests who return for quiet getaways again and again, it's an isolated collection of seven cedar-sided octagonal bungalows. The accommodations are simple but comfortable, spacious, and tidy; each has a kitchenette, lots of exposed wood, a ceiling fan, a porch, and a TV, but no phone. A sandy beach is a few steps away, and the inn offers an on-site saltwater pool along with a tennis court. You can rent cars, although the inn provides you with bikes and snorkeling gear.

One of the most appealing things about this place is **Dolcevita Restaurant and Lounge** — a destination for residents far up and down the length of Eleuthera. It has live Bahamian music twice a week and one of the most extensive menus on Eleuthera. The owners take pride that the menu hasn't changed much in 20 years — a fact that suits its loyal fans just fine. Table number two, crafted from a triangular teakwood prow of a motor yacht that was wrecked off the coast of Eleuthera in the 1970s, is a perpetual favorite of guests.

See map p. 298. Hatchet Bay. ☎ *800-688-0047 in the U.S. or 242-335-0294. Fax: 242-335-0294.* www.rainbowinn.com. *Rack rates: $140 double, $200–$225 two- or three-bedroom villas. MAP (breakfast and dinner) $45 per person extra. MC, V.*

Unique Village
$$ Palmetto Point

Located on a steep rise above the Atlantic coast of Eleuthera, this 14-room hotel is the creative statement of a Palmetto Point businessman who also owns the local hardware store (Unique Hardware). The hotel, built in 1992, offers everything from conventional single or double rooms to a one-bedroom apartment with a kitchenette to two-bedroom villas with full kitchens. All rooms come with air-conditioning. Wooden steps bring you to the beach, where a reef breaks up the Atlantic surf and creates calm waters on this sandy cove. There's a bar and restaurant, also called Unique Village (see our review in the "Dining Out" section later in this chapter), but few other luxuries. Although no sailing, scuba, or tennis is on-site, the staff can direct you to other facilities within a reasonable drive. (If you stay here, you'll probably want to rent a car; for more information on renting a car, see "Getting Around Eleuthera" earlier in this chapter.)

See map p. 298. North Palmetto Point. ☎ *888-820-8471 in the U.S. or 242-332-1830. Fax: 242-332-1838. Rack rates: $120–$130 double, $160 one-bedroom apt for two, $190 two-bedroom apt for up to four. MAP (breakfast and dinner) $35 per person per day. MC, V.*

Dining Out

Food on Eleuthera can be good and substantial, but don't expect fancy international restaurants. Your best bet for dining is at one of the few resorts. Branch out during the day to sample some "Bahama Mama" type places for island specialties. If you order as many Goombay Smashes as some of the locals do, you'll end up loving whatever is served.

Cambridge Villas
$ **Gregory Town   BAHAMIAN**

This restaurant occupies a large cement-sided room on the ground floor of a battered hotel (the accommodations aren't as appealing as the restaurant). Harcourt and Sylvia Cambridge, the owners, serve conch burgers, conch chowder, and sandwiches, usually prepared by Sylvia herself. This restaurant is just a simple spot where you may be entertained by the continually running soap operas broadcast from a TV over the bar.

See map p. 298. Main Street. ☎ *242-335-5080. Reservations not accepted. Sandwiches and platters: $5–$10. MC, V. Open: Mon–Sat 8 a.m.–9 p.m.*

Cigatoo Restaurant
$$ **Governor's Harbour   BAHAMIAN**

Set beside the swimming pool within the also-recommended Quality Inn Cigatoo, this is one of the more reliable and substantial dining areas within a town that isn't known for a wide variety of choices. Expect a mixture of Bahamian food with what you'd expect from an out-of-the-way steakhouse in Florida, with a choice of sandwiches, salads, and platters focusing on meats and catch of the day.

See map p. 298. In the Quality Inn Cigatoo, Queen's Highway. ☎ *242-332-3060. Sandwiches and salads: $8–$15; main courses: $17–$28. MC, V. Open: Daily 11:30 a.m.–3 p.m. and 6:30–10 p.m.*

The Cove
$$ **Gregory Town   BAHAMIAN/CONTINENTAL**

In the previously recommended hotel 2.5km (1½ miles) north of Gregory Town, this spacious dining room is your best bet in the area, featuring a gourmet Continental cuisine with local delights as well. The restaurant is decorated in a light, tropical style. Lunch begins with the inevitable conch chowder. We recommend you follow it with a conch burger, a generous patty of ground conch blended with green pepper, onion, and spices. Conch also appears several times in the evening, and we think this is the best cracked conch in town, tenderized, dipped in a special batter, and fried to a golden perfection. The kitchen serves the best fried chicken in the area, too.

See map p. 298. Queen's Highway. ☎ *242-335-5142. Breakfast: $8–$14; lunch: $8–$15; dinner main courses: $27–$32. MC, V. Open: Daily 8–10:30 a.m., 11:30 a.m.–2:30 p.m., and 6–8:30 p.m.*

Mate & Jenny's Pizza Restaurant & Bar
$$ Palmetto Point   BAHAMIAN/AMERICAN

This popular restaurant, known for its conch pizza, has a jukebox and a pool table. It's the most frequented local joint, completely modest and unassuming. In addition to pizza, the Bethel family prepares pan-fried grouper, cracked conch, or light meals, including snacks and sandwiches. Lots of folks come here just to drink. Try their Goombay Smash, Rumrunner, or piña colada, or just a Bahamian Kalik beer.

See map p. 298. South Palmetto Point, right off Queen's Highway. ☎ *242-332-1504. Pizza: $7–$27; main courses: $4–$28. MC, V. Open: Mon and Wed–Sat 11 a.m.–9 p.m., Sun 5:30–9 p.m.*

Muriel's Bakery
$ Palmetto Point   BAHAMIAN

Locals hail Muriel Cooper, a grandmother in her 70s, as the best baker in Eleuthera. Located across from the post office, her little bakery is simple yet warm and welcoming and filled with pictures of her grandchildren. You can stop in to stock up on freshly baked cakes, pies, tarts, rolls, and loaves of bread, which can be ideal for a picnic. Should some fishermen bring her fresh conch, she'll make a tasty chowder to go or else the island's best conch fritters. You'll fall for her rich, moist pineapple and coconut cakes as well.

See map p. 298. North Palmetto Point. ☎ *242-332-1583. Menu items: $1–$10. No credit cards. Open: Mon–Sat 10 a.m.–6 p.m.*

Pammy's
$ Governor's Harbour   BAHAMIAN

Tile-floored and Formica-clad, this restaurant is just a little cubbyhole with a few tables. At breakfast, you can order ham or corned beef and eggs, along with such sides as grits and bacon. Lunchtime features sandwiches, although you can also order hot plates of food (most often fried grouper). The dinner menu includes platters of cracked conch, pork chops, and either broiled or fried grouper. Don't expect anything fancy. It's a true local joint, serving up generous portions of flavor-filled food.

See map p. 298. Queen's Highway at Gospel Chapel Road. ☎ *242-332-2843. Reservations accepted for dinner only. Breakfast: $3.50–$7; lunch: $5–$10; dinner main courses: $14–$20. No credit cards. Open: Mon–Sat 8 a.m.–5 p.m.*

Sammy's Place
$ Rock Sound   BAHAMIAN

Hot gossip and cheap, juicy burgers make Sammy's the most popular hangout in Rock Sound — come here for a slice of local life. Sammy's is on the northeastern approach to the settlement in a neighborhood that even the owner refers to as "the back side of town." Sammy Culmer (who's assisted by Margarita, his daughter) will serve you drinks (including Bahama

Mamas and rum punches), conch fritters, Creole-style grouper, breaded scallops, pork chops, and lobster. If you drop in before 11 a.m., you may be tempted by a selection of egg dishes or omelets.

 This spot is primarily a restaurant and bar, but Sammy does rent four rooms with air-conditioning and satellite TV, plus two efficiency cottages with two bedrooms and a kitchen. These accommodations can be yours for $66 per night, double occupancy. An on-site cottage rents for $100 per night.

See map p. 298. Albury's Lane. ☎ *242-334-2121. Reservations recommended only for special meal requests. Breakfast: $5–$11; lunch: $5–$14; dinner main courses: $9–$25. No credit cards. Open: Daily 7:30 a.m.–10 p.m.*

Unique Village Restaurant & Lounge
$ **Palmetto Point   BAHAMIAN/AMERICAN**

This is the best place for food in the area, offering the widest selection. You can drop in for a Bahamian breakfast of boiled or stewed fish served with johnnycakes or steamed corned beef and grits. (You can also get "regular" breakfasts, such as hearty omelets.) Lunch offerings include zesty conch chowder and an array of salads. You can order burgers or the steamed catch of the day. At night, the choices grow, and you find the best New York sirloin available in mid-Eleuthera. Cracked conch fried in a light beer batter is one of the better versions of this dish on the island.

See map p. 298. In Unique Village hotel, North Palmetto Point. ☎ *242-332-1830. Main courses: $15–$36. MC, V. Open: Daily 7:30–11 a.m., 11:30 a.m.–5 p.m., and 6–9 p.m.*

Enjoying the Sand and Surf

Eleuthera possesses some of the finest beaches in The Bahamas, although none is as fine as the 5km (3 miles) of pink sands at Harbour Island (see Chapter 22).

Now relatively deserted, **Cape Eleuthera** was once home to a chic resort and yacht club that drew some of the movers and shakers from America's East Coast. They're all gone now, but the three splendid white sandy beaches remain the same, and locals claim the deep-sea fishing is as fine as it ever was. Directly north of the town of Tarpum Bay lies **Gaulding's Cay,** a lovely beach of golden sand with exceptional snorkeling.

 None of Eleuthera's beaches has facilities or lifeguards. Whatever you need on the beach, you should bring with you, including sunscreen and water. Don't expect any touristy kiosks selling drinks, snacks, or souvenirs — everything is pristine and undeveloped.

Even without its posh hotel, **Windermere Island** is worth a day trip. **Savannah Sound,** with its sandy sheltered beaches and outstanding snorkeling, is particularly appealing (bring your own gear). You also find excellent beaches for shelling and picnicking, and bonefishing is good — with some catches weighing in at more than 4.5 kilograms (10 pounds).

West Beach, a good place for sunning, swimming, and children, is about a ten-minute walk from the shut-down Windermere Club. The beach is on Savannah Sound, and this body of calm, protected water separates Windermere from the main island of Eleuthera.

Visitors can enjoy a number of activities, from bonefishing to windsurfing. The dockmaster at West Beach is well qualified to guide and advise you on bonefishing, or perhaps you prefer going deep-sea fishing for white marlin, dolphinfish, grouper, wahoo, Allison tuna, and amberjack. Because no permanent outfitter is on the island, you have to ask around locally about who can take you out.

At **Palmetto Point,** site of some villa rentals, you find **Ten Bay Beach,** one of the best beaches in The Bahamas, with its sparkling turquoise water and wide expanse of soft, white sand. The beach is a ten-minute drive south of Palmetto Point and just north of Savannah Sound. You won't find facilities here, only idyllic isolation.

Near the center of **Governor's Harbour** you find two sandy beaches known locally as the **Buccaneer Public Beaches;** they're adjacent to the Buccaneer Club, on the sheltered western edge of the island, facing Exuma Sound. Snorkeling is good here; it's best at the point where the pale turquoise waters near the coast deepen to a dark blue. Underwater rocks shelter lots of marine flora and fauna. The waves at these beaches are relatively calm.

On Eleuthera's Atlantic (eastern) side, less than a kilometer (a half-mile) from Governor's Harbour, is a much longer stretch of mostly pale pink sand, similar to what you find on Harbour Island. Known locally as the **Club Med Public Beach,** it's good for bodysurfing and, on days when storms are surging in the Atlantic, even conventional surfing.

Diving isn't a big sport on mainland Eleuthera. Outfitters come and go quickly, few getting enough business to hold out until another winter. But diving is excellent off Harbour Island, where you'll find some of the best scuba-diving experts in The Bahamas (see Chapter 22).

Exploring on Dry Land

We like to drive the full 161km (100-mile) length of Eleuthera, stopping wherever something enchants us. The island doesn't have any historical attractions, only those that nature created. We begin our tour in the south and head north.

Located in South Eleuthera, **Rock Sound** is a small, shady village. It is the island's main town and was once its most exclusive enclave. The closing of two old-time landmark resorts, the Cotton Bay Club and the Windermere Club, has — at least for now — halted the flow of famous visitors, who once included everybody from the late Princess Diana to a parade of CEOs. No reopenings are yet in sight, but that means you can have many of South Eleuthera's best beaches practically to yourself.

Rock Sound opens onto **Exuma Sound** and is located to the south of **Tarpum Bay.** The town is at least two centuries old, and it has many old-fashioned homes with picket fences out front. Once notorious for wreckers who lured ships ashore with false beacons, it used to be known as "Wreck Sound."

The **Ocean Hole,** which is about 2km (1¼ miles) east of the heart of Rock Sound, is said to be bottomless. This saltwater lake, which eventually meets the sea, is one of the most attractive spots on Eleuthera. You can walk right down to the edge of the water, and you can see many tropical fish here; they seem to like being photographed — but only if you feed them first.

After leaving Rock Sound, head south, bypassing the abandoned Cotton Bay Club, and continue through the villages of **Green Castle** and **Deep Creek.** At this point, you take a sharp turn northwest along the only road leading to **Cape Eleuthera.** Locals call this Cape Eleuthera Road, although you won't find any markings other than a sign pointing the way. If you continue following this road northwest, you'll reach the end of the island chain, jutting into Exuma Sound.

When you get back on the main road again, you can head north of Rock Sound for 14km (9 miles) until you come to **Tarpum Bay,** a charming old waterfront village. This tiny settlement, with its many pastel-washed, gingerbread-trimmed houses, is a favorite of artists, who have established a small colony here with galleries and studios.

Continue heading north, and you find **Windermere Island,** which lies between the settlements of Rock Sound and Governor's Harbour. To reach the island, you must cross a small bridge. Once the most exclusive vacation retreat in The Bahamas, many rich Americans still have second homes here, and security guards patrol the island.

You may have to do some sweet-talking to get past the security patrols. They generally let you drive along the island if they think you're a sightseer and not a burglar.

On the east side of Queen's Highway, south of Governor's Harbour, **North Palmetto Point** is a little village where visitors rarely venture (although you can get a meal here). This laid-back town will suit you if you want peace and quiet off the beaten track.

At some 300 years old, **Governor's Harbour** is the island's oldest settlement, reportedly the landing place of the Eleutherian Adventurers, the island's original settlers. The largest town on Eleuthera after Rock Sound, it's situated midway along the island. The town today has a population of about 1,500, with some bloodlines going back to the Adventurers and to the Loyalists who followed some 135 years later. Many old homes line streets amid the bougainvillea and casuarina trees.

Leaving Queen's Highway, you can take a small bridge, thought to be about 150 years old, to **Cupid's Cay.** As you explore the offshore island, you come upon one of the most interesting buildings in the area, an old Anglican church with its tombstone-studded graveyard.

Forty kilometers (25 miles) north of Governor's Harbour is the village **Hatchet Bay.** Hatchet Bay was once known for a sprawling British-owned plantation that had 500 dairy cattle and thousands of chickens. Today, the plantation is gone, and the village is now one of the sleepiest on Eleuthera, as you can see if you veer off Queen's Highway onto one of the town's ghostly main streets, Lazy Shore Road or Ocean Drive.

Gregory Town, north of Hatchet Bay, stands in the center of Eleuthera against a backdrop of hills, which break the usual flat monotony of the landscape. This village of clapboard cottages was once famed for growing pineapples. Although the industry isn't as strong as it used to be, the locals make a good pineapple rum out of the fruit, and you can visit the Gregory Town Plantation and Distillery where they produce it. You can sample it, and we almost guarantee that you'll want to take a bottle home with you!

Dedicated surfers come here from as far away as California and Australia to test their skills at **Surfer's Beach,** 3km (2 miles) south of Gregory Town on the Atlantic side. The waves are at their highest in winter and spring; even if you're not brave enough to venture out, the surfers are fun to watch.

South of Gregory Town on the way to Hatchet Bay are several caverns worth visiting, the largest of which is called simply **The Cave.** It has a big fig tree out front, which the people of Gregory Town claim that area pirates planted to conceal the cave because they had hidden treasure in it. Local guides (you have to ask around in Gregory Town or Hatchet Bay) can take you into the interior of the cave, where the resident bats are harmless (even though they must resent the intrusion of tourists with flashlights). At one point, the drop is so steep — about 3.6m (12 ft.) — that you have to use a ladder to climb down. Eventually, you reach a cavern studded with stalactites and stalagmites. At this point, a maze of passageways leads through the rocky underground recesses. The cave comes to an abrupt end at the edge of a cliff, where the thundering sea is some 27m (90 ft.) below.

After leaving Gregory Town and driving north, you come to the famed **Glass Window,** Eleuthera's chief sight and narrowest point. A natural rock arch once bridged the land, but it's gone now, replaced by an artificially constructed bridge. As you drive across it, you can see the contrast between the deep blue ocean and the emerald green shoal waters of Exuma Sound. The rocks rise to a height of 21m (70 ft.). Often, as ships in the Atlantic toss about, the crew looks across the narrow point to see a ship resting quietly on the other side (hence, the name "Glass Window"). American artist Winslow Homer was so captivated by this spot that he once captured it on canvas.

The inhabitants of **Current,** a settlement in North Eleuthera, are believed to have descended from a tribe of Native Americans. A narrow strait separates the village from **Current Island,** where most of the locals make their living from the sea or from plaiting straw goods. This small community often welcomes visitors. It has no crowds and no artificial attractions. Everything focuses on the sea, a source of pleasure for visitors, but a way to sustain life for the local people.

From Current, you can explore some interesting sights in North Eleuthera, including **Preacher's Cave,** where the Eleutherian Adventurers found shelter in the mid–17th century when they were shipwrecked with no provisions. (Note that your taxi driver may balk at being asked to drive there; the road is hard on his expensive tires.) If you do reach it, you'll find a cave that seems like an amphitheater. The very devout Eleutherian Adventurers held religious services inside the cave, which has holes in the roof to allow light to intrude. The cave isn't far from the North Eleuthera Airport.

Living It Up After Dark

Eleuthera is rather sleepy, but it does have a hot spot or two. The place to be in Gregory Town, especially on a Saturday night, is **Elvina** (☎ 242-335-5032), on Main Street. Owners Ed and Elvina Watkins make you feel right at home and practically greet you at the door with a cold beer. Their place has a funky charm, with local artwork, license plates, and surfboards as decorations. Surfers and locals alike flock here to chow down on burgers, Bahamian dishes, and Cajun grub, served daily from 10 a.m. to "whenever we close." Elvina's husband, "Chicken Ed," is from Louisiana, and does he ever know how to make a great jambalaya!

Also at Governor's Harbour, **Ronnie's Smoke Shop & Sports Bar** (☎ 242-332-2307), on Cupid's Cay, is the most happening nightspot in central Eleuthera. It's adjacent to the cargo depot of Cupid's Cay, in a connected cluster of simple buildings painted in combinations of black with vivid Junkanoo colors. Most folks come here just to drink Kalik beer and talk at either of the two bars. But if you want to dance, it has an all-black room just for disco music on Friday and Saturday nights. You also find the only walk-in cigar humidor on Eleuthera. If you get hungry, order up a plate of barbecue, pizza, chicken wings, or popcorn. The place is open daily from 9 a.m. 'til at least 2 a.m.

Going Beyond Eleuthera

Of course, the most enticing day trip is to **Harbour Island** (see Chapter 22). But **Spanish Wells** is intriguing, too, as a journey back to a distant past. Called a "quiet corner of The Bahamas," Spanish Wells is a colorful cluster of houses on **St. George's Cay,** less than a kilometer (a half-mile) off the coast of northwest Eleuthera. It's characterized by its sparkling bays and white beaches, sleepy lagoons, excellent diving, and fine fishing colony.

You can walk through the village and look at the houses — some more than 200 years old — which have New England saltbox styling but bright tropical coloring. You can see handmade quilts in many colors, following patterns handed down from generations of English ancestors. Homeowners display quilts for sale on their front porches or out their windows.

Regardless of the time of day you arrive, a ferryboat is either waiting for passengers or about to arrive with a load of them. (See "Getting Around Eleuthera" earlier in this chapter for more details.)

If you're on Spanish Wells at lunch, head for **Jack's Outback** (☎ 242-333-4219) along the harbor front. Unpretentious and well scrubbed, this little place stands along the waterfront in the heart of town. Known for its home-cooking, it offers the usual array of sandwiches and cheese-burgers, as well as Bahamian foods like cracked conch, conch burgers, and conch chowder. It also offers steaks, barbecued ribs, and cheesy shrimp poppers. The interior is air-conditioned, with views of the sea. Sandwiches cost from $4.80 to $12, with main courses priced from $11 to $25. It's open daily from 9 a.m. to 9:30 p.m. Credit cards aren't accepted.

Fast Facts: Eleuthera

American Express and ATMs

No Amex services are available on Eleuthera, but an ATM is available at the Bank of Canada (☎ 242-333-2230), on Dunmore Street near the library.

Emergency

Call ☎ 242-332-2111.

Hospitals

The Governor Harbour's Medical Clinic (☎ 242-332-2001), located on Queen's Highway, is open Monday through Friday

from 9 a.m. to 5:30 p.m. The clinic is also the site of a dentist's office. The dentist is here from 9:30 a.m. until 3 p.m., Monday through Wednesday and Friday only. Call for an appointment before going. A doctor and four resident nurses form the staff of the Rock Sound Medical Clinic (☎ 242-334-2226). Office hours are daily from 9 a.m. to 1 p.m.; after that, the doctor is always available to handle emergency cases.

Information

The Eleuthera Tourist Office (☎ 242-332-2142) is on Queens Highway. It's generally open Monday through Friday from 9 a.m. to 5 p.m.

Internet Access

Check with your hotel for Internet access. An Internet cafe has opened on the second floor of the Haynes Library (☎ 242-332-2877) at Governor's Harbour. The charge is $5 per hour, and the library is open Monday through Saturday from 9 a.m. to 5 p.m.

Pharmacy

Governor Harbour's Medical Clinic (☎ 242-332-2001) fills prescriptions. The clinic is located on Queen's Highway, and is open Monday through Friday from 9 a.m. to 5:30 p.m.

Police

If you need the police, call Governor's Harbour Police Station (☎ **242-332-2111**), located on Queens Highway.

Post Office

At Governor's Harbour, you can find a post office on Haynes Avenue (☎ 242-332-2060). Hours are Monday to Friday from 9 a.m. to 4:30 p.m.

Safety

Eleuthera is one of the safest Bahamian islands. Of course, take all the same precautions you would here that you would when traveling anywhere. Keep valuables in a safe place and don't wander into deserted, unfamiliar areas at night.

Taxis

Cabs meet incoming flights at all three airports. During your stay, your hotel staff can call a taxi for you.

Chapter 24

Exuma

In This Chapter

▶ Finding the best accommodations and restaurants
▶ Enjoying spectacular sailing and kayaking
▶ Exploring George Town, the charming harborside capital

*E*xuma — or the Exumas — is a string of some 365 cays, one for each day of the year. Most cays are either barely populated or completely uninhabited. The little archipelago is prime sailing, kayaking, fishing, scuba diving, and snorkeling territory.

Arriving at the Airport

Fourteen kilometers (9 miles) from George Town, **Exuma International Airport** is the official port of entry for this archipelago. Flights come in from Nassau and Florida (Miami, Ft. Lauderdale, St. Petersburg, and Sarasota). At the small, well-kept airport, you have to clear Customs unless you're coming from Nassau. Taxis wait just outside, and the cab fare to George Town hotels is about $25 for two passengers.

If you're going on to **Stocking Island,** an islet in **Elizabeth Harbour,** you can make prior arrangements with your hotel for boat transfers.

Choosing Your Location

George Town, on **Great Exuma,** the main island, is the easiest to reach. At the edge of Elizabeth Harbour, this postcard-pretty village isn't known for its beaches. However, just across the harbor from town, **Stocking Island** boasts some of the country's best sandy shores. A ferry links "mainland" hotels to this beach-rimmed island. If you want to stay on Stocking Island, your choice of hotels is limited to one: Hotel Higgins Landing. Although a few George Town hotels have their own beaches, the swimming is far better on Stocking Island. For guests of Higgins Landing, ferry service is free between this sandy harbor islet and George Town.

Sailing is excellent from any home base. Rent a boat, and you can anchor off some of the nearby uninhabited islets, where snorkeling and fishing

Great Exuma/Little Exuma

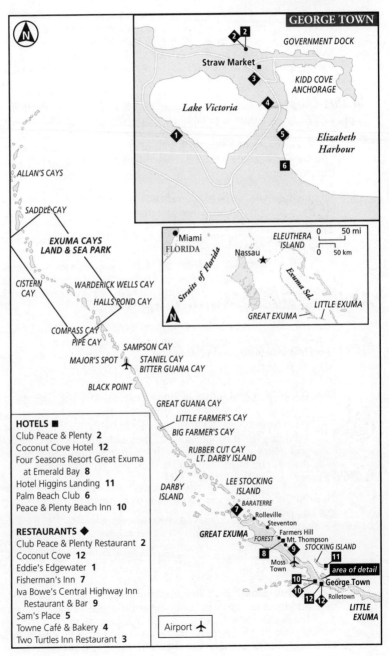

GEORGE TOWN

GOVERNMENT DOCK

Straw Market

KIDD COVE
ANCHORAGE

Lake Victoria

Elizabeth
Harbour

ALLAN'S CAYS

SADDLE CAY

EXUMA CAYS
LAND & SEA PARK

Miami
FLORIDA
Nassau

ELEUTHERA
ISLAND

0   50 mi
0   50 km

CISTERN
CAY

WARDERICK WELLS CAY

HALLS POND CAY

Straits of Florida

Exuma Sd.

LITTLE EXUMA

GREAT EXUMA

COMPASS CAY
PIPE CAY

SAMPSON CAY

MAJOR'S SPOT   STANIEL CAY
BITTER GUANA CAY

BLACK POINT

GREAT GUANA CAY

LITTLE FARMER'S CAY

BIG FARMER'S CAY

RUBBER CUT CAY
LT. DARBY ISLAND

DARBY
ISLAND

LEE STOCKING
ISLAND

BARATERRE

Rolleville
Steventon

GREAT EXUMA   FOREST   Farmers Hill
Mt. Thompson
STOCKING ISLAND

Moss
Town

George Town

area of detail

Rolletown

LITTLE
EXUMA

HOTELS ■
Club Peace & Plenty **2**
Coconut Cove Hotel **12**
Four Seasons Resort Great Exuma
   at Emerald Bay **8**
Hotel Higgins Landing **11**
Palm Beach Club **6**
Peace & Plenty Beach Inn **10**

RESTAURANTS ◆
Club Peace & Plenty Restaurant **2**
Coconut Cove **12**
Eddie's Edgewater **1**
Fisherman's Inn **7**
Iva Bowe's Central Highway Inn
   Restaurant & Bar **9**
Sam's Place **5**
Towne Café & Bakery **4**
Two Turtles Inn Restaurant **3**

Airport ✈

are top rate. No matter which hotel you select, you can arrange scuba diving and fishing.

When you're ready to explore dry land, George Town is the starting point for renting a car or taking a taxi tour. A bridge links Great Exuma to **Little Exuma,** which you can skip without suffering cultural deprivation. It's like wandering back into another day, because its heyday has been long gone with the wind.

Accommodations in Exuma are as distinct as they are small. If you like being in the middle of island action, book a room at Club Peace & Plenty in town. Guests who prefer a secluded, elegant eco-resort can choose solar-powered Hotel Higgins Landing on Stocking Island. (To find out more about both these hotels, see the section "Staying in Style" later in this chapter.)

No one has ever heard of the rat race in sleepy Exuma. Hotel rooms may not have phones, and the few TVs may get only a couple of centrally controlled channels (meaning that you watch whatever the bartender turns to). The liveliest entertainment "jumps up" on weekends, usually at Club Peace & Plenty, where the Saturday and sometimes Wednesday night dance parties are legendary. Hotels are close enough to each other that you can dine among them and mingle in a variety of settings. Some good local restaurants besides the ones in the hotels are also conveniently located in and around George Town.

Getting Around Exuma

Exuma is very accessible, and you don't have to rent a car.

- ✔ **Hoofing it:** George Town is designed for strolling, but don't expect sights that scream tourist attraction. This spot is a handsome little waterfront village where browsing at the tree-shaded straw market, sampling fresh conch salad at the dock, and mingling with residents and fellow vacationers over drinks and home-style meals are the big draws. The most idyllic walk is around **Lake Victoria.**

  Shuttle service is provided to town from **Peace & Plenty Beach Inn,** or you may want to walk the scenic mile.

  If you don't succumb to taking wheels, you can leisurely enjoy the glimpses of the turquoise and neon blue water through the wispy casuarina pines and bushy coconut palms lining **Queen's Highway.** "Highway" is a serious overstatement, so walking here is fine because traffic is sparse.

- ✔ **Taking a taxi:** You'll have no problems finding a taxi to take you to and from the airport, far-flung restaurants, or on-land tours around Great and Little Exuma. Your hotel can assist you. Fares are regulated, but drivers don't use meters, so agree on a price before setting out. Taxi driver **Kermit Rolle** (☎ 242-345-0002), who also farms and runs local restaurants, seems to know everything anyone could ever want to know about Exuma.

✔ **Boarding a boat:** For ferries between George Town and the beaches on Stocking Island, call **Club Peace & Plenty** at ☎ 242-336-2551. The twice-daily ferries are complimentary for Club Peace & Plenty guests. If you're not staying at the hotel, the cost is $10 round-trip and free for children under age 10. For renting boats, see "Climbing Aboard" later in the chapter.

✔ **Driving around:** Vacationers based in and around George Town have no real need to rent a car. If you want to see the rest of Great Exuma and Little Exuma, you can hire a taxi. But if you prefer striking out on your own, try **Thompson's Car Rental** in George Town (☎ 242-336-2442 or 242-345-4189), where autos begin at about $65 per day. Or try **Don's Car Rental** (☎ 242-345-0112), conveniently located right at the airport; daily rates start at $75.

The George Town area has two gas stations: one near Exuma International Airport and the other in Farmers Hill. They're generally open Monday through Saturday from 8 a.m. to 5 p.m., Sunday from 8 a.m. until noon, and on holidays from 8 to 10 a.m.

Staying in Style

Most hotels lie in and around George Town. Of the handful of hotels, most have fewer than 16 rooms. For escapists, one of Exuma's best accommodations is an offshore "one-to-one": one island, one resort.

Club Peace & Plenty
$$$ In the heart of George Town

This pink-and-white harborside hotel is the virtual social center of the Exumas. Club Peace & Plenty was once a private home built on the site of a slave market during Loyalist days when British supporters fled to The Bahamas after the Revolutionary War. A former kitchen has been transformed into a tavern decorated with old anchors, rudders, lanterns, and other maritime artifacts. During the National Family Island Regatta each April, visiting and local yachties flock to this hotel's cozy lounge.

The handsome two-story building faces the main road on one side and Elizabeth Harbour on the other. With balconies, satellite TV, and queen-size, double, or twin beds, the 32 bright guest rooms overlook the harbor, freshwater pool, or greenery. Although perfectly well maintained and comfortable, the rooms have a somewhat dated feel. Dine indoors or alfresco at Club Peace & Plenty's popular restaurant, where local seafood is the specialty. Twice a week, the hotel features a poolside cocktail party for guests. Snorkel gear is available, and a shuttle runs several times a day between the hotel and its closest sibling, **Peace & Plenty Beach Inn** (see the review later in the chapter). Guests can also take the complimentary ferry just across the water to Stocking Island beaches.

Peace & Plenty is Exuma's "chain" hotel. Peace & Plenty Beach Inn is about a half-kilometer (1 mile) up the road. Six kilometers (10 miles) southeast of George Town is **Peace & Plenty Bonefish Lodge,** an inn for anglers. The lodge serves dinner several nights a week, and guests of Club Peace & Plenty receive free transportation to it.

See map p. 315. Queen's Highway. ☎ **800-525-2210** *or 242-336-2551. Fax: 242-336-2093.* www.peaceandplenty.com. *Rack rates: $170–$205 double, $190–$310 suite. AE, DC, MC, V.*

Coconut Cove Hotel
$$$ George Town

Set about 1.8km (1 mile) west of George Town — on a seafront plot of land that's dotted with groves of coconut palms and palmettos and host to a brackish saltwater pond favored by bird life — this is a much-renovated incarnation of a hotel that has stood here for 20 years. Designed with three wings that radiate from a central core, much like the shape of an airplane propeller, it offers 11 simple but well-cared-for rooms, a bar where the rum-based Coconut Cove Specials are appropriately pink and heady, and a restaurant (see listing below in the "Dining Out" section) whose cuisine is praised as among the best on the island. The staff here can arrange access to island tours and watersports options.

See map p. 315. George Town. ☎ **242-336-2659**. *Fax 242-336-2658.* www.exuma bahamas.com. *Rack rates: $152–$262 double. Add $30 for extra person. AE, MC, V.*

Four Seasons Resort Great Exuma at Emerald Bay
$$$$$ North of George Town

The quiet Exumas emerged from a sleep of centuries with the official opening of this resort in the winter of 2004. Its sweeping ocean vistas and tropical beauty frame an experience unique in this part of the world; the Out Islands have seen nothing like this in their history, and the resort is expected to change the entire character of the archipelago.

All 183 accommodations here open onto private terraces and balconies with scenic views of the bay. You're given a choice of rooms, from generously proportioned gardenview units to oceanview rooms opening directly onto the bay. For the big spender, the resort also offers a series of executive suites and beachfront properties of one and two bedrooms.

So much goes on at this resort that you may never get around to exploring the surrounding islands. The most spectacular feature is a championship 18-hole golf course designed by Greg Norman. The full-service spa and health club is the finest in The Bahamas, and you can swim at the hotel's crescent-shaped white-sand beach or in its two pools. The best marina in the southern Bahamas is on-site. And the cuisine is among the best in the Out Islands, with both indoor and outdoor dining options and a selection of Italian, Caribbean, Bahamian, and international dishes.

Houseboats

The most offbeat way to stay in the Exumas is on a brightly decorated floating house-boat. Each boat is like a hotel suite that you can use to explore Elizabeth Harbour and the coast of the Exumas. In between moving your houseboat from anchorage to anchorage, you can go fishing, snorkeling, scuba diving, or just beachcombing. Each houseboat sleeps six to eight people and is fully equipped with air-conditioning, hot and cold running water, a marine radio, an inflatable dinghy, a fully equipped galley, all linens, purified water, and a propane barbecue grill. Boats range from an 11m (35-ft.) one-bedroom to a 13m (43-ft.) two-bedroom. You don't need a special license or even much experience to operate one of these boats. For reservations, contact **Bahamas Houseboats**, P.O. Box EX29031, Government Dock, George Town, Exuma, The Bahamas (☎ **242-336-BOAT**; fax 242-336-2629; www.bahamahouseboats.com). Rentals range from $360 to $490 per day, with a three-day minimum. American Express, MasterCard, and Visa are accepted.

See map p. 315. Emerald Bay. ☎ ***800-819-5053*** *or 242-366-6800. Fax 242-336-6081.* www.fourseasons.com. *Rack rates: $495–$995 double, from $995 suite. AE, DC, DISC, MC, V.*

Hotel Higgins Landing
$$$$$ **Stocking Island**

This intimate resort is on a tiny, virtually uninhabited, beach-rimmed island. Not only is it the only hotel on luscious Stocking Island, just a half-kilometer (1 mile) across Elizabeth Harbour from George Town, but it's also accessible only by ferry. No roads or cars are on the island, so feet and boats are the modes of transportation.

This upscale resort is solar powered. Hilly twists and turns along rocky paths lead to the five cottages, which sport large decks. Strategically placed to ensure both privacy and proximity to the beach, each unit is beautifully furnished with antiques, four-poster queen-size beds, and Oriental rugs. You're asked to conserve water, but you don't need to worry about running out. Ceiling fans cool the air, which circulates through glass-free screen windows. Cottages are equipped with enough voltage for fans and reading lights, but you have to go elsewhere at the resort to use standard 110-volt electricity. Instead of television, you can visit the hotel's little library. Bob Higgins, who runs the hotel with his wife, Carol, is in charge of breakfast, which the staff serves on a deck overlooking **Silver Palms Beach.** One day, Bob may whip up coconut pancakes; the next, eggs Benedict. The candlelit, multicourse dinner may be black mushroom soup followed by grilled beef or seafood and espresso chocolate custard. Room rates may seem high, but they include a gourmet dinner and hors d'oeuvres daily, the boat trip to and from the island upon arrival and departure, and a variety of watersports equipment. You can make arrangements for scuba diving, snorkeling, and fishing trips.

Smoking is not allowed inside the buildings, but it is permitted on your deck or at the beach bar. Children under 18 are not allowed unless you rent the entire resort.

See map p. 315. Across Elizabeth Harbour from George Town. ☎ *242-357-0008. Fax 866-289-0919.* www.higginslanding.com. *Rack rates: $350 and up. Rates include hors d'oeuvres and dinner. MC, V.*

Palm Beach Club
$$$ George Town

This is one of the most tranquil accommodations in the archipelago. Overlooking the waters of Elizabeth Harbour, this attractive 32-room resort offers beach-fronting villas, each featuring one of three options: a studio, a one-bedroom unit, or a more luxurious and spacious two-bedroom accommodations. The cottages are beautifully appointed, mostly with kitchenettes, cable TV, and Internet available. Each villa is individually decorated featuring queen-size or king-size beds, ceramic tile flooring, and comfortable tropical-style furniture. A shuttle bus carries visitors to and from George Town. Kayaks and paddle boats are available.

See map p. 315. Elizabeth Harbour, George Town. ☎ *242-336-2787.* www.palmbay beachclub.com. *Rack rates: $186–$285 double, $299–$355 two-bedroom unit. AE, MC, V.*

Peace & Plenty Beach Inn
$$$ Northwest of George Town

More subdued than its older sibling **Club Peace & Plenty** (see the review earlier in this "Staying in Style" section), this 16-room B&B sits on a small beach. Built in the early 1990s, it draws many snorkelers and bonefishermen. Everyone from newlyweds to families feel comfortable here. In the spacious, attractively decorated guest rooms, French doors open onto large patios or balconies overlooking the swimming pool and ocean. Steps from the saltwater pool lead down to the sand, with expansive views of Stocking Island across the water; guests can take the complimentary ferry to the beautiful beaches. Regular shuttles link Peace & Plenty Beach Inn with Club Peace & Plenty, the center of the George Town social scene.

See map p. 315. Queen's Highway, 1.6km (1 mile) northwest of George Town. ☎ *800-525-2210 or 242-336-2250. Fax: 242-336-2253.* www.peaceandplenty.com. *Rack rates: $170–$190 double. Ask about bonefishing package rates. AE, MC, V.*

Dining Out

Most of Exuma's restaurants are in George Town, but you can take a rental car, taxi, or hotel shuttle to some offbeat places in outlying areas. Visit hotel dining rooms for the most sophisticated and priciest dining. When these upscale accommodations serve local dishes, they often have Continental and American influences.

For the most authentic — and the least expensive — Bahamian cooking, try a local restaurant. The food stall near George Town's Government Dock makes a great fresh conch salad prepared to order, but its hours are limited: It's open only on Monday, Wednesday, and Friday.

Most hotels fix reasonably priced picnic lunches for beach excursions and other ramblings. Dining rooms in and outside hotels close between meals, and the smaller spots don't accept credit cards. **Peace & Plenty Beach Inn** (see the review under "Staying in Style" earlier in this chapter) provides shuttle service into town.

Club Peace & Plenty Restaurant
$$$ In the heart of George Town
BAHAMIAN/CONTINENTAL/AMERICAN

Go here for the finest island dining, with plentiful and good home-cooked meals that leave most guests satisfied. Boiled fish and grits is a popular breakfast choice at this hotel dining room with harbor views. But, you can also order eggs, French toast, and other American favorites. For lunch, try the conch burgers. Appetizers include a savory conch chowder, pumpkin soup, or hearts of palm salad. Grouper — pan-fried or steamed with peppers and onions — makes frequent evening appearances, along with Bahamian lobster and T-bone steak. You can also order pasta with shrimp or a spicy tomato sauce.

See map p. 315. Queen's Highway. ☎ *242-336-2551. Reservations required for dinner. Breakfast: $8.50; lunch: from $8; dinner main courses: $18–$30. AE, DISC, MC, V. Open: Daily 7:30.–10:30 a.m., noon–2:30 p.m., and 6:30–9:30 p.m.*

Coconut Cove
$$$ George Town   ITALIAN

Set on the premises of the previously recommended hotel, this dining room sits close to the sea, within a glassed-in, blue, white, and coral-colored dining room whose mahogany-and-glass doors slide open for maximum exposure to the breeze. American-born Palema Chimento, in cooperation with her Bahama-born assistant, Shelia, churns out well-flavored versions of Italian and Mediterranean-inspired food that's far removed from the usual Bahamian fare you may have expected. Starters include breaded calamari with oregano and parsley sauce, linguini marinara, jalapeño peppers, breaded mozzarella sticks, onion soup, and seafood salads. Main courses feature stone crabs, different preparations of shrimp, crawfish, poached salmon served with a tropical fruit salsa, and "cowboy steaks." There's also a choice of pizzas from a "pizza bar" on-site. Most dishes, except for lobster, are priced at the low end of the scale.

See map p. 315. In the Coconut Cove Hotel, George Town. ☎ *242-336-2659. Reservations recommended. Main courses: $24–$54; pizzas $12–$30. AE, DISC, MC, V. Wed–Sun 6–9 p.m.*

Fisherman's Inn
$$ Barraterre BAHAMIAN

This is the most isolated restaurant in the Exumas, a ramshackle, wood-sided hideaway that's set on a low ridge above the sea on the island of Barraterre, a 40- to 60-minute drive from George Town. Connected with two separate causeways to the "mainland" of Great Exuma Island, it's literally at the end of the line for motorists looking for a lonely, sun-bleached, and windblasted excursion from George Town. Don't come here with the assurance that there will be anything in the larder at the time of your arrival. If the season is slow, or if the supplies "didn't make it in that week," you may be faced with a smile and perhaps a somewhat erratic dialogue from the owner, and 'nary a crust of bread. To avoid disappointment, call ahead to survey the gastronomic lay of the land by discussing with the staff what may, or may not, be available that day. Expect a roster of fish, chicken, beefsteaks, soups, salads, and stews, lots of local color, and a genuine sense of the degree to which parts of The Bahamas archipelago are isolated from the rest of the world.

See map p. 315. Barraterre. ☎ 242-355-5016. Reservations required. Main courses: lunch $8–$10, dinner $20–$25. No credit cards. Daily 7 a.m.–midnight.

Eddie's Edgewater
$ George Town BAHAMIAN

On Monday nights, this is the place to be for the weekly "rake 'n scrape," when a band transforms rakes, saws, washboards, and other household items into instruments and turns the restaurant into a party — a wonderful, traditional Bahamian moment. At the edge of Lake Victoria, this casual hangout gets raves for its turtle steak and steamed chicken. If you have your heart set on either of those dishes, call ahead to make sure that they're on the menu that day. Other well-prepared dishes for lunch and dinner include okra soup, conch chowder, and pan-fried grouper. Breakfast is standard but reliable, with pancakes, French toast, and omelets, along with grits, ham, and bacon.

See map p. 315. Charlotte Street, by Lake Victoria. ☎ 242-336-2050. Main courses: $11–$15. MC, V. Open: Mon–Sat 7 a.m.–9 p.m.

Iva Bowe's Central Highway Inn Restaurant & Bar
$ Northwest of George Town BAHAMIAN

Islanders tell you that this restaurant is *the* place for that local favorite, cracked conch, and they're right. The chicken, fish, and lobster dishes are all excellent, too, and so are the crawfish salad and the shrimp scampi. The dining room isn't fancy, but the home-style food makes a trip — or two — here well worth your time. When you're tooling around Great Exuma, this eatery is a great choice for takeout.

See map p. 315. Central Highway, about a half-kilometer (¼ mile) from the International Airport. ☎ 242-345-7014. Main courses: $10–$12. Open: Mon–Sat 8 a.m.–11 p.m.

Eating with the locals

You can grab a quick meal at several casual joints in George Town. **Towne Café,** in the Marshall Complex (☎ **242-336-2194**) serves one of the best breakfasts in George Town. It's really the town bakery. Drop in any day but Sunday for a lunch of local Exumian specialties such as stewed grouper or chicken souse, or just a sandwich.

A former school bus was recycled and turned into **Jean's Dog House** along Queen's Highway in George Town. Here you'll find the island's best lobster burger in a cramped but spotless kitchen on wheels. Instead of eating our hotel dining room, we like to go here for breakfast and order the "MacJean," a robust sandwich with sausage or bacon, plus cheese, on freshly baked bread. Of course, she's also noted for her "dogs," or frankfurters. The owner is a well-loved personality known only as Jean. Visit her between 7 a.m. and 3 p.m. and don't bother bringing your credit card.

The best conch salad is found at **Big D's Conch Spot No. 2,** Government Dock (☎ **242-358-0059**). "Fresh, sexy conch," as it's called here, is served daily. They'll make it right in front of you, so you know exactly what's going into your salad. They're open Tuesday to Sunday noon to midnight. Reservations required only for large parties.

Sam's Place
$ George Town   BAHAMIAN/AMERICAN

Overlooking the marina in George Town, the broad veranda of this second-story restaurant provides a scenic setting for a morning, afternoon, or evening meal. The boating crowd comes here in droves to enjoy its ever-changing menu. Lunch may be conch chowder and a sandwich or maybe a succulent pasta dish. For dinner, your choices include local lobster tail, pan-fried wahoo (our favorite), tender roast lamb, or steamed chicken.

See map p. 315. Main Street, at the marina. ☎ *242-336-2579. Main courses: $12–$30. MC, V. Open: Daily 8 a.m.–9 p.m.*

Towne Café & Bakery
$ George Town   BAHAMIAN/BAKED GOODS

For a good alternative to breakfast at your hotel, stop at this bakery-plus. Bahamians come for the filling pancakes and the boil fish, cooked with onions and peppers and grits. The restaurant serves chicken souse with delicately sweet johnnycake (a mildly sweet bread). Coffeecake, fresh doughnuts, and bran muffins are the best choices for pastries here. Antique household items decorate the simple dining room. If the lunch menu includes grouper fingers, go for it.

See map p. 315. Marshall Complex, by the Shell gas station. ☎ *242-336-2194. Main courses: $8–$15. No credit cards. Open: Mon–Sat 7:30 a.m.–5 p.m.*

Two Turtles Inn Restaurant
$ George Town BAHAMIAN/AMERICAN

A popular meeting place, this hotel dining spot within view of the marina has the feel of a sidewalk cafe. Laid-back, but often busy, it is the only outdoor restaurant in town. Dishes prepared with fresh local seafood are excellent. For many years, the zesty Friday-night barbecues have been drawing scores of residents and those visitors who make the discovery — now you know all about it, too.

See map p. 315. Across from the village green and the straw market. ☎ *242-336-2545. Main courses: $12–$25. AE, MC, V. Open: Breakfast daily 9–10 a.m.; lunch daily 11 a.m.–3 p.m.; dinner Tues–Sun from 6 p.m.*

Enjoying the Sand and Surf

Most of the excitement on Exuma is all wet. However, you can spend a day driving to and through some of the drowsy settlements scattered along Great Exuma and the adjoining Little Exuma. If you don't, you end up missing some sights, such as historic gravesites, pink salt ponds, brightly painted tiny houses, a little museum-boutique, small farms, vestiges of plantation ruins, and plenty of island greenery.

Walking around George Town gives you plenty of opportunities to meet and greet residents and other vacationers. Instead of spending a whole day touring the island on dry land, you may have more fun seeing the sights by water — in a sailboat, speedboat, or kayak. This way, you can explore some of the smaller offshore uninhabited cays.

 The George Town–based **Starfish Activity Center** (☎ 242-336-3033) makes booking everything from kayaking to snorkeling as simple as one phone call.

Combing the beaches

George Town's best beaches aren't in George Town but are across Elizabeth Harbour on a pencil-thin slip of land known as Stocking Island. Not even 8km (5 miles) long and barely a kilometer (a half-mile) wide, Stocking Island protects the harbor from the open ocean. Club Peace & Plenty provides ferry service to this beach-rimmed island (free for guests of Club Peace & Plenty, $8 for non-guests, and free for children under age 10).

 You can traverse Stocking Island only by foot or boat. For the calmest swimming, your best bet is the soft, white sands on the harbor side of the island. If you prefer rougher surf, take the path across the island to the Atlantic coast; shelling is also ideal on the Atlantic side of the island. If you didn't pack a picnic lunch, just visit the snack bar. Scuba divers and snorkelers are lured to Stocking Island by the *blue holes* (ocean pools of fresh water floating on heavier salt water), coral gardens, and undersea caves. **Mystery Cave,** for example, meanders for some 121m (400 ft.) beneath this virtually uninhabited island.

Playing in the surf

Exuma's best asset is, of course, its surrounding sea. Here's a guide to the best watersports so you can get started on your ocean adventures.

Kayaking

You can best appreciate some of Exuma's most dramatic scenery from the peaceful perch of a sea kayak. In fact, many areas — including mangrove lakes, rivers, manta ray gathering spots, and bonefish flats — are too shallow for other boats to enter. Don't worry if you haven't hit the gym lately. Anyone in at least average physical condition — from children to seniors — can kayak with a smile. The **Starfish Activity Center,** based out of George Town (☎ **242-336-3033**), rents sit-on-top kayaks for singles and doubles. Singles cost about $10 an hour, $30 per half-day, $45 a day, or $160 a week. Doubles cost $15 an hour, $45 per half-day, $55 a day, or $180 a week.

For more adventure, book one of Starfish's guided kayak trips, which the company offers daily. You don't have to spend the whole time paddling your kayak. During half- and full-day excursions, you get lunch and beverages, and the price covers all gear, including snorkeling equipment. You may find yourself watching a blizzard of fish swarm a shipwreck, searching for sand dollars on a deserted beach, snorkeling into a sea

A regatta to remember

George Town may be known as a quiet, restful place, but in April the **National Family Island Regatta** changes all that. If you visit at this time of year, book your hotel room many, many months in advance. Although the regatta brings many a far-flung Bahamian back home for this week-long event, the maritime competition seems almost incidental to the festivities occurring on *terra firma.*

As the handcrafted sloops, owned and sailed by Bahamians, compete in Elizabeth Harbour, vendors along the waterfront sell grilled chicken, fried fish, and conch in all its varieties. Reggae fills the air. Men huddle around card tables, slapping dominos down with dramatic arcs of their arms. A Junkanoo parade — complete with loud drums and whistles, cowbells, and horns — pulses down the street. Spectators sit on the walls near the Government Building as cars with blaring horns festooned with rainbow-hued streamers pass in a slow line.

When the police band takes center stage in **Regatta Park,** people surge onto nearby steps for the best views. Band members look distinguished in their white tunics, wide red belts, red-banded hats, and black trousers with red side stripes. But nothing is formal about the way their lively music stirs up the crowd. Feet tap, fingers snap, and hips swing, whether they belong to tiny tots or elderly grandmothers.

cave, or finding out about bush medicine while you hike along a nature trail. Guided trips begin at $35 an hour for adults and $25 an hour for children.

Another good outfitter is **Ecosummer Expeditions** (☎ 800-465-8884). Ecosummer is especially skilled in exploring **Exuma Cays Land and Sea Park** (☎ 242-357-8344), a government-protected natural preserve with excellent wildlife viewing opportunities.

Scuba diving

Surrounding the Exumas, fields of massive coral heads, eerie blue holes, and exciting walls covered with marine life are exposed to scuba divers. Many excellent reefs are just 20 or 25 minutes away from the George Town area, so long boat rides don't cut into your underwater time.

For scuba divers, the great attraction here is the **Exuma Cays Land and Sea Park,** which is 35km (22 miles) long and 13km (8 miles) wide. It draws scuba divers to its 453 sq. km (175 sq. miles) of sea gardens with magnificent coral reefs, flora, and fauna. The park, inaugurated in 1958, lies some 35km (22 miles) northeast of **Staniel Cay.** Call your hotel to ask whether it offers a hotel/dive package or try **Exuma Scuba Adventures** (☎ 242-336-2893) at Peace & Plenty Beach Inn for information about scuba-diving excursions. A one-tank morning boat dive goes for $55, and a two-tank dive costs $75. You can also take an afternoon one-tank boat dive for $55 or a one-tank night dive for $60. A reef boat trip for snorkeling costs $25.

Snorkeling

The best bet for snorkeling is the magnificent waters off the coast of **Stocking Island,** across Elizabeth Harbour from George Town, a distance of 1.5km (1 mile). Stocking Island is a long, thin barrier island known for its crystal clear waters, white sands, and blue holes. The island is also ringed with a series of undersea caves and stunning coral gardens in rainbow colors. You can take a boat trip from George Town to Stocking Island; boats depart twice a day. Call **Exuma Scuba Adventures** (☎ 242-336-2893) if you want to snorkel around some of Exuma's most well-preserved reefs. These three-hour-plus excursions cost $25 per adult and $10 for children under 12.

Climbing aboard

If you like the water but want to keep your feet dry, George Town makes a good home base for skimming the waves.

Through the **Starfish Activity Center** (☎ 242-336-3033), based in George Town, you can rent *Hobie Waves,* high-performance sailboats that are easy to use. These stable, lightweight-yet-durable, 4.5m (15-ft.) catamarans are ideal for families, because they're simple to maneuver. With a minimum of two people, you can take a two-hour lesson for $30 per person. Renting one of these babies runs you $35 for two hours, $60 for a half-day, $85 for a full day, or — if it really looks good to you — $300 for a week.

If motor boats are more your speed, **Minns Water Sports** (☎ 242-336-3483 or 242-336-2604), based out of George Town, rents these 5-, 5.4-, and 6.7m (17-, 18-, and 22-ft.) boats for $85 to $195 per day, with daily rates dropping the longer you rent. **Exuma Dive Center** in George Town (☎ 800-874-7213 or 242-336-2390),where boat rentals start at $80 per day, also offers more economical rates when you keep a boat for a week or longer. With your boat, you can set out to sail the most stunning waters in The Bahamas, rivaled only by those in the Abacos. The best territory for recreational boating is the government-protected **Exuma Cays Land and Sea Park,** which stretches south from Wax Cay to Conch Cay, with their magnificent sea gardens and coral reefs.

Many visitors come to the Exumas just to go bonefishing, deep-sea, or bottom fishing, pursuing the likes of wahoo, dolphinfish, tuna, bonito, and kingfish, among other species. You can make arrangements for outings through **Club Peace & Plenty** (☎ 242-345-5555), the central office for the Peace & Plenty properties, located on Queen's Highway. The Exumas offer kilometers of wadeable *flats* (shallow bodies of water), where trained guides can accompany you. The resort also offers fly-fishing instruction and equipment.

Exploring on Dry Land

George Town is one of the prettiest settlements in the Out Islands. Spend some time wandering around this small village that borders both a harbor and a serene lake.

Touring George Town and Little Exuma

The **Government Building,** an impressive flamingo-colored edifice with white columns, stands at the harbor's edge. This location provides one-stop shopping for the post office, the police station, the courts, the jail, and the Ministry of Education.

Under the shady canopy of enormous trees out front of **N&D's Fruits and Vegetables,** women sit at their posts selling T-shirts, shell jewelry, various straw goods, and snacks. You can also stop for an inexpensive breakfast or some ice cream or other sweet treats.

Up the road a bit, **St. Andrew's Anglican Church** sits on a bluff. For a good view, go up the hill and around back to the gravesites. This resting place overlooks sparkling **Lake Victoria.** You may see small boats making their way toward the narrow opening that leads to the harbor. On your trek up the road, you pass small square houses with chickens running in front yards, a few mom-and-pop restaurants, and magnificent petite churches.

During your walk, you'll come to a table piled high with conch shells. Here you can watch this fish vendor hammer a shell, deftly cut out the dark mollusk and then skin it, exposing the white flesh that tastes so delectable in so many Bahamian specialties, such as cracked conch or conch chowder. Then spend some time sitting quietly on the pier at the water's edge.

Set aside part of a morning or afternoon for a taxi tour or a rental car drive down to **Little Exuma,** connected to Great Exuma by a bridge.

Little Exuma is a faraway retreat, the southernmost of the Exuma Cays. It has a subtropical climate, despite being in the tropics, and lovely white sand beaches. The waters are so crystal clear in some places that you can spot the colorful tropical fish more than 18m (60 ft.) down. Less than 1.6km (1 mile) offshore is **Pigeon Cay,** an uninhabited island. You can go snorkeling here and visit the remains of a 200-year-old wreck, right offshore in about 2m (6 ft.) of water. Visitors often come to Pigeon Cay for the day and later have a boat pick them up to take them back to Little Exuma. On one of the highest hills of Little Exuma, you can explore the remains of an old pirate fort. Several cannons are located nearby, but no one knows who built the fort or when. (Pirates didn't leave too many records lying around.)

Coming from Great Exuma, the first community you reach on Little Exuma is called **Ferry,** so named because the two islands used to be linked by a ferry service before the bridge was built. If anyone's around, see whether you can visit the private chapel of an Irish family, the Fitzgeralds, erected generations ago. Along the way, you can take in **Pretty Molly Bay,** site of the now-shuttered Sand Dollar Beach Club. Pretty Molly was a slave who committed suicide by walking into the water one night. Many locals have reported seeing her reincarnated as a mermaid sitting on a rock combing her hair.

Many visitors come to Little Exuma to visit the **Hermitage,** a plantation constructed by Loyalist settlers — the last surviving example of the many that once stood in the Exumas. The Kendall family, who came to Little Exuma in 1784, originally built it. They established their plantation at **Williamstown,** and, with their slaves, set about growing cotton. But they encountered so many difficulties in shipping the cotton to Nassau that in 1806 they advertised that the plantation was for sale. The ad promised "970 acres more or less" along with "160 hands" (referring to the slaves). Chances are a local guide will offer to show you around for a fee. Also ask to see several old tombs in the area. At Williamstown (look for the marker on the seaside), you can visit the remains of the **Great Salt Pond,** a shallow estuary separated from the ocean by a narrow barrier beach.

Keeping active

Four Seasons Resort Emerald Bay Golf Club (☎ **242-366-6800**) is one of the great oceanfront golf courses in the Caribbean. This Greg Norman–designed course features six oceanfront holes. The par-72 course stretches a challenging 6,284m (6,873 yards), yet accommodates golfers of various skill levels. The course uses environmentally friendly seashore paspalum grass and finishes on a rocky peninsula with a panoramic view of the bay. The club also boasts a pro shop. Greens fees are a steep $95 to $145 for 18 holes ($145–$175 for non-guests), and the club requires reservations. The resort also has six Har-Tru courts and a state-of-the art fitness center.

Living It Up After Dark

The best place to head for some after-dark diversion is **Club Peace & Plenty** (☎ **800-525-2210** or 242-336-2093), located in George Town. Although summer nights are slow here, something is usually happening here in winter, ranging from weekly poolside bashes to live bands that keep both locals and visitors jumping up on the dance floor.

Fast Facts: Exuma

American Express and ATMs

No Amex services are available in Exuma. You'll find an ATM at **Scotia Bank** (☎ **242-336-2651**), located on Charlotte Street in George Town. The bank is open Monday through Thursday from 9 a.m. to 3 p.m. and Friday from 9:30 a.m. to 4:30 p.m.

Emergencies and Police

Call ☎ **242-336-2666**.

Hospital

For medical care, contact the government-run clinic (☎ 242-336-2088), located on Queen's Highway, about 15 minutes west of Club Peace & Plenty in George Town.

Information

The Exuma Tourist Office (☎ 242-336-2457) is across the street from St. Andrew's Anglican Church, not far from Club Peace & Plenty in George Town.

Internet Access

Check with your hotel for access. You can also go to the ABC Exuma Internet Café at

the Exuma International Airport (☎ 242-345-6038).

Pharmacy

To fill a prescription, go to the clinic on Queen's Highway (see "Hospital" earlier in this listing).

Post Office

The post office is located in the Government Building in George Town. It's open Monday through Friday from 9 a.m. to 4:30 p.m.

Safety

The Exumas is one of the safest archipelagos in The Bahamas. Of course, the usual precautions are advised. Keep your valuables in a safe place and don't go into deserted, unfamiliar areas alone at night.

Taxis

You can find taxis easily, and your hotel's staff can assist you, but we recommend trying Kermit Rolle (☎ 242-345-0002).

Chapter 25

San Salvador

Drowsy San Salvador is so undeveloped that it has just two hotels and a handful of restaurants, most located at the larger hotel. Fabulous scuba diving brings most visitors to these tranquil shores. Beautiful empty beaches and easygoing, friendly residents also keep vacationers coming back. If bar hopping, nightclubbing, and eating at a different restaurant every night of the week is what you have in mind, then San Salvador isn't the island for you.

Arriving in San Salvador

San Salvador's small airport is a cinch to access. If you're staying at Club Med, you'll arrive on a direct charter flight from Miami or New York. Club Med's all-inclusive rates cover airfare. You can arrange charter flights through the Riding Rock Inn Resort and Marina as well. Both hotels provide their guests with group transportation to and from the airport. If you're flying into New Providence, you can catch a flight to San Salvador on **BahamasAir** (☎ 800-222-4262).

Choosing Your Location

Deciding where to stay on San Salvador is like choosing between pizza and filet mignon — the two beach hotels, **Club Med–Columbus Isle** and the **Riding Rock Inn Resort and Marina** — are both good, just different. The Riding Rock resembles a pleasant motel, while the larger Club Med resort is decked out in art and artifacts from around the globe.

The two beach hotels have one thing in common: They both offer excellent scuba-diving programs that allow you to take advantage of the island's main attraction — its underwater wonders. Some 40 well-preserved dive sites are no more than 45 minutes away from both hotels by boat. **Cockburn Town** (pronounced *Co*-burn), the sleepy capital of the island,

San Salvador

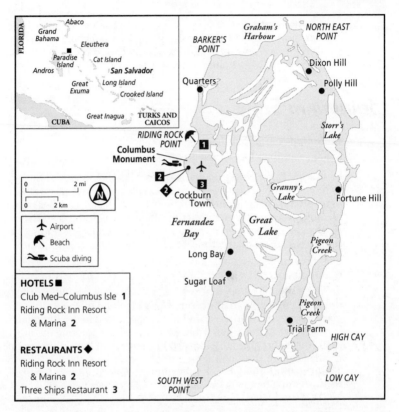

is a comfortable stroll or a quick bike or taxi ride away. However, calling the capital a town is like calling a caterpillar a snake. Cockburn Town features a restaurant, bar, and bank that's open once a week, but the chance to mingle with friendly residents is the real reason for heading to town.

Getting Around San Salvador

Renting a car isn't necessary in San Salvador. If you want to tour the island, ask your hotel staff to help you with arrangements.

- ✔ **Taking a taxi:** Your hotel staff can arrange taxi service for you. If you have the staff at **Club Med** (☎ **242-331-2000**) arrange an island tour for you, the cost is around $25 per person for a half-day ramble.

- ✔ **Driving around:** On San Salvador, you don't need to rent a car unless you want to explore far-flung places on your own. You can rent a car through **Riding Rock Inn Resort and Marina** (☎ 242-331-2631) for about $85 a day.

✔ **Pedaling bicycles:** Club Med guests have use of bikes for cycling around the property and for guided tours around the island. If you're not staying at Club Med, you can rent two-wheelers at Riding Rock Inn Resort and Marina for about $10 a day.

Staying in Style

Club Med–Columbus Isle
$$$$$ **North of Cockburn Town**

Until something better opens, this resort is the poshest, and it's far better than your typical Club Med vacation village. Set on the edge of one of the most pristine beaches in the archipelago, with 3km (2 miles) of white sand, it employs some 30 percent of the island's work force. This 280-room behemoth even operates on its own time clock: Clocks are set one hour earlier than eastern standard time to give late-rising guests another hour of daylight.

Built around a large free-form pool, the resort offers public rooms that are among the most lavish in the islands. Bedrooms contain a private balcony or patio, custom-made furniture from Thailand or the Philippines, sliding glass doors, and feathered wall hangings crafted in the Brazilian rain forest by members of the Xingu tribe. Rooms are large (among the most spacious in the entire hotel chain). Most rooms have twin beds, but you may be able to snag one of the units with a double or a king-size bed if you're lucky. The resort offers nightly entertainment presented in a covered, open-air theater and a dance floor behind one of the bars.

See map p. 331. 3km (2 miles) north of Cockburn Town. ☎ **800-CLUB-MED** *or 242-331-2000. Fax: 242-331-2458.* www.clubmed.com. *Rack rates: $1,300 per person to $1,900 for seven nights in a double room (price depends on what time of year you go and where you fly from). Rates include all meals, most beverages, most activities, gratuities, round-trip airfare, and ground transportation to and from San Salvador's airport. AE, DISC, MC, V.*

Riding Rock Inn Resort and Marina
$$ **North of Cockburn Town**

In stark contrast to the lavish Club Med, with its perky staff, Riding Rock Inn offers a more tranquil atmosphere. The 42 rooms are motel-like, but they're pleasantly decorated and outfitted with all the modern conveniences you need for a comfortable stay. The newer, two-story building houses are the best digs, and each room features two double beds, a TV, a refrigerator, and a balcony or patio with an ocean view. The hotel's older, smaller rooms overlook the pool. Most guests are avid divers who stay wet. (Riding Rock offers excellent scuba packages.) During the day while divers are away, this place seems downright empty. Nighttime is a different story, however. In fact, you could call Riding Rock Inn Resort and Marina San Salvador's social center. During the Wednesday night dance party, the joint is really jumpin', and Friday nights aren't so quiet, either.

See map p. 331. Just north of Cockburn Town. ☎ *800-272-1492 in the U.S., 954-359-8353 in Florida, or 242-331-2631 in The Bahamas. Fax: 242-331-2020.* www.riding rock.com. *Rack rates: $114–$141 double. Ask about the all-inclusive packages. MC, V.*

Dining Out

If you're staying at Club Med, room rates include all your meals. The resort offers reliable food, with all ingredients imported. The cuisine never reaches the sublime, but there is an effort to offer variety. Unlimited food, including snacks, is included, plus drinks during regular meal hours. However, you shouldn't leave the island without sneaking off campus for some local flavor.

Riding Rock Inn Resort and Marina
$$ Near Cockburn Town   BAHAMIAN/AMERICAN

Sit on the deck overlooking the water or eat inside; either way, you can dine on hearty portions of comfort food. Pancakes make a good choice for breakfast, and sandwiches are on the menu for lunch. The price-fixed dinners include soup, salad, main course, dessert, wine, and soft, chewy, just-baked Bahamian bread. Launch your meal with the well-seasoned conch chowder or okra soup and follow it up with steak, prime rib, veal, chicken, or fresh fish. Likewise, the Wednesday-night barbecues, featuring reggae music, are popular social events.

See map p. 331. Just north of Cockburn Town (within walking distance of Club Med). ☎ *242-331-2631.* www.ridingrock.com. *Reservations recommended. Breakfast: $12; lunch: $15; dinner: $28. MC, V. Open: Daily 7:30–9 a.m., 12:30–2 p.m., and 6:30–9 p.m.*

Three Ships Restaurant
$ Cockburn Town   BAHAMIAN

Since the early 1990s, Faith Jones, the owner, keeps visitors coming back for her cracked conch, steamed or fried grouper, and crab and rice, served with mounds of coleslaw, potato salad, or peas and rice. Spend some time here, and you're sure to strike up a conversation or two with Ms. Jones and the townspeople who stop in for food, drink, or just "to chew the fat" in more ways than one. Jones used to cater meals from her home next door before she opened this dining spot.

See map p. 331. In the heart of Cockburn Town. ☎ *242-331-2787. Main courses: $8–$15. No credit cards. Open: Daily noon–6 p.m.*

Enjoying the Sand and Surf

If you're looking for empty beaches or fantastic diving and snorkeling opportunities, you've come to the right place.

Combing the beaches

If you prefer finding a stretch of sand where the only footprints on it are your own, rent a car or a bike at Riding Rock Inn Resort and Marina or call a taxi. (See "Getting Around San Salvador" earlier in this chapter.) Empty beaches are everywhere. Just remember to take plenty of water and, of course, sunblock. You won't find much shade. Along the way, you can look for the island's various monuments to Christopher Columbus.

On the northeast coast, **East Beach** stretches for some 10km (6 miles). Crushed coral and shells turned the shore a rosy pink. The deep turquoise patches in the clear waters are coral heads, but the beach isn't good for snorkeling — people have spotted sharks here. Tall sea wheat or sea grass sprouts up from the sand. Off mile-marker number 24 on the main road, you can pick your way to the *Chicago Herald* Columbus Monument (see the "Exploring on Dry Land" section later in this chapter.)

Playing in the surf

Scuba divers flock to this remote island, which is a major dive destination with some **40 dive sites** that lie no more than 45 minutes by boat from either of the two resorts. San Salvador has such stunning sea walls around it that *wall diving* — diving where the sloping shoreline suddenly drops off steeply and plummets to the ocean depths — is a popular activity here.

Riding Rock Inn Resort and Marina (☎ 242-331-2631), just north of Cockburn Town, specializes in scuba packages and offers a good underwater photography program, as well as night dives on Tuesday evenings. For one of the best outfitters, call **Guanahani Dive Ltd.** (☎ 242-331-2631), based at Riding Rock Inn.

Club Med-Columbus Isle, also just north of Cockburn Town, should really be called an *almost*-all-inclusive resort, because scuba diving isn't included in its rates. Resort courses run $120, and certification courses are $400. A one-tank dive costs $40 and a two-tank dive costs $60.

Following in the footsteps of Columbus, snorkelers can find a rich paradise on this relatively undiscovered island, with its unpolluted and unpopulated kilometers of beaches that are ideal for swimming, shelling, and, of course, snorkeling. If you stay here a week, you've only begun to explore the possibilities. Places such as **Bamboo Point, Fernandez Bay,** and **Long Bay** all lie within a few miles of the main settlement of Cockburn Town on the more tranquil western side of the island. At the southern tip of San Salvador is one of our favorite places for snorkeling, **Sandy Point,** and its satellite of **Grotto Bay.** The elkhorn coral reefs off San Salvador are worth the trip to Sandy Point and Grotto Bay.

Exploring on Dry Land

For such a small island, San Salvador offers a great deal of history as well as some sights that merit a look.

Rent a bike, hire a taxi, or start walking, and see how many of the **Christopher Columbus monuments** you can hit. All these monuments are supposed to mark the place where Columbus and his crew anchored the *Niña, Pinta,* and *Santa Maria* early that morning in 1492:

✔ **Tappan Monument:** Just south of Cockburn Town, this small, four-sided stone pillar stands on the beach at **Fernandez Bay** (mile-marker no. 5 on the main road). The Tappan gas company embedded this monument here on February 25, 1951, in honor of Columbus.

✔ **A tall cross:** At mile-marker no. 6, about 5km (3 miles) south of Cockburn Town, stands the tall cross at the edge of the water, which is also a tribute to Columbus. This cross has been here since 1956, along with a third monument that lies hidden on the ocean floor.

✔ **The *Chicago Herald* Monument:** This monument is located at mile-marker no. 24 on the east coast. To reach it, turn off the main road and drive a half-kilometer (1 mile) to **East Beach.** Unless you meet a resident who can give you a ride in a four-wheel-drive car, you have to get out and walk. Turn right and hike 3km (2 miles) parallel to the beach until the sandy road ends. You'll see a cave to the left, at the water's edge. Follow the path to the right. Cupped by vegetation, a stone structure lies on the slice of land between the ocean and the bay. Although many historians dispute the claim, the marble plaque boasts, "On this spot Christopher Columbus first set foot upon the soil of the New World, erected by the *Chicago Herald,* June 1891." (Two reporters from the newspaper marked the site to commemorate the 400th anniversary of Columbus's landfall.) The only problem with the monument's claim is that the treacherous reefs here make this a dangerous — and highly unlikely — landing spot.

Another **monument,** located next to the Columbus cross south of Cockburn Town, commemorates the **1968 Olympic games** in Mexico. A spiral walkway leads to the top of this structure, where the bowl of the dark metal sculpture held the Olympic flame that was brought from Greece. The flame burned here until it was taken to the games in Mexico City.

In the northeastern portion of the island, the **Dixon Hill Lighthouse,** built in 1856, sends out an intense beam two times every 25 seconds. This signal is visible for 31km (19 miles). The oil-using lighthouse rises 49m (160 ft.) into the sky, and the lighthouse keeper still operates it by hand. For permission to climb to the top, just knock on the door of the lighthouse keeper, who's almost always in the neighboring house.

After huffing and puffing your way up, you'll be surprised when you see how tiny the source of light actually is. From the top of the lighthouse, you can take in a panoramic view of San Salvador's inland lakes, a distant Crab Cay, and the surrounding islets. Ask the lighthouse keeper to show you the **inspector's log**, with signatures that date back to Queen Victoria's reign. Be sure to leave at least a $1 donation when you sign the guestbook on your way out. The lighthouse lies about a 30-minute taxi ride from Riding Rock Inn Resort and Marina or Club Med.

Staying Active

Club Med–Columbus Isle offers ten **tennis courts** (three lit for night play), and Riding Rock Inn Resort and Marina has one (often empty) court. Fishermen test their skills against blue marlin, yellowfin tuna, and wahoo on fishing trips, which you can arrange through **Riding Rock Inn Resort and Marina** (☎ 242-331-2631), north of Cockburn Town. The trips run $400 for a half-day and $600 for a full day. Bonefishermen enjoy **Pigeon Creek,** and some record catches have been chalked up here. Rent a boat from a local or get your hotel to help set you up.

Living It Up After Dark

Club Med (☎ 242-331-2000), just north of Cockburn Town, keeps its guests entertained every night with musical revues and shows starring vacationers themselves. At **Riding Rock Inn Resort and Marina** (☎ 242-331-2631), also north of Cockburn Town, the Wednesday-night barbecue features reggae music, and many locals come to party. The hotel's **Driftwood Bar** is also hot on Friday nights (call ☎ 242-331-2631 in The Bahamas). If you're still game for some fun after the lodgings' festivities, head to the **Harlem Square Bar** (☎ 242-331-2777), across the road from Three Ships Restaurant in Cockburn Town. This friendly place is open daily from 9 a.m. to midnight.

Fast Facts: San Salvador

American Express and ATMs

No Amex services or ATMs are available on San Salvador.

Emergencies/Police

Call ☎ **242-337-0999** or 242-337-0444.

Hospital

The San Salvador Community Clinic (☎ 242-331-2105), a five-minute drive north of Club Med, is open Monday through Thursday from 8:30 a.m. to 4:30 p.m. and Friday from 8:30 a.m. to 4 p.m.

Pharmacy

The San Salvador Community Clinic (see "Hospital" earlier in this listing) fills prescriptions.

Safety

San Salvador is a safe island. However, you still need to take the same precautions that you should take anywhere you go: Keep valuables in a safe place; and don't go into deserted, unfamiliar areas alone at night.

Taxis

Your hotel staff can arrange taxi service for you. Island tours arranged through Club Med cost around $25 per person for a half-day ramble.

Part VII
The Part of Tens

The 5th Wave   By Rich Tennant

In this part . . .

We give you the ten most common misconceptions about The Bahamas. For example, if you ever thought that The Bahamas were a single, mountainous, casino-packed, Caribbean island, keep reading. We also share our top-ten picks for quintessential island activities, from walking underwater in The Bahamas — without the benefit of scuba gear — to snorkeling with stingrays.

Chapter 26

Top Ten Myths about The Bahamas

*I*n this chapter, we explain some of the most common misconceptions about these sunny islands. So the next time someone starts talking about wanting to go mountain climbing in The Bahamas, you can set him straight.

Columbus Definitely Landed at San Salvador

Historians aren't certain whether Columbus's three Spanish ships actually landed on San Salvador (which used to be called Watling's Island until the Bahamian legislature changed it in 1926). The Italian seafarer left no marker to indicate his landfall. Some geographers claim that the landfall occurred on one of the cays of Turks and Caicos; another site in the running is Cat Island. Artifacts of European origin, dating anywhere from 1490 to 1560, were found on San Salvador in 1983. But in a meticulously researched article, *National Geographic* published evidence in 1986 that the landfall occurred at Samana Cay, some 104km (65 miles) to the southeast of San Salvador.

The question will probably never be resolved. All we know is that at 2 a.m. on the moonlit night of October 12, 1492, Columbus and his men landed somewhere in the southern Bahamas and woke up some sleepy Lucayans who called them "men from Heaven." In time, when the Spanish killed or sold the Native Americans into slavery, the seafarers may have been more aptly called "men from Hell."

The Bahamas Are One Island

The Bahamas aren't one island — in fact, this archipelago is made up of more than 700 islands, from large landmasses to sandbars. People inhabit only about 30 of the islands, and just a handful of islands actually have hotels.

The Bahamas Are in the Caribbean

Sure, it begins with a *B*, just like Barbados and Bonaire, but The Bahamas (like Bermuda) are in the Atlantic Ocean, not the Caribbean Sea. The Bahamas are close enough that the weather most often feels like the West Indies. Scattered across some 258,998 sq. km (100,000 sq. miles) of ocean, the islands of the once-British Bahamas have their own special flavor. However, they share a West Indian heritage with their Caribbean neighbors. Therefore, you do find some similarities in architecture, food, music, dance, and the accents of the people.

Beach Weather Is a Given

The weather is *not* always warm enough for the beach. The Bahamas do cool off to often springlike temperatures around late December to March. Those months are much better for playing golf and tennis than for swimming and sunbathing. The weather can change quickly during this time of year, moving in a flash from beach days to cool days, and then back again.

The Islands Are Mountainous

In the low-lying islands, mountains are more like molehills. The highest point in all The Bahamas — on sleepy Cat Island — is just 63m (206 ft.). Unlike the often-majestic volcanic islands of the Caribbean, these Atlantic isles were created by coral reefs, which make for phenomenal scuba diving and snorkeling, starting in unusually shallow waters.

Palm Trees Are All Over the Place

Except around resorts and residential developments, where people planted palms, most of the trees you see are long-needled casuarina pines. Palms line some beaches, but wispy-looking evergreens (which lean in the direction of the prevailing wind) border the majority of beaches.

For Casinos and Hot Nightlife, Pick Any Island

If you want to gamble into the wee hours or dance 'til the sun comes up, you need to choose the island(s) you visit carefully. Head to Nassau, Cable Beach, or Paradise Island (all on or attached to the island of New

Providence), or to Freeport or Lucaya (on Grand Bahama Island). The rest of the islands don't have casinos, and what little nightlife they do have is liveliest on weekends.

All Bahamians Are of African Descent

On some islands, you find lots of locals with blue eyes and white skin. For example, almost everyone is of European ancestry on Spanish Wells, off the island of Eleuthera, as well as on Man-O-War Cay and Guana Cay, both in the Abacos. Most of these residents are direct descendants of some of The Bahamas' earliest settlers: the Eleutherian Adventurers. Arriving in Spanish Wells in the mid-1600s, these settlers came from Britain in search of religious freedom. In the late 1700s, after the Revolutionary War ended in America, Loyalists (Euro-Americans who sided with the British Crown) also fled to both Eleuthera and the Abacos.

Islanders Resent Tourists

Bahamians are some of the most personable folks around — that is, as long as visitors treat them with respect. For example, if you need to ask someone for directions, say "Hello" first, and don't assume that every local you see works at the resort, store, or restaurant that you're visiting. Strike up a conversation with a resident, and you're sure to come away with a tip about a popular nightspot or a little-known beach. You may even end up with a new friend.

Reggae Music Is the Local Sound

Although you certainly hear reggae music in The Bahamas, it was born in Jamaica, not in these islands. You also hear plenty of calypso (originally from Trinidad), plus lots of American pop, R&B, and rock. But along with all those imports, The Bahamas have their own sound. Traditionally played with cowbells, goatskin drums, whistles, and trumpets, fast-paced **Junkanoo** music is at the heart of the colorful carnival-like festival held on Boxing Day (Dec 26) and New Year's Day.

You may also hear the sounds of **Goombay** (a pared-down version of Junkanoo that's generally played without the elaborate festival costumes). Particularly in the Out Islands, some nightspots still have old-fashioned **rake and scrapes,** where bands turn things like washboards, saws, and barrels into instruments.

Chapter 27

Top Ten Bahamas Moments

*A*re you in the mood for a romantic stroll through manicured English-style gardens? Or is a ride in a horse-drawn carriage along the history-packed streets of Nassau more up your alley? Ever wondered whether pink sand is as soft as the snow-white variety?

Along with scuba diving and snorkeling — which are phenomenal all over The Bahamas — here are other unforgettable adventures you can consider putting at the top of your "to do" list.

Walking on the (Wet and) Wild Side

You can walk on the ocean floor without wearing scuba gear. You don't have to take lengthy classes, either — you just do it. While you're getting up close and personal with fish and coral, your face and hair stay dry. This fun activity is called **helmet diving.** To partake in this adventure, join one of Hartley's Undersea Walks in Nassau. To do so, you wear a lead and glass helmet as you descend a ladder into the ocean. A tank on the boat pumps air through a long tube into your aquatic helmet. For more information, see Chapter 13.

Taking a Carriage Ride through Nassau

Because Nassau, located on New Providence Island, is so full of the country's history, a good way to see this harborside city is from an old-fashioned horse-drawn carriage. You can take a leisurely ride along busy Bay Street (the main thoroughfare) past Parliament Square, with its 18th- and 19th-century Georgian-style government buildings (painted pink and white) and a statue of a young Queen Victoria, among other sights. Turn to Chapter 10 for details.

Wandering through Versailles Gardens

On Paradise Island, you can enjoy a setting that you'd expect to find only in the countryside of France. Studded with bright flowers, shady trees, a lily pond with turtles, and bronze and marble statues, **Versailles Gardens** (see Chapter 13 for details) is the site of a 12th-century monastery. Dramatically perched on a rise, it was built by the Augustinian monks in France. In 1962, Huntington Hartford, the island's original developer, had it moved to the island and reassembled, stone by stone.

Making a Date with Dolphins

Dolphin skin feels like warm, buttery leather. Pet one and you'll see what we mean. (Some marine studies, however, suggest that dolphins don't like human contact. They're such friendly animals, though, you don't get that impression.) You can commune with dolphins on Grand Bahama or an island off New Providence. Some sessions allow you to wade in the water with these mammals while trainers tell you everything you ever wanted to know about them. In other programs, you can scuba dive with Flipper's cousins in the open ocean. For more details, see Chapter 13 (on New Providence) and Chapter 17 (on Grand Bahama).

Feeding the Stingrays

If you find dolphins too tame, try feeding the stingrays that swim gracefully through the shallow waters around a tiny island off Green Turtle Cay in the Abacos (see Chapter 20). If you don't know how to snorkel, your guide can teach you on the spot, or you can take to the water dressed in scuba gear. Either way, you're also treated to a beach picnic after your captain grills the fish or lobster that he just caught.

Digging Your Toes into a Pink Sand Beach

Harbour Island's Pink Sand Beach may be only 2km (3 miles) long, but it seems to go on forever. The unusual color comes from shells and coral that the waves have pulverized over the years. This beach is pretty enough to make you roll out of bed in time to catch the sunrise. (Turn to Chapter 22 for more details.)

Watching the Sun Set on Dunmore Town

For some of the best sunsets in The Bahamas, head to Harbour Island's western coast. The spectacle is special here because of the glow that the sun casts on the 18th-century wooden cottages along the harborfront. Sip a Bahama Mama or a Goombay Smash at a waterside restaurant while you watch the show. (For more information, see Chapter 22.)

Visiting a Candy Cane–Striped Lighthouse

Sail through **Hope Town Harbor,** which is filled with small pleasure boats, or munch some conch fritters at the water's edge, and you can see the whimsical red-and-white striped lighthouse. For a sweeping view of narrow Elbow Cay, edged by fabulous beaches, climb to the top of the beacon, which has stood here since 1838. (See Chapter 19 for more information.)

Living It Up at Miss Emily's

In New Plymouth on Green Turtle Cay in the Abacos stands **Miss Emily's Blue Bee Bar,** the most famous watering hole in the Out Islands (see Chapter 20 for more information). The rum-laced drink, the Goombay Smash, may as well have been invented here. It's called the Abacos' answer to atomic fission. Miss Emily is gone now, but she left her secret recipe in the hands of her daughter.

Boating in the Abacos

No matter where you've boated before, nothing compares to sailing the Abacos in one of the vessels that you can rent at Marsh Harbour. (See Chapter 18 for details on how to do so.) Marsh Harbour is aptly known as "The Boating Capital of The Bahamas." In charge of your own vessel, you can visit uninhabited cays and seek out deserted beaches where you can go shelling, exploring, and picnicking in peace — and no one's around to witness if you want to go beachcombing in the buff.

Appendix

Quick Concierge

• •

Fast Facts

American Express

Representing American Express in The Bahamas is Destinations (☎ 242-322-2931), located on Shirley Street (between Charlotte and Parliament streets) in Nassau. Hours are 9 a.m. to 5 p.m. Monday through Friday. The travel department is also open Saturday from 9 a.m. to 1 p.m. If you present a personal check and an Amex card, you can buy traveler's checks here.

Area Code

On all islands, the area code for The Bahamas is **242**.

ATMs

To find an ATM near you, call or check the Web sites for Cirrus (☎ 800-424-7787; www.mastercard.com) and PLUS (☎ 800-843-7587; www.visa.com). See Chapter 5 for more information about using ATMs in The Bahamas.

Credit Cards

If your credit card gets lost or stolen, call the following emergency telephone numbers: American Express, ☎ 800-221-7282 collect; MasterCard, ☎ 800-307-7309; and Visa, ☎ 800-847-2911.

Currency Exchange

U.S. travelers don't have to swap their dollars for Bahamian currency because American green is accepted everywhere.

The exchange rate is $1 to $1, so you won't have any confusion. Other travelers can exchange currency at the Bank of Nova Scotia, with branches throughout The Bahamas (go to www.scotiabank.com for locations).

Electricity

Electricity is normally 120 volts, 60 cycles, AC. American appliances are fully compatible; British or European appliances need both converters and adapters.

Embassies and Consulates

The U.S. embassy (☎ 242-322-1181 or 242-328-2206) is on Queen Street, P.O. Box N-8197, Nassau. The Canadian consulate (☎ 242-393-2123) is on Shirley Street, Shopping Plaza, Nassau. The British High Commission (☎ 876-510-0700) is in Kingston, Jamaica, at 28 Trafalgar Road.

Emergencies

Throughout most of The Bahamas, the number to call for a medical, dental, or hospital emergency is ☎ **911**. In the Out Islands, the number is ☎ **919**. To report a fire, call ☎ **411**.

Etiquette and Customs

When you encounter someone, even a stranger in the Out Islands, exchanging greetings is customary. A "good morning" or "good afternoon" suffices. But that custom doesn't prevail in bustling Freeport and Nassau. Also, rushing up to someone and demanding that he supply you with directions to a place is impolite anywhere; Bahamians gently lead into conversations with a greeting and friendly comments before getting down to business.

Business in offices is conducted rather formally with exchange of business cards, elaborate handshakes, and the like. If you're doing business in The Bahamas, wear business clothes as you would to any office in America. Don't show up in resort wear or shorts for any formal meetings or functions.

When leaving the beach, men should put on a shirt and pants, even a pair of jeans, before heading into a town. Women should wear a cover-up over their bathing suit, or else slip into a tropical dress or pants.

If you're planning to attend religious services, wear the best clothes you brought along. Bahamians believe in dressing up for their "Sunday-go-to meeting."

Regardless of how colorful an islander may look, photographing anyone without permission is extremely rude.

Internet Access

Access is limited on the islands. Cybercafe, located in The Mall at Marathon (☎ 242-394-6254) in Nassau, is open daily from 10 a.m. to 8 p.m., charging 15¢ per minute; four computers are available. In the Out Islands, you can usually access the Web from your hotel. For more tips about staying in touch, see Chapter 9.

Liquor and Drug Laws

Liquor is sold in liquor stores and various convenience stores; it's readily available at all hours, although it's not sold on Sundays. The legal drinking age is 18.

Importing, possessing, or dealing in unlawful drugs, including marijuana, is a serious offense in The Bahamas that carries heavy penalties. Customs officers may conduct body searches for drugs or other contraband goods at their discretion.

Mail and Postage Rates

Most of the kiosks selling postcards also sell the Bahamian stamps you need to mail them, so you probably won't need to visit the post office. Sending a postcard or an airmail letter (up to ½-oz. in weight) from The Bahamas to anywhere outside its borders (including the U.S., Canada, and the U.K.) costs 65¢, with another 24¢ charged for each additional half-ounce of weight.

Mail to and from the Out Islands is sometimes slow. Airmail may go by air to Nassau and by boat to its final destination. If a resort has a U.S. or Nassau address, using it is preferable.

Police

Dial ☎ 911. In the Out Islands, the number is ☎ 919.

Safety

When going to Nassau (New Providence), Cable Beach, Paradise Island, or Freeport/Lucaya, exercise the same caution you would if you were visiting a large U.S. city like Miami.

Women, especially, should take caution when walking alone on the streets of Nassau after dark, particularly if those streets appear deserted. Pickpockets work the crowded casino floors of both Paradise Beach and Cable Beach. See that your wallet, money, and valuables are well secured.

If you're driving a rental car, always make sure that you lock the car door and never leave possessions in view. Don't leave valuables, such as cameras and purses, unattended on the beach while you go for a swim. If you're traveling with valuables, especially jewelry, don't leave them unguarded in hotel rooms. Many of the larger hotels provide safes. Keep your hotel room doors locked at all times.

You're less likely to be mugged or robbed in the Out Islands, where life is generally more peaceful. Some resort hotels, even today, don't have locks on the doors there.

Smoking

The Bahamas don't have any general restrictions against smoking in public places, so the smoking policy depends on the individual restaurant or bar. Most of them designate smoking versus nonsmoking areas and keep their premises well ventilated.

Taxes

Departure tax is $15 ($18 from Grand Bahama Island) for visitors ages 7 and up. You're also charged an 8 percent tax on hotel bills; otherwise, The Bahamas don't have sales tax.

Telephone

To call The Bahamas from the U.S. or Canada, dial 1-242 plus the seven-digit local number. From the U.K., dial 001-242 plus the local seven-digit number.

To make a direct international call from The Bahamas to the U.S. or Canada, dial 1 plus the area code and local number. To call other countries, dial 011 plus the country code (the U.K. is 44, for example), the area code (usually without its initial zero), and the local number.

For local calls within The Bahamas, simply dial the seven-digit number. To call from one island to another within The Bahamas,

dial 1-242 and then the seven-digit local number.

Old coin-operated phones are still prevalent in The Bahamas. Each local call costs 25¢; you can use either Bahamian or U.S. quarters. But those old phones are gradually being replaced by phones that use calling cards that come in denominations of $5, $10, $20, and $50. You can buy calling cards from any office of BATELCO (Bahamas Telephone Co.).

BATELCO's main branch (☎ 242-302-7000) is on Kennedy Drive, Nassau, although a popular local branch lies in the commercial heart of Nassau, on East Street off Bay Street.

To get directory assistance within The Bahamas, dial ☎ 916. To reach an international or a domestic operator within The Bahamas, dial 0. No distinction is made in The Bahamas between the two types of operators.

To reach the major international services of AT&T, dial ☎ 800-CALLATT from any phone, or head for any phone with AT&T or USA DIRECT marked on the side of the booth. Picking up the handset connects you with an AT&T operator. You often find these phones beside cruise-ship docks to help passengers disembarking on shore leave for the day. You can reach MCI at ☎ 800-888-8000.

Time Zone

All islands in The Bahamas are on eastern standard time. The islands also observe daylight saving time in the summer.

Water

Technically, tap water is drinkable throughout The Bahamas. But we almost always opt for bottled. Resorts tend to filter and chlorinate tap water more aggressively than other establishments; anywhere else, you can get bottled water at stores and supermarkets, and it tastes better than water from a tap.

On many of the Out Islands, rainfall is the main source of water. Definitely drink bottled water when you're there.

Weather

Call ☎ 915 to hear the forecast. Before your trip or if you have Internet access while in the islands, check out www. weather.com.

Weddings

See Chapter 8 for complete details about getting married in The Bahamas.

Where to Get More Information

Tourist offices

The best source to try before you leave home is **The Bahamas Ministry of Tourism Office.** You can browse the Web site at www.bahamas.com or call ☎ 800-BAHAMAS to request information. You can also go to or call the walk-in branch offices at the following locations:

- ✔ **Chicago:** 8770 W. Bryn Mawr Ave., Suite 1441, Chicago, IL 60631; ☎ 773-867-8377

- ✔ **Los Angeles:** 11400 W. Olympic Blvd., Suite 204, Los Angeles, CA 90064; ☎ 800-439-6993

- ✔ **Miami:** 1200 S. Pine Island Rd., Suite 750, Plantation, FL 33324; ☎ 954-236-9292

- ✔ **New York:** 60 E. 42nd St., New York, NY 10165; ☎ 212-758-2777

- ✔ **Toronto, Canada:** 121 Bloor St. E., Suite 1101, Toronto, ON M4W 3M5; ☎ 416-968-2999

- ✔ **London, U.K.:** 10 Chesterfield St., London W1J 5JL; ☎ 020-7355-0800

Web sites

The following is a list of our top picks for destination Web sites for The Bahamas. In addition to these sites, we recommend Frommers.com (www.frommers.com), which is full of travel tips, online booking options, and more comprehensive advice from *Frommer's Bahamas* (Wiley).

- ✔ The Bahamas Ministry of Tourism (www.bahamas.com)

- ✔ The Bahamas Out Islands Promotion Board (www.bahama-out-islands.com)

- ✔ Bahamas Tourist Guide (www.interknowledge.com/bahamas)

- ✔ Bahamasnet (www.bahamasnet.com)

Index

BUSINESS, CAREERS & PERSONAL FINANCE

0-7645-5307-0   0-7645-5331-3 *†

Also available:

- Accounting For Dummies †
  0-7645-5314-3
- Business Plans Kit For Dummies †
  0-7645-5365-8
- Cover Letters For Dummies
  0-7645-5224-4
- Frugal Living For Dummies
  0-7645-5403-4
- Leadership For Dummies
  0-7645-5176-0
- Managing For Dummies
  0-7645-1771-6

- Marketing For Dummies
  0-7645-5600-2
- Personal Finance For Dummies *
  0-7645-2590-5
- Project Management
  For Dummies
  0-7645-5283-X
- Resumes For Dummies †
  0-7645-5471-9
- Selling For Dummies
  0-7645-5363-1
- Small Business Kit For Dummies *†
  0-7645-5093-4

HOME & BUSINESS COMPUTER BASICS

0-7645-4074-2   0-7645-3758-X

Also available:

- ACT! 6 For Dummies
  0-7645-2645-6
- iLife '04 All-in-One Desk Reference
  For Dummies
  0-7645-7347-0
- iPAQ For Dummies
  0-7645-6769-1
- Mac OS X Panther Timesaving
  Techniques For Dummies
  0-7645-5812-9
- Macs For Dummies
  0-7645-5656-8
- Microsoft Money 2004 For Dummies
  0-7645-4195-1

- Office 2003 All-in-One Desk
  Reference For Dummies
  0-7645-3883-7
- Outlook 2003 For Dummies
  0-7645-3759-8
- PCs For Dummies
  0-7645-4074-2
- TiVo For Dummies
  0-7645-6923-6
- Upgrading and Fixing PCs
  For Dummies
  0-7645-1665-5
- Windows XP Timesaving
  Techniques For Dummies
  0-7645-3748-2

FOOD, HOME, GARDEN, HOBBIES, MUSIC & PETS

0-7645-5295-3   0-7645-5232-5

Also available:

- Bass Guitar For Dummies
  0-7645-2487-9
- Diabetes Cookbook For Dummies
  0-7645-5230-9
- Gardening For Dummies *
  0-7645-5130-2
- Guitar For Dummies
  0-7645-5106-X
- Holiday Decorating For Dummies
  0-7645-2570-0
- Home Improvement All-in-One
  For Dummies
  0-7645-5680-0

- Knitting For Dummies
  0-7645-5395-X
- Piano For Dummies
  0-7645-5105-1
- Puppies For Dummies
  0-7645-5255-4
- Scrapbooking For Dummies
  0-7645-7208-3
- Senior Dogs For Dummies
  0-7645-5818-8
- Singing For Dummies
  0-7645-2475-5
- 30-Minute Meals For Dummies
  0-7645-2589-1

INTERNET & DIGITAL MEDIA

0-7645-1664-7   0-7645-6924-4

Also available:

- 2005 Online Shopping Directory
  For Dummies
  0-7645-7495-7
- CD & DVD Recording For Dummies
  0-7645-5956-7
- eBay For Dummies
  0-7645-5654-1
- Fighting Spam For Dummies
  0-7645-5965-6
- Genealogy Online For Dummies
  0-7645-5964-8
- Google For Dummies
  0-7645-4420-9

- Home Recording For Musicians
  For Dummies
  0-7645-1634-5
- The Internet For Dummies
  0-7645-4173-0
- iPod & iTunes For Dummies
  0-7645-7772-7
- Preventing Identity Theft
  For Dummies
  0-7645-7336-5
- Pro Tools All-in-One Desk
  Reference For Dummies
  0-7645-5714-9
- Roxio Easy Media Creator
  For Dummies
  0-7645-7131-1

SPORTS, FITNESS, PARENTING, RELIGION & SPIRITUALITY

0-7645-5146-9   0-7645-5418-2

Also available:

- Adoption For Dummies
  0-7645-5488-3
- Basketball For Dummies
  0-7645-5248-1
- The Bible For Dummies
  0-7645-5296-1
- Buddhism For Dummies
  0-7645-5359-3
- Catholicism For Dummies
  0-7645-5391-7
- Hockey For Dummies
  0-7645-5228-7

- Judaism For Dummies
  0-7645-5299-6
- Martial Arts For Dummies
  0-7645-5358-5
- Pilates For Dummies
  0-7645-5397-6
- Religion For Dummies
  0-7645-5264-3
- Teaching Kids to Read
  For Dummies
  0-7645-4043-2
- Weight Training For Dummies
  0-7645-5168-X
- Yoga For Dummies
  0-7645-5117-5

TRAVEL

0-7645-5438-7   0-7645-5453-0

Also available:

- Alaska For Dummies
  0-7645-1761-9
- Arizona For Dummies
  0-7645-6938-4
- Cancún and the Yucatán
  For Dummies
  0-7645-2437-2
- Cruise Vacations For Dummies
  0-7645-6941-4
- Europe For Dummies
  0-7645-5456-5
- Ireland For Dummies
  0-7645-5455-7

- Las Vegas For Dummies
  0-7645-5448-4
- London For Dummies
  0-7645-4277-X
- New York City For Dummies
  0-7645-6945-7
- Paris For Dummies
  0-7645-5494-8
- RV Vacations For Dummies
  0-7645-5443-3
- Walt Disney World & Orlando
  For Dummies
  0-7645-6943-0

GRAPHICS, DESIGN & WEB DEVELOPMENT

0-7645-4345-8   0-7645-5589-8

Also available:

- Adobe Acrobat 6 PDF
  For Dummies
  0-7645-3760-1
- Building a Web Site For Dummies
  0-7645-7144-3
- Dreamweaver MX 2004
  For Dummies
  0-7645-4342-3
- FrontPage 2003 For Dummies
  0-7645-3882-9
- HTML 4 For Dummies
  0-7645-1995-6
- Illustrator cs For Dummies
  0-7645-4084-X

- Macromedia Flash MX 2004
  For Dummies
  0-7645-4358-X
- Photoshop 7 All-in-One Desk
  Reference For Dummies
  0-7645-1667-1
- Photoshop cs Timesaving
  Techniques For Dummies
  0-7645-6782-9
- PHP 5 For Dummies
  0-7645-4166-8
- PowerPoint 2003 For Dummies
  0-7645-3908-6
- QuarkXPress 6 For Dummies
  0-7645-2593-X

NETWORKING, SECURITY, PROGRAMMING & DATABASES

0-7645-6852-3   0-7645-5784-X

Also available:

- A+ Certification For Dummies
  0-7645-4187-0
- Access 2003 All-in-One Desk
  Reference For Dummies
  0-7645-3988-4
- Beginning Programming
  For Dummies
  0-7645-4997-9
- C For Dummies
  0-7645-7068-4
- Firewalls For Dummies
  0-7645-4048-3
- Home Networking For Dummies
  0-7645-42796

- Network Security For Dummies
  0-7645-1679-5
- Networking For Dummies
  0-7645-1677-9
- TCP/IP For Dummies
  0-7645-1760-0
- VBA For Dummies
  0-7645-3989-2
- Wireless All In-One Desk Reference
  For Dummies
  0-7645-7496-5
- Wireless Home Networking
  For Dummies
  0-7645-3910-8